CHANGING PERSPECTIVES
IN SPECIAL EDUCATION

edited by

Rebecca Dailey Kneedler

The University of Virginia

Sara G. Tarver

The University of Wisconsin

CHARLES E. MERRILL PUBLISHING COMPANY
A Bell & Howell Company
Columbus Toronto London Sydney

THE MERRILL PERSONAL PERSPECTIVES IN SPECIAL EDUCATION SERIES

edited by James M. Kauffman

This book was set in Schoolbook.
The production editor was Linda Hillis.
The cover was prepared by Will Chenoweth.

Published by
CHARLES E. MERRILL PUBLISHING COMPANY
A Bell & Howell Company
Columbus, Ohio 43216

Library of Congress Catalog Card Number: 76-58628

International Standard Book Number: 0-675-08529-2

2 3 4 5 6 7 8 — 81 80 79 78 77

Printed in the United States of America

SERIES EDITOR'S FOREWORD

As members and future members of the special-education profession, we are in many ways at an adolescent stage of development. We are being pulled in opposite directions, not really knowing whether we should separate ourselves from the educational mainstream and assert our independence or embrace and merge with the disciplines from which we spring. It is an awkward and painful stage that is full of conflicting urges and perplexing characteristics. We realize that our self-assurance is accompanied by self-doubt, that our growth is rapid and uneven, and that our desire to perform exceeds our knowledge and skill. We keenly sense our own tendency to be argumentative and we are constantly aware that our economic needs outstrip our ability to acquire financial support.

In order to survive this difficult period in our history, we may need to engage in serious introspection—not in a spirit of inducing biting self-criticism or remorse, but in order to clarify our origins, our current perspectives, and our future directions. We must realize that only by trying to determine where we have been and where we are going can we be certain that the process of getting there will continue to be rewarding.

The Merrill Personal Perspectives in Special Education Series is a project designed to facilitate this introspection and to communicate major points of view regarding issues and problems in the field. The series features original contributions from persons whose work has left an indelible mark on the profession. These individuals have contributed summaries of their professional development and current perspectives which are free of the vagaries and distortions which inevitably accompany interpretation by another writer. The mosaic created by their contrasting and complementary origins, experiences, ideas, and personalities provides a picture of the profession which should help us to see ourselves, our work, and our goals as special educators with greater clarity.

James M. Kauffman

The University of Virginia

PREFACE

The field of special education as a whole reflects the characteristics of the special students which it strives to serve. It is a discipline in which divergent perspectives result in the advocation of instructional approaches almost as varied as the individual learners themselves. Like the special child, special education is, at times, unpredictable and difficult to manage. It eludes concrete definitions or scientific classification systems, thus providing fertile ground for controversies and contradictory approaches. Finally, as in the case of the developing exceptional child, the field of special education is continually changing. Remarkable changes have occurred, most notably within the past fifteen years, in the efforts to find better ways to meet the educational needs of the special learner.

Special education today requires professionals who can reflect these characteristics. They must be equipped with the knowledge and skills of a variety of approaches. They should be comfortable amid disagreement, contradictions, and controversy. They must be able to sift through the many changes in the field and to identify those of greatest value. Most importantly, they must be able to change with a changing profession by being continually open and alert to new directions and efforts.

This book is designed to assist the student in special education to gain a broad perspective on the aspects of variety, controversy, and change which are influencing the profession. In addition, with the inclusion of diverse and, in some cases, incongruent perspectives, the text is intended to stimulate critical thinking among both prospective and current special educators. Finally, the contributors have been selected as models in a field in which creativity and commitment are essential attributes. Their chapters are described from a personal perspective and supplemented with bibliographical information in order to familiarize the student not only with the various topics but also with the unique individuals themselves.

The first and last chapters provide a background perspective on how the field has changed and a projection of the future impact of these changes. Chapters 2 through 5 present important new developments in teaching methods, curriculum, and educational technology. Major issues and efforts in the area of diagnosis and evaluation are described in Chapters 6 through 9. Chapters 10 through 13 present a variety of programming trends and considerations. Current research and its implications are discussed in Chapters 14 through 16.

CONTENTS

vii

PART 1

Past
Perspectives

1

How Special Education
Has Changed

Sara G. Tarver received a B.S. degree in education from North-east Louisiana State College in 1956, a M.A. in psychology from the University of Richmond in 1970, and a Ph.D. in special education from the University of Virginia in 1975. At present, she is assistant professor in the Department of Studies in Behavioral Disabilities at the University of Wisconsin—Madison. Dr. Tarver's experiences include teaching of both learning disabled and nondisabled children at the elementary and junior high levels. She held an assistant professorship at the University of Virginia prior to her present faculty appointment.

The title of this chapter implies that special education began at some specifiable point in time and that important changes have taken place since that time. Yet, both the exact birthdate of the field and the historical significance attached to changes vary with the perspective of the historian reporting them. Hewett and Forness (1974) pointed out that the roots of special education can be traced to the beginning of man himself when there was an awareness of special differences in people's behavior and appearance. It was not until the eighteenth century, however, that the groundwork was laid for the emergence of *education* for certain different individuals, and not until the nineteenth century that *special education* as we know it today really began. The twentieth century has been a time of increasingly rapid change, so much so that special educators, in recent years, have undoubtedly been the victims of their share of society's future shock.

Among the eighteenth century advances cited by Hewett and Forness (1974) were improved treatment for the mentally ill, the development of materials for teaching the blind to read and write, and the development of means of communication for the deaf. Education of the retarded began early in the nineteenth century with Itard's attempts to civilize and educate Victor, the Wild Boy of Aveyron (Robinson & Robinson, 1976). The recognition and special education of mildly handicapped children (e.g., educable mentally retarded, learning disabled, and emotionally disturbed) has been, in large part, a phenomenon of the twentieth century.

In this chapter, historical trends and changes in four areas— methodology, diagnosis and evaluation, programming and services, and research—will be summarized and discussed briefly. In keeping with the current trend toward noncategorization in special education, no attempt will be made to present these changes strictly from a categorical point of view. For more comprehensive categorical histories, the reader is referred to Robinson and Robinson (1976) and Blanton (1975) in the area of mental retardation, Kauffman (1976) and Lewis (1974) in the area of emotional disturbance, and Hallahan and Cruickshank (1973) and Wiederholt (1974) in the area of learning disabilities.

HOW METHODOLOGY HAS CHANGED

Cawley refers to methods as the *how* of teaching and to curriculum as the *what* of teaching. A number of changes in both of these aspects have occurred since the early 1800s and the relative emphasis placed on each has shifted back and forth. A strong emphasis on the how was evident in the early approaches of Itard, Seguin, and Montessori. A shift to interest in the what during the second quarter of the twentieth century was evidenced by an abundance of curriculum guides (Cawley).[1] A return to primary emphasis on specific teaching methods occurred in the 1960s.

Sensory training was an essential part of the classic methods developed in the eighteenth century. Itard (1962) relied almost totally upon sensory training in his attempts to educate Victor. Seguin's (1966) physiological method involved both sensory and muscle training. Montessori's (1912) method has been described as multisensory. Also incorporated into these early methods were many of the elements of the currently popular behavior modification and/or applied behavior analysis approaches. Kauffman (1976) described the methods of Itard and Seguin as amazingly modern ones which were "based on individual assessment; were highly structured, systematic, directive, and multisensory; emphasized training in self-help and daily living skills for the

---

[1] References to authors' chapters included in this volume are not followed by a date or listed in the References section.

severely handicapped; made frequent use of games and songs; and were suffused with positive reinforcement" [p. 342].

While the efforts of Itard and Seguin were directed toward the education of the severely and profoundly retarded, Montessori worked more exclusively with disadvantaged mentally retarded children who would probably be classified as educable mentally retarded today. It is not surprising, then, that she placed greater emphasis on teaching the basic academic skills of reading, writing, and arithmetic than did her predecessors. Montessori's book describing her method was published in 1912. Since that time, Fernald (1943), Lehtinen (Strauss & Lehtinen, 1947), and Gillingham and Stillman (1956) have developed multisensory methods of teaching basic academic skills which bear a strong resemblance to those of Montessori.

Increased efforts to expand curricula to nonacademic areas in the mainstream of education during the second quarter of the twentieth century resulted in decreased attention to the three r's. Since the typical curriculum for educable mentally retarded children enrolled in special classes was a slowed down version of that for normal children in the regular classroom (Robinson & Robinson, 1976), this general trend to de-emphasize the teaching of academic skills was reflected in special education.

It was also during the second quarter of this century—the 1930s and 1940s—that special methods of teaching brain injured, mentally retarded children were being developed within an institutional setting, the Wayne County Training School in Michigan. It was there that Werner and Strauss attempted to distinguish exogenous (brain injured) and endogenous (familial) mentally retarded children and to develop methods of structuring the classroom environment in order to eliminate extraneous distracting stimuli which were thought to interfere with the learning of the exogenous (Hallahan & Cruickshank, 1973). Their methods have been refined, adapted, and applied in public school settings in the Montgomery County Project for hyperactive, emotionally disturbed children (Cruickshank, Bentzen, Ratzeburg, & Tannhauser, 1961) and by Hewett as a part of his engineered classroom (Hewett, 1968; Hewett, Taylor, & Artuso, 1968) and The Madison School Plan (Hewett & Forness, 1974).

Concern for individual differences in learning was expressed in the writings of all of the special educators mentioned thus far in this chapter. As Keogh has so accurately stated, "the history of special education may well be viewed as a preoccupation with individual differences." It was not until the late 1950s and 1960s, however, that individual learning styles became the central theme of special education and concerted efforts were made to develop means for actually achieving the goal of individualization of instruction. This trend is reflected in the popular concepts of prescriptive teaching (Peter, 1965), diagnostic-prescriptive teaching (McIntosh & Dunn, 1973), intraindividual differences (Kirk, 1968), clinical teaching (Lerner, 1971), and remedial-diagnosis (Beery, 1968). Also inherent in these concepts are the notions that individualization of instruction must be based upon individual diagnosis and that diagnosis and remediation are continuous, ongoing processes (Wallace & Kauffman, 1973). Accordingly, much professional effort has been devoted to the development of diagnostic tests and corresponding teaching/training programs.

According to Paraskevopoulos and Kirk (1969), the concept of intraindividual differences brings remediation into focus because it implies delineation of specific deficiencies which become the focus of remediation. The need for a test designed to assess intraindividual, rather than interindividual, differences was recognized by Samuel Kirk and his colleagues in the 1950s. In an attempt to meet this need, they developed an experimental edition of the Illinois Test of Psycholinguistic Abilities (ITPA) which was published in 1961 and a revised edition which was published in 1968 (Kirk, McCarthy, & Kirk, 1961, 1968). Suggestions for remediation of the deficiencies revealed on the ITPA are included in Kirk (1966), Bateman (1968), Karnes (1968), and Bush and Giles (1960).

Two other assessment instruments developed in conjunction with corresponding programs of remediation in the 1960s were Marianne Frostig's Developmental Test of Visual Perception (Frostig, Maslow, Lefever, & Whittlesey, 1964; Frostig, Lefever, & Whittlesey, 1966; Frostig & Horne, 1964) and the Purdue Perceptual-Motor Survey (Roach & Kephart, 1966). Although the ITPA grew out of the early work of Kirk and his colleagues with mentally retarded children and Kephart's work began with "slow learners" (Kephart, 1960, 1971), all three of the diagnostic instruments described above—the ITPA, Frostig's DTVP, and the Purdue Perceptual-Motor Survey—came to be highly associated with the learning disabilities movement in the 1960s because they are designed to diagnose specific learning disabilities.

The first half of the present decade has been marked by controversies regarding the developments and trends of the 1960s. The basic concept of individualization of instruction has been called into question by reports of unsuccessful attempts to match diagnosed learning styles with corresponding teaching methods. In particular, the practice of assessing perceptual-motor and/or psycholinguistic processes thought to underlie academic achievement and prescribing process-oriented training on the basis of these findings has been under fire from a number of critics (Cohen, 1969, 1970, 1971; cf. Larsen; Mann, 1971). A recently published book, *Psycholinguistics in the Schools*, by Newcomer and Hammill (1976) is devoted to a review, analysis, and interpretation of much of the evidence pertinent to this controversy. The authors' interpretation of the evidence resulted in their taking "what is essentially a nonadvocacy position regarding the practical educational usefulness of the principle [sic] test, the ITPA, and training programs which represent the Osgood model" [p. *x*].

In contrast, an earlier review of studies evaluating the effectiveness of perceptual-motor training programs led Hallahan and Cruickshank (1973) to conclude that neither the negative nor the positive evidence is persuasive and that ultimate acceptance or rejection of these theories should be based on further empirical investigations. That this controversy has by no means been settled is indicated by a number of published rebuttals to the anti-process point of view (Bush, 1976; Frostig, 1969; McCarthy, 1976; McLeod, 1976; Minskoff, 1976) and subsequent responses to those rebuttals (Larsen, 1976; Newcomer & Hammill, 1976).

Taking a slightly different process-oriented approach to the individualization of instruction, a number of educators have attempted to assess individual differences in preferred learning modalities and match these preferences with different methods of teaching reading. To date, studies investigating the effectiveness of this type of matching procedure have failed to demonstrate success (Tarver & Dawson, in press). These negative findings are consistent with Engelmann's view that we "can't make a good case for 'different programs for different learning styles.' " He contends that effective teaching will be based on analysis of the task rather than on assessment of child variables. Similarly, Cawley states that in reference to most cases of reading disability we are dealing with content deficiencies rather than process deficiencies. Our real problem, he contends, is a lack of information about the task of reading rather than a lack of information about the learner's processes.

It is interesting to note that similar differences of opinion regarding the effectiveness of sensory training existed over a half-century ago. Binet argued that the time spent on sensory training such as that developed by Seguin would be better spent on teaching the retarded to read street signs and simple instructions (cf. Blanton, 1975). Binet's recommendation that sensory training be replaced by a more direct approach to the teaching of reading is much like the recommendations of many of today's critics of the process training approach. Stephens's (in press) directive teaching approach typifies current methods which emphasize the assessment of specific weaknesses and strengths in academic skills and remediation of each deficit through direct teaching. The paradox of this approach is discussed by Cawley. He points out that many children were being taught by this "head-on" approach at the time that they were found to have learning problems, that the process-oriented approach represented an attempt to alter instruction to fit the needs of the child, and that failure to demonstrate the effectiveness of this practice to date does not necessarily imply that a return to the original head-on approach is warranted.

Another seemingly paradoxical occurrence of the 1960s and 1970s was the concurrent increase of interest in individualization of instruction and behavior modification. The individualization concept is based on the assumption that individuals learn differently and should therefore be taught differently, while behaviorism is concerned with basic learning principles which apply to all organisms and all types of learning. A look at the development of these two contrasting trends reveals that they were advancing within different camps during the 1960s. Kauffman's (1975) review of the literature revealed that behavior modification techniques were applied primarily to the management of disruptive, hyperactive, aggressive, and inattentive behaviors during the 1960s. At that time, professionals advocating individualization of instruction were primarily concerned with deficiencies in academic skills. It was not until the early 1970s that an increase in the application of behavior modification to academic behaviors was evidenced in the literature. It was at this point that a need to integrate the two approaches became apparent.

The directive teaching trend of the 1970s may be viewed as a rapprochement of the concepts generally associated with the individualized instruction and behavior modification approaches. It incorporates many of the elements of behavior modification (e.g., precise measurement, reinforcement, task analysis) and, at the same time, involves individual assessment of skill weaknesses and strengths.

HOW DIAGNOSIS AND EVALUATION HAVE CHANGED

Diagnosis and evaluation have changed significantly in terms of both purposes and procedures during the last century. The primary purpose has changed from classification for placement to the acquisition of what has been called "educationally relevant" information about the child, and, finally, to the amassing of information about both the child and environmental variables which are thought to interact in a significant and meaningful way with child variables.

Prior to the twentieth century, classification and placement were the result of simple informal observations and subjective judgments of deviations from acceptable behavior and appearance. According to Crissey (1975), indices of mental development included head measurement, vital capacity, and the interviewer's personal "bias and sixth sense" [p. 803]. Individuals identified as "different" on the basis of these procedures would no doubt be classified as severely and profoundly handicapped today.

Mildly handicapped children were not generally identified as such and given a label to denote exceptionality until after the turn of the twentieth century. With the passage of compulsory school attendance laws in the late 1800s and early 1900s, more and more mildly handicapped children were enrolled in the public schools. Many educators felt that identification and segregation of these children in the early primary grades was a pressing need. Since these mildly retarded children were not easily distinguishable from normal children on the basis of observation and subjective judgment, an objective means of identification was needed. It was in response to this need that Alfred Binet was commissioned to devise a means of measuring mental development (Payne & Mercer, 1975). The intelligence scale devised by Binet and his colleague, Theodore Simon, in the first decade of this century has been revised several times and is known today as the Stanford-Binet Intelligence Scale (Terman & Merrill, 1960). Terman's 1916 revision was the first to introduce the concept of the IQ score, a quantification of the child's test performance. The practice of relying almost solely upon IQ scores for placement in special classes quickly became popular and remained so throughout the first half of this century.

It was near the midpoint of the twentieth century that a number of arguments against the use of intelligence testing were raised. Robinson and Robinson (1976) summarized the critics' major points as follows: (a) The tests do not measure what they are purported to measure, (b) people are unfairly labeled, (c) important decisions are based on these labels, and (d) these decisions become increasingly difficult to change because they determine the educational opportunities made available to the child. Increasing recognition of the potential detriment of intelligence testing led to a reaffirmation of the need to consider definitional criteria other than IQ scores in the identification of mental retardation; i.e., deficiencies in adaptive behavior manifested in the developmental period (Grossman, 1973; Heber, 1959). Two of the most widely used measures of adaptive behavior are the Vineland Social Maturity Scale (Doll, 1965) and the AAMD Adaptive Behavior Scale (Nihira, Foster, Shellhaas, & Leland, 1974).

Intelligence testing never played so crucial a role in the diagnosis and classification of other mildly handicapping conditions such as learning disabilities. There are several reasons for this difference in diagnostic practices. First, by the time learning disabilities was recognized as a category of exceptionality in the 1960s, the intelligence testing controversy was in full swing. Secondly, according to most definitions of learning disabilities, children in this category do not differ from normal children on intellectual potential; thus, IQ scores alone would not be expected to differentiate these children from normal children. However, to aid in distinguishing learning disabled from mentally retarded children and to affirm or refute the existence of a discrepancy between intellectual potential and academic achievement, intelligence tests have generally been included in diagnostic batteries administered to children referred because of learning difficulties in school. Third, and perhaps most importantly, views regarding the purposes of diagnosis changed drastically in the 1960s. The purposes of classification, labeling, and placement became secondary to the primary purpose of obtaining information about the child that could be used by educators to plan an individualized instructional program.

During the time that this change in purpose was evolving, many diagnosticians attempted to achieve the new purpose by using the same or similar diagnostic instruments; i.e., they attempted to glean from intelligence tests information on which they could base educational recommendations. The Wechsler Intelligence Test for Children (WISC), in particular, was used in this manner (Glasser, 1967) because it yields scores on ten subtests, a verbal IQ, and a performance IQ in addition to a total IQ. As other ability tests (e.g., the ITPA and the DTVP) gained popularity in the 1960s, educational recommendations were based more frequently on profiles from these tests and less often on those obtained from intelligence tests.

The controversy surrounding the use of ability tests and the subsequent shift to direct skill assessment and teaching were discussed in an earlier section of this chapter. Occurring along with this shift has been increased emphasis on the types of informal assessment procedures described by Larsen in his chapter in this volume.

Logan discusses two diagnostic models which are being developed currently. Both represent approaches concerned with the assessment of environmental, as well as child, variables. The first, Cromwell's ABCD model, provides for assessment of history, etiology, current behaviors, treatment, and prognosis. The second, the SOMPA model of Mercer and Lewis, focuses on the individual's social behaviors and the social systems in which he lives.

Despite the fact that classification and placement are no longer the primary purposes of diagnosis, they have been and still continue to be purposes which must be valued for pragmatic reasons. Bradley, in her chapter in this volume, expresses well the plight of educators vested with the responsibility of identifying handicapped children in order for them to receive special services.

HOW PROGRAMMING AND SERVICES
HAVE CHANGED

In the United States, education of exceptional children began in institutional or residential centers in the nineteenth century and moved into the public schools in the late nineteenth and early twentieth centuries (Van Osdol & Shane, 1974). Mental retardation was the first exceptionality recognized and provided for by the public schools. Included in this category were many deaf, blind, and multiply handicapped children whose condition of mental retardation was related to their other handicaps. Special classes were first organized for these children in 1896, yet by the end of the 1920s there were still only 222 special classes in the United States (Love, 1972). For the next 25 to 30 years or so, the majority of the severely handicapped continued to be institutionalized.

During these early years of the twentieth century, the mildly handicapped child was likely to be found in the regular classroom, and was described by many writers as unsuccessful, frustrated, humiliated, and ready to drop out of school at the first opportunity. In the late 1940s and 1950s, parents began to form organizations for the purpose of fostering public services for educable, as well as severely and profoundly, retarded children. The National Association for Retarded Children (NARC), now known as the National Association for Retarded Citizens, was successful at getting legislation passed which required school districts to provide special services for handicapped children. Since that time the growth of special classes for retarded children has been remarkable; e.g., between the years of 1953 and 1958 the increase in enrollment was 260 percent (Love, 1972).

It was during the 1950s and 1960s that parents and educators began to recognize a substantial number of children who were not mentally retarded, but who nevertheless were having difficulties functioning successfully in school; i.e., children who later came to be labeled "learning disabled" or "emotionally disturbed." Following in the steps of NARC, the parents of the learning disabled formed the Association for Children with Learning Disabilities and began lobbying for legislation. Because much of the groundwork had been laid by NARC, their purposes were achieved in a relatively short period of time and special classes for the learning disabled increased rapidly.

It seems almost paradoxical that, after fifty years of striving for the establishment of special classes, and at a time when progress toward that goal was taking place at an unprecedented rate, an about face and headlong rush toward mainstreaming occurred. This mainstreaming movement was brought about by a convergence of many related issues such as labeling, classification, definitions, the efficacy of special classes, racial segregation, child advocacy, and legislation and funding. Debates of these issues in recent court cases resulted in court decisions giving priority to regular class placement (LaVor). As discussed by MacMillan and Becker, these decisions were based not on evidence that the regular classroom *has been* effective in meeting the needs of exceptional children, but on evidence that the special class *has not*.

The assumptions underlying both special class and regular class placement for exceptional children have been summarized by Robinson and Robinson (1976). In the case of the special class placement, the assumptions are:

1. Children in special classes are homogeneously grouped.
2. Specialized curricula are used in special classes.
3. Special training has been provided teachers of special classes.
4. Class size has been reduced.

Assumptions underlying the regular classroom placement are:

1. Special class placement is a more isolating experience than regular class placement.
2. Exposure to models whose social and academic achievement is superior to that of the handicapped results in improved achievement on the part of the handicapped.
3. The regular classroom is more like the real world than is the special classroom.
4. Exposing normal children to handicapped children results in greater understanding and acceptance of the handicapped.

Robinson and Robinson (1976) pointed out that research to either refute or support these assumptions is meager in the case of both the special and the regular class placements.

As pointed out by MacMillan and Becker, most children with mild handicaps were experiencing failure in the regular classroom before they were placed in special classes. Unless it can be assumed that the typical regular classroom has changed significantly in recent years, a return to that environment could hardly be expected to provide solutions to the problems of most exceptional children. Proponents of the mainstreaming movement contend that such a change has taken place—that instruction has become more individualized in the regular classroom. They support the view that individualization of instruction, in combination with supplementary services of specialists such as resource teachers and/or learning disability specialists will effectively meet the needs of the mildly handicapped. It is interesting to note that the mainstreaming movement—a movement based largely on the assumption that individualization of instruction provides the key to the solution of most learning problems—seems to be reaching its stride at a time when the basic concept of individualized instruction is being questioned because of lack of evidence in support of its effectiveness.

HOW RESEARCH HAS CHANGED

Cattell (1966) discussed changes in the study of human behavior in terms of three phases. The first, which existed up until about a century ago, was called a literary and philosophical stage. The second, a clinical phase, gained prominence about 1870 and persisted for about half a century. The third phase, based on measurement and experiment, began about 1890 and has continued to gain momentum since that time. Within the third stage, two distinct methodological veins of development can be traced: the Wundt-Pavlov and the Galton-Spearman veins. Cattell (1966) described the methods stemming from the Wundt-Pavlov vein as bivariate, manipulative (controlled), atomistic, and "the old, familiar process of biting off a bit at a time" [p. 7]. In contrast, the Galton-Spearman experimental tradition was described as multivariate, nonmanipulative methodology which "enables wholistic real-life action to be analyzed without manipulative control" [p. 18].

Much of the applied and basic experimental research conducted in special education has been of the bivariate type. Included in this category are the comparative research studies in which the performance of a group of exceptional children is compared to that of a normal control group in order to investigate differences in some specific aspect of psychological processing. For reviews of this type of research, the reader is referred to Estes (1970) and Robinson and Robinson (1976) in reference to the mentally retarded, and Hallahan (1975) and Bryan and Bryan (1975) in reference to the learning disabled. Bivariate designs have also been used frequently to investigate the efficacy of methodological approaches and/or special placements; e.g., to compare the academic achievement of children exposed to perceptual-motor training to that of children receiving no such training and to compare the social and academic behaviors of children in special classes to those of children in regular classes.

Multivariate designs such as factor analysis, multiple regression, and discriminant analysis are so mathematically complex that they almost defy computation by hand; thus, their use was not widespread prior to the advent of the computer. They have become increasingly popular in recent years, however, and have been used to investigate a number of problems of particular interest to special educators. To cite a few examples, multiple regression has been used to delineate combinations of variables which predict academic success or failure; thus, this design has contributed to advancements in the early identification of high-risk children. Factor analysis has been used to investigate the validity of tests designed to assess specific weaknesses and strengths and to detect clusters of behaviors which are descriptive of certain subgroups of emotionally disturbed children.

The popular view that multivariate designs are more productive than bivariate designs in the study of individual differences (McCall, 1970) leads to the expectation that multivariate designs should predominate special education research. Research actuality, however, is more in line with Cattell's (1966) view that both bivariate and multivariate designs are essential to a complete understanding of individual differences in behavior. As a case in point, bivariate analysis of variance has been used in the aptitude-treatment interaction design employed to evaluate the effectiveness of matching individual learning styles with particular methods of teaching (Ysseldyke, 1973).

Other research methods which have particular relevance to special education have been developed by behavioral psychologists and educators over the last two decades. Kauffman (1975) stated that "perhaps the greatest single contribution of behavior modification to psychology and education has been the development of procedures for direct, continuous, and precise measurement of behavior" [p. 399]. He also pointed out that behavior modifiers have relied almost solely upon single-subject rather than group designs and described the three following single-subject designs which have been used frequently for behavior analysis in applied settings: (a) the reversal or withdrawal design; (b) multiple baseline designs involving multiple schedules, multiple responses, or multiple subjects; and (c) the changing criterion design. White, in his chapter in this volume, discusses the single-subject versus group design controversy and goes on to suggest that both types of designs contribute to our understanding of behavior and ways of modifying it.

Increased interest in the study of language development of exceptional children represents another important research trend of recent years. As research within the mainstream of psychology and psycholinguistics has demonstrated interrelations among perceptual, cognitive, social, and language development (McLean), the role of language in normal and delayed development has assumed new proportions.

Finally, the most obvious change in special education research during the last quarter century is the change in the quantity of research conducted. The tremendous increase in research related to the problems of exceptional children reflects not only the advances in methodology which have been discussed herein, but an increasing awareness on the part of educators of the value of research. The chapter by Tanis and James Bryan in this volume should serve to sharpen this awareness even more.

REFERENCES

Bateman, B. *Interpretation of the 1961 Illinois Test of Psycholinguistic Abilities.* Seattle: Special Child Publications, 1968.

Beery, K. E. *Remedialdiagnosis.* San Rafael, Calif.: Dimensions Publishing Co., 1968.

Blanton, R. L. Historical perspectives on classification of mental retardation. In N. Hobbs (Ed.), *Issues in the classification of children* (Vol. 1). San Francisco: Jossey-Bass, 1975.

Bryan, T. H., & Bryan, J. H. *Understanding learning disabilities.* Port Washington, N.Y.: Alfred Publishing Co., 1975.

Bush, W. J. Psycholinguistic remediation in the schools. In P. L. Newcomer & D. D. Hammill, *Psycholinguistics in the Schools.* Columbus, Ohio: Charles E. Merrill, 1976.

Bush, W. J., & Giles, M. T. *Aids to psycholinguistic teaching.* Columbus, Ohio: Charles E. Merrill, 1969.

Cattell, R. B. Psychological theory and scientific method. In R. B. Cattell (Ed.), *Handbook of multivariate experimental psychology.* Chicago: Rand McNally, 1966.

Cohen, S. A. Studies in visual perception and reading in disadvantaged children. *Journal of Learning Disabilities,* 1969, 2, 498-507.

Cohen, S. A. Cause and treatment in reading achievement. *Journal of Learning Disabilities,* 1970, 3, 163-66.

Cohen, S. A. Dyspedagogia as a cause of reading retardation: Definition and treatment. In B. Bateman (Ed.), *Learning disorders* (Vol. 4). Seattle: Special Child Publications, 1971.

Crissey, M. S. Mental retardation: Past, present, and future. *American Psychologist,* 1975, 30, 800-808.

Cruickshank, W. M., Bentzen, F. A., Ratzeburg, F. H., & Tannhauser, M. T. *A teaching method for brain-injured and hyperactive children.* Syracuse: Syracuse University Press, 1961.

Doll, E. A. *Vineland Social Maturity Scale: Condensed manual of directions* (1965 ed.). Circle Pines, Minn.: American Guidance Service, 1965.

Estes, W. K. *Learning theory and mental development.* New York: Academic Press, 1970.

Fernald, G. M. *Remedial techniques in basic school subjects.* New York: McGraw-Hill, 1943.

Frostig, M. Reading, developmental abilities and the problem of the match. *Journal of Learning Disabilities,* 1969, 2, 571-74.

Frostig, M., & Horne, D. *The Frostig program for the development of visual perception: Teacher's guide.* Chicago: Follett, 1964.

Frostig, M., Lefever, W., & Whittlesey, J. R. B. *Administration and scoring manual for the Marianne Frostig Developmental Test of Visual Perception.* Palo Alto: Consulting Psychologists Press, 1966.

Frostig, M., Maslow, P., Lefever, D. W., & Whittlesey, J. R. B. *The Marianne Frostig Developmental Test of Visual Perception, 1963 Standardization.* Palo Alto: Consulting Psychologists Press, 1964.

Gillingham, A., & Stillman, B. *Remedial training for children with specific disability in reading, spelling, and penmanship.* Cambridge, Mass.: Educators Publishing Service, 1956.

Glasser, A. J., & Zimmerman, I. L. *Clinical interpretation of the Wechsler Intelligence Scale for Children (WISC).* New York: Grune & Stratton, 1967.

Grossman, H. J. (Ed.) *Manual on terminology and classification in mental retardation.* American Association on Mental Deficiency Special Publication, Series No. 2, 1973.

Hallahan, D. P. Comparative research studies on the psychological characteristics of learning disabled children. In W. M. Cruickshank & D. P. Hallahan (Eds.), *Perceptual and learning disabilities in children: Psychoeducational practices* (Vol. 1). Syracuse: Syracuse University Press, 1975.

Hallahan, D. P., & Cruickshank, W. M. *Psychoeducational foundations of learning disabilities.* Englewood Cliffs, N.J.: Prentice-Hall, 1973.

Heber, R. F. A manual on terminology and classification in mental retardation. *Monograph Supplement American Journal of Mental Deficiency,* 1959, 64.

Hewett, F. M. *The emotionally disturbed child in the classroom.* Boston: Allyn & Bacon, 1968.

Hewett, F. M., & Forness, S. R. *Education of exceptional learners.* Boston: Allyn & Bacon, 1974.

Hewett, F. M., Taylor, F. D., & Artuso, A. A. The Santa Monica project. *Exceptional Children,* 1968, 34, 387.

Itard, J. M. G. *The wild boy of Aveyron.* New York: Appleton-Century-Crofts, 1962.

Karnes, M. B. *Helping young children develop language skills: A book of activities.* Arlington, Va.: Council for Exceptional Children, 1968.

Kauffman, J. M. Behavior modification. In W. M. Cruickshank & D. P. Hallahan (Eds.), *Perceptual and learning disabilities in children: Research and theory* (Vol. 2). Syracuse: Syracuse University Press, 1975.

Kauffman, J. M. Nineteenth century views of children's behavior disorders: Historical contributions and continuing issues. *Journal of Special Education,* 1976, 10, 335-49.

Kephart, N. C. *The slow learner in the classroom.* Columbus, Ohio: Charles E. Merrill, 1960.

Kephart, N. C. *The slow learner in the classroom* (2nd ed.). Columbus, Ohio: Charles E. Merrill, 1971.

Kirk, S. A. *The diagnosis and remediation of psycholinguistic disabilities.* Urbana: University of Illinois Press, 1966.

Kirk, S. A. The Illinois Test of Psycholinguistic Abilities: Its origin and implications. In J. Hellmuth (Ed.), *Learning disorders* (Vol. 3). Seattle: Special Child Publications, 1968, 395-427.

Kirk, S. A., McCarthy, J. J., & Kirk, W. D. *Illinois Test of Psycholinguistic Abilities* (Experimental ed.). Urbana: University of Illinois Press, 1961.

Kirk, S. A., McCarthy, J. J., & Kirk, W. D. *Illinois Test of Psycholinguistic Abilities* (Rev. ed.). Urbana: University of Illinois Press, 1968.

Larsen, S. C. Response to James McCarthy. *Journal of Learning Disabilities*, 1976, 9, 334-37.

Lerner, J. W. *Children with learning disabilities*. Boston: Houghton Mifflin, 1971.

Lewis, C. D. Introduction: Landmarks. In J. M. Kauffman & C. D. Lewis (Eds.), *Teaching children with behavior disorders: Personal perspectives*. Columbus, Ohio: Charles E. Merrill, 1974.

Love, H. D. *Educating exceptional children in regular classrooms*. Springfield, Ill.: Charles C Thomas, 1972.

Mann, L. Psychometric phrenology and the new faculty psychology: The case against ability assessment and training. *Journal of Special Education*, 1971, 5, 3-14.

McCall, R. B. The use of multivariate procedures in developmental psychology. In P. H. Mussen (Ed.), *Carmichael's manual of child psychology* (Vol. 1). New York: Wiley, 1970.

McCarthy, J. J. The validity of perceptual tests: The debate continues. *Journal of Learning Disabilities*, 1976, 9, 332-34.

McIntosh, D. K., & Dunn, L. M. Children with major specific learning disabilities. In L. M. Dunn (Ed.), *Exceptional children in the schools, special education in transition*. New York: Holt, Rinehart & Winston, 1973.

McLeod, J. A reaction to *Psycholinguistics in the Schools*. In P. L. Newcomer & D. D. Hammill, *Psycholinguistics in the Schools*. Columbus, Ohio: Charles E. Merrill, 1976.

Minskoff, E. H. Research on the efficacy of remediating psycholinguistic disabilities: Critique and recommendations. In P. L. Newcomer & D. D. Hammill, *Psycholinguistics in the Schools*. Columbus, Ohio: Charles E. Merrill, 1976.

Montessori, M. [*The Montessori method*] (A. E. George, trans.). New York: Frederick Stokes, 1912.

Newcomer, P. L., & Hammill, D. D. *Psycholinguistics in the Schools*. Columbus, Ohio: Charles E. Merrill, 1976.

Nihira, K., Foster, R., Shellhaas, M., & Leland, H. *Adaptive Behavior Scales: Manual*. Washington, D.C.: American Association on Mental Deficiency, 1969.

Paraskevopoulos, J. N., & Kirk, S. A. *The development and psychometric characteristics of the revised Illinois Test of Psycholinguistic Abilities*. Urbana: University of Illinois Press, 1969.

Payne, J. S., & Mercer, C. D. Intelligence and intelligence testing. In J. M. Kauffman & J. S. Payne (Eds.), *Mental retardation: Introduction and personal perspectives*. Columbus, Ohio: Charles E. Merrill, 1975.

Peter, L. J. *Prescriptive teaching*. New York: McGraw-Hill, 1965.

Roach, E. G., & Kephart, N. C. *The Purdue Perceptual-Motor Survey*. Columbus, Ohio: Charles E. Merrill, 1966.

Robinson, N. M., & Robinson, H. B. *The mentally retarded child*. New York: McGraw-Hill, 1976.

Seguin, E. *Idiocy and its treatment by the physiological method*. New York: Brandon, 1866.

Stephens, T. M. *Directive teaching of children with learning and behavioral handicaps*. Columbus, Ohio: Charles E. Merrill, 1976.

Stephens, T. M. *Teaching children with learning disabilities and behavior disorders*. Columbus, Ohio: Charles E. Merrill, in press.

Strauss, A. A., & Lehtinen, L. E. *Psychopathological education of the brain-injured child*. New York: Grune & Stratton, 1947.

Tarver, S. G., & Dawson, M. M. Modality preference and the teaching of reading: A review. *Journal of Learning Disabilities*, in press.

Terman, L. M., & Merrill, M. A. *Stanford-Binet Intelligence Scale: Manual for the third revision form L-M*. Boston: Houghton Mifflin, 1960.

Van Osdol, W. R., & Shane, D. G. *An introduction to exceptional children*. Dubuque, Iowa: Wm. C. Brown Co., 1974.

Wallace, G., & Kauffman, J. M. *Teaching children with learning problems*. Columbus, Ohio: Charles E. Merrill, 1973.

Wiederholt, J. L. Historical perspectives on the education of the learning disabled. In L. Mann & D. Sabatino (Eds.), *The second review of special education*. Philadelphia: Journal of Special Education Press, 1974.

Ysseldyke, J. E. Diagnostic-prescriptive teaching: The search for aptitude-treatment interactions. In L. Mann & D. Sabatino (Eds.), *The first review of special education*. Philadelphia: Journal of Special Education Press, 1973.

PART 2

Changing
Perspectives in
Methodology

2

Curriculum: One Perspective for Special Education

John F. Cawley

John F. Cawley received a B.S. degree from the University of
Rhode Island in 1953, a M.A. degree from the University of Connecticut
in 1956, and a Ph.D. degree from the University of Connecticut in 1962.
He is currently professor of education at the University of Connecticut
at Storrs.

Prior to his position at Connecticut, Dr. Cawley was assistant
professor at the University of Kansas, a fellow in mental retardation at
Syracuse University, and a teacher of the mentally retarded in Norwich,

Preparation of this chapter was aided in part by a grant from the Bureau of
Education for the Handicapped, "A Program Project Research & Demonstration
Effort in Arithmetic Among the Mentally Handicapped," OEG-0-70-2250(607)
#162008.

Connecticut. Dr. Cawley has written numerous articles and texts in the area of curriculum and instructional development. A selected bibliography of his works appears on page 45.

Special education is a complex and multivaried endeavor. Accordingly, I will limit this chapter to matters of curriculum as they apply to children generally referred to as emotionally disturbed, learning disabled, and/or mentally retarded.

For me, special education started rather simply on a field trip during my senior year in college. I was enrolled in a class in kinesiology and the instructor wanted us to have a first-hand look at the myriad of physical—primarily neuromuscular—problems which existed among handicapped children. Hence, the field trip to an institution for the severely multiply handicapped, nearly all mentally retarded. I was so turned on by the place that I even applied for a job there. No luck. They had needs, but no positions.

I took a position at the Norwich Free Academy in Connecticut. My first assignment consisted of teaching two sections of General Science, one section of General Math, one of Algebra, and one of Industrial Science; I was also to serve as assistant football coach and assistant track coach. The classes were homogeneously grouped in this large secondary school of over 3,000 students. The relative developmental expectancy of each class section was denoted in the teacher's schedule with letters: A = highest; D = lowest. Quickly, I found out that "D" really meant that the kids couldn't read, often manifested social conflicts with the school, occasionally displayed moderate emotional problems, and frequently demonstrated intellectual ability one to two or more standard deviations below average. Two things made sense. The first was to motivate the kids; the second was to find ways to teach science without letting their reading problems interfere (I had no idea how to handle the reading). Out went the books and in came the projects. We built everything, conducted every experiment, and tried anything. We collected snakes, pithed frogs, and built an electric chair. The kids learned their science and math, attendance was good, and discipline problems were few and far between.

Archie Goldberg was curriculum coordinator. During the course of the year he approached me about doing something for the "D" kids and also for kids of more limited ability who never got to secondary school. We discussed various options with Mr. George Shattuck, the principal. It was decided that we would hire a teacher who knew something about reading. I then would handle the kids for two hours a day in math and science and the reading specialist, Les Hartson, currently assistant headmaster at NFA, would have them for two hours a day in

English (reading) and social studies. The kids would use electives for the other two periods each day. In the second year, actually the tenth grade, the kids would be grouped for English and civics in a two-hour block, come to me for math for one period, and use three electives. The junior year had the kids grouped only for English and social studies and on their own for four periods. No program other than carefully selected teacher-pupil matches in scheduling was planned for the fourth year. One might say that the kids were "mainstreamed" for the senior year. It became necessary to hire additional teachers because the kids weren't dropping out of school. Meanwhile, I decided I should broaden my knowledge about the field so I enrolled in a program at the University of Connecticut. Bob Henderson, currently at the University of Illinois, Urbana, was the first and only special education faculty member, and it was his first year of teaching after completing his own doctorate. I became certified and functioned for the next six years as a teacher of the "mentally retarded." Actually, it was not until the early 1970s that more than one type of teacher certificate was offered in Connecticut; so my certification had nothing to do with the type of youngsters with whom I worked and learned.

Many times I wish that I could turn the clock back twenty years and return to the "good old days." Everything was so simple. The rules so easy. No complicated issues. No teacher or kid categories or labels to fight about. I often wonder if the real issue isn't *teacher categories* and not *kid categories* as we tend to infer. We only had one teacher category back then, so we simply took any kid who needed help and did the best we could. And these kids were generally as divergent a group of individuals as one could imagine. I think of Nancy, an epileptic with an alcoholic mother. Nancy was usually so overloaded with medication on the weekends that it took her until Wednesday to become alert enough to function—but function fairly well she did.

I think of Doris who was very bright but who had not been to school for four years because no school program was available at the nearby state hospital. I was leery the day that the psychologist approached me about his desire to get Doris out of the hospital and into school during the daytime at least. She wanted to go to school, but where? As usual Mr. Shattuck agreed. I figured "why not" and in came Doris.

And, there was John. His ability was above average, as measured by WISC-type tests; his achievement in the three r's was about zero; his behavior was pleasant. John's insight into electricity and his ability to build electrical devices was amazing. But he just couldn't make it in reading and math. We even sent him for a neurological examination because we seemed to be getting nowhere.

As I indicated, John was a pleasant character and he made every effort to be sociable. As a matter of fact, I recall one incident when

John invited one of the class to stay overnight at his house. Would you believe it? John wired the bed and during the night he shocked his guest. When I look back, I am convinced that the only reason John was sent for the neurological was because I had a teaching certificate in biology.

Also, there was Bernie. Figure 1 is a sample of one of his papers. I showed this to everybody, including a Polish speaking priest because I knew Bernie was Polish and I thought he might write only Polish.

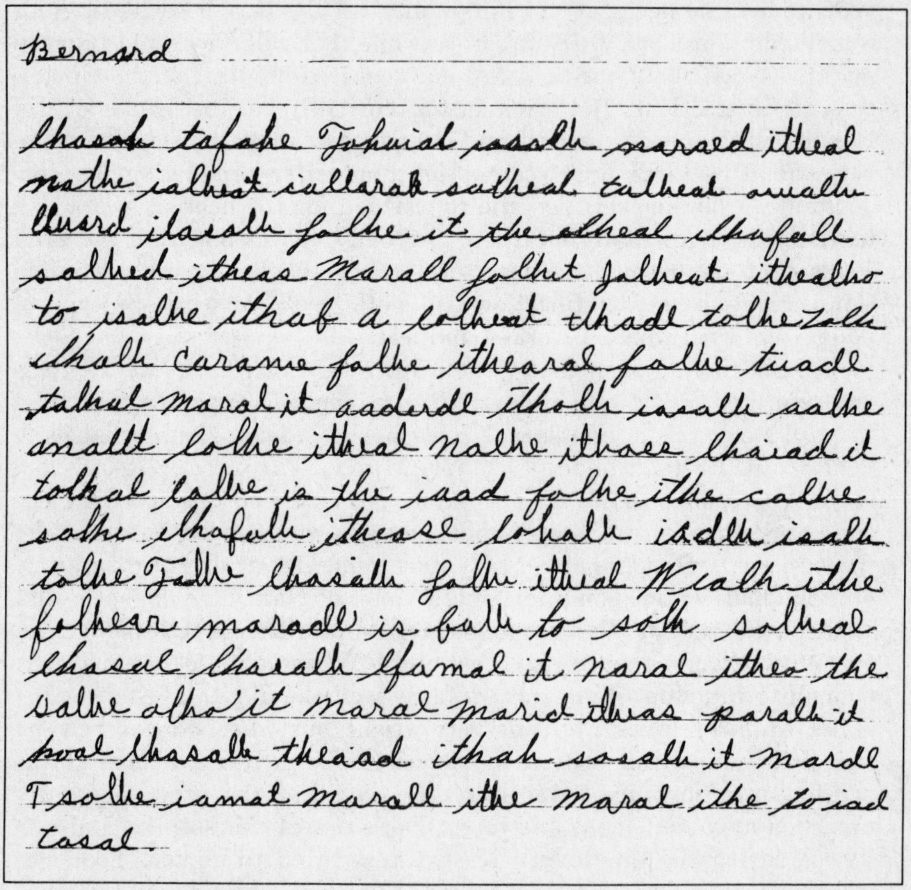

FIGURE 1: Example of the written production of one fourteen year old ninth-grade boy.

No way. It was straight-out gobbledygook. Anyway, Bernie was tested and his IQ was reported to be around 60. That explained everything. What else should we expect from a fourteen year old with a 60 IQ? Ultimately, this puzzled me because other fourteen year olds of comparable ability wrote reasonably well.

I also remember Lloyd. I insisted that these kids take all the same group tests that all the other kids did. The results didn't concern me, but I wanted their experiences to be similar to the others. Well, would you believe it! After one round of Otis IQ's a guidance counselor called me and suggested that we consider moving Lloyd to another section because he had an IQ score of 92. I told her to forget it because Lloyd had had the booklet upside down while reading the test. Later, I showed her a "get well" card Lloyd had sent me with his name spelled incorrectly.

Finally, there was Ernie who was unquestionably the most experientially deprived youngster with whom I had worked. Joe Levanto, currently the principal of NFA, had the "A plus" group. He and I decided to take his kids and my kids on a field trip to New York City. We collected scrap, saved our money (the middle-class "A plusers" got it at home), and were ready to go. About 3:00 A.M. on the day of the field trip my telephone rang. It was the local police and they had Ernie. Well, what happened was this. I had told Ernie that I would pick him up in front of the A & P store at 6:00 A.M. because this was near his house. The police picked him up at 2:30 A.M. Ernie was so afraid that I might miss him that he had planned to stay in front of the store all night.

At the professional level I hear many people talk about those "MR's" who are working in the fields of learning disabilities, emotional disturbance, and so forth. The reference is usually related to the experience and training of the "MR's" as a basis for involvement in other fields. Yet, as can be seen from the previous descriptions of the youngsters with whom I worked, the idea of my being "MR" or of their being "MR" is ludicrous. What am I? Frankly, I am not certain. What were they? Of that, I am less certain.

The issues that were raised in trying to help those kids with whom I worked remain issues today. Now we have more labels to affix to the kids and more terms with which to describe their strengths and weaknesses, but I don't believe we are much further ahead with respect to comprehensive curriculum planning. If there is one message that I would like to convey in this chapter it is the need for comprehensive curriculum development. I do not believe we have adequate curricular alternatives today. Nor do I believe that we have ever had adequate curricular alternatives.

I hate to think that Public Law 94-142, the Education for All Handicapped Children Act, which the Congress of the United States passed and President Ford signed into law is going to place millions of dollars into a system of education which has yet to validate alternative curricula models and programs to meet the needs of these children. I am sure that Herb Goldstein of Yeshiva, Bill Mayer of BSCS, Janet Wessel of Michigan State, Jim Lent of George Peabody, Ed Meyen of

Kansas University, and other curriculum developers would agree that there is a need to construct, validate, and compare alternative theoretical models and approaches.

Certainly, we have not satisfied the methodologists or "remedialologists" as the recent articles by Hammill and Larsen (1974) and Minskoff (1975) indicate. Neither does a dependency on remediation seem to be the answer as the Koppitz (1971) data suggest. We are not helping the kids as rapidly as we would like. One alternative to dependency upon remediation is to plan long-term endeavors which integrate developmental and remedial components into comprehensive curriculum designs.

With respect to Project MATH,[1] the demands of the system pushed us beyond our original limits and we have spent considerable time with the issues relating to specific learning disabilities and emotional disturbance. After eight years of continuous activity in this area of curriculum development, we think we have reached the point where we could extend our efforts and make a significant contribution, of a comprehensive nature, that will be of help to the entire field of special education.

COMPREHENSIVENESS DEFINED

I have raised the issue of comprehensiveness for three reasons. The first reason is that all children, including handicapped children, go to school for some twelve to fourteen years. The second reason is that the children are in school for periods of approximately five to six hours per day. A third reason is that human development is characterized by growth both in *processes*, or stages and in *knowledge* (Klausmeier et al., 1974).

Although we were not as sophisticated as the teachers of today, I am certain that those thousands of ditto masters that Les Hartson and I made at NFA were the basis of one approach to comprehensiveness. We planned for a full day, a full year, and for the basic processes and a reasonable set of knowledge. (I think of the time I placed carbon disulfide and sulphuric acid in a wastebasket to cause spontaneous combustion because I felt it had to be demonstrated as well as talked about.)

Minimally speaking, comprehensive programming will have to include:

[1] The development of this product was funded by a grant from the Bureau of Education for the Handicapped, "A Program Project Research and Demonstration Effort in Arithmetic Among the Mentally Handicapped," OEG-0-70-2250(607) #162008, John F. Cawley, Project Director, University of Connecticut, Storrs, Conn. 06268.

1. Contrasting approaches based upon different curriculum models such as subject-matter vs. broad-fields vs. child-centered.
2. Varying approaches to the selection, development, and presentation of content; for example, within the broad areas of social studies and science.
3. Different approaches to basic skills such as those in language arts and mathematics.

I believe in the development of alternative approaches because (a) that is what general education offers to its participants, (b) no single school of thought has proven its superiority in meeting the needs of handicapped children, and (c) the needs of some handicapped children may be better met via one approach than by another.

The ingredients for every approach should be:

1. Procedures for individual assessment in both individual and group situations.
2. Assignment to and selection of instructional practices that are linked to assessment.
3. Procedures for continuous assessment.
4. Long-term patterns of organization of the scope and sequence of content.
5. Appropriate sets of instructional materials and provisions for inservice training.
6. Some modest pre-implementation evaluation.

Curriculum development is heavily rooted in values—values which influence the way in which we think and feel about children. My major doctoral advisor was a curriculum specialist. He thought and wrote (Pritzkau, 1959) extensively about values and the role values play in curriculum development. I have always been influenced by some of his notions, a few of which are listed below:

1. Reluctance to alter established organization limits admission of children's values.
2. Curriculum should provide laboratory conditions for idea evolvement.
3. Learning conditions must relate subject areas to people and behavior.
4. Conditions demand sacrifice for ideas.
5. To put it bluntly, the content which is designed to help individuals attain competence in the workaday world should, in

every respect, receive the same attention and carry the same level of meaning as that which supposedly prepares one for college; to separate college-bound students from life-bound meanings constitutes a "watering down" of content for the college-bound group.

I wonder what Annie Inskeep (1938) would think of the last item listed above. Pritz was somewhat of a radical and there are times when I feel the same way about myself. My first funded research project was *Productive Thinking Among Mentally Retarded and Average Children.*[2] I followed this with another effort[3] because I wanted to see if there was anything to the fixation that an IQ of 90 or above was a basis for distinguishing learning disabilities and mental retardation. We ran the study using the paradigm presented in Figure 2 (Cawley, Goodstein, & Burrow, 1968), employing a host of psychoeducationally identified variables.

	Average		Retarded	
Good Reader	CA $\overline{X}$:	121.52	CA $\overline{X}$:	167.96
	MA $\overline{X}$:	124.68	MA $\overline{X}$:	113.44
	IQ $\overline{X}$:	102.56	IQ $\overline{X}$:	68.00
Poor Reader	CA $\overline{X}$:	121.68	CA $\overline{X}$:	164.32
	MA $\overline{X}$:	120.00	MA $\overline{X}$:	114.24
	IQ $\overline{X}$:	98.36	IQ $\overline{X}$:	69.80

FIGURE 2: Developmental characteristics of good and poor readers among mentally retarded and average children.

Basically, we found that:

1. Children of average ability who were good readers (reading age = mental age) were better than all other groups on nearly everything.

2. Children who were poor readers (reading age 2.5 years less than mental age) were poorer than good readers (reading age = mental age) regardless of IQ level on just about everything.

3. Poor readers of either ability level were not significantly different from one another in anything. If you had a learning disability you had it at IQ 100 and at IQ 70.

[2] Cawley, J. *Productive thinking in retarded and non-retarded children.* USOE Project No. S-8106-2-12-1, 1967.

[3] Cawley, J., Goodstein, H., & Burrow, W. *Reading and psychomotor disability among mentally retarded and average children.* Storrs: University of Connecticut. A project funded by the Connecticut Research Commission.

Our conclusions:

1. Positive traits are positively related. You got it, you got it.
2. Poor readers of different ability levels are up the creek.
3. Defining LD in terms of 90 IQ is a problem for us because we had so little IQ effect between our groups of poor performers.

I have generally tried to maintain a research framework with the above paradigm in mind because it tends to keep me thinking about all the kids.

METHODS VS. CURRICULUM

In 1965, Vincent J. Glennon, a noted mathematics educator, proposed a theoretical model for mathematics education (Glennon, 1965). Glennon suggested that mathematics educators could not afford the luxury of being students of subject matter *only*, nor could they be students of the process for transmitting subject matter *only*. He felt that mathematics educators had to concern themselves with both the *process* and the *product*, the *how* of teaching and the *what* of teaching. Glennon suggested that the *what* question is the easier question to answer; the *how* question being much more difficult. What Glennon cited as an issue for mathematics education may be cited as an equivalent issue today for special education: Special education cannot afford the luxury of being concerned with the *how* without equivalent attention to the *what*.

METHODS ISSUES

Historically, the emergence of the methods trend in special education began with a concern for specific language disabilities among wounded soldiers and with a concern for the more totally developmentally disabled. I have elected to separate the specific language disabled and the more totally developmentally disabled because of the nature of the individuals who manifested the problems. The sample which consisted mainly of soldiers who suffered brain damage as a result of battle wounds were individuals who could speak and understand one day but were unable to do so the next. On the other hand, Victor, the so-called "Wild Boy of Aveyron" who, incidentally, did not come from Aveyron (Lane, 1976), was developmentally disabled in that he had never acquired language prior to his being presented to Itard (1932).

The soldiers and the boy were severely, almost totally, disabled. The method concept, that is to remediate process-type deficiencies, had considerable validity because the individuals clearly lacked the process. The issue was bimodal: process or no process.

Today, the matter is not quite so basic because the individuals with whom we often work are differentiated on a continuum where some have more, or less, of something than do others. I am referring, of course, to norm-referenced diagnosis rather than to clinical diagnosis as practiced with the soldiers and the boy.

Let me illustrate this problem with an example as it relates to the field of psycholinguistic training. My reference point here is the discussion between Hammill and Larsen (1974) and Minskoff (1975). Hammill and Larsen (1974) reviewed 39 studies which focused upon the efficacy of psycholinguistic training. The general conclusion of these authors here and elsewhere (Newcomer, Larsen, & Hammill, 1975) is that psycholinguistic training will not substantially modify the status of the learner, either in the designated psycholinguistic processes or in other processes such as reading and spelling. Minskoff (1975) feels that the nature of the research which led to this conclusion is suspect and in need of improvement in many areas. Let us accept the validity of the consensus relative to the research and go one step further by suggesting that minimally, the 15 criteria proposed by Minskoff must be adhered to in order to evaluate the impact of remediation. I ask you then, Do we have any acceptable research evidence relative to the efficacy of this type of training? I think not!

On the other hand, Newcomer, Larsen, and Hammill (1975) suggest that if they had a child with an expressive language problem "we would design an individualized sequenced program to teach the use and understandings of words in sentences" [p. 147]. I talked recently with Don Hammill and he was strong in his feelings that we should be looking at instructional (I'll include curriculum) provisions that are more directly related to reading, arithmetic, spelling, language, and writing. Here, of course, is the paradox—namely, the rationale that led to the development of various psycholinguistic, perceptual, motor, and related types of diagnostic and curriculum material endeavors. For years children had been approached "head-on" in the areas of reading, math, etc. Yet, a significant number of kids were not making any progress. Efforts were made to look somewhat differently at these kids (i.e., psycholinguistically, perceptually, and so forth), with the idea in mind that instruction in some of these areas might facilitate the status of the learner to a point where direct instruction in reading, spelling and so forth might be undertaken. These latter tactics do not seem to be meeting the need, so a return to the more "head-on" approach is now being suggested.

It seems incredible, but we really aren't much further ahead now than we were years ago. We still don't know "how much of what" is necessary in order for a child to read, to do mathematics, or to spell. But it seems as though I went down this road before in working on *The Slow-Learner and the Reading Problem* (Cawley, Goodstein, & Burrow, 1972). The title of our reading text was deliberately selected in order to suggest that our real problem rests in a lack of information about *reading* and not in the slow learner. With respect to other groups of handicapped children (ED/LD) and to other areas of basic skills, I feel that our status is similar.

Regardless of the position that one might take personally, we are still faced with the problem of how to use "psycholinguistic forms of diagnostics" and suggested remedial and developmental strategies on an all-day basis. How do we translate the assessed needs of the child to the teacher in order that they might be incorporated into the instructional activities during science, social studies, physical education, and so forth. In other words, it is my contention that unless this can be satisfactorily accomplished, neither the diagnostics nor instructional programs will be appropriate to the all-day needs of the child. Remedial efforts which take place for brief periods of time during the day would not appear to have the same potential for impact as those which take place on an all-day basis. As a matter of fact, as part of the requirements for the course I taught during the spring semester, 1976, I had the students:

1. Construct behaviorally (process) based diagnostic instruments using subject matter as the content.
2. Conduct an analysis of the reading skills contained in subject matter texts. We found that it was possible to take a science text and do a reading skills analysis of the material.
3. Write, as seen in Figure 6, instructional tasks that are linked to specific behavioral objectives.

In order to deal with this issue we must propose a most delicate question; namely, Are we attending to *process* or *content* needs? I submit that the utility of the process orientation is limited because (a) we have not clearly defined or experimentally validated the processes that we tend to rely upon and (b) that we are dealing more with content deficiencies than we are with process deficiencies. Take the following:

A child, among other measures, has been administered the Auditory Reception Test of the Illinois Test of Psycholinguistic Abilities. The child has a CA of 6-4, a raw score of 15, scaled score of 26, and language age of 4-3. He responded correctly to 15 of the 26 items necessary to provide a scaled score of 36 ($\overline{X}$ = 36; SD 6).

This youngster responded correctly to more than one-half the items expected of his age group and, as a matter for illustration, he got 14 of the first 15 items correct.

What I fail to understand is the "process deficiency." The youngster described above used the process correctly fifteen times. That is, when given a question aurally, he was able to respond "Yes" or "No." It is my feeling that most of the so-called process deficient youngsters do not have process problems at all. What they lack is experience, familiarity with or understanding of the content that is used in measuring the specific behaviors. I believe that this is true in most instances of individual assessment and, for this reason, I believe we should attend much more to subject matter (curriculum) as a means of facilitating the status of the handicapped child. I don't know of any "process" as operationalized on diagnostic instruments that I can't relate to subject matter.

As a matter of fact, one of the things we attempt to accomplish in our inservice training institute is to have the participants develop proficiency in subject-based diagnosis. I attempt to demonstrate this with, among other illustrations, a homemade facsimile of the ITPA. I developed this using ITPA behaviors as the "process" reference and electricity as the "content" reference. It's fun!

I am of the opinion that special education is going to have to moderate its short-term ameliorative emphasis and turn much more toward long-term planning. Something keeps telling me that the continuous development of instructional materials that are aimed at remediating a specific behavior or process is a tactic that will make only a minimal contribution to special education. My colleague, Dr. Anne Marie Fitzmaurice, a mathematics educator, called my attention to the extensive display of instructional materials at a recent convention. She pointed out the lack of comprehensiveness and the lack of integration with diagnostics that was characteristic of many of the materials. I feel as she does—that instructional materials must be linked to curriculum and to assessment. In a sense, what we need to do is to "put it together." This is what we have tried to do with Project MATH and with the Mainstream Series.[4] It is akin to what Herb Goldstein and his associates at Yeshiva University have done with the *Social Learning Curriculum*. Bill Mayer and his group at the Biological Sciences Curriculum Study, Boulder, Colorado, have used a different approach in preparing various science programs for use with handicapped children.

Long-term planning will involve *compensation*—the practice of avoiding a child's disabilities in one area while teaching him via another. The child who cannot read during reading cannot read during mathematics, science, social studies, and so forth. A reading disability should not limit the child's participation in other areas because a major

[4] Publications of Educational Progress Corporation, Tulsa, Okla.

component of all can be dealt with without reading. In effect, we should seek out relative strengths within the child or select alternative channels of communication with him when teaching content areas.

I lean in this direction because of (a) the work of individuals such as Elizabeth Koppitz (Koppitz, 1971) whose five-year follow-up of children shows varying degrees of progress, (b) the emphasis on the need for secondary school programs which, to me, is more indication that the ameliorative effort is a long-term proposition, and (c) the mass of confusion which exists among the methodologists.

At times I have the feeling that we in special education have been somewhat overzealous. It often seems that we have made "recognition of a problem" synonymous with "having provided a solution to that problem." In effect there is a tendency to fail to distinguish between "what we need to do" and "what we are able to do." To illustrate, in the area of disabilities in mathematics, I would submit that the level of our knowledge and competence derived from research and practice is near zero. We lack adequate diagnostic procedures (Goodstein, 1975); we have only limited linkages between diagnostics and effective instructional practices built upon diagnostics. Is it necessary, as has been proposed (Cawley, 1977), to have the diagnostic-instructional model built around a form of content × mode × algorithm triad? Should the child, for example, use a nonconventional algorithm (his own set of rules), or should we insist upon the conventional rules? What kind of instructional model can we generate that will be acceptable throughout the K-12 range? These and many other methods issues remain in mathematics. I suspect that just as many exist in reading, language, and other areas.

Curriculum Issues

Education in general and special education in particular have not been effective in the area of curriculum development. While the problem for general education is troublesome, the problem for special education is acute. Children enrolled in general education programs tend to demonstrate comparable, and typically satisfactory attainment, regardless of the nature of the curriculum or the type of curriculum model being used. The reason for this is that the child is ordinarily intact with regard to his developmental characteristics. The curriculum developer, most often the commercial entrepreneur, has been able to provide curricula for nonhandicapped children because he is able to select content and prepare a scope and sequence for that content based upon reasonable assurances that the child derives substantial benefits from the program.

Handicapped children are, by definition, children whose developmental characteristics are not intact. Something is amiss with each one of these children. For some, it is developmental delay and overall slower rates of development; for others it may be sensory impairments; others may have identifiable or nonidentifiable specific learning disabilities; and for some children the source may be emotional. With regard to handicapped children, the matter of curriculum development becomes more than the selection of content and the organizing of this content into a scope and sequence. Curriculum development for the handicapped must stand the rigors of the requirement that suggests that the handicap(s) be (a) prevented, (b) ameliorated, or (c) compensated for.

Historically, curriculum development in special education has been minimal. Rather than being the target of the commercial organizations, which basically control curricula anyway, the needs of handicapped children have been ignored. The result was that our system of comprehensive curriculum consisted of locally or regionally developed curriculum guides of varying degrees of sophistication, a few generalizations from our methods texts, and a teacher, prepared or unprepared, who was waiting to staff the unit.

When I think back to the marvelous start we had, I wonder why we don't have it all wrapped up today. My reference here is, of course, to the work of Maria Montessori. Montessori's efforts impress me as one of the more substantive attempts at comprehensive curriculum planning. While we have generally come to think of Montessori in relationship to the *Montessori Method*, the fact is that she took a rather extensive approach to education. Montessori focused on reading, mathematics, music education, and metrics (poetry, its rhythms and rhymes). And she did more than write about these areas. She selected content, organized a scope and sequence, prepared materials, trained the teachers, and conducted individual assessments, as well as experiments, to explore and validate curricula. She even computed baselines (Montessori, 1929) which she called "curves." She collected data for both individual and group "curves." Based upon one "Curve of Work," she had this to say about a child:

> The child in question (O) seemed to have a tendency to learn from others; he ran away from work or was attracted to it only for a brief moment; and seemed incapable of receiving direct teaching. If any attempt was made to teach him something, he grimaced and ran away. He wandered about, disturbing his companions and seemed quite intractable; but he listened attentively to the lessons the teacher gave to the other children [p. 101].

Obviously, individual performance standards and related classroom management (motivation and on-task behavior) were integral concerns.

Montessori (1928) dealt with many of the specifics with which we concern ourselves today. In the area of language she gave a great deal of attention to nouns (labels), adjectives, adverbs, conjunctions, disjunctions, and structure. In writing about interjections, she stated that "because the children are now able to recognize different parts of speech, it is no longer necessary to make sentences containing only those parts of speech which the children know" [p. 114]. Later, under sentence analyses, she wrote about simple sentences with and without modifiers, verb forms, complex sentences, and other permutations. When looked at as a combination of a method by content interaction, I have the feeling that truly she would have been a hybrid coming off Distar and transformational linguistics.

The striking thing about Montessori is the way in which she put it all together, regardless of how one might feel about her specific approach. Montessori operationalized the system. Her writings are about *what she had done* and not about *what one should be doing.*

Some Bases for Curriculum

As indicated earlier in this chapter, there is a necessary concern for both method, the *how*, and curriculum, the *what*. The Glennon paper (Glennon, 1965) contains a discussion of what he identified as three somewhat polarized views of curriculum. There is the *psychological* view of curriculum which holds that curriculum should eventuate from the needs and interests of the learner; there is the *sociological* view of curriculum which advocates the selection of curriculum content on a basis of its usefulness at the adult social level; and there is the *logical* perspective of curriculum which holds that content should be selected and taught because of the values inherent within the content itself.

There was a period of time in special education when a primary concern was on *what to teach*. The work of Inskeep (1938) reflects this, as does the work of Ingram (1968) and the efforts of Meyen (1972). This emphasis was most noticeable during the middle thirties through the sixties. Every school system developed a curriculum guide; every graduate student wrote at least one guide in some course; many states developed curriculum guides.

Sometime in the sixties the trend changed from the *what* to the *how*. Methods texts have become abundant. All kinds of diagnostic instruments have come upon the scene. And, of course, instructional materials have flooded the market.

I believe the seventies, as the evidence indicates, will begin to produce systems of instruction which link the *how* and the *what*. Our own effort in Project MATH does this. It seems to me that the future will produce alternative curricula which also link the psychological, the sociological, and the logical views of curriculum.

To begin with, the psychological perspective must be considered. The handicapped child is an individual who is defined in terms of needs —needs which have been identified by differing, but generally equivalent, forms of psychoeducational assessment. It is my contention that special education is going to have to rely more upon content to meet the psychoeducationally determined needs of the handicapped child.

The sociological perspective is an inherent component of curriculum for the handicapped. I would modify its basis somewhat and suggest that content should not be based solely on those items thought valuable and necessary for adult life. I would include everyday issues relevant to the age and experiences of the child.

Last, but not least, I would hold that there is considerable merit in viewing curriculum development from a basis of the logical structures and knowledge of the content itself. This does not seem to pose a problem when one wants to undertake a task analysis of the addition of two single-digit numbers. Yet, we tend to slough off when it comes to a comparable undertaking relative to spontaneous combustion. Which is more important? I submit that there are fewer fatalities resulting from an inability to add two single-digit numbers than there are from spontaneous combustion.

AN INTEGRATING DESIGN

Throughout this chapter I have suggested the need to integrate the diagnostically determined needs of the learner with the content encountered in the subject matter areas. Accordingly, I would like to proceed in this chapter with a description of one strategy which facilitates this integration. The design of the *Desired Learner Outcome* (DLO) constitutes the basis for the *Behavior Resource Guide* which I put together with a number of colleagues (Cawley, J., Calder, C., Mann, P., McClung, R., Ramanauskas, S., & Suiter, P., 1972). The DLO is a simple three-part behavioral statement that is content free; that is, it can be used with any content or subject matter. Unlike the typical behavioral or instructional objective, the DLO only signals input-output behaviors. There is no content, no criteria, no conditions. DLO's were developed for twenty-two agreed-upon areas, with a total of 266 included in the *Behavior Resource Guide*. A few illustrations are presented in Figure 3.

Code #	Standard	Learner response/action
ARG-1	a word	identify from among two or more choices the picture of object which represents meaning in standard
VAS-1	an object or picture of an object	name or describe the object
VAS-10	a picture of an object and two or more choices	identify picture which has highest associative relationship to standard after standard has been removed
AOP-1	a single word	state an acceptable definition using descriptive, function or classification terms

FIGURE 3: Illustration of desired learner outcomes.

The *Behavior Resource Guide* correlates over 300 diagnostic subjects to behaviors such as those listed above and then cross-correlates the behaviors to curriculum materials. ARG-1 is representative of the Peabody Picture Vocabulary Test, VAS-1 is representative of the Verbal Expression Test of the ITPA, VAS-10 is representative of the Visual Reception Test of the ITPA, and AOP-1 is representative of the WISC Vocabulary Test.[5]

Figure 4 illustrates, with the "fuse" and the "heart," how an instructor can use or vary either content or process. If ARG-1 is used with the "fuse" and the "heart," subject matter (electricity, anatomy) differs. If the "fuse" is used with ARG-1, VAS-1, and AOP-1, content is held constant and behavior or process varied.

Figure 5 contains a task from our inservice institute, *Meeting the Learning and Behavioral Needs of Handicapped Children via a Subject Matter Emphasis*. This is part of a two- or three-day institute which serves to train individuals to translate diagnostic information into instructional activities based on subject matter. What we have done in all of this is to delineate behaviors that can be used during subject matter instruction (you know—that thing that takes place in the mainstream!). Notice in the activities that the third is a group activity. I feel this is important because my personal inclination is that handicapped children are better educated in groups and also, group activity is more efficient in terms of teacher time and effort.

The biology illustration serves only to focus attention upon the use of subject matter under controlled behavioral (process, if you will) learning experience. If the learner fails to respond satisfactorily, the instructor has the option to change the content or to keep the content the same and change the behavior; e.g., go to ARG-1, VAS-1, or so forth, as per Figure 4.

Finally, Table 1 contains a set of activities developed in three subject areas for three test-related and DLO-interpreted behaviors. This task was done by Kathleen McGrath, one of our students at the University of Connecticut.

PROJECT MATH: A CURRICULUM DESIGN

Curriculum development is an extensive proposition. I no longer believe it to be a "grass roots" procedure, although curriculum selection, modification, and implementation are clearly local concerns. Curriculum development must be undertaken by a team of experts who can devote the necessary time and effort to produce, field test, revise, and disseminate a curriculum. It has taken us (Cawley, Goodstein, Fitzmaurice, Lepore, Sedlak, & Althaus, 1976) approximately eight years to trans-

---

[5] ARG = Aural Recognition; VAS = Visual Association; AOP = Oral Production.

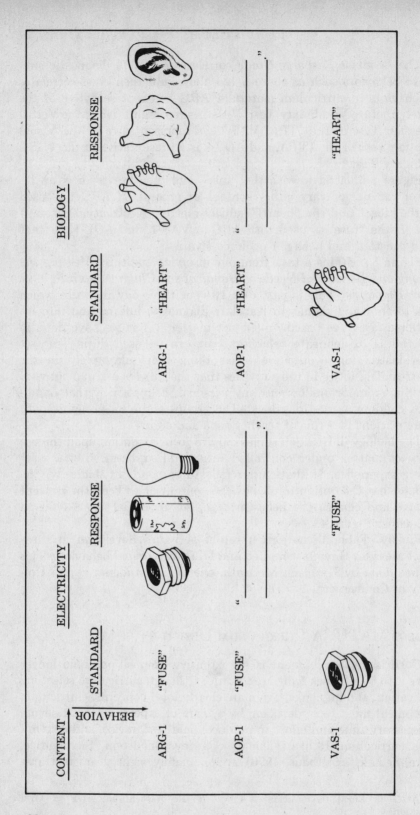

FIGURE 4: Examples of curriculum activities which are conducted within the same content area across the DLO (↓) or across different content areas within the same DLO (→).

Desired learner outcome		
Code # VAS-10	Standard a picture of an object and two or more choices	Learner response identify picture which has highest associative relationship to standard after standard has been removed

Instructional activities
1. Obtain a picture of woodlands area, show it to the child, remove it, and then show him 3 pictures—one of a squirrel, one of a giraffe, and one of a fish. Instruct him to point to the picture of the animal that belongs with the woodlands picture.
2. Obtain a picture of a freshwater pond. Show it to the child, remove it, and show him 3 pictures—one of a bear, one of a frog, and one of a horse. Instruct him to point to the picture that belongs with the picture of the pond.
3. Prepare a ditto master which contains a number of rows, with three or more pictures to a row. Each picture should reflect something relative to the present topic, Biology/Animal Habitats. Collect a set of stimulus pictures for your use. Distribute the activity sheet to each child and have him cover the paper with another paper. Display your standard, remove it, and instruct the learner to expose the first row of his paper and to mark the picture that goes with the standard you displayed. Continue throughout the activity sheet.

FIGURE 5: Translation of desired learner outcome into instructional activities in biology. Note that the DLO is representative of the Visual Reception Test of the ITPA.

form a set of ideas into a finished product. What we have accomplished is generally depicted in Table 2. What we started with were a variety of concepts and biases about the need to improve the quality of mathematical learnings and mathematically related experiences of handicapped children.

Consistent with the ideas expressed by Mayer (1975) we recognized that curriculum development should be initiated by the development of a model. Our model was a composite of a list of strengths and weaknesses of handicapped children coupled with the identification of a strategy that would enable us to work with the strengths of a learner, while minimizing the influence of weaknesses. The goal of our approach was to develop a means that would allow the nonreader to demonstrate proficiency in mathematics without being impeded by a lack of reading ability. We accomplished this by devising an interactive unit (Cawley & Vitello, 1972) which was modified from a nine-unit behavioral system to its current sixteen-unit status (see Figure 6).

The unit provides the instructor with four approaches through which instruction can be given; it provides the learner with four alternatives to demonstrate proficiency. The unit was the instructional basis for the Multiple Option Curriculum, while the selection of six mathe-

TABLE 1: Diagnostically related instructional illustrations for science, mathematics, and geography.

DLO	Science	Math	Geography
I. Vocabulary (WISC: Vocabulary) AOP-1. a single word — state an acceptable definition using descriptive, function, or classification terms	1. What does *sharp* mean? 2. What does *float* mean? 3. What does *stem* mean?	1. What does *set* mean? 2. What does *square* mean? 3. What does *add* mean?	1. What does *map* mean? 2. What does *ocean* mean? 3. What does *desert* mean?
I. Verbal Opposites (Detroit: Verbal Opposites) AOP-16. a single word — name a word that is the opposite of the standard	1. hot — cold 2. float — sink 3. root — stem	1. add — subtract, take away 2. circle — square 3. whole — part	1. north — south 2. east — west 3. desert — jungle
I. Similarities (WISC: Similarities) AOP-17. the names of two or more objects or things — state ways in which they are similar and/or different	1. whale/beaver (both animals) 2. jet/helicopter (vehicles that fly) 3. spider/bee (both insects)	1. one/four (both numbers) 2. circle/square (both geometrical shapes) 3. ½ - ¼ (both fractions or parts)	1. Atlantic/Pacific (both oceans) 2. U.S./Canada (both countries; both are next to each other) 3. Hartford/Boston (both cities)

TABLE 2: Components of project MATH.

	Level I	Level II	Level III	Level IV
I. Evaluation and Teaching				
Mathematics Concept Inventory	1	1	1	1
Learner profile	18	18	18	18
Class profile	1	1	1	1
II. Multiple Option Curriculum				
Instructional guides	358	420	420	325
Activity booklets	A, B, C	A, B, C	A, B, C	A, B, C
Supplemental activities	1	1	1	1
Booklet for instructor				
Manipulatives	192 blocks 400 chips	256 blocks 500 chips 3 geoboards 32 fractional pieces 8 rulers	3 geoboards 1 balance scale 8 rulers 32 fractional pieces	8 rulers 32 fractional pieces
III. Verbal Problem Solving				
Administrative guide	1	1	1	1
Story mats	18	20	—	—
Object cards	228	246	—	—
Line drawings	—	32	—	—
Money cards	—	111	—	100
Problem cards			100	100
IV. LABS			30	60
V. Administrative Guide	1	1	1	1

41

				Interactive unit			
Input	Do	See	Say	Construct	Present	State	Graphically symbolize
Output	Do	See	Say	Construct	Identify	State	Graphically symbolize

Definitions

Construct (Do)	to pile, build, arrange, manipulate two- or three-dimensional objects or materials.
Present (See)	to display in fixed representations either two- or three-dimensional stimuli.
Identify (See)	to point to or otherwise mark nonsymbolic options in a multiple-choice task.
State (Say)	to orally state.
Graphically symbolize (Say)	to write with symbols (letters/numerals) or to draw.

FIGURE 6: The interactive unit.

matical strands (geometry, patterns, sets, numbers and operations, measurement, and fractions) formed the basis for the content. We felt that some form of content-related assessment was also essential in order to screen and place the learner. This resulted in the development of the *Mathematics Concept Inventory*.

Verbal problem solving was as an enigma to us at the outset. I think we were led astray in this area because of our conventional thinking. At some point we recognized that the typical verbal problem was, in reality, a computation task with words around it (Goodstein, 1972). Furthermore, after DeVard (1973) found out that kids could read problems they could not solve and solve problems that they could not read, we recognized a need for an alternative approach to verbal problem solving. The result is that we treat it from an informational processing perspective and distinguish the instructional activities from those contained in the Multiple Option Curriculum.

Finally, we learned that mathematically based activities could be used to structure experiences to facilitate the development of social skills and behaviors. Thus the LABS came into being. These are mini units which last from periods of a few days to several weeks. Some of the topics covered are:

1. *Metrics:*   The learners build instruments and models which can be used in metric measurement activities.

2. *Calculators:* The learners compare, select, and operate hand and desk calculators in performing mathematical tasks.

3. *Telephones:* The learners experience using the telephone under different conditions and become familiar with different costs connected with the use of the telephone.

4. *Popular Songs:* The learners conduct their own poll to find the "top ten" in their classroom and experience the procedure by which such polls are carried out.

There is a heavy emphasis on individual responsibility in each LAB. There is also the need for some degree of proficiency in selected mathematical operations. These are the main reasons for including LABS at Levels III and IV only.

Briefly, then, one framework of curriculum design has taken eight years to develop. This is reasonably consistent with what it takes a commercial developer to go from the idea to the product stage. The significance of our efforts will have to be determined in the future as we look for reactions from the field, gather data upon which to evaluate the program, and obtain suggestions for modification and improvement.

SUMMARY

Personal opinions are personal opinions. My hope is that reaction to this chapter can provide some impetus toward the following goals:

1. Comprehensive planning for handicapped children.

2. Integration of the *how* and the *what* of the all-day educational experience of the child.

3. Means by which our diagnostic capability can be extended and interpreted to better serve handicapped children.

4. Integration of behavioral management strategies with curriculum.

The last one seems an appropriate basis for an anecdote with which to conclude this chapter.

I'll never forget the day I was sitting in a math class observing some of the kids with whom I was doing diagnostics and remediation. The teacher asked one of the kids to go to the board and put his homework problem on display. The kid indicated that he didn't do his homework. The teacher asked, "Why not?" and the kid replied, "That page is missing in my book." Without a moment's hesitation, six to eight kids tore the pages from their books and went over and handed them to the other youngster. There has to be a message here!

REFERENCES

Cawley, J. F. An instructional design for children with learning disabilities: Emphasis on secondary school mathematics. In L. Mann, L. Goodman, & J. L. Wiederholt (Eds.), *Learning disabilities: Meeting the challenge in our secondary schools*. Boston: Houghton Mifflin, 1977.

Cawley, J. F., Calder, C., Mann, P., McClung, R., Ramanauskas, S., & Suiter, P. *The behavior resource guide*. Tulsa: Educational Progress Corporation, 1972.

Cawley, J. F., Goodstein, H. A., & Burrow, W. H. *The slow learner and the reading problem*. Springfield, Ill.: Charles C Thomas, 1972.

Cawley, J. F., Goodstein, H. A., Fitzmaurice, A. M., Lepore, A., Sedlak, R., & Althaus, V. *Project MATH*. Tulsa: Educational Progress Corporation, 1976.

Cawley, J. F., & Vitello, S. Model for arithmetical programming for handicapped children. *Exceptional Children*, 1972, 39, 101-10.

Glennon, V. J. Method—A function of a modern program as a complement to content. *The Arithmetic Teacher*, 1965, 12 (3), 179-80.

Goodstein, H. A. Assessment and programming in mathematics for the handicapped. *Focus on Exceptional Children*, 1975, 7 (7), 1-11.

Goodstein, H. A., Bessant, H., Thibodeau, G., Vitello, S., & Vlahakos, I. The effect of three variables on the verbal problem solving of educable mentally handicapped children. *American Journal of Mental Deficiency*, 1972, 76 (6), 703-9.

Hammill, D. D., & Larsen, S. The effectiveness of psycholinguistic training. *Exceptional Children*, 1974, 41, 5-16.

Ingram, C. *Education of the slow-learning child*. New York: Ronald Press, 1968.

Inskeep, A. *Teaching dull and retarded children*. New York: MacMillan, 1938.

Itard, J. M. G. [*The Wild Boy of Aveyron.*] (G. M. Humphrey, trans.). New York: The Century Co., 1932.

Klausmeier, H., Ghatala, E., & Frazer, D. *Conceptual learning and development: A cognitive view*. New York: Academic Press, 1974.

Koppitz, E. *Children with learning disabilities*. New York: Grune & Stratton, 1971.

Lane, H. The wild Boy of Aveyron. *Horizon*, 1976, 18, 32-38.

Mayer, W. *Planning curriculum development.* Colorado: Biological Sciences Curriculum Study, 1975.

Meyen, E. *Developing units of instruction: For the mentally retarded and other children with learning problems.* Dubuque: Wm. C. Brown Co., 1972.

Minskoff, E. Research on psycholinguistic training: Critique and guidelines. *Exceptional Children,* 1975, 42, 136-43.

Montessori, M. *The advanced Montessori Method I.* London: William Heinemann, 1928.

Montessori, M. *The advanced Montessori Method II.* London: William Heinemann, 1929.

Newcomer, P., Larsen, S., & Hammill, D. D. A response. *Exceptional Children,* 1975, 42, 144-50.

Pritzkau, P. T. *Dynamics of Curriculum Improvement.* Englewood Cliffs, N.J.: Prentice-Hall, 1959.

A SELECTED BIBLIOGRAPHY OF WORKS BY JOHN F. CAWLEY

Cawley, J. F. Teaching arithmetic to mentally handicapped children. *Focus on Exceptional Children,* 1970, 2, 4.

Cawley, J. F. Special education: Selected issues and innovations. In A. Roberts (Ed.), *Educational innovations: Alternatives in curriculum and instruction.* Boston: Allyn & Bacon, 1975.

Cawley, J. F., & Goodstein, H. Components of a system of initial reading instruction. In N. G. Haring (Ed.), *Improvement of instruction.* Seattle: Special Child Publications, 1971.

Cawley, J. F., Goodstein, H. A., & Burrow, W. *The slow learner and the reading problem.* Springfield, Ill.: Charles C Thomas, 1972.

Cawley, J. F., & Vitello, S. A model for arithmetical programming for handicapped children. *Exceptional Children,* 1972, 39, 101-10.

Cawley, J. F. et al., *The behavior resource guide.* Waterford, Conn.: Educational Sciences, 1973.

Goodstein, H. A., Cawley, J. F., Gordon, S., & Helfgott, J. Verbal problem solving among educable mentally retarded children. *American Journal of Mental Deficiency,* 1971, 76, 238-41.

3
Sequencing Cognitive and Academic Tasks

Siegfried E. Engelmann is professor of special education at the University of Oregon and visiting research associate for the Oregon Research Institute. Mr. Engelmann is senior author of the well-known Distar instructional programs in reading, arithmetic, and language. He has participated in numerous USOE research and/or grant projects. In addition, he has delivered over 300 public addresses including presentations at state and national conferences and major institutions of higher learning. Mr. Engelmann received the B.A. degree in 1955 from the University of Illinois. A selected bibliography of his works is found on page 61.

Perhaps 90 percent or more of the children who are labeled "learning disabled" exhibit a disability not because of anything wrong with their perception, synapses, or memory but because they have been seriously mistaught. Learning disabilities are made, not born.

The solution to the problem involves adequate instruction. The teacher must do what is required to teach, correct, and reinforce. The teacher frequently must avoid doing what comes naturally. The program that is used to teach the child must be designed so that it buttresses against all possible "misrules" or misunderstandings. Finally, the program must also provide for adequate practice of the skills taught and sufficient "applications" of what is taught.

My job, in the following pages, is to abstract those principles and procedures that relate to only part of the solution—the sequencing of tasks. It is impossible to provide more than a brief introduction to the various principles, and the end result may be to create more confusion than clarification.

The guiding principle for constructing workable sequences is that the presentation must be consistent with one and only one possible interpretation. If the demonstration is consistent with more than one interpretation, some learners will fix on the wrong one. This fact can be illustrated with a simple presentation of examples. Let's say that the instructor presents each example below and identifies each as *glerm*.

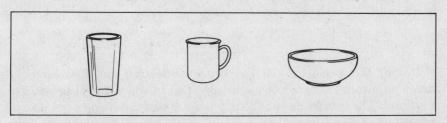

Clearly, you could generalize to a new example (identifying it as either glerm or not-glerm) if you understand what glerm means. But does the demonstration let you know precisely what glerm means? If you concluded that glerm means container, you would generalize in one way. If you concluded that glerm means any object, you would generalize in another. Here's the principle: if the presentation has more than one interpretation, some learners will fix on one that is not intended. This principle is not trivial, because:

1. It is impossible to present any single example of a concept that is consistent with only one interpretation.
2. A group of positive examples is never consistent with only one interpretation.
3. Therefore, a group of positive and negative examples must be presented and the group must be carefully constructed.

Before we examine the properties of a demonstration that is consistent with only one interpretation, let's make it clear that the glerm example is structurally similar to other concepts that are taught to naive learners. When you teach the concept of *under*, you cannot explain it verbally (since the learner doesn't understand any synonyms for under); therefore, you must simply present examples and label them. The same situation obtains for teaching *red*, *the next word*, *vowel*, *the title of the story*, *higher than*, *little*, and a host of other concepts.

To design a presentation of examples that is consistent with only one interpretation, we must show the learner which features of the example are irrelevant, which are relevant to classification of the examples as a positive example, and which are relevant to classification as a negative example. Although these criteria seem imposing, there is a simple sequencing technique that will meet them, called a dynamic presentation. A dynamic presentation involves a single object that is changed so that it becomes a positive or a negative example. Below is a dynamic presentation that is capable of teaching glerm. A real cup, positioned in different ways, is used to create the examples.

| No | No | Yes | No | Yes | No | Yes | No | No | Yes |

Following the demonstration (in which the teacher identifies each example as either glerm or not-glerm) is a test in which the examples are repeated. The learner has not completed the basic teaching until he can respond to all test examples.

The demonstration comes very close to being consistent with only one interpretation.

1. It shows which features are relevant to glerm. The slight change from the second example to the third results in the example changing from not-glerm to glerm; therefore, the difference shown in example three is relevant to glerm. The features observed in this example are confirmed by subsequent examples of glerm.

2. The demonstration also shows what is relevant to not-glerm. The only possible conclusion about what makes an example not-glerm is that it is not oriented so that the opening is directly above the bottom of the cup.

3. The demonstration shows which features are irrelevant to glerm. All features that are present in both positive examples and negative examples can't be features that determine glermness.

The fact that the cup is presented at a particular height can't be relevant to glermness if the same height is observed in both positive and negative examples. The fact that the container is round can't be relevant if the roundness is present in both positive and negative examples. Since all examples (both positive and negative) are presented using the same object, all features other than orientation are irrelevant to glermness.

Another important point about the demonstration is that since it is consistent with only one interpretation, we can predict that the learner who passes the "test" on the examples presented above will be able to generalize to a new example, one that he has never been tested on before. This is not a statement about the learner. Rather, it is a statement about the demonstration. If the demonstration clearly implies what the concept is, the learner (any child who doesn't have a very serious brain disorder) will generalize. He will generalize with both positive examples and negative examples.

1. If we presented this example the learner would identify it as not-glerm. If and are negative, must be negative also.

2. Similarly, the dynamic presentation assures that the learner will be able to identify new positive examples of the concept. Let's say we present an example that is held higher than any preceding examples, or an example that involves a cup of a different color. The learner would most probably identify the new example as glerm. The reason for the generalization is similar to the reason for the generalization of negative examples. If the only examples of glerm are upright cups, the uprightness will generalize to new examples.

There is one problem with the dynamic presentation. Although it provides a demonstration that is consistent with one and only one interpretation, it runs the risk of implying that perhaps glerm is limited to a specific context. To show what is relevant and irrelevant to glerm, the dynamic presentation uses a single object. The single object has the advantage of "isolating" those features that are relevant to glermness. But the demonstration may imply that glerm applies only to cups, only to cups of a certain shape, only to cups in a particular environmental context, etc. So we must follow the initial demonstration and test of glerm with some scattered examples of glerm and not-glerm to show that glerm is not limited to the object used in the initial demonstration. For example, we may present a couple of examples with a bucket, a couple with a picture of a bathtub, and a couple of other examples. Although this step is important, it is relatively easy because the learner already knows what controls glerm. The scattered examples merely show him that what he has learned about glerm applies over a large range of irrelevant features. (The specific features of the container are irrelevant.)

One last point about the dynamic presentation. There is an educational myth that different children learn in different ways and that somehow different children need a different form of information. The suggestion that *all* children who demonstrate prerequisite skills could learn from the same presentation is treated as educational heresy. I submit that it is educational heresy to suggest that virtually *all* children could not learn from the same presentation. Consider the facts. All children are naive, giving no behavioral indication that they understand a concept (such as glerm) before the teaching. The concept glerm is the same for all children. All children must have the same basic information about what glerm is and what glerm isn't if they are to understand the concept. Ask yourself: If I were a Martian with an IQ of 600, could I get by with less information than the information provided in the dynamic demonstration of glerm? If I were a kid with an IQ of 48, could I get by with less information? If you can postulate *any* possible mechanism other than chance or pure mysticism that could account for somebody learning a concept from a presentation that is *consistent with more than one interpretation*, you have a good case for the need for "different programs for different learning styles." However, I don't think you can.

Note that I am *not* suggesting that there is only one possible demonstration that would work with all naive learners. We could have demonstrated glerm with a different container. We could have changed the sequence of the examples. In other words, we could have constructed an indefinitely large number of demonstrations, each of which would work. But all these demonstrations would have had to meet certain basic presentation requirements. All would have had to "isolate" the variable that makes an object an example of glerm, and all would have had to show what kind of minimum change converts an example of glerm into an example of not-glerm.

I am not suggesting that there would be no difference in the performance of different learners. Different children would require different amounts of practice before they would pass the test on the initial examples of glerm. For some children, the instructor would have to repeat the demonstration and perhaps correct extensively on the "test" before the learner could perform adequately. After he had passed, however, he would be able to generalize to new examples of glerm and of not-glerm.

(The generalization is not primarily determined by the child but by the demonstration.)

Now we come to the question, How can the basic dynamic presentation be used? The answer: Use it to demonstrate any basic discrimination. For example, if you work with a child who can't discriminate between *b* and *d*, print *b* on a transparency. First demonstrate the concept with a series of examples, such as:

ꓒ	b	b	ꓒ	d	ꟼ	b	d	ꟼ	b
NO	YES	YES	NO	NO	NO	YES	NO	NO	YES

(You create each example simply by turning the transparency.) Present a series of test examples in which the child indicates whether what you show him is *b* or not-*b*. After he is quite firm at identifying *b* and not-*b*, identify *d*. If the learner has never been introduced to *b* and *d*, he'll learn quite quickly. If he has been confused and been guessing for some time, the firming of *b* and *d* may take quite a bit of repetition.

The dynamic presentation is powerful because it shows the child something that he may never have been taught; i.e., the object is called *b* only when it is in a particular orientation. A change in the orientation changes the name. Once the child has been taught what controls *b* and *d*, the basic demonstration can be augmented with exercises in which the child writes *b* or *d* from dictation, etc.

Other examples of the demonstration could be used to show the learner the meaning of *next word*, *next line*, *beginning of the word*, *ending sound*, etc. For example, to teach next line, the instructor would demonstrate that touching the next word or another word on the same line is not the next line, thereby showing the basic difference between next word and next line.

Variations of the basic dynamic presentation can be used to teach more sophisticated rules, such as: When air gets hotter, it expands. You could hold your hands out, as if you were grasping an imaginary ball about the size of a basketball. After firming the children on repeating the rule, you say, "Okay. Pretend that I have a mass of air. It's this big. Tell me if it gets hotter." Without changing the size of "the ball" you ask, "Did it get hotter?" You make the ball a little bigger. "Did it get hotter?" A little smaller. "Did it get hotter?" and so on.

In other words, there are hundreds of basic language concepts (and concepts in reading) that can be taught very effectively through dynamic presentations. And if they are presented in the right way, all children learn. However, not all basic discriminations lend themselves well to a dynamic presentation. Examples involving parts of speech, words, mathematical symbols, and the like can't be manipulated the way a book can be when you're teaching under and not-under. For these more cumbersome examples, there is a sequencing technique called the *AB* set procedure. It is particularly applicable when you have taught the children one discrimination or concept and they are now ready to learn a new concept that is systematically related to the familiar one. For example, the children may know how to read and interpret fractions, but may not understand corresponding decimals. To use the *AB* set procedure, you would make up two basic sets of items. The items in set *A* would be fractions (with denominators of 100). Set *B* would consist of decimals that correspond to the different members of set *A*. Below is the major variation for sequencing the two sets.

A	B	A	B	Random AB
$\frac{4}{100}$	.12	$\frac{6}{100}$	.03	$\frac{24}{100}$
$\frac{17}{100}$	.98	$\frac{94}{100}$	.07	.06
$\frac{2}{100}$	.02	$\frac{3}{100}$	.28	.17
$\frac{98}{100}$	.04		.97	$\frac{4}{100}$
$\frac{6}{100}$	.17		.04	.81
$\frac{12}{100}$	.06			.03
				etc.

You would present the examples in order (down each column). The child would identify each example of the first *A* set. At the beginning of the *B* set (second column) you would explain about the decimal notion. "Here's another way to write twelve hundredths. When we write hundredths this way, we must have a decimal point and *two numbers* after the decimal." You would then run the child through the remaining examples in order. If he has trouble *at any point in the series*, you would provide the answer, back up three or four examples, and continue in the series. Note that the sequence is designed to teach the discrimination. The last example in the first and second columns corresponds to the first example in the next column. This feature provides the learner with information about the critical differences between the decimals and fractions. The range of *B* examples (in the second column) reinforces the explanation that there must be two numbers. Finally, after the learner is presented with *A*, *B*, *A*, and *B*, he would identify random examples from *B* and from *A*. Further firming would be needed, but the learner who completes the basic *AB* series should be able to handle randomly ordered examples.

Variations of the *AB* design can be used to teach discriminations that are not easily explained. For example, let's say that the goal is to teach students the grammatical label, *prepositions*. Let's assume that the students are reasonably well versed in adjectives, nouns, and verbs. Let's further assume that they don't know adverbs (which is a quite safe assumption). Here would be examples that teach the critical features of prepositions:

Example:	You say:
A { He went *outside*.	*Outside* is not a preposition.
That happened *before*.	*Before* is not a preposition.
He was *near*.	*Near* is not a preposition.
B { He was *near* the door.	*Near* is a preposition.
That happened *before* the king.	*Before* is a preposition.
He went *outside* the house.	*Outside* is a preposition.

Following the presentation of the preceding examples would be a repetition of part of the *A* set, all of the *B* set, and then a series of random examples. (Actually, the presentation would be better if the *A* set and the *B* set contained more examples than those in the illustration.)

By constructing the members of the *A* set so that each example is most easily confused with members of the *B* set (prepositions), we can show the learner the essential features of prepositions. If we were to try to describe these features verbally, we would probably have to spend an enormous amount of time explaining what we mean by "objects of prepositions," etc. Yet, with paired examples, we can show what prepositions are quite dramatically. Note, the *AB* series for prepositions is not complete and it does not adequately teach all the preposition discriminations the learner would be expected to master. It does show, however, that prepositions are structurally determined and that in all positive examples the name of an object (or event) follows the preposition.

To review: the dynamic presentation is most applicable for situations in which you can achieve a continuous change between positive and negative examples. The *AB* set procedure is best for situations in which conversion from one example to the next is cumbersome. If you wanted to teach the student *faster than*, you would use a dynamic presentation (with one object moving at a constant rate and the other object at a changing rate so that it is moving relatively faster or not faster than the constant-rate object). If you wanted to teach the discrimination between maple leaves and sweet gum leaves, the *AB* set procedure would probably be most appropriate (with the last member of the *A* set most similar to the member of the *B* set).

Both the *AB* set and the dynamic presentation deal with basic discriminations or examples that can be classified as either positive or negative. In addition to teaching basic concepts, however, there are "operations." These involve the "chaining" of responses. The construction of operations is somewhat more complicated than the construction of discriminations. One reason is that operations involve responses. We can teach the discrimination of *higher than* or *maple leaves* without requiring the learner to do more than nod his head, say "yes" or "no," or use any pair of stable responses to indicate which examples are positive and which are negative. Operations are different. The learner is now required to produce specified responses, particularly the "outcome" response (the final answer or response).

Despite the differences between discrimination teaching and operational teaching, operations must be designed so that they adhere to the basic principle of being consistent with one and only one interpretation.

Our examination of operations will be limited to symbolic operations; i.e., operations such as those involved in solving a simple addition problem of the form: $3 + 5 = \Box$; or reading a regular word, such as *man*. But before we begin, it is important to note that there are critical differences between symbolic operations and nonsymbolic operations (such as cutting meat with a knife and fork, tying a shoe, throwing a ball, etc.). These differences have apparently not been considered by many educational theorists, and the result has been the development of perfectly inadequate sequences.

Here are the most critical differences:

1. With nonsymbolic operations, the steps that lead up to the outcome are always overt. A person cannot throw a ball or tie a shoe without performing the overt steps that will lead to the outcome. In contrast, the steps that lead to the outcome of symbolic operations are not necessarily overt. In fact, the steps that are perhaps most critical are never overt. A child can identify the number of objects in a set of four without overtly counting the objects. A child can read a word "silently," or even solve the problem $30 + 20$ without performing overt steps that would show us the operational steps that precede the outcome.

2. With nonsymbolic operations, there is a feedback-correction system that relates the outcome to the steps preceding the outcome. A child who does not follow the necessary operational steps involved in throwing a ball will not achieve the desired outcome. A child who does not appropriately carry out the indi-

vidual steps in tying a bow will not tie a bow. With all non-symbolic operations, the outcome can be achieved only if certain operational steps are performed. The environment, in other words, requires the learner to perform these steps. A violation in the operational steps results in failure. The child who is learning to ride a bike can provide dramatic testimony to this fact. With symbolic operations, on the other hand, there is no automatic link between observable operational steps and outcome. The child can identify the word *man* as "the"; yet the environment permits the outcome to occur without any negative sanctions. The child is not prevented from saying, "the." In other words, symbolic operations (which are the construction of man, not nature) do not provide the learner with the same kind of precise feedback that is provided with non-symbolic operations. Therefore, the learner may perform the wrong operational steps, arrive at the wrong outcome, and never receive information that either the outcome or the operational steps are wrong.

We can construct symbolic operations that meet the requirement of being consistent with only one interpretation if we model the structure of the symbolic operations after nonsymbolic operations. This involves:

1. Making all aspects of the operation overt.
2. Closely relating the operational steps to the outcome (so that the steps are indeed functional in arriving at the outcome).
3. Providing a correction-feedback system that assures that the learner is performing the appropriate operational steps.

Point 2 above is particularly important. The operation must serve the learner in all the situations that he encounters. However, it can serve him in all situations only if the symbols that are used in the operation have a constant value. We can illustrate the problem by referring to reading. Let's say that we teach the learner a sounding-out procedure. This operation satisfies the requirements of being overt, allowing for precise feedback at every step, and leading to the appropriate outcome *if* the symbols in the words he reads have a constant value. But what happens if the learner, who has been taught that *a* makes the sound aa (as in *at*), encounters the word *all*? By following the operational steps that he has learned, he will identify the word as "al." Since he arrived at the wrong outcome by following the operational steps, the operational steps are suspect. The learner will soon discover that there must be some other "operation" (such as guessing) that will serve him better than the one he has been taught. To prevent this situation, we must adjust the universe of examples that the learner encounters, or we must "misspell" words so that he can use the operation we have taught. (We might spell *all* as awl, for example.) The approach that we choose will be determined by economy of teaching. The approach that involves the fewest "transition steps" is the most desirable because it involves the least amount of teaching. In either case, we must assure that the learner will be exposed only to those words that are consistent with the operation we have taught.

The procedure for designing sequences that teach the application of an operation is to *start with the critical operation*, not with the preskills. Many program writers make the serious mistake of either starting with terminal reading behavior (silent, comprehension reading) or starting with the individual components that are involved in some unspecified operation. Both approaches lead to inefficient sequencing of skills. Start with the critical operation. First identify it. It is the operation that will allow the learner to achieve the desired outcome with any member of the set in which the symbols maintain a constant value. You identify this operation in much the same way that you identify the "concept" for simple discriminations. First ask, "What do all the examples of reading regular words have in common?" Then make a list:

1. All have symbols that correspond to one sound.
2. All follow the code that the first sound corresponds to the left letter.
3. All involve sequencing these sounds or saying the word at a normal speaking rate.

Now make up an operation that incorporates all those features. The basic operation might be that the learner sounds out the word *without pausing* between the sounds. We could prompt the left-to-right direction by putting an arrow under the word: man→

As part of the initial operation, we would require the teacher to touch under each sound as the learner says, "mmmaaannn." The teacher touches the ball of the arrow and says, "Sound it out," touching under each sound as the child says, "mmmaaannn." The teacher says, "Say it fast." The convention of not pausing between the sounds is introduced to demonstrate that the sounded-out word has the same basic set of features as the word produced at a normal speaking rate. One important feature of words that are spoken at a normal speaking rate is that there are no pauses between the sounds. Therefore, we eliminate pauses between the "sounds" of the sounded-out word and make the similarities between this word and the regularly pronounced word more obvious. The reason for requiring the teacher to touch under each symbol as the child responds verbally is that we want to make the operation overt and amenable to precise corrections for each operational step.

The value of specifying the operation is that it shows us precisely what we must teach before the learner is presented with the operation. We can identify these prerequisite skills by asking two qustions:

1. Is there a form of the response that involves coordinating fewer behaviors?
2. Does the operation involve elements?

We can identify a number of "preskills" by applying the questions above. For example, an easier form of blending is a verbal task in which the student first says the word slowly (without pausing between the sounds) and then says the same word at a normal speaking rate. "Listen: aaaammmm. Say that. . . . Now say it fast. . . ." A variation that involves even fewer behaviors would be: "Listen: aaaammmm. Say it fast."

We can also identify the various symbols that are involved in the word, including the arrow under the word. The skills involved in "following the arrow," sequencing events that are depicted on the arrow, and identifying the "sounds" that are used in the operation—all are preskills which should have been taught before the learner was introduced to the operation. Note that these preskills are identified on one basis. They are implied by the basic operation that we specify. The wording in the basic operation, "Follow the arrow . . . sound it out . . . say it fast," are words that would be used in the preskills. The components of the operation that can be presented in a "simpler" form (requiring fewer behaviors that must be coordinated) are identified as preskills. The basic operation is the only source for identifying these preskills. And the basic operation implies not only which skills must be taught, but the form that they must assume (the wording used to present them).

After the basic operation has been taught (which means that the learner is facile in using it) the steps can be "faded," which means that part of the operation now becomes covert. Also, new operations can be introduced; e.g., reading irregular words, or reading words that begin with stop sounds and cannot therefore be presented easily in the basic operation. (For the stop-sound-first word, the teacher would cover the first letter of a word such as *tip* and instruct the child to sound out and identify the ending "ip." The teacher would then say, "This word rhymes with ip," and point to the t. The child says, "Tip.")

As with the original operation, this operation implies preskills, specifically, the symbols that might be involved in the task and a simpler form of the rhyming (one that involves coordinating fewer behaviors). An easier example would be one in which the teacher simply presented a letter, such as *m*. After the child identifies the letter, the teacher says, "You're going to rhyme with *at*. What are you rhyming with? . . . Rhymes with *at*." The teacher touches under the *m* as the child says, "mmm." The teacher slashes right and the child says, "mmmat." Finally, the child says it fast.

The procedures for identifying all operations involve the same steps. First you must identify the critical sameness that all positive examples have in common. (In the case of the words that begin with stop sounds, the whole word rhymes with the beginning.) Next, you write out the critical operation. Now examine the operation that is spelled out for words, concepts, and possibly simpler forms of the operation. Be careful not to go out into left field. Limit yourself to preskills that are actual behavioral components of the operation.

The application of the principles that I have so rapidly discussed frequently yields programs and sequences that are substantially different from those that are traditionally used. For example, let's say that we wanted to teach the learner how to solve all basic algebra problems similar to:

$$3D = \frac{1}{3}$$
$$2D =$$

The analysis of the universe of examples discloses that each problem requires the learner to change a number into another number through multiplication. (In the problem above, the 3 must be changed into a 2.) Since this feature is shared by all problems of the form above, we would teach the following operation for solving the problem:

The learner writes: $\qquad \frac{3}{1} (\qquad) = \frac{2}{1}$

Next, he changes $\frac{3}{1}$ into 1: $\qquad \frac{3}{1} (\frac{1}{3}) = \frac{2}{1}$

On the left side of the equal is 1. On the right side is 2. The learner can see that he must multiply by 2 on the left side to make the sides equal:

$$\frac{3}{1} (\frac{1}{3} \cdot \frac{2}{1}) = \frac{2}{1}$$

The value that is inside the parentheses is the answer: $\frac{2}{3}$. If 3 is multiplied by $\frac{2}{3}$, you'll end up with 2.

The learner multiplies both sides of the original equation by $\frac{2}{3}$

The left side is now 2. The right side equals $\frac{2}{9}$, which is the answer.

$$\frac{2}{3}(\ 3D\ )\ =\ (\frac{1}{3})\frac{2}{3}$$

$$2D\ =\ \frac{2}{9}$$

This operation works for a full range of problems, such as:

$$\frac{5}{7R}+4\ =\ 12$$

$$\frac{1}{3R}\ =$$

Note that the emphasis of the operation is on the solution, not on application of the "associative law" and the like, which are highly suspect because they don't provide the learner with any guidance about how to solve the problem, or how to tell when he is closer to the solution. The identification of the basic operation also assures that the learner will not learn the serious misrule that the problem is always to be solved for $1X$ or $1R$. Once the critical operation is specfied, we see precisely which skills must be taught before we introduce the operation.

Earlier, we mentioned that operations involve responses. There are sequencing principles that apply to responses, and these are somewhat different from the principles that we have discussed. The primary principle is that we must "turn on" the learner through reinforcement if at all possible. Next, we must design the sequence so that he is responding appropriately at least 70 percent of the time (or on 70 percent of the trials). If the ratio of reinforceable responses to wrong responses drops much below 70 percent, the learner's progress will be quite lumpy.

One sequence that is very useful in achieving a relatively high ratio of reinforceable responses is the "memory sequence." The memory sequence is based on the simple assumption that the same task can be presented in varying contexts which make that task easier or more difficult. For simplicity, here are four levels of "memory" difficulty:

Level	*Test*
1. *A* --- (pause) --- *A*	
2. *A* --- *B* --- *A*	
3. *A* -- *B* *C* *D* -- *A*	
4. *BCDEF* --- *N* -------- *A*	

A stands for the task that you are teaching, *B, C, D* . . . stand for other familiar tasks. Let's say that the task is responding to "What's your name?"

Level 1 is the easiest form of the task. You tell the child the answer. Then you present the task, pause a moment or two, and repeat the same task. "What's your name?"

Level 2 is more difficult because instead of simply pausing after the student responds appropriately to A, you present a different task, "Touch your head." Then you return to the A task, "What's your name?"

Level 3 is still more difficult because a larger number of tasks are interpolated before the test: ". . . Yes, your name is Tom. . . . Stand up. Sit down. . . . Touch your nose. . . . What's your name?"

The level-4 task is the most demanding on the memory. This level does not begin with the A task. It begins with a series of stimuli to which the student responds. He catches a ball, yells at a dog, kicks a can, greets his buddy, goes into the classroom, etc. Then the teacher says, "What's your name?" and has trouble understanding how the child could fail the very same task that he performed so well on the day before. The answer is that the task was not the same in terms of memory difficulty.

For some students, you may have to present hundreds of repetitions before they master basic discriminations (or relearn them appropriately) or learn to produce basic responses. Some children have a great deal of difficulty remembering letter names or numeral names. Some have a great deal of initial difficulty saying words or sentences. (Many are preempted from reading comprehension because they can't say the important sentences that they read.) The memory sequence is very useful in working with these students. It allows for all the repetition they need and can still allow for a correct response level of at least 70 percent. You continue to work on level 1 until the student has produced at least two or three consecutive correct responses. You then move to level 2. If the student fails, return to level 1 and present a few more examples (reinforcing the student for each correct response). Again return to level 2. Repeat level 2 until the student produces at least two or three consecutive correct responses. Then proceed to level 3. Your goal is to reach level 4, but the student's errors tell you when he's ready to attempt a level-4 task. His performance also tells you what level you should return to. If he is quite consistent on level 3, you don't have to return to levels 2 or 1. Work on 3 and 4, always maintaining a correct response criterion of at least 70 percent. He'll learn.

We have barely scratched the surface of sequencing principles and applications; however, this chapter must end. In conclusion, I would like to make the following points.

The principles that I have so laconically outlined make a big difference. Although my associates and I have worked with thousands of children labeled "learning disabled," we have never seen a child who could not learn to read, learn arithmetic, or learn more complicated skills. Not one. The learning disability should more appropriately be labeled a teaching disability. But the learning disability will remain so long as teachers (and publishers) present demonstrations that are consistent with more than one interpretation (such as the picture on the page that always corresponds to the words and encourages the poor, naive reader to think that perhaps he is supposed to read the word by looking at the picture) or operations that are covert (such as "intuiting" the number of the set without counting) and in general violation of every principle of sequencing skills. There is no magic to instruction. If the instruction is carefully designed, if the demonstrations are consistent with only one interpretation, if the operations are initially overt and perfectly clear, if the preskills are identified and taught (without teaching other skills that "may be" important) you will succeed. Remember, don't start by observing the child. Start with the task.

A SELECTED BIBLIOGRAPHY OF WORKS BY SIEGFRIED E. ENGELMANN

Engelmann, S., & Engelmann, T. *Give your child a superior mind*. New York: Simon & Schuster, 1966.

Engelmann, S. Relating operant techniques to programming and teaching. *Journal of School Psychology*, 1968, 6, 89-96.

Engelmann, S. *Conceptual learning*. San Rafael, Calif.: Dimensions Publishing Co., 1969.

Engelmann, S. *Preventing failure in the primary grades*. Chicago: Science Research Associates, 1969.

Engelmann, S. Concepts and problem solving. In K. E. Berry & B. Bateman (Eds.), *Dimensions in early learning series*. San Raphael, Calif.: Dimensions Publishing Co., 1969.

Engelmann, S. How to construct effective language programs for the poverty child. In F. Williams (Ed.), *Language and poverty: Perspectives on a theme*. Chicago: Markham Publishing Co., 1970.

Engelmann, S. The effectiveness of direct verbal instruction on IQ performance and achievement in reading and arithmetic. In J. Hellmuth (Ed.), *The disadvantaged child* (Vol. 3). New York: Bruner-Mazel, 1970.

Engelmann, S. Does the Piagetian approach imply instruction? In D. R. Green, M. P. Ford, & G. B. Flamer (Eds.), *Measurement and Piaget*. Carmel, Calif.: California Test Bureau, 1971. Pp. 118-26.

Engelmann, S. Accountability. In M. Csapo & B. Poutt (Eds.), *Education for all children*. Vancouver, B.C.: Federation of the Council for Exceptional Children, 1974. Pp. 106-20.

Engelmann, S., & Bereiter, C. *Teaching disadvantaged children in the preschool*. Englewood Cliffs, N.J.: Prentice-Hall, 1966.

Engelmann, S., & Rosov, R. Tactual hearing experiment with deaf and hearing subjects. *Exceptional Children*, 1975, 41, 243-53.

4
Behaviorism in Special Education: An Arena for Debate

Owen R. White is coordinator of planning and evaluation for the Experimental Education Unit, Child Development and Mental Retardation Center (CDMRC), University of Washington. He also serves as both project manager of field-initiated research studies on hearing and instructional hierarchies and principal investigator of field-initiated research studies on the impact of evaluation in special education at CDMRC, University of Washington. Prior to his appointment at the University of Washington, Dr. White held research assistantships and directorships at the University of Oregon and served as a consultant to school districts in Oregon.

Dr. White received the B.A. in psychology from Willamette University in Oregon in 1967. From the University of Oregon, he obtained the M.A. in 1970 and the Ph.D. in 1971 with majors in special education

and minors in behavioral psychology, statistics, and research design. A
selected bibliography of works by Dr. White appears on pages 82-83.

Had I written this chapter ten, or even five, years ago, it would
have taken a far different form. Like most behaviorists, I would have
reacted to an implied obligation to engage in a defense of the fledgling
science, to present it in the best possible light, and to ignore the diversity of opinion and debate which exists within the field of behaviorism
per se. Far more eloquent writers than I have already undertaken that
task, however, and at regular intervals have responded to a variety of
questions and attacks (e.g., Skinner, 1953; Sidman, 1960; Dukes, 1965;
Baer, Wolf, & Risley, 1968; Risley & Wolf, 1972; Birnbrauer, Peterson,
& Solnick, 1974; Edgar & Billingsley, 1974). Today, although far from
universally adopted, the position of behaviorism as a basic and applied
science is relatively well established. From that somewhat secure position, I and others feel far more comfortable in questioning the specific
forms and applications of our own work. This chapter was written to
illustrate the types of questions that are being raised.

Having decided to expose the behavioral flank, as it were, I had
some difficulty in isolating the questions which concerned me most. In
deference to the forum in which they will be presented, I selected those
which I felt had the greatest relevance to classroom teachers and applied
educational researchers. They are (not necessarily in order of importance): (a) whether it is more important for the applied practitioner
to become well versed in previously established "behavioral principles"
or, alternatively, the skills with which to continuously monitor and
analyze behavioral change; (b) whether the visual analysis of charted
performance records is sufficiently explicit and reliable for educational
and/or scientific purposes; and (c) whether data concerning the behavior of large groups have any significance in a behavioral approach
to education.

I would like to begin with a few words of caution. First, I will be
assuming that the reader has had some exposure to material concerning
basic behavioral principles and methodologies. If that is not the case,
much of what follows will be somewhat confusing, and I would recommend that the reader direct his or her attention to one or more of the
references cited earlier and/or a basic introductory text (e.g., Millenson,
1967). Secondly, the questions I am raising *are questions*. At the moment, there are no definitive answers. I shall provide at least a sample
of data and some personal opinion concerning each question. I urge the
reader to distinguish carefully between the data and the opinions, to
weigh the former more heavily, and to wait until more definitive data
have been made available before taking an inflexible stand on any of
the issues discussed. Finally, it will not be possible to examine all facets

of each issue in the space allowed. I will be content, however, if I can simply illustrate the various logics which have been applied in each case and the questions which are yet to be resolved.

ANALYSIS OR APPLICATION?

Nearly all of the earliest dissertations on behaviorism stressed the *methodology* of defining, studying, and analyzing behavioral phenomena. One might say the early behaviorist was more interested in how better to study behavior than in what those studies revealed. Skinner, for example, once said that he would rather be remembered for the development of the cumulative recorder[1] than for the initial formulation of the principles of reinforcement.[2,3] The concern for methodological development was and is based on the premise that, if given a better tool with which to study behavior, better methods for prediction and control of behavior are simply a matter of persistence in the application of those tools. Methodological development continues today, of course, but represents a smaller proportion of the total behavioral literature (e.g., Skinner, 1976; Carman, 1976; Jones et al., in press; White, in press).

The best illustration of a basic development/methodological approach to applied behaviorism may be found in Ogden Lindsley's *Precision Teaching* (e.g., Lindsley, 1964; Haughton, 1969; Kunzelman, 1970; White, 1971a). In Precision Teaching, practitioners are trained almost exclusively in precise and highly systematized methods for the description of behavior, the specification of relevant environmental events, daily measurement of behavioral performance, charting behavioral records, and analyzing the charted data. Virtually no mention is ever made of previously established "behavioral principles" (e.g., conditioning, shaping, schedules of reinforcement, extinction). It is assumed that a teacher who carefully documents and analyzes a pupil's responses to an instructional plan will *derive* all of the "principles" he or she needs; that giving too much attention to the results of other people's work will simply increase the frequency with which the teacher applies a "bag of tricks" (e.g., "praise," "ignoring," "time-out," "M&Ms"), decreasing the frequency with which the child's actual performance is critically examined and analyzed. After all (a person without a commitment to data may reason), when something has been studied so thoroughly in the past, it *must* be effective. If it is, why bother to

[1] The cumulative recorder is a device for automatically recording and graphing the distribution of responses over time (White, 1971a).

[2] Personal communication, University of Oregon Conference, Summer 1969.

[3] In any event, many would say that the principles of reinforcement are simply more precise and useful *re*formulations of Thorndike's "laws of effect": reformulations made possible by Skinner's impressive advances in methods for the study of behavior.

document it one more time? Without the continuous analysis of the child's performance, however, if the child *does* run into trouble, the problem may grow to grand proportions before it is recognized.

On the other side of the coin, it is difficult to ignore all of the established principles of behavior and the specific examples of their successful application in educational settings. If precise behavioral research demonstrates that a particular instructional tactic has a very high probability of facilitating learning, why not communicate that information to teachers? Why should they have to "derive" all of those principles and procedures through the application of their own measurement and analysis tools? Based on this logic, Siegfried Engelmann has taken an entirely different "tactical" approach to applied behaviorism.

In his book, *Preventing Failure in the Primary Grades* (Engelmann, 1969), Engelmann devotes only about ten percent of the text to the consideration of what might be called "behavioral investigation strategies," less than one percent to specific procedures for data collection or analysis, and provides absolutely no information about potentially useful charting tactics—all of which are very important in Lindsley's Precision Teaching. Most of the text is spent in describing and illustrating certain specific procedures which have proven of significant value with most children in developing reading and computational skills (e.g., ". . . give each child four index cards, each marked to indicate the top of the card. . . ." [p. 199]). Engelmann himself employs very precise behavioral research strategies in developing his techniques. The continuous analysis of pupil progress is a very important part of that research. When attempting to develop behavioral skills in teachers, however, emphasis is placed on the *application of specific instructional tactics* rather than on the measurement and analysis skills with which the teacher might continue to refine and develop those tactics, should the need ever arise.

Both Lindsley and Engelmann are highly respected and successful behaviorists, but their personal approaches to teacher preparation are almost diametric. One obviously operates under the assumption that it is better to provide teachers with a means of continuously monitoring and analyzing child progress, while the other finds it better to instruct teachers in the application of procedures which others have developed and tested. Which of these approaches is "best"? Available data do not, unfortunately, provide any real answers.

Studies investigating the impact of measurement and evaluation per se on the behavior of teachers and children have been conducted with some regularity (e.g., Surratt et al., 1969; Hall et al., 1971; Fixen et al., 1972; Bohannon, 1975). Most of these studies, however, were relatively short-term and concentrated on the "first-person" impact; that is, they assessed the effects of "self-recording" or "self-monitoring." Of the studies listed above, only Bohannon's analyzed the impact of teacher collected and analyzed data on the performance of children (i.e., the procedures most representative of the Precision Teaching approach). Also, with the exception of Bohannon's work, most studies concerning the impact of measurement and evaluation have not specified exactly how the data analysis process was to be conducted. It is impossible, therefore, to determine exactly how the data were treated, if at all, and to separate the impact of skills in measurement from the impact of skills in data analysis.

Lindsley has provided some rather informal data to the effect that, on their first attempt, roughly 80 percent of the teachers he trains are able to decide *what* to change in a program to produce increased learning once they are provided with the measurement and analysis skills for deciding *when* to change. Of those who are not successful on their first attempt, a second program change will be sufficient with an additional 15 percent of his trainees, and nearly all of the remaining 5 percent will be successful no later than their third attempt.[4] My personal experiences tend to confirm those data,[5] with one qualification. Until the advent of specific "data decision rules" to help the teacher determine precisely when a program change should be instituted, I found that many teachers would allow a program to remain in effect long after its usefulness had been exhausted. In other words, simply collecting progress information did not necessarily ensure that a teacher would react to it. On the other hand, if the teacher did react to the progress data differentially, there appeared to be a high probability that they would develop effectively flexible programs to meet the special needs of individual learners (White, 1971b). Now that specific rules have been developed for analyzing classroom data (Liberty, 1975; White & Haring, 1976), the impact of measurement and analysis on a child's progress appears to be more uniform and generally *quite* desirable (Bohannon, 1975).

Studies concerning the application of specific instructional tactics are more numerous (see, for example, *Exceptional Children*, 1972-76; *Journal of Applied Behavior Analysis*, 1968-76), but also have their faults. In most such studies the teacher is not directly involved in the collection or analysis of data, but only rarely is it made clear whether the teacher has access to that information. Even if the teacher is not influenced by the data, there is always the possibility that the child is affected by the daily assessment (e.g., Bohannon, 1975). The assessment of a particular instructional procedure may very well be confounded with the impact of evaluation, therefore, and be of little or no value in answering the question of "application vs. analysis."

Finally, even in cases where there is an overwhelming amount of data to indicate the general impact of an instructional procedure per se (e.g., as is the case with Engelmann's DISTAR reading program),

[4] Personal communication, University of Oregon Conference, Summer 1969.

[5] In more than 100 trainees during the years 1969-72, I only experienced one teacher who was unsuccessful in devising an effective program change within three attempts.

there is little evidence to indicate that teachers will faithfully follow even the most explicit procedural guidelines (Haring, in progress). Convenient variations, adaptations, and simple sloppiness in a teacher's adherence to an instructional plan cast doubt as to whether the tactic which was planned is the actual tactic which the teacher employs. Despite the high probability of differences between planned and applied tactics, however, instruction in how to apply certain procedures apparently *can* increase the probability of teacher effectiveness. It might be that the procedures in question are so powerful that slight variation in application make little difference, or, alternatively, that teachers are reacting to informal assessments of the child's progress and the variation in application is actually appropriate—*increasing* the power of the procedure. If the former is true, it would support Engelmann's tactically prescriptive approach to teacher training. If the latter is true, it would indicate that Lindsley's concern for continuous progress assessment is appropriate.

My own opinion, based on the informal assessment of my own training successes and the successes of others, is that *both* Lindsley and Engelmann are "correct." It all depends upon how you examine the problem. When teaching a class in general principles of behavior and specific instructional procedures, I find that I can generate a rapid change in teacher behavior and, indirectly, rapid change in the behavior of pupils. If the procedures which I suggest to my teacher trainees are successful, however, I find that they are less likely to collect or analyze data of their own to refine those procedures. If problems develop at some time in the future, they either turn to me for further help or conclude that the general principle involved does not apply (e.g., "I reinforced Billy consistently with praise, but he did not improve; reinforcement must not work with Billy"). The price of an efficient, initially high "turn-on" rate with a tactically prescriptive approach in teacher training may be teacher dependency, stagnation, or even a high eventual turn-*off* rate.

With Precision Teaching, my problems and rewards are almost reversed. Teachers will generally not encounter "instant success" when taught how to collect and analyze pupil progress information. It will take time to master the skills involved and more time to collect enough data to begin deriving useful information for program refinement. My "teacher turn-on" rate tends, therefore, to be much lower.[6] Teachers who do end up applying the measurement strategies in their own classes, on the other hand, tend to be more independent in the deriva-

[6] With a one-quarter course following Precision Teaching, I can usually count on at least 3-15 percent of the teachers maintaining some of the measurement and analysis strategies as a regular feature of their instruction *after* my involvement with them has been concluded. My batting average appears to be improving, but in courses where I discuss specific instructional tactics, I am likely to produce a semi-permanent (albeit less adaptive) change in over 50 percent of the trainees.

tion of appropriate program modifications to meet the special needs of individual pupils.

Each approach to training applied behavioral educators appears to have its own advantages and disadvantages: initially high impact with reduced independence and flexibility vs. low initial impact with a high level of independence and flexibility. Ideally, one would combine the best of both, but that is not as easily accomplished as it might seem. An initial emphasis on measurement skills is likely to reduce the number of teachers who will actually complete the training sequence and/or apply their new skills in their own classrooms. An initial emphasis on highly prescriptive tactics is likely to reduce the probability that the teachers will ever become fully involved in the measurement and analysis process. As a result of this conflict, it has been my experience that most proponents of either system advocate the dogmatic acceptance of their approach and the rejection of the other approach.

During the 1960s and early seventies, the majority of teachers and their trainers appeared to prefer a tactically prescriptive approach to behaviorally based education, though continuous assessment strategies certainly gained their share of converts as well. Now that trend appears to be reversing. In a recent survey by the American Association for the Education of the Severely/Profoundly Handicapped, between 34 percent and 56 percent of the respondents indicated a need for further training in initial assessment, setting goals and objectives, planning programs, managing programs, or applying specific program strategies; whereas between 74 percent and 78 percent of the respondents indicated an interest in learning more about the use of daily performance measures for the analysis of pupil progress and program effectiveness (Lynch, 1976). Indeed, "continuous evaluation skills" was the only general area of training which was given a high priority by a significant majority of the respondents.

Personally, I am pleased with this sudden increase in the number of people showing interest in basic behavioral methodology, but I sincerely hope that it does not indicate a simple "flip-flop" of preferences with the same old "one-or-the-other" philosophy. Some attempts have already been made to integrate the two approaches, and at least one recently funded training grant promises to systematically evaluate one such program on a relatively long-term basis.[7] The results of such studies are likely to have dramatic impact on the form of applied behaviorism and the methods for training new practitioners. Before we

[7] Personal communication with Dr. William Wright of Greeley, Colorado, concerning a three-year teacher inservice training and follow-up program recently funded by the Bureau of Education for the Handicapped. According to Dr. Wright, part of the program will be to differentially analyze the impact of each component in *Exceptional Teaching*, a multimedia program which combines the continuous assessment and tactically prescriptive teacher training approaches (White & Haring, 1976).

know the precise manner in which differing approaches might best be combined, however, there is still a great deal of work which remains to be done.

IS SEEING BELIEVING?

I mentioned earlier that simply collecting continuous progress information does not necessarily ensure that a teacher will react to that information, or, if a reaction does occur, that it will be appropriate.[8] The same might be said of the behavioral researcher.[9] Typically, the behavioral researcher has chosen to analyze the learning patterns of experimental subjects on an individual basis. By attending to only one or, at most, a few subjects at any given time, it is generally easier to control the relevant variables, to react quickly to unexpected circumstances or results, and to avoid the often confused "composite" or "average" picture of performance so common in large-group studies (Sidman, 1960; Dukes, 1965; Baer, Wolf, & Risely, 1968; Yates, 1970; Kazdin, 1973; Birnbrauer, 1974). When analyzing single-subject or time-series data (so called because a series of data are generated by a single subject over a period of time), the behaviorist has traditionally relied upon a simple visual inspection of the charted or graphed performances. If enough people can agree that they "see" a change in the subject's performance as a result of the experimental manipulations, "then the conclusion is proclaimed a scientifically sound one." (Baer, in press.)

When the single-subject research strategy was introduced, there was really no alternative to the procedure of visual analysis. Statistics available for the analysis of group data at that time were all based on an assumption of "independency" (i.e., that no single score in any given phase of the analysis would determine, in part or whole, the value of any other score). When working with a single subject, all of the data come from the same person. The performance on one day is very likely to be at least partially dependent upon the performances achieved on preceding days. Unless the possibility of this sequential dependency is taken into account, the application of formal statistics can be more misleading than helpful. Still, the lack of appropriate statistics was of little matter, since the control one was able to exert over a single subject's behavior was usually so great that the results of most experiments were quite clear. The application of formal statistical analyses, no matter how appropriate, would have added nothing (Sidman, 1960;

---

[8] "Appropriate," in the case of a classroom decision, has been defined as the extent to which the decision demonstrably facilitates a child's learning (White, 1971b; White & Haring, 1976).

[9] "Appropriate," in the case of a research analysis decision, will be defined for the purposes of these discussions as the extent to which reliable changes in performance and the determinants of those changes are accurately identified.

Michael, 1974a). Behaviorists essentially remained quite content with the state of their analytic art for more than 30 years (Michael, 1974a).

As it happens, however, behavioral research is not the only situation in which data of interest might be collected on a single "subject." Weather forecasts, analyses of stock market trends, and even the "yield cycles" in a particular wheat field all involve information which violates the assumptions of traditional group statistics. Out of interest for these other phenomena, new statistics were developed which accounted for the unique characteristics of single-subject data (e.g., Anderson, 1942; Bartlett, 1935; Box & Jenkins, 1970; Glass, 1968). Eventually, some behavioral researchers began to suggest the application of those statistics to the analysis of their own data (e.g., Edgington, 1966, 1967, 1969; Glass et al., 1973; Gottman, 1971; Thoreson & Elashoff, 1974; Jones et al., in press). The stage was set for one of the biggest debates that I have ever known in the field of behaviorism.

The opening shots in the debate, at least those which appeared in the behavioral literature, were rather modest affairs. Stevens and Savins (1962) simply suggested that some of the charts and graphs used in visual analyses might be reworked to more accurately reflect the behavioral learning process. They were, for all intents and purposes, ignored; as was Revusky (1967) when he presented a proposal for a conservative statistical approach to the analysis of multiple baseline data. Of some interest is the fact that those two initial attempts at the reexamination of analytic procedures were published in the *Journal of Experimental Analysis of Behavior* (the *basic* research journal which should show the greatest interest in methodological advance). It was not until an article appeared in the *Journal of Applied Behavior Analysis* (Gentile et al., 1972) that people sat up and took notice.

Gentile, Roden, and Klein (1972) suggested that a simple analysis of variance could be applied without ill effects to the analysis of single-subject data. Immediately (or as immediately as is possible with publication delays), five articles of rebuttal appeared in the same journal (Kratochwill et al., 1974; Hartmann, 1974; Thoresen & Elashoff, 1974; Keselman & Leventhal, 1974; Michael, 1974b). A sixth article was also published by Michael (1974a) at the same time, but served mainly as an introduction to the others. All of the rebutting authors reacted negatively to Gentile, Roden, and Klein's specific suggestion for at least one common reason: the sequential dependency in single-subject data is not taken into account by a simple analysis of variance. Four of the five articles were not negatively inclined to the *concept* of statistical analysis, however, and the authors offered their own suggestions for alternative approaches: Keselman and Leventhal suggested an analysis of variance with a *repeated measures* model; Hartmann suggested the use of analysis of variance only in situations where it was demonstrated that there was no sequential dependency; Thoresen and Elashoff mentioned certain descriptive and nonparametric procedures (i.e., White,

1971b, 1972); and Hartmann, Thoresen, and Elashoff, and Kratochwill et al. all suggested the use of time-series statistical analyses developed specifically for use with sequentially dependent data (e.g., Glass, Wilson, & Gottman, 1973).[10] Of all the authors, only Michael rejected the notion of statistical analyses entirely.

Michael (1974b) presents many arguments against the use of statistical procedures, but the main thrust of his thesis appears to rest on the assumption that single-subject research, if well designed and executed, should produce such clear-cut results that nothing more than a visual analysis will be necessary. If the results are not clear-cut, he implies, then the study should be rejected. Attending specifically to the logical counterargument that current applied investigations cannot always achieve the same level of control as experiments with animals or institutionalized people,[11] Michael suggests that sufficient levels of control are, indeed, possible, and that in order to maintain the level of "motivation" necessary to gain that control, we must avoid falling back on a statistical crutch to sort out our research design inadequacies. In short, statistical procedures should not only be unnecessary, they might actually encourage sloppy research and inhibit the rapid advance of the science. Michael certainly presents a number of interesting hypotheses, but they rely upon words like "should" and "might" instead of data. In recognition of this problem, he stated:

> From an empirical point of view, it would be desirable to have some data comparing the scientific or practical results achieved when significant tests are used with those when judgments are otherwise based. I know of no information of this sort [p. 648].

"Round two" of the debate involved a change of characters. In defense of time-series analysis, Jones (in press) decided to provide at least a portion of the data which Michael requested. Baer (in press) took up Michael's role in the rejection of those procedures.

After explaining the basic concepts and procedures for (statistical) time-series analysis, Jones attempted to illustrate its potential usefulness by applying the procedures to previously published data (Boren & Colman, 1970; Ingham & Andrews, 1973; Phillips et al., 1971; Baer et al., 1973; Wincze et al., 1972). In several cases, the analyses merely confirmed what the authors had already concluded as a result of their

[10] Personally, I do not think that the application of an analysis of variance model with repeated measures solves the basic problem of sequential dependency, or that the restriction of such analyses to cases in which no dependency exists is the answer. Too many behavioral studies would not meet that criterion. Regarding the other suggestions, I am favorably prejudiced with respect to the descriptive and nonparametric procedures mentioned (i.e., White, 1971b, 1972) and can objectively support the application of formal time-series analyses of the type referenced (e.g., Glass, Wilson, & Gottman, 1973).

[11] That is, the type of study typical of early behavioral research and which is the major focus of the *Journal of the Experimental Analysis of Behavior.*

visual analyses. In other cases, the statistics helped to clarify the type of change which occurred in a subject's performance (e.g., suggesting that an apparent change in the level of a subject's performance was really due primarily to a change in trend or rate of progress). However, in at least one case with every study, the statistics indicated that what the authors had concluded was an effect of the experimental manipulations, might only be the result of some other process or "chance." In other words, there were times when the results of the studies were apparently not clear-cut and where the application of formal statistics would have resulted in more *conservative* conclusions. Of course, whether those conservative conclusions would be more appropriate (i.e., lead to more productive applied work or further research) cannot be determined from Jones' analyses. Modestly, Jones concludes that "probably no statistical method will ever replace human judgment (Michael, 1974b), but as a supplementary tool, time-series analysis deserves a place in the operant methodologist's armamentorium" [ms. 20].

Baer (in press) disagreed:

> A comparison of differences treated by skeptical examination by eye and by computation of the probability that they arose by chance from a zero-difference population suggests strongly that much smaller and less consistent differences can be validated by computation than by inspection [ms. 5].

If visual inspection is employed, Baer claims, only very large and clear-cut differences will be accepted as evidence of a variable's effect. Conversely, the application of formal statistics will result in undue attention to "the less basic, less general, less dependable, less consistent, and less usable aspects of behavior" [ms. 10]. The existence of empirical evidence to support those statements is implied, but Baer neither provides nor references those data explicitly. This is particularly curious in light of the fact that when Jones (in press) analyzed some of Baer's own data (Baer et al., 1973), the results of the time-series analyses were *more* conservative than were Baer's conclusions in three out of five cases.[12] That would suggest that Baer is seeing "clear" differences when the statistics do not (exactly the opposite of what Baer claims *should* happen). Of course, Jones undoubtedly selected examples of studies in which such incongruencies did occur. There is no guarantee

---

[12] The experiment involved one major change with three children and one additional change with two of those children—a total of five opportunities to test Baer's hypotheses. Regarding the first change, Baer concluded that "for each child, [the tested] technique resulted in clear and useful increases," and with the second change (applied to only two children) he concluded that "further increases . . . were produced" [pp. 298, 297]. The statistics failed to confirm that a significant change occurred in one of the first three cases and found no significant differences in either of the two latter cases.

that those results are representative of what would happen in most, or even a reasonable proportion, of the published literature.

Some of the apparent incongruency between the statements of Baer and Jones might be explained through a closer inspection of their arguments. At one point, for example, Baer (in press) states:

> Individual-subject-design practitioners, operating without calculation of the pertinent probabilities, *necessarily* fall into very low probabilities of Type 1 errors and very high probabilities of Type 2 errors, relative to their group-paradigm colleagues [ms. 8, italics added].[13]

According to Baer, then, single-subject researchers, operating without statistics, *must* be more conservative. At first glance, it would seem that Jones' data (in press) completely destroys that statement. To prove that something is not *necessarily* so, one only needs to produce a single case in which it is not so. Jones provided several examples. But look more closely at what Baer said. In his last phrase, Baer made reference to "*group*-paradigm colleagues." Jones studied the impact of statistics on *single*-subject research. I may think that Baer is still making a rather tenuous statement, but I cannot use Jones' data to refute it.

Baer makes reference to group research in several places (as, indeed, Michael did in his 1974b article), which raises the question of its relevance in a discussion of statistics applied to single-subject research. Are the statistical procedures in each case essentially the same? Do they both try to provide the researcher with the same information? To a certain degree, yes; but in one very important respect, I think that group and time-series analyses are very much different. Traditional group-statistical models and time-series analyses both attempt to assess the "overlap" between sets of data. If the overlap is small, a conclusion of "significant differences" may be warranted. If the overlap is large, one must conclude that apparent differences might simply be the result of "chance variation." The way in which overlap is assessed in each case is quite different, however.

In a group study (where the data are independent), one can simply look at the overall level of each group. If all of the scores in one group are higher than the scores in the other group, for example, then statistics are not even necessary: if there is no overlap between the levels of the two groups, the difference has to be statistically significant (given a reasonable sample size). Assume, however, that we are studying a single child and that his performances are steadily improving from day-

[13] A Type 1 error is committed when one says that a significant difference has been obtained when, in fact, the difference may not be significant or meaningful. A Type 2 error is committed when one says there is no real difference when, in fact, there is.

to-day. Each performance is better than the last. At some point, we change the child's program, but the daily improvement simply continues at the same rate. Because the child's scores are always improving, all of the scores in the second phase of our experiment are higher than the scores in the first phase. There is no overlap, at least in terms of the overall level of performance. Does that mean that the new program produced a significant effect? No—the child simply continued to grow at the same rate at which he was *already* growing. Based on the pattern of his performance during the first phase, we would have predicted that he would continue to improve even without the new program. In short, the overlap between where we would predict the child to be (had no program change been made) and where he actually ended up is quite high. We must conclude that the program had no effect.

A pattern of steady, continued growth is relatively easy to spot. It is not likely that many researchers would fail to notice such a trend and take it into account when analyzing the impact of their programs. Patterns of learning in applied situations are not always that smooth, however, and may involve complex combinations of cycles, trends, changes in variability, and random variation. In the analysis of time-series data (either statistically or visually), one must attempt to identify *all* of the elements in such patterns and to account for them when deciding if the performances in one experimental phase are simply the logical extension of the performances in a preceding phase. The question is not, therefore, whether the performances are "different" (e.g., higher or lower, more or less variable), but, rather, whether they can or cannot be explained by some process or factor other than the experimental manipulations. Examined in this light, it seems more reasonable that a powerful tool (e.g., statistical analysis) which accounts more precisely for the preexisting patterns in a child's learning, might just as easily negate a conclusion of significant difference as support one.

Finally, both Michael (1974b) and Baer (in press) appear concerned with the fact that, especially in applied situations, a "statistically significant" result might not be "practically significant." As Baer puts it, "If a problem has been solved, you can *see* that; if you must test for statistical significance, you do not have a solution" [ms. 9]. The potential conflict can be stated the other way around, however: all solutions need not be statistically significant or have scientific relevance! Jones' (in press) analysis of Baer's (1973) data did not refute the fact that the children were better after the first program change was introduced. The statistics only suggested that, at least in one case, the "solution" might be explained by a preexisting upward trend in the subject's performance and might have nothing to do with the new program at all.

In my opinion, the question of practical significance is entirely separate from the question of statistical significance or scientific relevance. The former might be answered through visual inspection of the data, but in answering the latter, statistical time-series analyses may be of use. Being basically a conservative, I might go even further than either Michael (1974) or Baer (in press) in my cautions about the use of formal statistical procedures. While I think they might be valuable, I would suggest that they be used primarily to negate conclusions of experimental impact. Unless both a visual inspection of the data and a formal statistical analysis clearly support the experimental hypotheses, it is my opinion that one should draw a conclusion of "no significant and/or practical difference."

The place of formal statistical procedures in the behavioral sciences has yet to be determined. Certainly before all of the questions of practical and scientific relevance can be answered, many more studies of our analytic options and their impact must be completed. I would hope, however, that future debates turn more frequently to empirical evidence of the sort provided by Jones (in press) rather than to the continuation of rhetoric filled with statements of what "might" or "should" be.[14]

ONE AT A TIME, OR ALL TOGETHER?

As Baer's article (in press) reveals, questions of behavioral methodology are very frequently reduced to the issue of group vs. single-subject research per se. Traditionally, group researchers reject single-subject data as invalid or, at best, "quasi-experimental" (Campbell & Stanley, 1963), and single-subject researchers ignore group data as misleading and generally irrelevant (Sidman, 1960). At present, each discipline appears quite convinced of its own superiority, and all of the debate occurs between the two groups, not within them. I would like to change that. Although I am primarily a single-subject researcher, I believe it is time for a reassessment of the role of group data in placing single-subject results in perspective.

First, it is my opinion that the process of continuous data collection and analysis is an integral part of any behavioral program, whether in research or application. An examination of the recent behavioral literature will reveal, however, that an increasing number of people are making highly prescriptive suggestions regarding instructional tactics, with little or no reference to the possible role of measurement in the success of those tactics. The implication, it seems to me, is that the procedures in question will usually work and that it is not necessary for the practitioner to monitor the program with any exactitude. If, indeed, that is what those researchers are suggesting, then it would

[14] Recently, I received notification from the Bureau of Education for the Handicapped that my proposal for a five-year study of evaluation and research methodologies in special education had been accepted. To facilitate the formulation of specific hypotheses and the interpretation of results, a panel of several well-known behavioral researchers will serve as regular consultants. Both Jones and Baer have consented to sit on that panel.

seem advisable for at least some data to be collected on: (a) the actual role of measurement in determining the effects of the program, and (b) the degree to which the results of the program are generalizable over some relatively well-defined population of potential subjects.

Generalizability of results can be satisfactorily established through the systematic replication of single-subject studies (Sidman, 1960), but the contribution of continuous measurement can only be adequately determined by comparative studies in which the impact of the program is analyzed in a situation where assessments are held to an absolute minimum. Some people might suggest the use of covert assessment, but of course human rights legislation requires that the subject (e.g., the teacher employing the method) be at least aware that the observations are being made. The effects of that knowledge could be significant. If a behaviorist wishes to be tactically prescriptive, therefore, there may be a time when the overall impact of a program should be assessed via a group study in which a simple randomized posttest-only or pretest/posttest design (Campbell & Stanley, 1963) is employed to minimize assessment requirements, while still providing sufficient data for meaningful analysis of the procedure's generalizability.

Second, although one of the major advantages of single-subject research lies in the fact that it can more readily account for slight individual differences and thereby reveal more clearly the general patterns of learning common to all or most subjects (Sidman, 1960), it would seem desirable at times to explicitly assess the degree to which subjects *are* similar or different. By manipulating variables in a classroom until each individual's learning pattern reflected the same basic characteristics as the composite group learning pattern, it might be possible to more precisely determine which variables have the highest degree of generalized impact.

Third, many people have stressed the importance of having specific goals or aims for each applied behavioral program (e.g., Pascal, 1976). Presumably, each goal is established at a level which represents "success," but the definition of success is rarely explicated. In many cases, it is obvious that success has been equated with "normalcy," or at least the performance of a child's nondeviant peers. The establishment of such criteria certainly requires the assessment of at least *some* group of children.

Even if criteria are more functionally determined, there may still be an advantage to the analysis of group data. In one case, for example, a teacher set a child's aim in a "say sound" program at 40 correct sounds per minute with no errors—a goal which reflects a "comfortable normal performance." The child reached the aim within a few weeks, and the program was terminated. After a month, however, a follow-up assessment revealed that the child's performance had slipped to roughly one-half of the aim, so the program was reinstated. After reaching the aim for a second time, the program was again terminated. A second follow-up assessment one month later indicated that the child had slipped even more than before. Finally, the teacher doubled the aim and brought the child to a criteria of 80 sounds per minute (well above "normal" performances). Thereafter, the child had no difficulty in maintaining her skill (at 80 sounds per minute) over long periods without practice (White & Haring, 1976). It would appear that an objective of 80 sounds per minute had functional relevance to that child, whereas 40 sounds per minute did not. While it is fortunate that the little girl's teacher was responsive enough to the problem to discover a functional aim, it is unfortunate that more data were not available to suggest an appropriate aim before the program began. It certainly seems reasonable that there might be general guidelines or rules for establishing functional criteria which would work for most children—at least within some of the more highly refined curricula and task ladders (e.g., computation skills). To discover those functional criteria, however, certain group analysis procedures will have to be employed (e.g., discriminant analyses or Gottman scalability analyses).

Finally, there are certainly many members of the educational system who must be concerned with groups. Principals, district administrators, state superintendents, and other educators are constantly faced with decisions which must, for all intents and purposes, be applied to the entire population of pupils in their charge (e.g., which textbooks should be purchased). In the past, relatively static analyses of group performances have been conducted to facilitate those decisions (e.g., a simple pretest/posttest design to determine the overall impact of a new program). After a few specific samples have been analyzed, the assessment program is usually dropped. There are definite flaws in such short-term investigations (e.g., see Thomas & Pelavin, 1976), but interest in developing viable alternatives has been lacking. I would hope that the measurement expertise and familiarity with learning processes which single-subject researchers possess could be applied to this problem.

There are other cases in which I believe the analysis of group data might be helpful to the single-subject researcher, but those I have just listed are sufficiently representative for my purposes here. By group analyses, however, I do not necessarily mean the type which has been traditionally employed. The application of inferential statistics, for example, may not be necessary at all. The time is approaching when whole "populations" of children could be assessed on a regular basis. If an entire population were to be assessed, there would hardly be any need to determine the generalizability of results.[15] Group monitoring systems

---

[15] Some approximations of "whole population" systems already exist. The Oregon State Mental Health Division, Programs for the Mentally Retarded and Developmentally Disabled, for example, maintains a system in which every trainable mentally retarded child in the state is assessed with a uniform, teacher-developed, criterion-referenced checklist twice annually. The data are summarized

conceivably could be based on a compilation of daily classroom per-formance measures, thereby enabling the precise analysis of individual pupil progress and the consideration of that progress in higher level group summaries. But, before such systems can be realized in any num-bers, a great deal of work must be done in building uniform data collection systems, standard (or at least comparable) curricula, and in training of teachers who would ultimately be responsible for mak-ing the system work. Moreover, it will be necessary to conduct a great deal more research concerning methods which enable the compilation of individual performance records into group summaries without sacrificing that most valuable quality of single-subject data—the ability to analyze the *process* of learning—as opposed to its simple product.

I think it is time that single-subject researchers reexamine the value of group data. It will be interesting to see which force will be most important in determining how many will end up in agreement with me—the traditional dislike for all things associated with groups and group analyses, or the challenge of developing new ways for applying process analyses to the study of human behavior.

IN CONCLUSION

When I entered the behavioral field, first as a psychologist and later as an educator, I was resigned to a rather "dull" career. I thought that all of the major pioneering work—all of the exciting work—had already been completed. All that was left was the painstakingly slow process of application and refinement. Not true! Behaviorism is a young, vibrant, rapidly changing field. There are more than enough fascinating "break-throughs" still to be made and certainly enough controversy to go around. I have only been able to touch upon a few of the more recent issues here—and only briefly at that. If I have succeeded in whetting your appetite for debate and your desire for empirical data with which to resolve those debates, however, I will have achieved my purpose. Debate and controversy have characterized almost every major scientific development in the history of mankind; and, when it comes to debate,

---

by individuals, classes, schools, districts, intermediate districts, and age groups within the state. These data are arranged to show the level of each child and group, their progress since the time of the last assessment, and the relationships of their performances to those of their chronological peers; that is, age-mates who were tested at the same time throughout the state. The results of those assess-ments have been used to determine the impact of inservice training, new curricu-lar materials, teacher-pupil ratios, and a variety of other things of concern to educational administrators. There is even a "legislative summary" which helps assess the impact of funding patterns. I find systems of this type extremely excit-ing, for they enable educational administrators to make and evaluate decisions based on the *actual performance of children*—perhaps for the first time in their administrative careers.

it has been my experience that the application of behavioral principles and methods in the field of special education is the biggest arena of them all.

REFERENCES

Baer, A. M., Rowbury, T., & Baer, D. M. The development of instructional control over classroom activities of deviant preschool children. *Journal of Applied Behavior Analysis,* 1974, 7, 643-46.

Baer, D. M. Perhaps it would be better not to know everything. *Journal of Applied Behavior Analysis,* in press.

Baer, D. M., Wolf, M. M., & Risley, T. R. Some current dimensions of applied behavior analysis. *Journal of Applied Behavior Analysis,* 1968, 1, 91-97.

Birnbrauer, J. S., Peterson, C. R., & Solnick, J. V. Design and interpretation of studies of single subjects. *American Journal of Mental Deficiency,* 1974, 79, 191-203.

Bohannon, R. M. *Direct and daily measurement procedures in the identification and treatment of reading behaviors of children in special education.* Unpublished doctoral dissertation, University of Washington, 1975.

Boren, J. J., & Colman, A. D. Some experiments on reinforcement principles within a psychiatric ward for delinquent soldiers. *Journal of Applied Behavior Analysis,* 1970, 3, 29-37.

Campbell, D. T., & Stanley, I. C. *Experimental and quasi-experimental designs for research.* Chicago: Rand McNally, 1963.

Carman, J. B. Detection of water level in inverted bottles. *Journal of Experimental Analysis of Behavior,* 1976, 25, 278.

Dukes, W. F. $N = 1$. *Psychological Bulletin,* 1965, 64, 74-79.

Edgar, E., & Billingsley, F. Believability when $N = 1$. *Psychological Record,* 1974, 24, 147-60.

Edgington, E. S. Statistical inference and nonrandom samples. *Psychological Bulletin,* 1966, 66, 485-87.

Edgington, E. S. Statistical inference from $N = 1$ experiments. *Journal of Psychology,* 1967, 65, 195-99.

Edgington, E. S. *Statistical inference: The distribution-free approach.* New York: McGraw-Hill, 1969.

Engelmann, S. *Preventing failure in the primary grades.* Chicago: Science Research Associates, 1969.

Fixen, D. C., Phillips, E. L., & Wolf, M. M. Achievement place: The reliability of self-reporting and peer-reporting and their effects on behavior. *Journal of Applied Behavior Analysis,* 1972, 5, 19-32.

Gentile, J. R., Roden, A. H., & Klein, R. D. An analysis of variance model for the intrasubject replication design. *Journal of Applied Behavior Analysis,* 1972, 5, 193-98.

Glass, G. V., Willson, V. L., & Gottman, J. M. *Design and analysis of time-series experiments.* Boulder: Laboratory of Educational Research, University of Colorado, 1973.

Gottman, J. M. *Time-series analysis in the behavioral sciences and a methodology for action research.* Unpublished doctoral dissertation, University of Wisconsin, 1971.

Hall, R. V., Fox, R., Willard, D., Goldsmith, L., Emerson, M., Owen, M., Davis, F., & Porcia, E. The teacher as an observer and experimenter in the modification of talking-out behavior. *Journal of Applied Behavior Analysis,* 1971, 4, 141-50.

Haring, N. G. (principal investigator). *Learning and instructional hierarchies in severely and profoundly handicapped children.* Bureau of Education for the Handicapped, University of Washington (Grant G00-75-00-593), in progress.

Hartman, D. P. Forcing square pegs into round holes: Some comments on "An analysis of variance model for the intrasubject replication design." *Journal of Applied Behavior Analysis,* 1974, 7, 635-38.

Haughton, E. Counting together: *Precision teaching rationale—69.* Eugene: Instructional Materials Center, University of Oregon, 1969.

Ingham, R. J., & Andrews, G. An analysis of a token economy in stuttering therapy. *Journal of Applied Behavior Analysis,* 1973, 6, 219-29.

Jones, R. R., Vaught, R. S., & Weinrott, M. Time-series analysis in operant research. *Journal of Applied Behavior Analysis,* in press.

Kazdin, A. E. Methodological and assessment considerations in evaluating reinforcement programs in applied settings. *Journal of Applied Behavioral Analysis,* 1973, 6, 517-39.

Keselman, H. J., & Leventhal, L. Concerning the statistical procedures enumerated by Gentile et al.: Another perspective. *Journal of Applied Behavior Analysis,* 1974, 7, 643-46.

Kratochwill, T., Alden, K., Demuth, D., Dawson, D., Panicucci, C., Arntson, P., McMurray, N., Hempstead, J., & Leven, J. A further consideration in the application of an analysis of variance model for the intrasubject replication design. *Journal of Applied Behavior Analysis,* 1974, 7, 629-34.

Kunzelman, H. P. (Ed.). *Precision teaching.* Seattle: Special Child Publications, 1970.

Liberty, K. A. *Decide for progress: Dynamic aims and data decisions.* Seattle: Experimental Education Unit, Child Development and Mental Retardation Center, University of Washington, 1975. (Working paper 56.)

Lindsley, O. R. Direct measurement and prosthesis of retarded behavior. *Journal of Education,* 1964, 147, 62-81.

Lynch, V., Shoemaker, S., & White, O. Training Needs Survey. *Review: The American Association for the Education of the Severely/Profoundly Handicapped*, 1976, 1, 1-16.

Michael, J. Statistical inference for individual organism research: Some reactions to a suggestion by Gentile, Roden and Klein. *Journal of Applied Behavior Analysis*, 1974, 7, 627-28. (a)

Michael, J. Statistical inference for individual organism research: Mixed blessing or curse? *Journal of Applied Behavior Analysis*, 1974, 7, 647-53. (b)

Millenson, J. R. *Principles of behavioral analysis*. New York: MacMillan, 1967.

Pascal, C. E. Using principles of behavior modification to teach behavior modification. *Exceptional Children*, 1976, 42, 426-31.

Phillips, E. L., Phillips, E. A., Fixsen, D. L., & Wolf, M. M. Achievement place: Modification of the behaviors of pre-delinquent boys within a token economy. *Journal of Applied Behavior Analysis*, 1971, 4, 45-49.

Revusky, S. H. Some statistical treatments compatible with individual organism methodology. *Journal of the Experimental Analysis of Behavior*, 1967, 10, 319-30.

Risley, T. R., & Wolf, M. M. Strategies for analyzing behavioral change over time. In J. Nesselroade & H. Reese (Eds.), *Life-span developmental psychology: Methodological issues*. New York: Academic Press, 1972.

Sidman, M. *Tactics of scientific research*. New York: Basic Books, 1960.

Skinner, B. F. *Science and human behavior*. New York: Macmillan, 1953.

Skinner, B. F. Farewell, my lovely! *Journal of the Experimental Analysis of Behavior*, 1976, 25, 218.

Stevens, J. C., & Savin, H. B. On the form of learning curves. *Journal of the Experimental Analysis of Behavior*, 1972, 5, 15-18.

Surratt, P. R., Ulrich, R. E., & Hawkins, R. P. An elementary student as an engineer. *Journal of Applied Behavior Analysis*, 1969, 2, 85-92.

Thomas, T. C., & Pelavin, S. H. *Patterns of ESEA Title I reading achievement*. A 1976 report to the Policy Development Office of the Department of Health, Education and Welfare. Copies may be obtained from E-105, Stanford Research Institute, 333 Ravenswood Avenue, Menlo Park, Calif., 94025.

Thoresen, C. E., & Elashoff, J. D. An analysis-of-variance model for intra-subject replication design: Some additional comments. *Journal of Applied Behavior Analysis*, 1974, 7, 639-42.

White, O. R. *Glossary of behavioral terminology*. Champaign, Ill.: Research Press, 1971. (a)

White, O. R. *A manual for the calculation and use of the median slope: A technique of progress estimation and prediction in the single case*. Eugene: Regional Resource Center for Handicapped Children, University of Oregon, 1972. (Working paper 15.)

White, O. R. *Pragmatic approaches to the progress in the single case.* Unpublished doctoral dissertation, University of Oregon, 1971. (b)

White, O. R. Evaluating education progress. In J. D. Cone & R. P. Hawkins (Eds.), *Behavioral assessment: New directions in clinical psychology.* New York: Brunner-Mazel, in press.

White, O. R. & Haring, N. G. *Exceptional teaching: A multimedia training package.* Columbus, Ohio: Charles E. Merrill, 1976.

White, O. R., & Liberty, K. A. Evaluation and measurement. In N. G. Haring & R. Schiefelbusch (Eds.), *Teaching special children.* New York: McGraw-Hill, 1976.

Wincze, J. P., Leitenberg, H., & Agras, W. S. The effects of token reinforcement and feedback on the delusional verbal behavior of chronic paranoid schizophrenics. *Journal of Applied Behavior Analysis,* 1972, 5, 247-62.

Yates, A. J. *Behavior therapy.* New York: Wiley, 1970.

A SELECTED BIBLIOGRAPHY OF WORKS BY
OWEN R. WHITE

White, O. R. *Proposed evaluative system for rehabilitation projects with the mentally retarded: User's manual—short form.* Eugene: Rehabilitation Research and Training Center in Mental Retardation, University of Oregon, 1970.

White, O. R. *Glossary of behavioral terminology.* Champaign, Ill.: Research Press, 1971.

White, O. R. *A physician's introduction to behaviorism.* Paper presented to the pediatricians of Eugene, Oregon in partial explanation of the "Special Training for Exceptional Parents" (STEP) program, January 1972.

White, O. R. The identification of handicapped students through the Northwest Regional Resource System and its relation to the Hawaii State Resource System. In *Report of Education of the Handicapped Part D Special Studies Institute for Administrators in Special Education: Orientation to Education for Moderately and Severely Handicapped Students.* Department of Education, Office of Instructional Services, Special Education Branch, Honolulu, 1973.

White, O. R. Some additional considerations in the use of a precision teaching approach for a broad-based data management system. In D. Sailes (Chair), *Precision teaching: A means for process and produce evaluation.* Symposium presented at the 2nd annual meeting of the Washington Educational Research Association (WERA), Seattle, May 23-24, 1974.

White, O. R. *Evaluating the educational process.* Working paper available through the Experimental Education Unit, Child Development and Mental Retardation Center, University of Washington, 1974.

White, O. R. *Principles of behavioral technology*. Paper presented at the ESD Workshop for the Severely/Profoundly Handicapped, Experimental Education Unit, Child Development and Mental Retardation Center, University of Washington, August 11-13, 1975.

White, O. R. *Program evaluation*. Paper presented at the ESD Workshop for the Severely/Profoundly Handicapped, Experimental Education Unit, Child Development and Mental Retardation Center, University of Washington, August 11-13, 1975.

White, O. R. Evaluating educational progress. In J. D. Cone & R. P. Hawkins, (Eds.), *Behavioral assessment: New directions in clinical psychology*. New York: Brunner-Mazel, in press.

White, O. R., & Haring, N. G. *Exceptional teaching: A multimedia training package*. Columbus, Ohio: Charles E. Merrill, 1976.

White, O. R., & Liberty, K. A. *Practical classroom measurement: Precision teaching*. Working paper available through the Experimental Education Unit, Child Development and Mental Retardation Center, University of Washington, 1975.

White, O. R., & Liberty, K. A. Evaluation and Measurement. In N. G. Haring & R. Schiefelbusch (Eds.), *Teaching special children*. New York: McGraw-Hill, 1976.

5

The Current and Future Role of Educational Technology

G. Phillip Cartwright

G. Phillip Cartwright is presently professor and chairman of the graduate program in the Department of Special Education at Pennsylvania State University. His previous professional positions include that of assistant director of the Computer Assisted Instruction Laboratory at Penn State, assistant project director for research and evaluation of instructional materials for Science Research Associates, and teacher of primary and secondary classes for the mentally retarded. Dr. Cartwright has written extensively in the areas of identification and diagnosis as well as on numerous topics pertaining to educational technology.

Dr. Cartwright received his B.S. degree in psychology from the University of Illinois in 1960 and his M.S. degree in education from the University of Illinois in 1962. In 1966, he obtained a Ph.D. in special education research from the University of Pittsburgh. A selected bibliography of works by Dr. Cartwright appears on pages 101-102.

I thought of preparing this chapter in programmed text format. Although such a format would be in keeping with the topic, I discarded the idea because writing programmed instruction is even more dull than reading it.

Flow charting crossed my mind, too, and I always keep a few all-purpose flow charts handy in case of emergency. For a short while my plan was to use a series of criterion-referenced tests followed by appropriate branches around familiar material. Finally, I settled on a suitable technologically oriented gimmick: a free demonstration of our magic computer assisted instruction system here at Penn State. So, the next time you're in central Pennsylvania, stop in and see me and I'll give you the Grand Tour, the Good Lord willing (to say nothing of the provost, the dean, IBM, and BEH).

So much for the gimmick; on with the substance.

EDUCATIONAL TECHNOLOGIST VS. EDUCATOR WITH TECHNOLOGICAL SUPPORT

I approach educational technology from the vantage point of a special educator; i.e., as a special educator interested in efficient and effective methods of instructing the handicapped and, especially, in instructing personnel to work with the handicapped. Such a vantage point presents a different (not necessarily better) perspective from that of an educational technologist or instructional media specialist who may, from time to time, apply his skills to problems in special education. My vantage point has led me to try various methods of instruction and instructional devices (especially programmed instruction, television, and computer assisted instruction) in attempts to reach different sets of objectives with handicapped children and educational personnel.

Historically, the media specialist became a specialist in relatively well-circumscribed media areas partly because of personal interest and partly because it is difficult and time-consuming to acquire expertise in more than one or two facets of media. The tendency is to concentrate on one or two areas and, as problems present themselves, the usual reaction is to solve the problems using the tools (media) with which the specialist is most familiar. Because of single-mindedness and an over-zealous, even evangelistic commitment, proponents of media have in some instances done themselves a disservice by overpromoting media or overgeneralizing media's effectiveness. As Welliver (1973) puts it, "The people who did the most to destroy the educational impact of a particular technological tool were the individuals who worked most vigorously to promote the educational uses of that tool" [p. 2].

In fairness to educational technologists and media specialists, let me hasten to add that the single all-purpose medium approach is fast disappearing. Although it is impossible to keep up with all the literature relating special education and technology, my perception is that the media specialists of today are much less prone to push one or two favorite devices. In fact, their emphasis is increasingly upon problem solving and in using media only where appropriate.

EDUCATIONAL TECHNOLOGY: 1961

The early years (late 1950s, early 1960s) of media in education were characterized by the single-device approach and the results were not especially satisfying. I recall relatively little use of media in my own school days but I recollect vividly the use to which NDEA media funds were put during my first year of teaching a special class of seven-year-old retarded children. My little semirural school consisted of seven classes: grades 1 through 6 and my special class. Every Monday morning at 9:15 was film time. The superintendent of schools personally delivered 50-75 minutes of film, threaded the projector, and showed the films. All 150 children in the school gathered in the "auditorium" to watch. The teachers had no advance notice of content and had no choice but to attend and bring the children. I enjoyed some of the films, but 95 percent of them were not even remotely related to my curriculum and the week's instructional activities. A bad example? Sure, but not an uncommon one.

Congreve (1971) writing in a massive report by the Commission on Instructional Technology stated the case well:

> Technology as it is used in schools today is not an integral part of the program. Rather it is an appendage to the "tried and true" (tired and predictable) methods in which the teacher is the dominant figure and the student is the homeostatic stimulus-reducing organism [p. 545].

Such was the state of educational technology in the programs for the handicapped in the 1960s and, to a great extent, it is still the same today. With few exceptions, development and use of technology in education programs for the handicapped is limited to efforts that are fragmentary and often irrelevant. It is apparent from even a cursory examination of the literature related to technology and the handicapped that the pattern during the 1950s and 1960s was to develop hardware for hardware's sake and to use readily available software; e.g., films, slides, and tapes produced for various nonhandicapped audiences instead of systematically developing total instructional systems for handicapped children.

EDUCATIONAL TECHNOLOGY DEFINED

Following customary procedures, I will now attempt to define the term of interest: *educational technology*. I'll not tackle the definition of *education* except to say the education and education programs about which I am personally concerned deal with basic objectives: promulgation of societal culture for the community at large; and, for the individual, acquisition of skills, knowledges, and attitudes useful in helping him/her gain personal dignity and worth. Education programs need not be formal and they need not have formal meeting times or places.

According to the *Oxford English Dictionary* the word *technology* is from the early Greek language and means "systematic treatment" or "the scientific study of the practical and applied arts."[1] The first recorded use of the word was in the early 1600s. The *Random House* dictionary defines technology as "that branch of *knowledge* that deals with industrial arts, applied science, engineering, etc."[2]

It is significant that none of these primary definitions refer directly to objects, machines, or devices. Rather, the definitions refer directly to process and terminology. This usage is in contrast to the popular conception of technology as it is applied to education. If you were to ask 100 educators to tell you what comes to mind at the mention of educational technology, I would wager that 80 of them would include "audiovisual," "machines," "hardware," and the like in their responses, and would *not* include references to process or systematic treatment.

Those working in instructional media and in educational technology are keenly aware of the process-machine distinction. Media technologists and instructional (nee educational) technologists go to great lengths to stress and elaborate this distinction. The most often quoted definition of instructional/educational[3] technology is that by Tickton (1970) in a report by the Commission on Instructional Technology:

> Instructional technology can be offered in two ways. In its more familiar sense, it means that media born of the communications revolution which can be used for instructional purposes alongside the teacher, textbook and blackboard. In general, the Commission's report follows this usage. In order to reflect present-day reality, the

[1] *Oxford English Dictionary*, 1971, s.v. "technology."

[2] *Random House*, Dictionary of the English Language, 1967, s.v. "technology."

[3] For the moment, please regard instructional technology and educational technology as synonymous.

Commission has had to look at the pieces that make up instructional technology: television, films, overhead projectors, computers, and the other items of "hardware" and "software" (to use the convenient jargon that distinguishes machines from programs). In nearly every case, these media have entered education independently, and still operate more in isolation than in combination.

The second and less familiar definition of instructional technology goes beyond any particular medium or device. In this sense, instructional technology is more than the sum of its parts. It is a systematic way of designing, carrying out, and evaluating the total process of learning and teaching in terms of specific objectives, based on research in human learning and communication, and employing a combination of human and nonhuman resources to bring about more effective instruction. The widespread acceptance and application of this broad definition belongs to the future. Though only a limited number of institutions have attempted to design instruction using such a systematic comprehensive approach, there is reason to believe that this approach holds the key to the contribution technology can make to the advancement of education. It became clear, in fact, as we pursue our study that a major obstacle to instructional technology's fulfillment has been its application by bits and pieces [pp. 21, 22].

Welliver (1973) identifies the two parts of the Tickton definition as Technology I, tools, and Technology II, processes. He goes on to explain:

Tools were defined as the machines or the hardware of technology. The processes refer to a thorough, comprehensive, systematic approach to instruction. Under this concept, the processes of technology focus upon the needs of the learner and experiences are designed on the basis of these needs. The tools of technology play a subordinate role and are called into play only when they can be effectively brought to bear on identified learner needs as part of the total system for satisfying those needs [p. 1].

Welliver (1976) also points out that the processes of technology should be used by persons who are not necessarily specialists in the tools of technology. In fact, the greatest danger in using technological tools is from their application in absence of the processes of technology.

Technology, as a concept, is not limited to education; educational applications are a miniscule part of the uses of technology in society. To many persons the advance of technology is an associated if not a causative factor in the decline of humanism. They identify technology not merely with various machines but rather with a menacing spectre of a future holocaust or, at least, a harbinger of a computer-controlled mass of robots. By far, the majority of quotations about technology in the *International Thesaurus of Quotations* (Tripp, 1970) carry clear implications: the need for caution in its further development and use, and the need to regard the human as the evolutionary pinnacle of a superordinate technology; viz., John F. Kennedy's remarks on May 21, 1963, "Man is still the most extraordinary computer of all."

Technology is blamed for many of man's current problems, and its critics are ready to blame current technological advances for problems which have not yet surfaced. Educational applications of technology do not escape these criticisms.

EDUCATIONAL TECHNOLOGY, AUDIO VISUAL AIDS, AND ADAPTIVE EDUCATION

Although many people use the terms *educational technology* and *instructional technology* interchangeably, others have found a distinction between them to be useful. My colleague, Paul Welliver, when pressed, provided an analog with educational and instructional television. Instructional television is oriented toward the teaching of specific instructional objectives. Generally, it operates in a relatively well-structured setting and is geared toward assisting a fairly specific group of students to reach certain relatively well-defined educational objectives. Educational TV usually is regarded as a public affairs, noncommercial service which broadcasts symphonies, plays, town forums, etc. in the general interest of the public. The intended audience is generally much larger and less well defined than the intended audience of instructional TV. The objectives of educational TV programs in general are more diffuse, less specific. The broader educational TV network, however, may be the vehicle through which the instructional TV service is offered. In this conception, instructional TV is a subset of educational TV.

To complete the comparison, then, instructional technology is the more specific, goal-oriented, subsidiary to the wide-ranging technology related to education.

The term *audio visual aids* may stimulate the vision of a movie projector showing something like the "Life Cycle of the Honey Bee" to a group of fourth graders. AV usually refers to some educationally oriented materials presented by a machine of some kind such as a tape recorder, slide projector, overhead projector, or movie projector. The educational materials are usually content oriented, usually have some level of educational objectives or outcomes associated with them, and often have some vague statement about the intended audience. The onus is on the teacher to see to it that the materials fit the learners' needs. The AV approach is, thus, *materials* oriented.

The educational technology approach is *learner* oriented. The application of a systematic and comprehensive technology of education starts with the needs, characteristics, and objectives of the learner and creates a long-range instructional program for that learner. Thus the emphasis of instructional technology is to establish a match between the learner and the most appropriate methods of instructing that learner. According to Stolurow (1970), "individualization as it relates to the new education means prescriptive instruction, not isolated learning experience. Possibly personalization is a more descriptive term than individualization" [p. vi].

Mitzel (1970), in discussing adaptive education and instructional technology, says that "individualized instruction suggests that something unique about the learner has been taken into account in a dynamic way to build an instructional sequence" [p. 24]. Furthermore, his definition of *adaptive education* is at once a goal of all education as well as a methodological challenge to educators and technologists:

[Adaptive education is] the tailoring of subject-matter presentations to fit the special requirements and capabilities of each learner as an individual. The ideal is that no learner should stop short of his full potential to grasp a subject because of any idiosyncratic difficulties he may have in learning style, or in sensory receptivity, or in organization [pp. 23-24].

For convenience, the concepts embodied by the terms *adaptive education*, *personalized instruction*, and *individualized instruction* may be regarded as equivalent and may be viewed as goals as well as methods. Instructional/educational technology provides the processes and tactics (software) for the concepts; and audio visual aids provide the machinery (hardware).

TECHNOLOGY AS AN AID TO LITERATURE REVIEW

It is not the purpose of this chapter to provide an extensive review of the literature relating technology and the handicapped. I considered a review of some interesting applications important, though, so I decided to call upon the services of CEC-ERIC to assist me in reviewing the relevant literature.

I have been quite satisfied with the results of computer-based information services such as CEC-ERIC and I encourage our graduate students to use such services for papers and theses. One of our master's degree students, Richard Regan, assisted me in using the Lockheed/ DIALOG system to search the CEC-ERIC data base. We chose to do the initial query in "real time" so that we would have immediate feedback about (a) the number of abstracts of studies and reports we would get using different combinations of descriptors, and (b) the "hit rate";

i.e., the usefulness of the abstracts produced using the various combinations of descriptors.

We used two sets of descriptors. Set A defined the handicaps in which we were interested; in this case all handicaps were included. Set B contained descriptors which related to educational technology such as instructional media, computer, systems analysis, audio visual, instructional technology, etc. We asked the computer to select all abstracts which were described by at least one term from set A and one term from set B.

The entire search history is too long and complex to present here so I'll summarize and, I hope, illustrate how the computer search saved many hours of manual literature search. To me, this search dramatizes how one facet of educational technology can assist the professional educator.

Shortly after we signed on to the system, we were informed that set A contained 22,604 abstracts and set B contained 14,369 abstracts. Limiting our search to abstracts which contained at least one descriptor from set A and set B produced a total of 639 abstracts. That is, the CEC-ERIC file contained 639 references in which educational technology and the handicapped were linked in some way. We read about 20 abstracts on a cathode ray tube display and decided the descriptors and procedures were satisfactory.

About a week later, the printout of the 639 abstracts arrived. In general, we were quite satisfied with the results. The abstracts obtained in such a search vary in quality and detail, but usually enough information is present to help the investigator decide whether or not the content of the abstracted article is such that the original document should be reviewed. The biggest drawback to the CEC-ERIC data base for those of us interested in technology is that technical and semitechnical literature from related disciplines is not abstracted.

As we reviewed the 639 abstracts and some of the original documents, it became very apparent that there were great differences in the uses of technology with different handicapped groups. We found that, for the most part, educational technology has been used with deaf children. Nearly one-third of the 639 abstracts we reviewed dealt with technology and deafness. This figure is even more startling when it is noted that (using set A descriptors alone) our computer search turned up 2,498 abstracts of articles dealing with the disturbed, 2,359 dealing with the learning disabled, and 958 about the deaf. When set A and set B descriptors were used together, 196 abstracts were found which included some reference to the deaf. Only 31 abstracts related to the uses of technology with the learning disabled were found and only 28 abstracts related to using technology with the disturbed were found. This phenomenon; i.e., relatively greater use of media and technology with the deaf and hearing impaired was also noted by Lance (1973). He pointed out, and I concur, that much of the early emphasis on providing media resources for the deaf was stimulated by financial and moral encouragement from the Bureau of Education for the Handicapped, United States Office of Education. (BEH's contribution to technology in special education is noted in more detail in the next section.)

In summary, the use of computer searches of the literature is a remarkable application of technology to education just now coming into its own. Its future is assured not only for the professional literature but for child-based materials as well, as witnessed by the development of the National Instructional Materials Information System (NIMIS). The NIMIS system is housed within the National Center on Educational Media and Materials for the Handicapped at the Ohio State University. The ultimate goal of this interactive "real-time" system is to develop a computer-based system which will permit and encourage teachers and parents from any state to immediately locate instructional materials appropriate for use with individual handicapped children.

BUREAU OF EDUCATION FOR THE HANDICAPPED

The Bureau of Education for the Handicapped (BEH) has stimulated the use of media with the handicapped by example, by unsolicited grant programs, and by solicited contractual arrangements. Technology applications have been centered primarily in the BEH Media Services and Captioned Films branch, although all its branches have encouraged and supported innovative media applications. One of the major goals of the BEH technology program is to put effective instructional materials into the hands of educational personnel who work with handicapped children and into the hands of children themselves. Actually, the goal goes far beyond the mere delivery of instructional materials to teachers and children. According to Lance (1973), the vision of special educator/technologists both within BEH and in the field is the development and implementation of a sophisticated instructional system including

> provisions for insuring the identification of handicapped children, a proper educational diagnosis, and an ongoing prescriptive process which would match each student's learning requirements with the most appropriate educational program. This program would include the media and materials and competent teacher to complete the final step in delivering services to children [p. 17].

To that end, BEH has established an elaborate network of learning resource centers and specialized offices at local, state, and regional levels. The various units provide a variety of functions related to the provision of technological services to teachers and children. The present and planned services are impressive and everyone interested in the education of the handicapped should be aware of the BEH Learning Resources System. Further information can be obtained from BEH, Office of Education, Washington D.C.

In addition to the Learning Resources Systems network, BEH has financed numerous research, development, and demonstration projects in which media/technology plays an important role. Most of the projects reported in the next section were sponsored by BEH.

SOME PROMISING APPLICATIONS

A risk in taking a futuristic look at a developing field is to overlook significant past achievements which are still pertinent and are likely to remain so for some time to come. Fortunately, a good summary of the uses of instructional media with the handicapped through 1974 is available to chronicle many important technological projects (Lance, 1973). Projects covered in that publication will not be repeated here. Likewise, computer uses in special education up to 1974 were covered in an extensive review by Cartwright and Hall (1974) and will not be repeated. That which follows is a brief review of some interesting ideas which I feel bear watching.

Recently, I spent some time reviewing the work of some engineers at Scope Electronics, Reston, Virginia. They have developed a system they call VDETS—Voice Data Entry Terminal System.

VDETS makes it possible to access virtually any computer by spoken commands. Functionally, this means that the computer can "recognize" and respond appropriately to the human voice. A trivial use of this device would be to turn on a TV set and command it to display channel seven, for example. A more important use is reported by Glenn, Miller, and Broman (in press). Several quadraplegic youths and adults have been trained as computer programmers and use VDETS instead of a conventional computer terminal. That system would be a natural for interactive instructional programs for homebound, severely disabled persons.

A project which directly addresses homebound instruction for handicapped children is Tel-Catch. Tel-Catch is an application of TICCIT (Time-shared, Interactive, Computer-Controlled Information System), a computer-based instructional system developed by the MITRE Corporation also of Reston, Virginia. A demonstration of the system in 1976 provided instruction to 100 children who are severely physically handicapped, emotionally disturbed, and neurologically impaired, as well as chronically ill and hospitalized. The system uses a telephone and standard TV linked to the community cable TV system. The TV delivers instructional material, and the student communicates with the computer by means of a simple keyboard linked with the telephone (*Communication News*, 1976).

Whereas VDETS is a voice-in system, the Kurzweil Reading Machine is a voice-out system. Kurzweil Computers Products, Inc., of Cambridge, Mass., has developed a device which can translate ordinary printed materials into full-word English speech. The speech is synthetic or synthesized by a computer from small units but is readily comprehensible. It promises to be a major breakthrough in reading for blind people.

A relatively simple audio device is available for blind people to allow them to vary the rate of prerecorded cassettes. The Varispeech II looks like a standard cassette deck but it has an additional control which permits the listener to increase or decrease the presentation speed at will. Speeds up to three times the normal speech rate are possible with no change in pitch and little difference in comprehension. This device has promise for use with sighted nonreaders and can be used in conjunction with conventional packaged slide-tape presentations.

Another device designed for use by blind persons which caught my eye recently is a "talking calculator" called Speech Plus. This calculator is similar in size and appearance to the thousands of minicalculators which have become available in all sizes and price ranges and can be purchased in places ranging from your corner drugstore to Neiman Marcus. Its major difference is the inclusion of synthesized voice output. For example, punching the equation $2 \times 4.3 = 8.6$ will produce the words "two times four point three equals eight point six" with each key press. It is a simple, nearly foolproof device which could provide an extremely valuable service to blind persons and be a valuable teaching tool as well. Silicon chip technology has made low price (less than 400 dollars) and compactness a reality in this instance.

An entirely different conceptual aid for teaching the blind is the Tactile Vision Substitution System (TVSS). Scadden (1974) reports that the TVSS "converts the visual image from a narrow-angle television camera to a tactual image on a 5-inch square, 100-point display of vibrators placed against the abdomen of the blind person" [p. 394]. The device has also been described as a "Tummy Tickler" that is useful with normal and retarded readers as well as dyslexics (*Mosaic*, 1975). Research support for this assertion is weak, however, and further study is needed to establish the system's effectiveness.

The TVSS is the conceptual and technical cousin to the more popular Optacon. The Optacon converts standard printed symbols into a three-dimensional representation of the symbols which are "read" by the blind person's fingertips. The Optacon has been the subject of numerous reports (e.g. Bliss & Moore, 1974; Moore & Bliss, 1975).

A remarkable catalog listing over 1,000 aids and appliances for the blind has been published by the American Foundation for the Blind.

Most of preceding examples are geared to assisting blind and partially sighted persons. Some interesting applications with deaf populations have been reviewed by Boothroyd (1975). He provides a survey of technological devices which have been developed to help the deaf with communication, warning, education, and entertainment.

Meierhenry (1974) reviews developments in educational media for teaching the deaf during the period 1961-74. His article is in a special issue of *American Annals of the Deaf* (October, 1974) which focuses on technology and the deaf and includes reports of activities at Gallaudet College (which continues to be a living laboratory for the development and demonstration of educational technology for the deaf), the National Technical Institute for the Deaf, the Media Services and Captioned Films Branch of BEH, and at several state schools. Also included are examples of various media such as TV, overhead projectors, computer-assisted instruction, and the Talking Typewriter; and a review of Project LIFE (Language Improvement to Facilitate Education.)

SYSTEMATIC INSTRUCTION: SOME INTERESTING ILLUSTRATIONS

For the most part, technological applications with the blind and deaf have emphasized sensory aids to enhance communications. Other handicapped children, presumably near-normal in sensory acuity, have benefitted greatly from the organization and systematization of knowledge associated with good examples of educational technology.

Systematization of instruction is not unique to educational technology, as non technologists quickly point out. However, the *process* of creating software or programs for use with any kind of device usually has great benefits. Packaging of mediated instruction forces the developer to fully conceptualize the final product. The developer must think through the objectives, strategies, materials, etc., and prepare them in such a way that a nonspecialist in the area—or a machine—can deliver the instructional pitch reliably and accurately. The less sophisticated and "intelligent" the teaching machine, the more attention must be given to the development of the software. The most intelligent, adaptable, and responsive machine (in other words—the live teacher) can get by with less careful software development.

Project MORE (Lent, 1975) is an example of how a special education problem area is finding solution through the use of media. This approach is in contrast to that of starting with a given medium of instruction and seeking problems that can be solved by that medium. Project MORE (Mediated Operational Research for Education) is a systems-oriented project using educational technology to help instruct trainable mentally retarded persons in survival skills. I expect the impact of this project to be strong regardless of whether or not implementation of its concepts depends upon the use of media.

Even further removed from the hardware side of technology is *Precision Teaching*. Precision Teaching is an application of behavioral technology and does not depend upon electromechanical devices, although such devices can often be used to good advantage. A relatively old, but still important, review of this application can be found in *Teaching Exceptional Children*, Spring 1971. Also important is the work of Tawney at the University of Kentucky. He uses operant technology in conjunction with computer-based devices to provide systematic instructional sequences to severely retarded children (Tawney & Schedgick, 1974).

As an indicator of the pervasiveness of the "systematic treatment" definition of educational technology, consider the bibliography published by the Kansas Neurological Institute. The work is titled *Educational Technology for the Severely Handicapped* (Guess, Sailor, & Lavis, 1975) and is described as a comprehensive bibliography of educational programs for the severely handicapped. The references in the bibliography are included in a computer-based retrieval system which can provide abstracts of the programs, research data, costs, etc. I estimate that fewer than 25 percent of the programs, projects, and articles included the use of media in any significant way. A much higher percentage of the entries reflect that attention was given to systematization of instruction.

I am fond of referring to the work of Schwartz and Oseroff of Florida State University as an excellent example of the system analysis approach applied to teacher training in special education. They have produced that rare item: a replicable, apparently cost-effective model of teacher training. It has all the buzz words of the early 1970s: *systems analysis, technology, computer-managed instruction, cost benefits*, etc. Their project has an even rarer product: data. What's more, the concepts and ideas are out in plain view (at last), and the potential user can see in advance what the project is all about. A full description of this project is given in the final report to BEH (Schwartz & Oseroff, 1975).

Another union of technology and special education is in the training program directed by Hofmeister at Utah State University. Hofmeister's (1973) program is designed to train graduate-level special educators in the application of educational technology in working with handicapped children.

Also involved in the preparation of special educator technologists is Thiagarajan at Indiana University. His group has produced a fascinating and comprehensive *Sourcebook* to assist teachers in developing instructional materials for handicapped children (Thiagarajan, Semmel, & Semmel, 1973).

CARE—COMPUTER ASSISTED REMEDIAL EDUCATION

You would be surprised if this chapter didn't mention my own work in applying educational technology to the problems of the handicapped, so I won't disappoint you. That which follows is a brief summary of the Penn State CARE projects, 1969-76.

CARE is really a series of development and dissemination projects designed to assist regular educational personnel to screen and accommodate mildly handicapped children in general education situations. The format is computer-assisted instruction at the college level. Four complete college courses have been developed under the sponsorship of the Bureau of Education for the Handicapped. The courses are: CARE 1: Early Identification of Handicapped Children; CARE 2: Diagnostic Teaching of Preschool Children; CARE 3: Diagnostic Teaching of Primary Children; and CARE 4: Education of the Visually Handicapped. Each of the courses is a "self-contained" CAI course; i.e., students take the entire course by CAI with no need for a human instructor. Average completion time is 30 hours (*SD*—6 hours) for CARE 1, 2, and 3, and about 10 hours for CARE 4.

There have been two principal applications of these courses: resident instruction and continuing education (off campus). Penn State has a 32-station IBM 1500 Instructional System which offers the courses as part of the regular college curriculum for special education and elementary education majors and for students in several related areas. At the time of this writing slightly more than 5,000 students have completed one or more of the CARE courses at the University Park location.

The continuing education program is now in its sixth year of operation. In this application, a 16-terminal IBM 1500 Instructional System is housed in a 40-foot van which is expandable to a width of 17 feet. The CARE van is hauled to various locations in the nation and parked for six to eight weeks. During that time 100-150 teachers can take one or more of the CARE courses. As with the University Park installation, the van is open day, night, and weekends to accommodate the varying schedules of individual students. The students can take instruction when it is convenient for them and are not bound by conventional classroom schedules.

Regular Penn State credit is given for the successful completion of the courses. Alternative arrangements are often made to allow teachers to receive credit from local colleges or universities. Up to now, nearly 5,000 students have taken one or more CARE courses by CAI in one of the three Penn State CARE vans.

The CARE courses use a wide variety of instructional strategies to assist students in reaching the course objectives. All the strategies are interactive and all require active involvement on the part of the learner. The most prevalent strategy used in the courses is the *tutorial* approach. The tutor presents information, asks penetrating questions, and carefully analyzes the student's responses to the questions. On the basis of the student's demonstrated understanding or lack of understanding of a given concept, the tutor provides alternative courses of instruction, remedial sequences of instruction, or even enrichment material. The tutor can move a capable or well-informed student through a course of instruction very rapidly. Similarly, the tutor can tailor a sequence of instruction to meet the needs of a student who is not as capable or who does not have a good background of experiences or preparation.

The second major strategy used in the CARE courses is the *inquiry* approach. This type of activity is used in the latter stages of a course to draw together all the concepts acquired by the teachers throughout the course. This strategy includes *simulation* of regular classroom problems as well. In essence, the inquiry and simulation approaches as used in the CARE courses are directed problem-solving strategies. For example, teachers are told that they have access to information about a class of first-grade children. One or more of the children in the class may be handicapped or have an educational problem of one kind or another. It is the teacher's task, in effect, to screen the class for children with educational problems, identify those children with existing or potential problems, and deal with the problem by modifying the child's educational program or making an appropriate referral. Thus, while CARE is predominantly a tutorial program, other modes of CAI are introduced for specific instructional needs.

At the time of this writing, plans are being made to change the CARE curriculum in two ways. First, a different computer-assisted instruction system (hardware) will be used. The IBM 1500 system was experimental and has outlived its usefulness. Criteria for selection of a replacement system include low student/terminal hour cost, high reliability of interface devices, and capability for including a wide variety of pedagogical models (including facilities for audio, graphics, still or motion photography, or VTR).

A more fundamental (and interesting) change will be in the software. In addition to updating the content, the curriculum will be converted to a modular system instead of a full-length course format. Modularization of the content will permit users to pick and choose among the various modules and tailor-make a course or part of a course to meet individual needs.

Three significant contributions to education have emerged from the CARE projects. First, those persons who have completed a CARE course have had extended interaction with a computer system. They have experienced a sophisticated technology firsthand and the vast majority have become advocates. I believe the experience will enable them to be more receptive to new technologies as they emerge.

Second, the CARE series has demonstrated that it is possible to implement a "stand alone" CAI course in the field without daily attention from content specialists and computer specialists. Some would argue that it would be better to have a content specialist travel with the vans to provide practicum experiences for those taking the computer courses. I agree. But costs would be extremely high. We made the decision to focus on knowledge and application objectives for this series because of the additional costs involved in providing practicum experiences.

The most important contribution of the projects has not been the hardware. Rather, it has been the development of conceptual, reproducible models for dealing with the educational problems of the handicapped. The Diagnostic Teaching Model, as we call it, is the core of our special education undergraduate and graduate training programs. Most of the courses and activities in the master's degree program relate directly to the model. A number of related studies have emerged as a result of the CARE series and the concepts are being employed in school districts and other training programs. Reports about the various components of the project are numerous (e.g., Cartwright, Cartwright, & Robine, 1972; Cartwright & Cartwright, 1972; Cartwright & Cartwright, 1973; Cartwright, Cartwright, & Ysseldyke, 1973; Hall & Mitzel, 1973; Hall, Mitzel, & Cartwright, 1974; Cartwright & Cartwright, 1975).

CLOSING CHORDS

Max Morath, ragtime historian and performer, occasionally introduces songs with a bit of history to place the song into the proper context. One of his favorite selections is "Heaven Will Protect the Working Girl," a typical humorous, but chauvinistic, turn-of-the-century ballad which chronicles the trials and tribulations of a farm girl who goes to work in the city. The conventional wisdom of that innocent era would have it that there was only one reason that a young unmarried woman would leave her small village for the big city: sin. If not in her past, then definitely in her future! Happily, our heroine wards off temptations, villains, taxicabs, and trolleys, and all ends well.

American society has begun to appreciate the contributions of women to the extent that the lyrics of this particular song now appear ludicrous. Although there is still a long way to go before the full contributions of women may be realized, at least a substantial start has been made. So it is with technology. A change in basic attitudes is paving the way for rapid advances. Educational technology may not have played much of a role in your past, but I predict that it will in your future.

REFERENCES

Bliss, J. C., & Moore, M. W. The Optacon reading system, Part I. *Education of the Visually Handicapped*, 1974, 6(4), 98-102.

Boothroyd, A. Technology and deafness. *Volta Review*, 1975, 77(1), 27-34.

Cartwright, C. A., & Cartwright, G. P. Competencies for prevention of learning problems in early childhood education. *Educational Horizons*, 1975, 53(4), 151-57.

Cartwright, G. P., & Cartwright, C. A. Gilding the Lilly: Comments on the training based model. *Exceptional Children*, 1972, 39, 231-34.

Cartwright, G. P., & Cartwright, C. A. A computer assisted instruction course in the early identification of handicapped children. *Journal of Teacher Education*, 1973, 24(2), 128-34.

Cartwright, C. A., Cartwright, G. P., & Robine, G. G. CAI course in the early identification of handicapped children. *Exceptional Children*, 1972, 453-59.

Cartwright, G. P., Cartwright, C. A., & Ysseldyke, J. E. Two decision models: Identification and diagnostic teaching of handicapped children in the regular classroom. *Psychology in the Schools*, 1973, 10(1), pp. 4-11.

Cartwright, G. P., & Hall, K. A. A review of computer uses in special education. In L. Mann & D. Sabatino (Eds.), *The second review of special education*. Philadelphia: JSE Press, 1974. Pp. 307-50.

Glenn, J. W., Miller, K. H., & Broman, M. T. Voice terminal may bring jobs to the disabled. *American Journal of Occupational Therapy*, in press.

Guess, D., Sailor, W., & Lavis, L. *Educational technology for the severely handicapped*. Kansas City: Kansas Neurological Institute, 1975.

Hall, K. A., & Mitzel, H. E. CARE: Computer assisted renewal education— an opportunity in Pennsylvania. *Audio Visual Instruction*, 1973, 18, 35-38.

Hall, K. A., Mitzel, H. E., & Cartwright, G. P. A triumph for CAI education. *Phi Delta Kappan*, 1974, 56, 70-72.

Hofmeister, M. *Final report: Instructional technology training programs in special education*. Logan: Utah State University, 1973. (Mimeo, 34 pp.)

International Catalog of Aids and Appliances for Blind and Visually Impaired. American Foundation for the Blind, 15 West 16th Street, New York, N.Y. 10011.

Lance, W. D. *Instructional media and the handicapped*. Stanford, Calif.: Stanford University, ERIC Clearing House on Media and Technology, December 1973.

Lent, J. R. The severely retarded: Are we really programming for their future? *Focus on Exceptional Children*, 1975, 7(1), 1-11.

Meierhenry, W. C. Developments in educational media: The past and the future. *American Annals of the Deaf*, 1974, 119(5), 466-71.

Mitzel, H. E. Computers and adaptive education. *American Education*, 1970, 6, 23-26.

Moore, M. W., & Bliss, J. C. The Optacon reading system, Part II. *Education of the Visually Handicapped*, 1975, 7(1), 15-21.

Peabody, Ralph L., Cartwright, G. P., & Ward, M. E. *Final report: A computer assisted course in the education of visually handicapped children for rural regular classroom teachers*. University of Pittsburgh, 1972.

Scadden, L. A. The Tactile vision substitution system: Applications in education and employment. *New Outlook for the Blind,* 1974, 68(9), 394-97.

Schwartz, L. & Oseroff, A. *The clinical teacher for special education.* Tallahassee: Florida State University, 1975. (2 vols.)

Stolurow, L. M. Instructional technology. In P. L. McDonald, E. R. Blum, & P. E. Barker (Eds.), *Kaleidoscope: Emerging patterns in media: Action highlights of the December 1970, CEC San Antonio Conference.* Arlington, Va.: Council for Exceptional Children, 1971.

Tawney, J. W. and Schedgick, R. *Operant technology applied to the development of teaching environments for children with severe developmental retardation.* Lexington: University of Kentucky, 1974. (Mimeo, 24 pp.)

Thiagarajan, S., Semmel, M. I., & Semmel, D. S. *Sourcebook on instructional development for training teachers of exceptional children.* Bloomington: Indiana University, 1973.

Tickton, Sidney. *To improve learning: An evaluation of instructional technology. Part 1: A report by the Commission on Instructional Technology.* New York: Bowker, 1970. Pp. 21-22.

Tripp, R. T. *International thesaurus of quotations.* New York: Thomas Y. Crowell, 1970. Pp. 630-31.

Tummy Tickler: A tactile technique. *Mosaic,* 1975, 6(1), 10-15.

Ward, Marjorie E. *Examination and application of formative evaluation for author utilization during the preparation of a CAI course.* Unpublished doctoral dissertation, University of Pittsburgh, 1972.

Welliver, P. W. Don't judge technology by the "technologist." *Faculty Forum,* College of Education, Pennsylvania State University, August 14, 1973. (Mimeo, 2 pp.)

Welliver, P. W. Personal communication, February 16, 1976.

A SELECTED BIBLIOGRAPHY OF WORKS BY
G. PHILLIP CARTWRIGHT

Cartwright, G. P., & Cartwright, C. A. (Eds.). *Early identification of handicapped children.* University Park, Pa.: CAI Laboratory, 1971.

Cartwright, G. P., & Cartwright, C. A. Gilding the Lilly: Comments on the training based model for special education. *Exceptional Children,* 1972, 39, 231-34.

Cartwright, G. P., & Cartwright, C. A. An undergraduate computer-assisted instruction course in the early identification of handicapped children. *Proceedings of the 1972 Conference on Computers in Undergraduate Curricula.* Southern Regional Education Board, Atlanta, Ga., June 1972. Pp. 167-75.

Cartwright, G. P., & Cartwright, C. A. A computer-assisted instruction course in the early identification of handicapped children. *Journal of Teacher Education,* 1973, 24(2), 128-34.

Cartwright, G. P., Cartwright, C. A., & Robine, G. G. CAI course in the early identification of handicapped children. *Exceptional Children,* 1972, 38, 453-59.

Cartwright, G. P., Cartwright, C. A., & Ysseldyke, J. E. Two decision models: Identification and diagnostic teaching of handicapped children. *Psychology in the Schools,* 1973, 10(1), 4-11.

Cartwright, G. P., & Hall, K. A. A review of computer uses in special education. In L. Mann and D. Sabatino (Eds.), *The second review of special education.* Philadelphia: JSE Press, 1974.

Hall, K. A., Mitzel, H. E., & Cartwright, G. P. Computer-assisted remedial education. *Phi Delta Kappan,* 1974, 56(1), 70-72.

Ward, M. E., Cartwright, G. P., Cartwright, C. A., & Campbell, J. (Eds.). *Diagnostic Teaching of Preschool and Primary Children.* University Park, Pa.: CAI Laboratory, 1973.

PART 3

Changing
Perspectives in
Diagnosis and
Evaluation

6
Diagnosis: Current and
Changing Considerations

Don R. Logan

*Don R. Logan is professor and chairman of special education.
at the University of Louisville. Prior to his present appointment, he was
associate professor of special education and educational administration,
University of Utah. Dr. Logan's earlier public school experiences include
speech therapist, school psychologist, and director of special education.
Dr. Logan has also served as coordinator and/or principal investigator
for numerous USOE grants and as consultant and/or speaker at local,
state, and national meetings. He holds editorships and consultantships
with several leading professional journals and has been a member of the
research committees of both the American Association of Mental Deficiency and the Council for Exceptional Children.*

*Dr. Logan received the B.S. degree in psychology from North Texas
State College in 1957, the M.Ed. in counseling psychology from North*

Texas State College in 1964, and the Ed.D. in special education from the University of Oregon in 1968. A selected bibliography of works by Dr. Logan can be found on page 121.

INTRODUCTION

In my attempt to conceptualize the content of this chapter many thoughts came to mind. Because of the nature of the book, I felt that the writing approach should not be simply a recounting of past work, but a blend of personal feelings and statements about some current and future trends in diagnosis. The assigned title certainly provides expectations about content and an indication of necessary constraints in organization. However, the area of diagnosis is a broad one that can be approached from many vantage points. As such, the problem is not one of lack of conceptual frameworks but an abundance of avenues from which to work. Consequently, in organizing my thoughts and attempting to decide on what to include and what to leave out, I found myself frequently in a "yeahbut" position. That is, as I thought about diagnosis and considering what is the state of the diagnosing "art" (factoralists, forgive me) I found myself saying, "Yeah, but what about philosophical influences; yeah, but what about litigation; yeah, but what about test validity"; ad infinitum (or so it seemed).

Not being completely unfamiliar with the writing process, I was not unduly concerned about such a disorganized and possibly even chaotic beginning. After much obvious procrastination, I finally decided that there were four interrelated topics I wanted to cover:

1. What is diagnosis and what does it imply?
2. What is the relationship between diagnosis and teachers?
3. What are some philosophical controversies related to diagnosis?
4. What are some future trends in diagnosis?

While I still retain some anxiety about many related "yeahbuts" that were left out or cursorily attended to, I feel that my primary concerns can be explored. Therefore, the balance of this chapter, logically enough, will be headed by descriptors that parallel the preceding four topics. In addition, there will be a concluding statement.

DIAGNOSIS: PURPOSE AND PROCESS

The term *diagnosis* is in my mind a multifaceted abstraction that like many television and newspaper ads (and some college courses) often promises more than is or can be produced. It has a ring of authority and learnedness that promises rewards if we can only correctly align the assessment tumblers into a diagnostic combination. The concept of diagnosis infers a concreteness in which a decision is reached about a condition based on a thorough examination of symptoms. While diagnosis is probably most directly tied to medicine in most peoples' minds, it has been, relatively speaking, increasingly used in psychoeducational circles. The obvious implications are that we study the symptoms of a student's learning and/or behavioral problems, arrive at a logical conclusion as to cause, and prescribe an approach (prescription) to remediate the condition. Nothing could be more straightforward; few things any more misleading when applied in behavioral settings.

The assumptions of the above approach are that (a) we are sophisticated in the understanding and use of the terms engendered in the process, (b) we possess adequate (i.e., valid and reliable) instrumentation, and (c) we have fully conceptualized the ramifications associated with educational problems in all situations, with all types of children, from all types of environments.

It is this writer's opinion that due to a lack of specificity in terminology (i.e., interchangeableness of terms: *diagnosis, testing, assessment, evaluation,* etc.) both within and between so-called diagnosticians and practitioners, we frequently mislead ourselves. That is, we too frequently profess knowledge that is without understanding. For example, we have a number of sacrosanct words that are repeatedly used in parrot-like fashion that seem to serve as professional identifiers. These words seem to have a magic connotation that not only provides status to the user but frequently terminates conversation—often to our profound relief. Such was the case some years ago when I was first employed as a school psychologist. Being flushed with excitement at my first full-time professional position (not job!), I could hardly wait to begin my duties. To my chagrin and bewilderment I was stopped a number of times by teachers who stated that they had a child they were going to refer for a "psychological." I nodded assuredly and went on only to find that the referral did specify a "psychological" with no other information or direction. Not only was I perplexed, but being new (and obviously naïve) I was in the uncomfortable position of being employed in a "role" in which I suddenly felt incompetent. Everyone seemed to know what a "psychological" was but the psychologist. Undaunted after my initial shock, I decided that certainly something as high-sounding as "psychological" must include more than a WISC or Stanford-Binet. So in my naïveté I concluded that my arsenal should include a Bender-Gestalt and a Wide Range Achievement Test among other things. With considerable trepidation I ventured forth with my black bag of tricks to solve the problems of the beseech'ng teachers. To my pleasant surprise my reports were received with due respect and, at times, even open admiration. With such reinforcement I concluded that my initial fears were unfounded and that I truly had a contribution to make. The appreciation of my colleagues spurred me on to greater efforts, and I was soon being further rewarded with comments about my diligence, industry, and most importantly about my final written reports that kept psychological jargon to a minimum. After a period of not only relief that I did understand what a referral for a "psychological" implied and that I was obviously competent in the eyes of my contemporaries, a spectre of self-doubt began to intrude on my consciousness. My concern intensified as it became apparent to me that my labors, while still being reinforced by others, were actually of limited value. The removal of a child from a regular class to a special class was evident activity, but beyond that my reports were merely duly noted, filed and forgotten. Again, I began to question what was meant by a "psychological," but this time, bolstered by my past success, in a more direct way. Through questioning of teachers, principals, and supervisors, it became increasingly clear that the referral for a "psychological" basically meant one of two things: either it expressed a desire to have a child placed in a special education class; or it was used as a catch-all term because my colleagues had no other referral term to use either through lack of training or because of limited expectations; and one term was as good as another. I was able to overcome these problems to a considerable degree through inservice training and by the simple procedure of spending time talking to the teacher prior to my seeing the referred child. My suspicions about teachers (and principals and supervisors) not knowing what to ask for were confirmed as I worked with individual teachers in attempting to be specific about their real interests in learning about a particular child. To my surprise and relief I was able to reduce my testing activities by approximately one-half as I found that in working with teachers I could frequently dispense with formal tests altogether or limit such activity to a quick verification of what the teacher felt she was seeing in class. The emphasis in my work shifted to a more challenging and fruitful intervention with teachers about learning and/or behavioral problems in the classroom.

This experience coupled with many other such experiences has had much to do with my present attitude regarding diagnosis—an attitude that has ranged from cynical to slightly bemused to hopeful. I would like to think that the preceding narrative was only a tale of yesteryear but my experience is otherwise. By this I do not mean that most school psychologists and teachers are quite as naïve today as we were then, but we still too often blindly use tests without consideration as to purpose, too frequently think a child is diagnosed on the basis of a single test, and refrain from asking obvious questions. It seems, therefore, that we still have not adequately delineated the diagnostic process for teachers (or psychologists) or become consistent in our use of terms. We have still continued to exclude the teacher from the diagnostic process and have in many subtle ways communicated that the process is of such intricacy that it must be conducted in a separate place from the classroom. Teachers have long begun to suspect that the "emperor has no clothes." Perhaps, if we can convince the "emperor" that he is embarassing us all we can correct our shortcomings and *together* take a more mature approach to a vital problem.

DIAGNOSIS: THE ROLE OF THE TEACHER

This writer shares with others (Gillespie & Sitko, 1976; Hammill, 1971) the belief that the teacher should be the person who directs the diagnostic process at least in the early stages and that the teacher should be included throughout the total process. This in no way lessens the responsibilities of such ancillary school personnel as psychologists and social workers. The classroom teacher is the one person primarily responsible for the educational and social needs of children in the school situation. As such, she/he is the only one in direct day-to-day contact with the child. It is too often the case that the teacher can only refer a child and then await the arrival of someone to carry out the diagnostic process. This approach conceptually minimizes the teacher's importance in diagnosis and additionally omits important information about a child. A school psychologist or educational diagnostician (or whatever title you prefer) can only respond in limited and predictable ways if a generic "psychological" is requested. By including the teacher as the facilitator of diagnosis and the user of the data generated, an important bridge is built that is presently too often ignored.

A good teacher is involved in diagnosis, programming, and evaluation as a part of the teaching process. Gillespie and Sitko (1976) put it as follows:

> If the diagnostic process is in situ, it should focus on the teacher. The teacher should be constantly modifying his/her program based on new information—every lesson can be part of the assessment procedure. The teacher should be able to field problems (Hammill, 1971) and to assess the methods and materials used in the educational program. This is a radical departure from traditional diagnostic treatment procedures because it gives the teacher a central role in the diagnostic process. Furthermore, this view considers decision making or problem solving as an integral part of the development of instructional strategies [p. 401].

The teacher's role in the diagnostic process should be that of identifying the learning and/or behavioral problem of a particular child through observation and informal tests (Hammill, 1971); developing strategies for educational programming based on these observations and informal tests; and then again observing the child, once the program is underway, to assess if any behavioral changes could be directly attributed to the intervention. At this point, additional information would have been gained which could lead to the continuation of the previously developed program or to the decision that additional assistance is needed. In the latter case, such ancillary school personnel as a school psychologist, speech therapist, or reading specialist could be consulted. The teacher should be able to tell the ancillary person (e.g., psychologist) specifically what is being observed, share the information collected, and cooperatively identify what further information is needed. After a report is received the teacher and the psychologist should discuss the additional information that has been generated relative to educational implications and then, with this data, alter the teaching strategy as required. After attempting the new approach based on the psychologist's data it may be decided that the problem has now been sufficiently identified and the original concern is being remediated, or it could be that additional input from both the psychologist and a reading specialist is necessary. This approach would be continued until a successful educational program is developed. As indicated, it may well be that a number of persons need to be involved both from within the school and the community at large (physician, audiologist, social worker, etc.). The point is that it is the teacher who is responsible for the educational strategies that lead to a child's learning. With special children there is no question that a team approach to diagnosis is required. As Hammill (1971) has previously indicated, "teachers and others charged with the diagnostic functions must recognize that instruction and evaluation are not separate worlds, but they are inseparably meshed" [p. 149]. The attitude that the initial diagnostic placement is an end to the process has left many children in a kind of educational limbo. Diagnosis must be an ongoing cooperative venture of all educational activities and is best expressed and validated only when the child learns.

I strongly feel that many of our brighter teachers leave the classroom, and sometimes education, due to our disregard for them as responsible people who have a distinct contribution to make. If we are to move toward professional status we must provide not only quality preparation programs but allow teachers to develop as the key to all of our educational efforts. To do otherwise cheats the educational enterprise, deprives children of the best education possible, and drives the best teachers out of the classroom.

For the balance of the chapter *diagnosis* will refer to *the total process* engendered in investigation of a perceived or identified school-related problem. *Assessment* will refer to *the use of various instruments* (e.g., tests, inventories, observation, etc.) utilized in ascertaining progress or in identifying skill levels. Other such frequently used concomitant terms as *evaluation, testing, psychological*, etc. will be used restrictively in this chapter in the interests of clarity.

DIAGNOSIS: THE CONTROVERSY

Diagnosis and the process contained therein are very much involved in a philosophical controversy. This controversy has its roots in all theoretical conceptualizations about behavior in which measurement has been attempted. The debate basically is only a quasi-controversy and centers about the degree with which measuring instruments are efficacious. Nunally (1967) uses the terms *objects* (i.e., intelligence, learning, memory, creativity) and *attributes* (i.e., a supposed feature of objects) in describing two ingredients in test building. Objects, in the preceding sense, are not directly measurable; they are concepts. In order to measure a concept (or object) the test maker must be able to define the concept and then isolate those tasks (or attributes) that are felt to make up the concept (e.g., learning). The attributes must be measurable in order that inferences can be made regarding the degree or amount of a concept that is present within a given individual. The degree to which this is accomplished is the essence of a "good" test.

The controversy in educational diagnosis centers about two diagnostic models: the *ability training* approach and the *task analysis* approach (Ysseldyke & Salvia, 1974). Although apparently in opposition to one another the two approaches differ more in degree than in kind which, not surprisingly, has been found to be true in most quasi-categories. The ability training approach emphasizes usage of tests that supposedly identify the various strengths and weaknesses in a child's learning and/or other behavioral repertoire. That is, if we have a child who is demonstrating difficulty in remembering spoken messages, and if this is verified by a test that purports to measure auditory memory, then it is concluded that the child is in need of skill development in this ability area. The instructional plan would then be oriented toward remediating the deficit in auditory memory. This approach assumes that the test is a valid index of auditory memory and stresses the identification of the processes suspected of causing inadequate skill development.

Those persons taking a task analysis approach, on the other hand, see the problem somewhat differently. The approach would be task oriented utilizing observable behaviors in skill development and would not attempt to identify the *cause* of the observed differences. The ability testing approach is essentially a norm reference approach and the task analysis is primarily a criterion referenced approach (Drew, Freston, & Logan, 1972).

The primary difference between ability training adherents (Bannatyne, 1968; Bateman, 1967; Frostig, 1967; Kirk, McCarthy, & Kirk, 1968; McCarthy, 1972) and task analysis proponents (Bijou, 1970; Cohen, 1969; Gold, 1968; Mann, 1971) is on whether causality is a valid issue in the diagnostic-prescriptive approach. The ability training group takes the position that causality is important and must be attended to if remediation is to be successful. The task analysis group counters that the tests devised to identify cause of a deficit are not sufficiently rigorous (valid and reliable) to allow us *at this time* to utilize them in educational programming with any confidence. Ysseldyke and Salvia (1974) provide reliability data on various tests currently in use in diagnosis (e.g., Developmental Test of Visual Perception, Illinois Test of Psycholinguistic Development, Bender Visual Motor Gestalt Test, etc.). The test-retest reliability coefficients range from .12 to .90 on the subtests of the Illinois Test of Psycholinguistic Ability; between .29 and .74 on the Frostig; and between .39 and .66 on the Bender Gestalt. Only two reliability coefficients reached .90: the Graham-Kendall Memory for Designs Test and the Auditory Association subtest of the ITPA. It is pointed out by Ysseldyke and Salvia (1974) in a quote from Nunally (1967) that in applied settings a reliability coefficient of .90 is a minimum, and that .95 should be a standard when important program decisions are made. The case, therefore, is well taken that the use of tests in decision making is somewhat suspect relative to reliability. The validity of the measures is open to question. The counter to the reliability argument by those taking an ability training approach is that the measures are still better than chance. Ysseldyke and Salvia (1974) computed the forecasting efficiency of each of the tests and found that the percent increase over chance ranged from "less than 1 percent to 59 percent depending on age and instrument" [p. 182].

It is obvious that current tests are not as sufficiently rigorous as we would like them to be. However, despite relatively low reliability coefficients, the forecasting efficiency of the tests is for the most part improved over the level of chance and does tell us something. The primary lesson to be learned is that we must be extremely cautious in making decisions about a child and his/her educational program based on tests alone. We deal in approximations and probabilities and there is always a danger that we are making decisions about children that can have both positive and negative influences on their lives. As was pointed out in the preceding section, we need to do a much better job in preservice and inservice training programs for teachers relative to the careful use of tests and the inclusion of teachers in the diagnostic aspects of remediation. For an excellent discussion of this "controversy" I would recommend the series of articles in *The Journal of Special Education*, 1971, under the heading of Symposium No. 4.

DIAGNOSIS: FUTURE CONSIDERATIONS

During the past few years a number of events have transpired that have had and will continue to have a profound influence on education in the years to come. A listing of the most important "happenings" as related to diagnosis would have to include the following:

1. a "renewal" of the realization that a single test or score on a test is not of real benefit to the educator;

2. the fact that many standardized tests are biased against minority groups

3. the concept of "least restrictive" classroom setting for handicapped children;

4. the move toward mainstreaming;

5. the litigation that has led to schools providing services for previously excluded children; and

6. the move toward accountability in education.

These and other factors have produced a need and a demand for increased sophistication in many educational areas. Diagnosis is one area that is crucial if we are to make decisions about placement and for effective educational programming. That children have been misplaced through inadequate diagnosis is a given fact. The literature and the personal experience of many school personnel amply testify to the damage that has been done to innumerable children through inadequate diagnosis either at the time of initial placement or in failing to continue the process after placement.

That we are ill-equipped to effectively account for all of the variables and interactions involved in the teaching-learning process is apparent. We are not, however, as diagnostically unsophisticated as practice would sometimes indicate. There are current efforts that have impressed me as possibly being harbingers of change not only in the way we diagnose but in the way we look at children. Central to all in my mind is the work of Jean Piaget who has reconceptualized the methods with which we evaluate. Through a developmental approach Piaget has focused on the process involved in arriving at responses to a task. Guilford (1967) in a different framework has been and will be influential in intellectual assessment. And there is the work of Labov (1972) who has through his studies on black language cast doubt on the "cultural deprivation" concept. He has found that black language is not a deficient or concrete dialect, even though it differs from standard English. Rather, "[it] has equivalent ways of expressing the same logical content" [p. 238]. Work related to Labov's in cross-cultural frameworks (Ginsburg, 1972; Kleinfeld, 1973; Levi-Strauss, 1966) has demonstrated the importance of understanding the child's milieu before diagnostic decisions are made. Indeed, our knowledge about cultural and subcultural aspects is still so limited regarding learning and behavior patterns that diagnosis of children from minority groups should be undertaken only with extreme caution. One book with somewhat more sophisticated concepts than have been previously made available relative to understanding and diagnosing behavior of different cultural groups is *The Cultural Context of Learning and Thinking* by Cole, Gay, Glick, and Sharp. Published in 1971, this book is actually the report of a massive study in which the authors have reported the cultural effects of learning and thinking at various age levels of Kpelle tribal members in Africa and American students. The authors have used a combined anthropological, linguistic, and experimental psychology approach to the understanding of cognition. They have concluded that "cultural differences in cognition reside more in situations to which particular cognitive processes are applied than in the existence of a process in one cultural group and its absence in another" [p. 233]. The importance of this work to diagnosis is in its influence on diagnostic approaches to minority groups. In light of the existing cross-cultural research, to continue to say that a child from a minority group is limited in his ability to learn only demonstrates a stereotype that has been reinforced by the use of inadequate assessment tools and educational provisions that are often biased.

During the past year I have been impressed by two approaches to diagnosis: the work of Rue Cromwell at the University of Rochester and that of Jane R. Mercer and June F. Lewis at the University of California at Riverside.

Cromwell (1976) has devised a diagnostic construct based on four components he refers to simply enough as the *A B C D's*. As a result of previous work on emotional disturbance, Cromwell received a grant from the U.S. Office of Education to further develop the diagnostic potential of four classes of data. The letters represent four aspects of a diagnostic process: A—antecedent events (history, etiology); B—current behaviors; C—treatment; and D—prognosis. For each class, Cromwell developed assessment measurements and then collected data on 500 disturbed children and a control group of 250 normal children. Through the use of multivariate techniques the interrelationships among the many variables in the four classes were analyzed.

Cromwell felt that there were four findings of particular importance:

1. that his original belief in a single-level classification system was naïve. A child's level of cognitive development is manifestly different from one age level to another and this must be taken into account in any diagnostic procedure;

2. that behavior that is often called "acting out," even when the same or similar characteristics are evidenced, was not a priori the same type of emotional behavior. That is, there are many different factors that can cause a child to "act out," but they are not necessarily caused by the same underlying stimulus;

3. that intercorrelations between two or three of the four factors were not uncommon. A surprising finding was that A C D combinations were frequently more useful than B C D combinations.

That is, A factors (background history and child rearing) were found to be significantly more important than B factors (current behavior) for treatment and prognosis. "There were seven A C D factors and no B C D factors unless A was also present in a total A B C D complex" [p. 44];

4. that some C D combinations were efficacious without being related to A and B. "Some treatments are related to favorable prognosis (and others to unfavorable prognosis) independently of any diagnostic information about a child. For example, peer opinion of a given disturbed behavior, as compared to the response or attitude of an adult . . . can produce an unusually positive and enduring influence on a disturbed child" [p. 44].

I must admit to being somewhat overwhelmed by Cromwell's research in its approach, scope, and implications. His demonstration of the possibility of developing tight relations between the four components only serves to underscore how far we are from being able to apply similar approaches in educational intervention in special education. The finding that the factor of past history is possibly more important than a child's current behavior in determining treatment and for prognosis is notable in and of itself. Of particular importance in my mind is Cromwell's separation of value judgments from the empirical A B C D relations and his stressing the importance of knowing the difference. This is only sound research procedure but it has rarely been demonstrated so well in practice in applied settings. Coupled with this is his demonstration of the need for longitudinal research that is related to past history, current behavior, and treatment. If nothing else is gained from Cromwell's work, which I seriously doubt, the possible stimulation of longitudinal research on A B C D variables in the classroom would be sufficient. Indeed, Cromwell's research should have sufficient heuristic value in a number of areas, particularly in stimulating continued research that should have direct implications for diagnosis.

The contribution of psychology to special education, particularly in diagnosis, is well known, but as a result of the work of Jane R. Mercer and June F. Lewis, sociology may add new dimensions to the diagnostic process. In a work currently in the final stages of refinement, the authors have described a diagnostic system they refer to as a "System of Multi-Cultural Pluralistic Assessment" (SOMPA). Dr. Mercer and Mrs. Lewis allowed me access to Chapter 2 of the *Technical Manual* which provides an overall description of the three models basic to the SOMPA.

The SOMPA model requires a conceptualization of assessment utilizing three different conceptual models: Medical, Social System, and Pluralistic. Mercer and Lewis feel that current diagnostic procedures are hampered by undifferentiated definitions of *normal-abnormal* that are not only used interchangeably but also are based on different assumptions about normality. The authors have attempted to carefully specify the definition of each of the three models in respect to normal-abnormal, list the assumption of each model, state the properties of the statistical characteristics of the three models, define the characteristics of each model's appropriate measures, specify how scores on the measures are interpreted, and identify the appropriate tests (measures) taken from each model that make up the total SOMPA measures.

The following descriptions of each model are taken from the material provided by Mercer and Lewis and are condensed for this chapter. Due to space limitations I was unable to provide the complete rationale behind each aspect of the SOMPA model and the clearly detailed explanation of the assumptions used in developing the SOMPA measures.

The Medical Model is based on the belief that a disease is an outward manifestation of some underlying biological condition. This model does not inherently consider socio-cultural factors in determining diagnosis or treatment. It is a deficit model that is oriented toward pathology and is not bound by environmental influences except as they directly cause or produce biological changes. This model has been adapted by diagnosticians in the behavioral sciences in ascertaining mild behavioral pathology (emotional disturbances, mental retardation, etc.). Mercer and Lewis, however, have defined it in the strict sense of medical usage in order to escape the problems inherent in adaptation and to differentiate it from other models. The measures taken from the Medical Model to be included in the SOMPA battery are: (a) physical dexterity tasks, (b) Bender Gestalt Test, (c) health history inventories, and (d) weight by height.

The Social System Model requires the user to look at behavior from a completely different perspective. This model is drawn from the social deviance view in sociology. The approach is oriented toward the social organization in which a person lives and the role(s) the person has within such social systems. The focus is on a person's social behavior as it relates to the expectations of the social systems. These social systems are complex and interrelated and are composed of (a) social statuses (third-grade student, oldest child, baseball player, etc.), (b) social roles (these vary according to activity and in relation to social statuses), and (c) social norms (each role in relation to each status carries behavioral expectations of the social system).

There are, consequently, multiple definitions of *normal* depending on the person's social status, social role, and the particular social norms of the social system of which the person is a member. This model, as opposed to the medical model, contains not only a deficit aspect but also possesses asset components. Judgments of ability are determined by social norms of the social system in relation to a child's status and associated roles. Two measures were used for the Social System Model: the WISC-R and the Adaptive Behavior Inventory for Children (ABIC).

The WISC-R was used as a measure of academic performance. The published norms were utilized and the child's score is to be interpreted as a measure of his current School Functioning Level (SFL). The Adaptive Behavior Inventory for Children (ABIC) was developed to obtain information about a child in his/her "role performance in the family, the peer group, the community, non-academic school roles, earner-consumer roles and self maintenance roles."[1] The mother is used as the informant in that it was felt that she would be in the best position to see the child "from the perspective of his own family, neighborhood and sociocultural group."[2]

The Pluralistic Model is a third way of viewing a child's behavior. Mercer and Lewis use this model to provide a view of performance from another perspective and as a supplement to the other two models rather than as a distinct assessment model. It utilizes the child's sociocultural group as the normative population for assessment. After reviewing approaches to assessment of children from different sociocultural backgrounds, the authors decided on WISC-R as the measuring instrument. The method, using multiple regression equations, was to (a) identify the family background characteristics that are related to WISC-R performance, (b) decide the optimum weight each background characteristic should be given for predicting performance on the WISC-R and (c) to ascertain a score which could be predicted for a child from his/her sociocultural background. That score was used in establishing pluralistic norms from the WISC-R. Detailed information will be provided as to exactly how the norms were established for each measure when the material is published by the Psychological Corporation.

In taking this approach Mercer and Lewis made the assumption that

> pluralistic assessment does not change the content or language of the WISC-R nor does it modify the test procedures. Instead, it assumes that all tests including the WISC-R are achievement tests which measure learning and that all tests are culture bound. It is based upon the fundamental premise that an achievement test can be used to make inferences about a child's aptitude *if* his performance is compared only with others who have come from a similar sociocultural setting and, presumably, are equivalent on the five assumptions listed earlier: opportunity to learn, motivation to learn, test taking experience, emotional condition, and physical condition. *The technical problem is one of identifying as precisely as possible the appropriate normative framework within which to interpret each child's performance so that he is being compared only with others*

[1] From the preliminary manuscript of *SOMPA: System of Multi-Cultural Pluralistic Assessment*. Reprinted with kind permission of the authors.

[2] Ibid.

who have come from a similar sociocultural setting [italics in original].[3]

Based on the sociocultural group norms, a child's score on the WISC-R can be compared to others from his same background by converting his test score into a standard score. The standard score (or a percentile score if desired) can then be translated into what Mercer and Lewis have called the child's Estimated Learning Potential (ELP). In this way it is hoped that a child from a particular sociocultural background will not be handicapped by being subjected to having his/her score compared to those of others from other backgrounds, but will be compared to age peers in the same sociocultural group.

The WISC-R was chosen as the measuring instrument "because it is the most widely used, individually administered test in the United States and, consequently, is the most important instrument used in educational placement and program planning in the country."[4]

Obviously the SOMPA approach is a very ambitious undertaking that promises to provide a wealth of data not heretofore tapped. The inclusion of community and/or sociocultural data as they relate both to social behavior and learning potential based on background should be an extremely valuable addition to diagnosis. The utilization of a three-model approach is unique and conceptually sound and indicates the complexity involved in ascertaining developmental and learning-potential levels. That the use of the SOMPA will greatly increase the time required for data collection seems apparent. However, if the application of the model proves as valuable in practice as it does conceptually, there is no doubt that the time involved in administration and interpretation will be a very minor consideration.

CONCLUSION

The word *conclusion* has a finality about it that I certainly don't feel. Perhaps "Random Thoughts" or "Musings" would be a more appropriate heading for this final section.

The content of this chapter raises many philosophical issues that must be addressed and are continually controversial. One obvious issue is the teacher's role in the diagnostic process. This is not only an issue in and of itself; it also leads to other related topics such as teacher preparation, finance, role protection (as in *territorial prerogatives*), and the value of education. The continuing practice of having the teacher handle the mundane tasks that are often presently required not only minimizes his/her role but prevents the teacher from being actively engaged in facilitating diagnoses and implementing learning prescrip-

[3] Ibid.
[4] Ibid.

tions in a professional manner. This view is seemingly not shared by many school administrators, possibly the community, and perhaps even by some teachers. Be that as it may, we pay the price of limiting our profession and minimizing children's opportunities when we fail to continually seek new instructional strategies as we evaluate our present teaching *and* diagnostic techniques.

As a profession, education has been relatively slow in developing into a science of education. McKenna (1976) has addressed this topic in asking why there is a science of medicine and engineering but not of education. Building on some of Piaget's work, McKenna raises the issue of the lack of researchers within education: "Why is it that other professions owe their developments chiefly to researchers within their own ranks but education does not?" [p. 405]. He goes on to point out many reasons, such as lack of understanding of the complexity of pedagogy, the politics involved in education, the lack of a scientific framework, the reliance on related disciplines for theory, etc.

The demand for "quick-fix tools" has fostered so many educational bandwagons in the past few years that I am left somewhat dazed. On the one hand we decry theory as not relevant and we then turn around and involve ourselves in teaching approaches that are primarily theoretical anyway. I am reminded of the time I worked in speech pathology with stutterers who would come to therapy essentially seeking a "shot" so they could go about their lives sans stuttering. Some educators strike me the same way—give me a quick shot of whatever it is I need so I can go "change" the children. It is apparent from both the Cromwell research and the Mercer and Lewis SOMPA that the diagnostic approach (as only one aspect of education) is and has to be a very painstaking procedure. The complexities involved are manifest. However, the decisions that are to be made in education affect lives and we cannot afford simplistic approaches.

It is apparent that education must assume a more active role in what McKenna (1976) calls "philosophico-scientific inquiries" in a disciplined way. We have the methods, we have the technical skills, we have the resources. Cromwell (1976) states that educators need to face the reality that decisions are too frequently being made on the basis of conflicting societal values and not facts; certainly not on the basis of "all the A B C D relations established, all the t's crossed, i's dotted, and *p* values available" [p. 45]. But the need and the challenge is there for education to become a profession.

REFERENCES

Bannatyne, A. Diagnostic and remedial techniques for use with dyslexic children. *Academic Therapy Quarterly*, 1968, 3, 213-24.

Bannatyne, A. Diagnosing learning disabilities and writing remedial prescriptions. *Journal of Learning Disabilities,* 1969, 1, 242-49.

Bateman, B. Three approaches to diagnosis and educational planning for children with learning disabilities. *Academic Therapy Quarterly,* 1967, 3, 11-16.

Bijou, S. What psychology has to offer education—Now. *Journal of Applied Behavior Analysis,* 1970, 3, 65-71.

Cohen, S. Studies in visual perception and reading in disadvantaged children. *Journal of Learning Disabilities,* 1969, 2, 498-507.

Cole, M., Gay, J., Glick, J., & Sharp, D. *The cultural context of learning and thinking.* New York: Basic Books, 1971.

Cole, M., & Scribner, S. *Culture and thought: A psychological introduction.* New York: Wiley, 1974.

Cromwell, R. Ethics, umbrage and the A B C Ds. In the issue *Mainstreaming: Origins and implications. Minnesota Education,* 1976, 2, 42-47.

Drew, C., Freston, C., & Logan, D. Criteria and reference in evaluation. *Focus on Exceptional Children,* 1972, 4, 1-10.

Frostig, M. Testing as a basis for educational therapy. *Journal of Special Education,* 1967, 2, 15-34.

Gillespie, P., & Sitko, M. Training preservice teachers in diagnostic teaching. *Exceptional Children,* 1976, 42, 401-2.

Ginsburg, H. *The myth of the deprived child.* Englewood Cliffs, N.J.: Prentice-Hall, 1972.

Gold, M. *The acquisition of a complex assembly task by retarded adolescents.* Urbana: University of Illinois, Children's Research Center, 1968. (Mimeo)

Guilford, J. *The nature of human intelligence.* New York: McGraw-Hill, 1967.

Hammill, D. Evaluating children for instructional purposes. *Academic Therapy,* 1971, 6, 341-53.

Kirk, S., McCarthy, J., & Kirk, W. *Illinois Test of Psycholinguistic Abilities* (Rev. Ed.). Urbana: University of Illinois Press, 1968.

Klienfeld, J. Intellectual strengths in culturally different groups: An Eskimo illustration. *Review of Educational Research,* 1973, 43, 341-60.

Labov, W. The logic of non-standard English. In F. Williams (Ed.), *Language and poverty: Perspectives on a theme.* Chicago: Markham Publishing Co., 1970, 153-87.

Levi-Strauss, C. *The Savage Mind.* Chicago: University of Chicago Press, 1972.

Mann, L. Psychometric phrenology and the new faculty psychology: The case against ability assessment and training. *Journal of Special Education,* 1971, 4, 3-13.

Mercer, J., & Lewis, J. *SOMPA: System of multi-cultural pluralistic assessment.* New York: Psychological Corporation, in press.

McCarthy, D. *Manual for the McCarthy Scales of Children's Abilities.* New York: Psychological Corporation, 1972.

McKenna, F. Piaget's complaint—and mine: Why there is no science of education. *Phi Delta Kappan,* 1976, 57, 405-9.

Nunally, J. *Psychometric Theory.* New York: McGraw-Hill, 1967.

Ysseldyke, J., & Salvia, J. Diagnostic-prescriptive teaching: Two models. *Exceptional Children,* 1974, 41, 181-85.

A SELECTED BIBLIOGRAPHY OF WORKS BY DON R. LOGAN

Chinn, P. C., Drew, C. J., & Logan, D. R. *Mental retardation, a life cycle approach.* St. Louis: C. V. Mosby, 1975.

Drew, C. J., Freston, C. W., & Logan, D. R. Criteria and reference in evaluation. *Focus on Exceptional Children,* 1972, 4, 1-10. Reprinted in Jones, R. L., & MacMillan, D. L. *Special education in transition.* Boston: Allyn & Bacon, 1974.

Drew, C. J., & Logan, D. R. Extra list errors in paired associate learning by retarded and normal children. *Psychological Reports,* 1970, 26, 467-71.

Drew, C. J., Prehm, H. J., & Logan, D. R. Paired associate learning performance as a function of association value of materials. *American Journal of Mental Deficiency,* 1968, 73, 294-97.

Logan, D. R. Linguistic development of the mentally retarded. *The Torch,* Instructional Materials Center, University of Oregon, 1967, 1, 47-53.

Logan, D. R. Paired associate learning performance as a function of meaningfulness and response times. *American Journal of Mental Deficiency,* 1969, 74, 249-53.

Logan, D. R. The teacher's role? *Perceptions* (Guest editorial), The Northwestern Utah Multi-District Service Center, 1971. Reprinted by the Southwestern Utah Multi-District Service Center, 1972.

Logan, D. R., Prehm, H. J., & Drew, C. J. Effects of unidirectional training on bidirectional recall in retarded and non-retarded subjects. *American Journal of Mental Deficiency,* 1968, 73, 493-95.

Prehm, H. J., & Logan, D. R. Effects of warm-up on the rote learning performance of retarded and non-retarded subjects, *Exceptional Children,* 1972, 38, 623-27.

7

The Educational Evaluation of Handicapped Students

Stephen C. Larsen is associate professor and coordinator of the learning disabilities program at The University of Texas at Austin. Prior to his post master's training at the University of Kansas, he was assistant professor of special education at the University of Nebraska at Omaha. Dr. Larsen is president-elect, Division for Children with Learning Disabilities (DCLD), Council for Exceptional Children. His contributions to the professional literature have been numerous.

Dr. Larsen received both the B.S. degree in speech pathology and elementary education in 1965 and the M.S. degree in speech pathology in 1966 from the University of Nebraska at Omaha. He obtained the Ed.D. in learning disabilities from the University of Kansas in 1971. A selected bibliography of his works appears on pages 141-42.

The educational evaluation is an indispensable ingredient of effective teaching. To be of maximum use for handicapped pupils, evaluation strategies must yield data that is directly applicable to the formulation of viable instructional programming. It is an unfortunate occurrence that the educational evaluation in today's schools is all too often undertaken to satisfy generally irrelevant administrative demands that are extraneous to the main purpose of teaching. It is impossible to estimate the amount of time, effort, and money that are expended annually to (a) "label" students and (b) justify their placement in special education. There can be little doubt that these two functions of current evaluation efforts, while perhaps necessary for legislative and financial purposes, provide little, if any, information that can be readily transferred to remedial instruction.

It is imperative that professionals now involved with educational planning for handicapped students become aware of the major limitations of traditional evaluation practices and be provided with alternate methodologies for the generation of educationally relevant information. New and innovative techniques must be continually developed which permit the expanded evaluation of a handicapped pupil in relation to his/her environment as well as the curricular areas in which the school failure is being exhibited. The purpose of this chapter is to delineate the primary components of current evaluation strategies with particular emphasis upon their major shortcomings for educational programming. In addition, some emerging trends in the assessment of students exhibiting school related problems are discussed with implications for expanding the concept of "handicapping" conditions.

THE EDUCATIONAL EVALUATION IN TODAY'S SCHOOLS

The educational evaluation in today's schools, while differing in format from school system to school system, consists of several major components. This section will discuss the purpose of the educational evaluation, the organizational structure by which it is typically implemented, and the two types of evaluation procedures that are commonly utilized to assess handicapped learners. The educational usefulness of current evaluation practices will be reviewed, with implications for expanding optimal evaluation strategies in the future.

PURPOSES OF THE EDUCATIONAL EVALUATION

The purpose of an educational evaluation is threefold. These purposes are: (a) to determine if placement in special services is justified, (b) to apply the most appropriate classification or categorical label, and

(c) to provide information that is useful in developing an instructional program for the student. When placing a pupil into some aspect of special education, it is necessary to demonstrate that the placement is justified. All states have now adopted guidelines or criteria by which a student may be judged eligible to receive special services.[1] Typically, all pupils admitted into special services programs must exhibit certain specified "deficits" (e.g., in achievement, intelligence, social development, and sensory acuity) which can be documented through the use of some formal assessment device. Most educators are all too aware that failure to comply with the state criteria for placement of students into special programs may result in the loss of federal, state, and/or local subsidies.

The second purpose of the educational evaluation is to determine the classification or categorical label which seems most appropriately applied given the test scores and school performance of a particular student. It has now become apparent that the classification applied to a pupil is of little instructional value. Traditionally, the use of such labels as *mentally retarded, emotionally disturbed, brain injured, deaf, visually impaired,* etc., has been primarily to estimate the prevalence of various types of exceptionalities as well as to determine the amount of monies to be allocated for the administration of special service programs.

The final purpose in the evaluation of students is to provide data which will be helpful in planning an educational program for a learner. At this point, it is essential to delineate what specific academic and/or social skills and subskills the student needs to master in order to perform at a level near his maximum potential. For example, if a second-grade pupil is experiencing particular difficulty in arithmetic, it would be necessary to assess competency in areas such as numeration, addition, subtraction, fractions, measuring, and time concepts in order to compile a precise profile of what actually needs to be taught to promote proficiency in mathematical computations. Obviously, this phase of the evaluation is most efficiently conducted by the individuals who will be responsible for planning and carrying out the instructional program with the pupil. Informal assessment devices are typically utilized to determine which skills will comprise the instructional content of the remedial program.

ORGANIZATIONAL STRUCTURE OF THE EDUCATIONAL EVALUATION

While the purposes of the educational evaluation are relatively consistent across most school systems, the format or structure by which it is actualized is quite variable. In most instances, however, evaluation is typically keyed by the referral of a student with some suspected edu-

---

[1] Readers are referred to Gillespie, Miller, and Fiedler (1975) for an example of state criteria required for admission into programs for the learning disabled.

cational problem. The referral may come from a regular classroom teacher, parent, social worker, neighbor, or any interested adult. In any event, it is important to note for later discussion that the referral is predicated upon someone in the student's immediate environment making a judgment that certain observed behaviors are possibly deficient, deviant, or abnormal. After the relevant information pertaining to the pupil's perceived problem has been collected from the person making the referral, more in-depth testing will usually follow.

Once the complexity of a pupil's problem has been shown to exceed the expertise of the regular teacher (or parent, social worker, etc.), a series of assessment devices is usually administered to justify and document that placement in some special service program is warranted. In order to accomplish this task, a battery of formal tests are frequently employed to probe the factors of (a) intelligence; (b) achievement; (c) perceptual, process, and/or psycholinguistic functioning; and (d) social/emotional development. If such placement is viewed as being justified by meeting prescribed criteria, a categorical label is applied and informal assessment techniques are utilized to facilitate educational planning. The formal and informal evaluations are usually conducted as two discrete processes but, when taken together, comprise the total evaluation in today's schools. It is an infrequent occurrence when any additional effort will be expended to further investigate a given student's problem. According to Hammill (1971), at its most efficient level, the total educational evaluation will

(1) identify children who are likely to have trouble in school;
(2) refer children for medical or psychiatric attention when needed;
(3) isolate specific areas of difficulty . . . ; and (4) probe, in depth, the parameters of these particular problems [p. 120].

At the conclusion of the total evaluation, an educational plan is developed which, hopefully, is based upon the assessment data that have been collected relevant to the pupil's diagnosed disorder. In most situations the educational plan should contain three primary components: the goals and objectives to be achieved by the student over a specific period of time; the techniques or strategies of intervention that have been judged to be most appropriate for a given pupil; and the instructional materials which will most adequately facilitate the acquisition of those objectives that have been selected as being of top priority. To be viable, the educational plan should have input from the regular and special educators who will be ultimately responsible for its implementation. In some instances, however, the plan is largely useless as a result of being written by noninstructional personnel who frequently focus upon presumed etiological factors which are of no help to the teacher. In addition, unrealistic classroom demands are sometimes stressed with excessive interpretations of educationally irrelevant data. In any event, it should be noted that the educational plan is the final product of the combined formal and informal evaluations. Educators must be aware of the components of each in order to effectively assess and critique current evaluation practices in today's schools. The following sections will briefly discuss the elements of the formal and informal evaluations and offer a summary of their effectiveness for providing information useful in effecting maximum service for handicapped students.

TYPES OF EDUCATIONAL EVALUATION

The types of educational evaluation available to educators may be divided into many different classifications. In general, the most logical division includes two major approaches. The first approach necessitates the use of instruments primarily for documentation and labeling of handicapped students (formal evaluation). The second stresses the application of techniques which are designed to provide information that facilitates viable instructional programming (informal evaluation).

Formal evaluation: The formal evaluation is characterized by the use of *standardized* tests and may be conducted in settings other than the regular classroom by individuals specifically trained in the testing of children or in the classroom by the teacher who has some formal training in the assessment of pupils. In this instance, standardized tests refer to those instruments with known reliability and validity and which are specifically used to compare a student's score with some normative data that have been collected on a national or regional level. The results of the formal evaluation are usually reported in terms of grade equivalents, scaled scores, stanines, or percentiles and are used to determine if a student meets the specific criteria for admission into a particular special service program. As a result of the nature and purpose of the formal evaluation, the scores obtained are quite general in scope and offer little direct assistance to individuals who are responsible for initiating an instructional program. The areas of mental functioning which are typically tapped include intelligence; perceptual, process, and/or psycholinguistic functioning; academic achievement; and social/emotional development.

The number of tests which are available for the formal evaluation are practically limitless. In the measurement of intelligence the most frequently used instruments include the Wechsler Intelligence Scale for Children, the Stanford-Binet Intelligence Scale, the Slosson Intelligence Test for Children and Adults, the Peabody Picture Vocabulary Test, and the Leiter International Performance Scale. A sample of tests which purport to profile perceptual, process, and/or psycholinguistic functioning are the Illinois Test of Psycholinguistic Abilities, the Wepman Auditory Discrimination Test, the Bender Visual-Motor Gestalt Test, the Frostig Developmental Test of Visual Perception, the Screening Test for Auditory Perception, and the Developmental Test of Visual-

Motor Integration. Achievement batteries designed to measure general abilities in academic subject areas include the California Achievement Tests, the Metropolitan Achievement Tests, the Stanford Achievement Tests, the Wide-Range Achievement Tests, the Gates-McKillop Reading Diagnostic Tests, the Key Math Diagnostic Arithmetic Test, and the Screening Tests for Identifying Children with Specific Language Disability. Social-emotional development is commonly assessed by the Pupil Rating Scale, the Thematic Apperception Test, the House-Tree-Person Projection Technique, and the Cain-Levine Competency Scale. Interested readers are encouraged to consult Buros (1972) or Hoepfner, Strickland, Stangel, Jansen, and Patalino (1970) for a critical evaluation of these instruments.

In school practice the majority of formal tests are administered by specially trained personnel in settings other than the regular classroom. This is particularly true for measures of intelligence, social-emotional development, and most perceptual, process, and/or psycholinguistic functioning. At the conclusion of the formal testing, a report is written which is utilized in the administrative decision as to whether the student is qualified to receive special services. At best, the formal evaluation will negate or suggest the presence of mental retardation; indicate general levels of academic underachievement; point out the possibility of some problems in social development; identify dysfunctions in perceptual, process, or psycholinguistic functioning; and recommend areas where more precise evaluation needs to be undertaken.

As has been mentioned previously, the formal evaluation is of little, if any, assistance in the planning of specific educational programs for a particular student. However, the results of formal tests do have the advantage of being objective and may provide useful instructional information of a global nature when attempting to document a pupil's achievement over a given period of time. At present, it seems that this type of educational evaluation is primarily used as an administrative convenience to justify placement and attach the most appropriate label. Professionals who are concerned with the gathering of more educationally relevant data must resort to the informal evaluation which is usually undertaken by an educational diagnostician, special or regular classroom teacher.

Informal evaluation: The informal evaluation is that part of the diagnostic process that focuses upon the student's observed educational problem and is used to specify steps by which it may be remediated. At this point, no attempt is made to further label or classify a pupil. Rather, according to Hammill and Bartel (1975) the goals of the informal evaluation are

> to detect areas of weakness and strength; to verify, probe, or discard the conclusions and recommendations of the formal evaluation; to deduce the child's particular instructional and behavioral needs; and to formulate a remedial program for him [p. 7].

It is apparent to even the most casual observer that the teacher or educational diagnostician must utilize a number of techniques in order to fully explore the various parameters of a particular school-related problem. In general, educators will employ a number of non-norm referenced measures to gather pertinent information related to the diagnosed disorder. For example, anecdotal records will be perused; various rating scales, checklists, personality inventories, attitude scales, and interviews with the student's teacher and parents may be taken into account to provide a core of background information that will be helpful when formulating an instructional program. More importantly, a systematic analysis of the pupil's responses to a series of educational tasks must be accomplished. This analysis is directly related to the specific academic and/or social skills the student needs to master and the instructional methodology which will facilitate the acquisition of these skills.

The process by which teachers determine the specific content of an educational program has been variously termed as *prescriptive teaching*, *diagnostic teaching*, or *task analysis*. Regardless of the term applied, the primary focus of this approach is on (a) delineating the sequence of skills that needs to be mastered in order to perform a given task, (b) determining a precise profile of the student's ability to perform these skills, (c) devising an instructional program to teach the skills that have not yet been mastered, and (d) evaluating the effectiveness of the educational program and initiating modifications when necessary. To illustrate this process, a teacher may wish to determine if a student can identify the "plus," "minus," and "equal" signs as a prelude to minimal competency in mathematical calculations. In order to assess performance on this task, the following sequence of skills was developed. The pupil will be taken through each subskill to evaluate competency on this task.

Instructional Objective: The student will identify the plus, minus, and equal signs upon command.

Subskill 1. The student will be able to point to the plus sign when asked to do so when shown the number sentence $3 + 5 = 8$.

Subskill 2. The student will be able to point to each subtraction problem when asked which problems are "take-away" problems when shown a page of ten addition and subtraction problems.

Subskill 3. The student will be able to use the plastic pieces to construct an addition and subtraction problem when asked to show two plus five and then six take away one when given plastic numerals and a plus and a minus sign.

Subskill 4. The student will be able to point to each equal sign when asked to do so when shown five number sentences.

Subskill 5. The student will be able to read each sentence correctly; i.e., "six plus three equals nine" or "eight take away two equals six" when given a worksheet with ten number sentences, addition or subtraction, with solutions; i.e., $6 + 3 = 9$ or $8 - 2 = 6$.[2]

The use of this *skill ladder* allows the teacher to evaluate the student's ability to identify the plus, minus, and equal signs. In addition, it is also possible, when failure is encountered, to specify where the pupil is experiencing difficulty and suggest where instruction needs to be initiated. The method of instruction which is undertaken by the teacher may take many forms and is considered effective as long as the various skills are mastered by the learner. Consistent monitoring of the progress made by the student is essential to ensure that remediation remains effective.

The informal evaluation just described has several advantages in that it is designed by the individuals who will be responsible for its implementation and tends to focus upon the demonstrated problem exhibited by the student. There are several potential drawbacks to this method, however, that should be kept firmly in mind. Obviously, the viability of the method depends entirely upon the competency of the teacher. In some instances, a great deal of time may be wasted by teachers analyzing and teaching skills which have no logical or empirical relation to school success. In addition, the effective usage of the method implies that the teacher is able to efficiently observe a learner and pinpoint areas that require more precise analysis. The reliability of some personnel to perform this task is certainly questionable. While the potential hazards of informal evaluation need to be clearly noted, apparently it is the best single method in today's schools to individualize instruction for those students who are experiencing academic and/or social difficulties.

In conclusion, the most commonly employed strategies for the administrative and instructional assessment of students entails both the formal and informal evaluation. Currently, these types of evaluation are the best available given the structure and policies of today's schools and the level of training of educational personnel. During the past few years, however, I have become increasingly aware of definite shortcomings inherent in both the formal and informal evaluations as they are presently implemented. In my opinion, these weaknesses seriously limit their effectiveness in providing maximum service to handicapped stu-

---

[2] The content for this task ladder was derived from the experimental edition of the *Instructional Based Appraisal System*, Learner Managed Designs, Inc., 1973.

dents. The final portion of this section will delineate these weaknesses and suggest alternative procedures that will promote a clearer understanding of the learner and his school failure.

SHORTCOMINGS OF THE EDUCATIONAL EVALUATION

From my point of view, the major shortcomings of the educational evaluation in today's schools are (a) the inordinate amount of time and effort expended upon instructionally irrelevant formal evaluation, (b) the emphasis placed upon the assessment of ill-defined psychological constructs that are presumed to underlie many instances of school failure, and (c) the tendency to ignore the significant variables of the student's immediate environment in causing and maintaining academic and/or social problems. As has been previously discussed, the formal evaluation comprises a substantial portion of the total evaluation effort while providing little or no data that are directly applicable to instructional programming. Undoubtedly, many educational administrators will argue that the time, money, and effort devoted to the labeling of students is necessary for the efficient operation of special service programs. It has been my impression, however, that the excessive concern with documentation and labeling is extremely restrictive and provides little solace to those individuals who must spend a major portion of each day instructing a student who is in need of some special service.

Most regrettably, it is readily apparent that many university training programs and inservice activities inappropriately focus upon how various norm-referenced instruments (i.e., tests of intelligence, perception, psycholinguistics, etc.) can be used in planning instruction for students. This type of training is questionable at best and is usually done at the expense of teaching more educationally relevant informal techniques. The result of this training process perpetuates the reliance of teachers upon noninstructional personnel to "solve" the majority of their problems. For example, I am personally aware of a situation where a special education teacher delayed the initiation of remedial instruction for three months until receiving the psychologist's report (the formal evaluation). The report, when it did arrive, stressed that the student evidenced signs of "minimal cerebral dysfunction," suffered from dyslexia, and, consequently, was labeled as learning disabled. Since the pupil was obviously reading two grade levels below his peers, this "diagnostic" finding and label was of little practical assistance. The teacher's reluctance to begin instruction was based upon her own insecurity and lack of training as well as the belief that some test scores were essential before a meaningful educational plan could be developed. This seeming inability or fear of many regular and special teachers to effectively manage even the most mild academic or social problems is certainly not a rare occurrence.

Being somewhat of a realist, I am aware that, for many reasons, the formal, norm-referenced evaluation will be with us for some time to come. I do feel, however, that much can be done to mitigate its effects by expanding teacher training and inservice activities—to mainly stress those techniques that have been demonstrated to have a logical and empirical basis for remediating school-related problems. Teachers continually need to be made aware that they are the ones who must assume major responsibility for the evaluation and programming of handicapped learners. Consequently, only those procedures that are directly applicable to their immediate environments should be emphasized. Anything less than teacher trainers (preservice and inservice) being accountable for the *success of their products when working with students* will result in the continued use and reliance upon instructionally irrelevant evaluation strategies.

The second shortcoming of current evaluation practices is the stress placed upon the measurement and interpretation of psychological constructs that are thought to be factors in many instances of school failure. More specifically, I am referring to the use of those assessment devices that purport to assess "perceptual," "process," or "psycholinguistic" abilities. The tests that are commonly employed to evaluate these areas have been mentioned in the previous section of this chapter. The extent to which these types of instruments are currently employed is immediately apparent when considering that most states now require that a student be shown to exhibit some deficit in these areas as a prelude to being labeled as learning disabled (Gillespie, Miller, Fiedler, 1975). In addition, pupils who are classified as emotionally disturbed and mentally retarded are frequently thought to suffer from some perceptual, process, or psycholinguistic disorder which is hypothesized to exacerbate their academic and/or social problems.

As a result of current research, it is my opinion that the continued use of assessment devices which purport to measure these areas of psychological functioning should be carefully reconsidered or, perhaps, eliminated completely until some evidence is presented that substantiates its usefulness in school practice. A mere sampling of research over the past seven years casts doubt as to whether frequently used perceptual, process, and/or psycholinguistic tests (a) actually measure skills that are essential to academic or social behavior, (b) possess the necessary power to differentiate between handicapped and normal students, and (c) can effectively predict school success (Cohen, 1969; Hartman & Hartman, 1973; Hammill & Larsen, 1974; Black, 1974; Bryan, 1974; Larsen & Hammill, 1975; Vellutino, Steger, DeSetto & Phillips, 1975; Newcomer & Hammill, 1975; Larsen, Rogers, & Sowell, 1976). An additional conclusion is that many training programs which are designed to remediate perceptual, process, or psycholinguistic deficits have been less than successful (Robinson, 1971; Hammill, 1972; Hammill & Wiederholt, 1973; Hammill, Goodman, & Wiederholt, 1974; Hammill & Larsen, 1974; and Larsen, Parker, & Sowell, 1976). Based upon these and other research studies it appears that little evidence is now available to support the continued use of these tests for any purpose. In the future, I sincerely hope that the advocates of this method of diagnosis and remediation will conduct research in an attempt to demonstrate the effectiveness of their tests and training materials. Until this information is available, definitions of various handicapping conditions should be modified to either exclude the necessity of "demonstrating" deficits in these areas or, at least, make the documentation of such hypothesized problems optional.

The third major shortcoming of the educational evaluation in today's schools is the tendency to center only upon the assessment of the observed academic and/or social problems of the student, and ignore the potentially potent effects of the environment in causing and maintaining the school failure. In particular, I refer simply to the need for some analysis of the student that takes into account the many environments in which the pupil operates as well as his/her interactions within those environments. It is apparent that the tendency of educators to disregard this phase of the pupil's school life will result in definite limitations when initiating meaningful instructional programs for handicapped students.

The rationale for my concern with the evaluation of the environment as well as the student stems from the results of a research study with which I was involved. The intent of this study was to follow a large group of first-grade students through their first four months of school while systematically observing every formal academic teaching situation to determine both the quality and quantity of teacher-student interactions. Before the school term began, each teacher was interviewed to ascertain which student characteristics she preferred and which student behaviors she felt designated the "bright" child who would do well during his academic career. Teacher A explained that she enjoyed the child who was "outgoing," "alert," and "not afraid to speak his mind." Once the school year began, some children enrolled in her classroom did exhibit these gregarious qualities, but others did not. Johnny was a child who tended to be generally shy and retiring. In the course of all teaching activities during the four months, Teacher A called upon or interacted with Johnny on only three occasions; and two of these were the result of Johnny asking a question. Only once did the teacher direct a question to him! It was apparent that the child was not learning, primarily because he was not being taught.

In early December, Johnny was referred to special education (a newly established resource room) because he was "not learning to read" and had begun to "withdraw." He was administered a battery of tests and was subsequently labeled "learning disabled." Add to this the fact that Johnny possessed normal intelligence, adequate language skills (determined by tests administered independently of the school system), and had scored in the upper 15th percentile on the Metropolitan Readiness Tests and the problem takes on even more ominous overtones. Apparently, this child's failure was due to a deficit present in the instructional style of his teacher rather than to some fault of his own. He did not live up to the expectancies of his teacher and, as a result, was subjected to negative treatment patterns.

A myriad of additional research has been conducted which emphasizes the role of the school, teacher, and peer culture in initiating or maintaining school problems. For example, many characteristics of students have been found to influence teachers' patterns of interactions with them. Race, ethnic background, sex, handicapping conditions, personality, physical attractiveness, seating location, writing neatness, and speech and language patterns have all been demonstrated to be strong determinants of teacher behavior (Readers are referred to Good & Brophy (1973) and Brophy & Good (1975) for excellent reviews and discussions of research related to this topic.) It is obvious that several significant advantages will accrue from evaluating the student as a part of the environment in which he/she is experiencing failure. The means for accomplishing this type of evaluation will be specified in the following section.

EMERGING DIRECTIONS IN THE EDUCATIONAL EVALUATION

It is my opinion that the educational evaluation in today's schools must be expanded to include the systematic analysis of how a student *interacts* with his/her environment. It should be clearly noted that I do not suggest that all current practices in evaluation should be discontinued or even extensively modified. There is no doubt that much useful information is derived from traditional procedures. It is apparent, however, that the general tendency to look at the pupil only to determine the cause of his/her school failure is extremely restrictive. In addition, this approach may result in a distorted perception of the complexity and extent of the observed problem as well as the most effective method for remediation.

The advantages of studying the interactions between the student and the environment are obvious. This type of evaluation permits the professional to determine if the school problem is manifested in more than one educational setting. It is also important to determine if the academic and/or social disorder is exhibited in only one or two curriculum areas, with certain teachers, or at specific times of the day. Additionally, the specific features of each environmental setting which appear to facilitate or impede learning should provide educators indispensable information when planning a remedial program. This data would also be of substantial value when attempting to "carry over" the remedial activities to the regular classroom. While the positive benefits of an environmental analysis are too many to be listed here, any experienced professional will have little difficulty in estimating its worth.

A reasonable structure for undertaking an *ecological assessment* has been developed by Laten and Katz (1975). They recommend that the initial focus of this evaluation should be upon the student's involvement with the many environmental systems in which he/she must interact. Furthermore, the expectations that the pupil has for him/herself and that others have for him/her must also be collected for study. Laten and Katz's model for ecological assessment is as follows:

A. Referral
 1. Engaging the environment for data collection on perceptions of the problem
 2. Gathering information from the system that triggered the referral
 3. Gathering information from the systems which support the referral
 4. Gathering information about the systems which do not support the referral
 5. Mapping the information
B. Expectations
 1. Gathering information about expectations in problematic situations
 2. Gathering information about expectations in successful situations
 3. Mapping the expectations
C. Behavioral Descriptions
 1. Data collection on the interactions and skills of the people involved in the problematic situations
   a. present data
   b. historical data
   c. interactional analysis
   d. functional analysis
 2. Data collection on the interactions and skills of the people involved in successful situations
   a. present data
   b. historical data
   c. interactional analysis
   d. functional analysis
 3. Assessment of skills in specific settings
D. Summary of Data
E. Setting Reasonable Expectations [Pp. 40-41]

Upon perusal of this model, one is immediately aware that many of the components listed are already accomplished by the competent educator or educational diagnostician during the routine investigation of school-related problems. This is particularly true for the Referral (Level A) and Expectations (Level B) where simple interviews with parents and regular teachers (plus a large measure of common sense) will yield much useful information. However, concise "Behavioral Descriptions" are somewhat more difficult to generate in that they require the utilization of relatively precise evaluation techniques. This section will discuss some evaluation strategies which permit the systematic study of the student's interactions within the regular classroom. Specific interactions to be considered include the pupil with (a) the teacher and (b) the curriculum.

TEACHER-STUDENT INTERACTIONS

The task of evaluating teacher-student interactional patterns is a relatively arduous undertaking for the professional with little expertise or training in this area. Good and Brophy (1973) stress this point when they state:

> The maze of interacting behaviors occurring in classrooms is rich and complex, and can be understood only if the observer can see and assess a wide variety of classroom factors. Many important events go unnoticed unless the observer is looking for them. For example, as John Holt (1964) points out in *How Children Fail,* untrained observers often focus their undivided attention on the teacher. They seldom look at students. . . . Observers often fail to notice clues that describe the interest and involvement of the students in the task at hand [p. ix].

It is axiomatic that any professional attempting to investigate teacher-student interactions must have access to at least several observational systems which permit the reliable collection of data. Since space limitations prohibit a detailed discussion of the many diverse systems currently available, I will briefly describe some of the useful devices I have employed for research and evaluation purposes. Readers are encouraged to study these procedures in more detail, and select for use those that are most directly applicable to the environment in which they find themselves.

In those situations where it is important to gain some idea of the quality of teacher behaviors emitted, professionals may choose to employ several already published techniques or develop their own. Herbert and Attridge (1975) have provided an in-depth guide for developers and users of observational systems. Two methods that provide observational data have been developed by Hughes (1959) and Perkins (1964). Basically, these techniques do not require extensive training of the observer, and provide a *general* analysis of how the teacher functions within the educational environment in which the handicapped student is located. Both systems focus upon categorizing those overt teacher behaviors which are presumed to elicit or impede school learning. I have used each of these procedures as a means to structure my general observations of both regular and special classrooms. While specific evaluative information is not forthcoming when applying these methods, they do provide a basis for the selection of more specific and precise observational systems for more in-depth study of an educational environment.

One classroom observational instrument which has shown considerable promise is the Observation Schedule and Record (OScAR 5) developed by Medley, Schluck, and Ames (1968). The OScAR technique requires the observer to watch for five-minute intervals and then record in the various cells until a half-hour of observation has been completed. Categories delineate (a) four types of pupil behavior, (b) four types of teacher questions, (c) several modes of response to pupil behavior (from unqualified support to criticism), (d) problem structuring, (e) feedback provision, and (f) several procedural and managerial teacher behaviors.

The OScAR system is capable of providing a large amount of classroom interactional data which directly relate to the way that the student and teacher are engaged in the instructional process. It should be noted that this instrument is sensitive to the actions of the learner as well as to those of the teacher. It will determine specific estimates of what actually transpires within the classroom and may point out areas where the handicapped pupil is receiving significantly more negative interactions than are his/her achieving peers. Ideally, this information will be extremely valuable in counseling teachers, providing optimal learning environments for the students, and directing remedial efforts outside of the resource room or a special class.

Another observational system that I have found quite useful is the Dyadic Interaction System (Brophy & Good, 1972). This technique is capable of coding in excess of 150 distinct teacher-student verbal interactions. However, I have found that five basic patterns of interactions will yield a fairly concise description of what goes on in the classroom while significantly reducing the demands on the observer. The five different types of dyadic interactions include:

1. Response opportunities—in which the student publicly attempts to answer a question by the teacher;
2. Recitation—in which the pupil reads aloud, describes some experience or object, goes through arithmetic tables, or makes some other extended oral presentation;

3. Procedural contacts—in which the teacher-student interaction concerns permission, supplies and equipment, or other matters concerned with the pupil's individual needs or with classroom management;

4. Work-related contacts—in which the teacher-student interaction concerns seat work, homework, or other written work completed by the pupil; and

5. Behavioral contacts—in which the teacher disciplines the student or makes individual comments concerning his/her classroom behavior.

These five broad categories of teacher-student interactions permit observers to note whether the initiator of the verbalization was the teacher or student. In addition, the quality and quantity of the teacher's message or response to the pupil during the total interaction is also recorded. The coding of response opportunities and recitation turns focuses primarily upon the type of question asked and the quality of the student's response, both of which are specified before coding the nature of the teacher's feedback. An important feature of the Dyadic Interaction System is that it preserves the sequential order of interactions so that the chain of action and reaction sequences within these categories are maintained.

It is my belief that any comprehensive educational evaluation must include the assessment of teacher-student interactions. This information is very useful when attempting to determine if the cause of the school problem lies within the pupil, the instructional style of the teacher, or both. Obviously, having this data available will significantly influence content and structure of any intervention strategies. Hopefully, future evaluation efforts will include these methods in the routine investigation of academic and/or social problems.

INTERACTIONS WITH THE CURRICULUM

Perhaps the single most important variable in evaluating the environment of a student who is exhibiting school failure is determining the particular curricula demands which may be exacerbating the academic and/or social problem. It is quite unfortunate that very few techniques are available that permit a reliable assessment of how a student is managing the scholastic demands of a classroom. One procedure which has shown a great deal of promise is Applied Behavior Analysis (ABA). While ABA is not a strictly evaluative system, it does permit a succinct estimation of the factors which influence the manner in which learners deal with various curricular tasks. Lovitt (1975a,

1975b) provides an excellent discussion of the philosophical underpinnings and practical uses of this approach.

According to Lovitt (1975a), the application of ABA is comprised of five main processes. These components include:

1. Direct measurement—the specific analysis of what tasks the student is currently attempting to master;

2. Daily measurement—a systematic baseline of a student's performance of a given period of time;

3. Replicable teaching procedures—a precise description of how a task is presented;

4. Individual analysis—the maintenance of graphic data on *each* pupil experiencing difficulty; and

5. Experimental control—the establishment of a functional relationship between the teaching method and pupil gain.

The consistent use of the five major elements of ABA provides educators with an accurate and easily employed method for the study of the learner in relation to the appropriateness of the school curriculum.

In some instances, educators may wish to utilize ABA techniques in the diagnostic teaching of various skills. Several specific procedures for instituting this process have been developed by Lovitt (1975b) and Wright (1968). In general, these procedures are predicated upon the identification of the specific behavior and level to which it will be taught, study of observed error patterns, selection of the most appropriate contingency systems, ability to generalize, and the programming of self-management behaviors.

The advantages of ABA lie primarily in its flexibility. This system will permit analysis of most of the variables which relate to basic academic and social skills. One student characteristic may be selected for study with the consequent simplification of measuring only one teaching procedure at a time. This trait of ABA is eminently preferable to the relatively global and nonspecific procedures of informal assessment that are currently being employed in the schools today. The data accrued from ABA should provide professionals with a reliable foundation for the planning and implementation of remedial procedures for handicapped pupils.

CONCLUDING STATEMENTS

There can be little doubt that the evaluation procedures currently employed in the schools are inadequate to gain a clear understanding of a particular student's academic and/or social problems. Several techniques have been described in this chapter that will broaden the scope of the traditional evaluation to include the assessment of various interaction patterns within the educational environment which have supported a student's referral for special services. It should not be thought, however, that the utilization of only those procedures discussed will result in a precise description of those variables which may negatively affect school learning. Educators may also find it necessary to investigate the professional climates of schools to ascertain if academic and social failure are the norm or exception in a given educational environment. Fox, Schmuch, Van Egmond, Ritvo, and Jung (1975) have developed thirty instruments which assess a wide variety of potential trouble spots in the typical school situation.

An additional area of classroom functioning which may prove fruitful to educators is the evaluation of peer interactions. When assessing these types of interactions, the sociogram (Redl & Wattenberg, 1959) and behavior rating scales (Sheltzer & Stone, 1971) may provide reliable data in an efficient and effective manner. The advantages of these evaluation strategies are that they aid the teacher in identifying cliques in class groups, pinpoint isolates in the classroom, provide clues in how to deal with disciplinary problems, and indicate those students who are out-of-school learners.

In summary, the educational evaluation is an extremely difficult undertaking for even the most experienced professional. Much research is needed to clarify those variables which may influence a pupil's school achievement and, consequently, the evaluative procedures necessary to fully assess their role in individual cases of reported failure. It is possible at this time, however, to improve on-going systems of evaluation by upgrading current preservice and inservice teacher training programs. Professionals who conduct these programs should make every effort to keep current on changing educational philosophies and, more importantly, the research that either supports or questions traditional evaluation practices. To do otherwise is to ensure the continued use of essentially unproven and, very probably, erroneous techniques that will yield no practical data regarding a student's school failure.

REFERENCES

Black, F. W. Achievement test performance of high and low perceiving learning disabled children. *Journal of Learning Disabilities*, 1974, 7, 179-82.

Brophy, J., & Good, T. *Teacher-student relationships: Causes and Consequences*. New York: Holt, Rinehart & Winston, 1974.

Bryan, T. Learning disabilities: A new stereotype. *Journal of Learning Disabilities,* 1974, 7, 304-9.

Buros, O. K. *The seventh mental measurements yearbook.* Highland Park, N.J.: Gryphon, 1972.

Cohen, S. Studies in visual perception and reading in disadvantaged children. *Journal of Learning Disabilities,* 1969, 2, 498-507.

Fox, R., Schmuck, R., Van Egmond, E., Ritvo, M., & Jung, C. *Diagnosing professional climates of schools.* Fairfax, Virginia: NTL Learning Resources Corporation, 1975.

Gillespie, R., Miller, T., & Fields, V. Legislative definitions of learning disabilities: Roadblocks to effective service. *Journal of Learning Disabilities,* 1975, 8, 660-66.

Good, T., & Brophy, J. *Looking in classrooms.* New York: Harper & Row, 1973.

Hammill, D. D. Evaluating children for instructional purposes. *Academic Therapy,* 1971, 6, 53-58.

Hammill, D. D., & Bartel, N. *Teaching children with learning and behavior problems.* Boston: Allyn & Bacon, 1975.

Hammill, D. D., Goodman, L., & Wiederholt, J. L. Appropriateness of the developmental test of visual perception when used with economically disadvantaged children. *Journal of School Psychology,* 1971, 9, 430-35.

Hammill, D. D., & Larsen, S. C. The effectiveness of psycholinguistic training. *Exceptional Children,* 1974, 41, 5-14.

Hammill, D. D., & Larsen, S. C. The relationship of selected auditory perceptual skills to reading ability. *Journal of Learning Disabilities,* 1974, 7, 429-36.

Hammill, D. D., & Wiederholt, J. L. Review of the Frostig visual perception test and the related training program. In L. Mann & D. Sabatino (Eds.), *The first review of special education* (Vol. 1). Philadelphia: JSE Press, Grune & Stratton, 1973, 33-48.

Hartman, N. C., & Hartman, R. Perceptual handicap or reading disability? *The Reading Teacher,* 1973, 26, 684-95.

Herbert, J., & Attridge, C. A guide for developers and users of observational systems and manuals. *American Educational Research Journal,* 1975, 12, 1-20.

Hoepfner, R., Strickland, G., Stangel, G., Jansen, P., & Patalino, M. *Elementary school test evaluations.* Los Angeles: Center for the Study of Evaluation, UCLA Graduate School of Education, 1970.

Hughes, M. *Development of the means for the assessment of the quality of teaching in elementary schools.* Salt Lake City: University of Utah Press, 1959.

Larsen, S. C., & Hammill, D. D. The relationship of selected visual perceptual abilities to school learning. *Journal of Special Education,* 1975, 9, 282-91.

Larsen, S. C., Parker, R., & Sowell, V. *The effectiveness of the MWM program in developing language abilities.* Unpublished manuscript, University of Texas, 1976.

Larsen, S. C., Rogers, D., & Sowell, V. The use of selected perceptual tests in differentiating between normal and learning disabled children. *Journal of Learning Disabilities*, 1976, 9, 85-91.

Laten, S., & Katz, G. A theoretical model for assessment of adolescents: The ecological/behavioral approach. *Occasional papers,* Madison, Wisconsin Public Schools, June 1975.

Lovitt, T. Characteristics of ABA, general recommendations, and methodological limitations. *Journal of Learning Disabilities*, 1975, 8, 432-43. (a)

Lovitt, T. Specific research recommendations and suggestions for practitioners. *Journal of Learning Disabilities*, 1975, 8, 504-18. (b)

Medley, D., Schluck, C., & Ames, N. *Assessing the learning environment in the classroom: A manual for users of OScAR 5.* Princeton, N.J.: Educational Testing Service, 1968.

Newcomer, P., & Hammill, D. D. *Psycholinguistics in the schools.* Columbus, Ohio: Charles E. Merrill, 1976.

Perkins, H. A procedure for assessing the classroom behavior of students and teachers. *American Educational Research Journal*, 1964, 2, 251-57.

Redl, F., & Wattenberg, W. *Mental hygiene in teaching* (2nd ed.). New York: Harcourt, Brace & World, 1959.

Robinson, H. *Perceptual training—Does it result in reading improvement?* Paper presented at the annual convention of the International Reading Association, Atlantic City, April 1971.

Shertzer, B., & Stone, S. *Fundamentals of guidance.* Boston: Houghton Mifflin, 1971.

Vellutino, F., Steger, J., DeSetto, L., & Phillips, F. Immediate and delayed recognition of visual stimuli in poor and normal readers. *Journal of Experimental Child Psychology*, 1975, 19, 223-32.

Wright, H. F. *Recording and analyzing child behavior.* New York: Harper & Row, 1968.

SELECTED BIBLIOGRAPHY OF WORKS BY STEPHEN C. LARSEN

Hammill, D. D., & Larsen, S. C. The relationship of selected auditory perceptual skills and reading ability. *Journal of Learning Disabilities*, 1974, 7, 429-36.

Hammill, D. D., & Larsen, S. C. The effectiveness of psycholinguistic training. *Exceptional Children*, 1974, 41, 5-14. Reprinted in M. Lahey & L. Bloom (Eds.), *Selected Readings in Childhood Language Disorders.* New York: Wiley, 1976.

Larsen, S. C. The influence of teacher expectations on the school performance of handicapped children. *Focus on Exceptional Children,* 1975, 6, 1-14.

Larsen, S. C. Learning disabilities specialist: Roles and responsibilities. *Journal of Learning Disabilities,* in press.

Larsen, S. C., & Bagley, M. T. Teacher expectancy and academic achievement. *Perceptual and Motor Skills,* in press.

Larsen, S. C., & Hammill, D. D. The relationship of selected visual skills to school learning. *Journal of Special Education,* 1975, 9, 281-91.

Larsen, S. C., & Hudson, F. Oral kinesthetic sensitivity and the perception of speech, *Child Development,* 1973, 44, 390-94.

Larsen, S. C., Parker, R., & Jorjorian, S. A comparison of self-concept in learning disabled and normal children. *Perceptual and Motor Skills,* 1973, 37, 510-11.

Larsen, S. C., Rogers, D., & Sowell, V. The usefulness of selected perceptual tests in differentiating between normal and learning disabled children. *Journal of Learning Disabilities,* 1976, 9, 85-91.

White, L. A., & Larsen, S. C. The predictive validity and reliability of the Basic School Skills Inventory. *Journal of Learning Disabilities,* in press.

8

State Education Agency
Considerations in
Identification of the Handicapped

Carol Bradley

Carol Bradley is learning disabilities consultant for the Iowa Department of Public Instruction, Des Moines, Iowa. She is a member of the National Board of Trustees, Division for Children with Learning Disabilities, Council for Exceptional Children, and a member of the board of the Iowa Association for Children with Learning Disabilities. She has presented at national and state conferences and serves as a consultant to several state education agencies.

Ms. Bradley received the B.A. degree in education from the University of Iowa in 1967, the M.A. in special education from the University of South Dakota in 1972, and is presently enrolled in the Ph.D. program in special education administration and learning disabilities at the University of Iowa.

State education agency personnel are often viewed as reactionary. It appears to be almost fashionable to consider a state education agency and its department or division of special education as a necessary bureaucratic evil. We seem to be generally seen as those who continually are in the way of innovation, wear blue coats, carry big sticks, and speak in thou shall nots.

I remember as a beginning special education teacher I had vague notions about our own Iowa Department of Public Instruction and state education agencies in general. I had very little knowledge about our SEA's function or its effect on me, my classroom, or whom I taught in that classroom. I doubt that many special educators today or in the near future will have so little knowledge of their respective state education agencies. Events of the last ten years have caused most special educators to feel their effects ever more directly. Federal and state legislation, litigation, and civil rights action seems to indicate this trend is not soon going to reverse.

State education agencies and their divisions of special education are usually charged with the promotion, development, and evaluation of special education instructional programs and support services. They are also charged by the federal government and their own state legislatures with monitoring full services mandates and insuring that due process procedures are implemented. In addition, federal funds are channeled through state education agencies to intermediate units and local school districts. State education agencies are also charged in many states with review and approval of local education agency or intermediate unit plans for special education services before state funds can be generated and expended.

Identification of the handicapped is one responsibility ultimately laid at the doorstep of state education agencies. It is often viewed as the most controversial—a damned if you do or damned if you don't dilemma.

In this chapter I will consider three of the many questions which I believe state education agencies must deal with in meeting their responsibilities for identification of the handicapped. These questions are:

1. Is it really necessary to label students as handicapped?
2. What are the legislative and funding realities?
3. How can a state education agency best meet its responsibilities in identification of the handicapped?

IS IT REALLY NECESSARY TO LABEL STUDENTS AS HANDICAPPED?

It is difficult to pick up professional literature in special education today without finding an article that addresses the evils of labeling children as handicapped and glowingly praises the practice of defining the special needs of children instead. One example of this recent barrage is an article entitled "Legislative Definitions of Learning Disabilities: Roadblocks to Effective Service" (Gillespie, Miller, & Fiedler, 1975). According to the authors, they requested the state laws, rules, and regulations relevant to special education from the fifty state education agencies. From this review of the legislation, they concluded that the major emphasis by the fifty state education agencies was on defining special children rather than special needs. It seems from the title of the article that the reader is to assume the authors also came to the conclusion that this emphasis represents a roadblock to effective service. The article also states that "in sum, legislation should provide alternative plans for meeting the special needs of exceptional children [p. 67].

While I personally agree wholeheartedly with that conclusion, I am still at a loss as to how legislation can be written on alternative plans for meeting the special needs of exceptional children without first defining exceptional children. Admittedly, it is much easier to develop alternative plans for meeting special needs than it is to define exceptional children. For example, in Iowa we have described and written into our legislation alternatives ranging from the educational strategist (a consulting teacher model) to a self-contained special class model with a teacher/pupil ratio of one to five. Resource teaching programs may be operated categorically or as cross-categorical programs depending on the individual district's needs. However, we are still faced with the question, Who are all these alternative models designed to serve? Answers to that question are much more difficult. For example, a physically handicapped child is obviously, to the eye, handicapped. But sometimes, by simply removing physical barriers and providing access to the general education classroom, the child is no longer handicapped in obtaining an education. Without the ease of an arbitrary I.Q. cutoff point, how can mental retardation be defined? How many articulation errors constitute a handicap? What in the name of heaven are learning disabilities?

Some would have us answer that any child who would profit from special education is entitled to it and thus resolve our definitional issues. May I suggest that I personally could profit from unemployment compensation, food stamps, increased tax exceptions, and any number of other social services. But, am I entitled to them? I believe not, because I can survive and make progress without those important services, at least at this point in my life.

It seems that the same is true in approaching the question of identification of the handicapped. Our primary responsibility as special educators is to identify and appropriately serve those youngsters who are so handicapped in obtaining an education that they will not make educational progress without the provision of a special education instructional program or support service. The real question then becomes, Will the program or service that accrues to the handicapped child more than offset the possible negative effects of being labeled as handicapped in obtaining an education? Answering that question, child by child, is the ethical dilemma we face.

Let me hasten to add that the handicapped students of whom I speak represent no more than ten to twelve percent of the general school age population. When we speak of student populations in excess of that approximate incidence, I, too, seriously question the practice of labeling. In fact, it seems to me that we are not then speaking of young-sters who should be the primary instructional responsibility of special educators. Special education has an obligation to youngsters with needs in our schools, but that responsibility should take the form of indirect service. Some examples of indirect service are inservice training for general education faculties; expanded consultation from school psychol-ogists, speech clinicians, categorical consultants, school social workers, etc.; demonstration teaching in general education classrooms and obser-vation in resource rooms; and special classes by general education faculty members. For example, in Iowa we recommend that special education resource room teachers be free of direct teaching to mildly handicapped students the equivalent of one-half day per week. During that time, these teachers may work with general classroom teachers to develop plans for students who present instructional problems to the teacher. Such students, though, are not viewed by the classroom teacher as handicapped or necessarily at risk.

It seems to me that special educators in their rush to mainstream, eliminate labels, and generally do good things, are inadvertently en-couraging general education to either ignore its handicapped students or drastically narrow its concept of normalcy. Strange as this statement may seem, all one has to do is spend a couple of days out in a school district to see what I mean. I have been told by slyly smiling personnel of school districts who have provided next to nothing for any of their handicapped pupils that special educators are finally catching up with them. On the opposite end, but just as distressing, are the districts who suddenly decide twenty or thirty percent of all their students are handi-capped when it is not necessary to label them as such. Some of this latter phenomenon can be explained by a school district's recognition of a need for program adjustments, wider curriculum offerings, and updated equipment and materials. However, if we continue to loosely take more and more children into direct service special education alter-natives, I think we can expect a backlash in the form of viewing special education as out of hand. The old "tail wagging the dog" argument will, no doubt, surface again. If *I* were a general education principal or school superintendent today, I would fear that at some future point all monies requested to effect any improvement in educational practices would have to be called for in the name of special education. We, as special educators, must not be party to this if we conceive of ourselves as truly part of the total education community.

WHAT ARE THE LEGISLATIVE AND FUNDING REALITIES?

It's no secret to anyone in public school education that the education dollar is getting tighter and tighter. Costs of school plant operation, transportation of students, and personnel salaries have increased sharply. At the same time, many school districts are still in a steady period of enrollment decline. Taxpayers find it difficult to see the need for increased budgets when fewer children are presenting themselves for enrollment. Bond issues are repeatedly voted down and even the hallowed institution of boys' high school athletics has had rough sledding financially.

Because local education agency budget resources are limited, many states have accepted the responsibility of developing legislation which provides most of the excess costs of educating handicapped students primarily through state reimbursement. Recently, new state legislation has also included mandatory right to education clauses and full service goal statements.

To expect state legislatures to pass good comprehensive special education legislation and to authorize the necessary dollars to support appropriate programs for the handicapped without clearly stating who these exceptional children are is, in my estimation, the height of naïveté. In addition, when legislation includes mandatory and full services elements, legislators do ask and expect a response to how many handicapped students there are in the state. For example, estimates of the number of children with learning disabilities which range from one to fifteen percent would never suffice in the eyes of the legislators. Why should we expect anything different? How could legislators be responsible to taxpayers in authorizing funding for special education programs for such a wide range of incidence estimate? The cost could be x or fifteen times x. There just isn't that much flexibility in state budgets.

Reality must be faced not only at the state legislature level but also at the federal level. Public Law 94-142, the Education for All Handicapped Children Act, indeed a landmark piece of legislation, clearly sets limits. Under that law no state may count more than twelve percent of the number of all children aged five to seventeen as handicapped for purposes of receiving federal funds. In addition, no more than one-sixth of that twelve percent may be counted as children with learning disabilities. This last statement, I'm sure, reflects the concern of Congress for the possibility of unlimited numbers of youngsters being viewed as handicapped. Public Law 94-142 also requires the reporting of numbers of handicapped students by *handicapping condition* to the federal government twice a year. In addition, the procedural safeguards or right to due process sections in this law seem to me to clearly indicate that euphemisms such as a "special need" or a "little problem" are not going to be tolerated. Identification procedures, evaluation processes, and educational placement decisions are all subject to due process procedures. These due process requirements must include provisions that allow for: (a) examination of all relevant records; (b) independent evaluations, written prior notice for any change in school program; (c) opportunity to present complaints and have an impartial due process hearing; (d) right to be accompanied by counsel and expert witness; (e) right to cross-examine, present evidence, and compel attendance of witnesses at a hearing, etc.

As difficult as all of this may seem operationally, I, for one, welcome the challenge. It translates into accountability. We, as special educators, must clearly state for whom we are primarily responsible, get about the business of providing appropriate special education options, and demonstrate our intent and efficacy in the form of *individual* child plans and documentation of progress.

HOW CAN A STATE EDUCATION AGENCY BEST MEET ITS RESPONSIBILITIES IN IDENTIFICATION OF THE HANDICAPPED?

Special educators generally agree that identification of the handicapped is a complex and multidimensional task. Procedures and instruments available to us are just not as valid as we would like. We also recognize that our professional skills and competencies vary widely. Most important certainly is the realization that children do not come in neat, well-ordered packages of strengths and weaknesses.

For these reasons, state education agencies must select mechanisms to be used in the identification of handicapped children that will meet the intents of their individual state legislatures and yet allow room for professional judgment and review. There are a number of mechanisms typically available to state education agencies; i.e., laws or statutes, rules or regulations, standards, guidelines, general best practice statements, position or concept papers, etc. Public school educators have no choice but to meet the letter and intent of a law or statute. Rules or regulations and standards generally have the force and effect of law. Guidelines, general best practice statements, and position or concept papers are generally seen as recommendations from the state education agency which local school districts and intermediate units may choose to adopt as policy within their own agencies.

The *Code of Iowa* (1975) states that "children requiring special education means persons under twenty-one years of age, including children under five years of age, who are handicapped in obtaining an education because of physical, mental, emotional, communication, or learning disabilities or who are chronically disruptive, as defined by the rules of the department of public instruction" [section 281.2].

Thus, the law simply contains a list of handicaps and directs our state education agency to define the handicaps in rules of special education. As with most definitions, these statements are two and three paragraphs in length and define the handicapping condition conceptually but not operationally.

For example, *communication disability* is defined in the 1974 rules as the inclusive term denoting deficits in language, voice, fluency, articulation, and hearing. Impairment in articulation is defined as "defective production of phonemes which interferes with ready intelligibility of speech" [p. 3]. Most would agree that this statement does conceptually define impairment in articulation. However, to operationally define an impairment in articulation that constitutes a handicap is much more complex. Questions such as the following would have to be answered:

1. How many errors are there in phoneme production?
2. What kind of errors?
3. How frequently do those phonemes appear in the vocabulary needed at the chronological age of the child?
4. When is the child's speech readily intelligible?
5. What if one teacher can understand the child and another cannot?

Developing an operational definition of mental retardation has long plagued and eluded us. Iowa's rules, as do those of most of the other states, speak to significant deficits in adaptive behavior and sub-average general intellectual functioning. Sub-average general intellectual functioning can be defined operationally and arbitrarily by some score on an individual test of general intelligence. However, defining maladaptive behavior operationally is extremely complex—although the work of Jane Mercer (1973) offers us hope in this area.

The 1974 rules also require the "compilation or acquisition of a comprehensive educational evaluation for each pupil which includes recent evaluations of vision, hearing, language and speech, intellect, social functioning, academic status, health history, and other elements deemed appropriate by the diagnostic-educational team [p. 3]. Thus, in Iowa's rules, we define the handicapping conditions conceptually and specify the areas of evaluation necessary to make a determination of eligibility for services under the rubric of special education. The rules do not generally contain arbitrary criteria statements that operational definitions must contain to be useful.

It seems to me that operational definitions coming from a state education agency are best kept in guideline or recommendation format. If the necessary arbitrary criteria statements were in rules, they would have the force of law and leave little room for professional judgments. Just as importantly, guidelines or recommendations can be modified more quickly than laws or rules as we acquire more accurate information through research in clinical settings and in the schools.

The field of learning disabilities as a part of special education has received its fair share of criticism for not stating clearly how one determines a child is handicapped. Since learning disabilities is my direct responsibility in our state education agency, let me use it as an example of what I believe belongs in laws, rules, and recommendations. Our law simply lists learning disabilities as a handicap. It is defined conceptually in our 1974 rules as

> the inclusive term denoting deficiencies which inhibit a pupil's ability to learn efficiently in keeping with his potential by the instructional approaches presented in the usual curriculum and require special education programs and services for educational progress.
>
> These deficiencies occur in the acquisition of learning skills and processes or language skills and processes, including but not limited to the ability to read, write, spell or arithmetically reason and calculate. These deficiencies may also be manifested in an inability to receive, organize, or express information relevant to school functioning.
>
> The deficiencies displayed by pupils with learning disabilities are not primarily due to sensory deprivation, mental disabilities, emotional disabilities, or a different language spoken in the home [p. 3].

You will remember that the areas of evaluation for the determination of eligibility and service in our special education programs are specified in rules also. The operational criteria that I have developed for identification of students with learning disabilities (1976) combine the rule required areas of evaluation with the concepts in the definition statement.

IOWA'S RECOMMENDED OPERATIONAL CRITERIA
FOR IDENTIFICATION OF STUDENTS
WITH LEARNING DISABILITIES

Sensory Criteria

1. Hearing Sensitivity
   Hearing sensitivity must be within normal limits after correction. However, students who may be experiencing a temporary loss or whose loss is noneducationally relevant; i.e., high-frequency losses above the speech range, should not automatically be excluded.
2. Visual Acuity
   Visual acuity must be within normal limits after correction; i.e., acuity better than 20/70.

Intellectual Criteria

Students whose primary handicapping condition is due to learning disabilities must score above the minus one standard deviation on a *major* instrument that is recognized as a valid measure of intellectual functioning. When placement in a special class or assignment to a resource room is being considered, the student must have been administered an individual or series of individual intelligence tests which are taken into consideration in making a written statement concerning the student's overall intellectual potential.

Occasionally, there is reason to suspect the test results are not true indices of a particular student's ability. In these cases, other data supporting the professional judgment that intellectual potential is above minus one standard deviation must be submitted in written form.

Mental Health Criteria

Students with learning problems primarily due to emotional disabilities are not eligible for services on the basis of learning disabilities. Although this differentiation is primarily one of professional judgment at this time, the staffing team should consider each student's behavior in the following areas:

1. Behavior problems apparent in social relationships including peer relationships, student-teacher relationships, student-parent relationships and student-sibling relationships.
2. Behavior problems apparent in various settings including the regular classroom(s), playground, study hall and other unstructured time, special subject areas such as music and art, the home and community.

Students with learning disabilities, however, may evidence behaviors which are characteristic of social-emotional problems. They may often miss or confuse nonverbal cues in the behavior of others and have little understanding of subtle language used in puns, slang expressions, etc. They may not be able to attend to tasks in group settings. As the student with learning disabilities grows older, particularly if he has been undiagnosed and unserved, he/she often will have a less than adequate self-concept and be difficult to motivate.

Academic Discrepancy

1. The extent of a student's academic deficiency is determined by his performance on individual or group standardized tests. To satisfy the academic discrepancy criteria, a child must be significantly under-achieving in one or more of the following basic skill areas: preacademic (readiness skills), reading, spelling, written expression, math, by the following amounts when first identified:
   a. Preschool—by performance on standardized readiness measures of minus 1 standard deviat'on.
   b. First Grade—by performance on standardized readiness measures or appropriate achievement measures of minus 1 standard deviation.
   c. Second Grade—by one grade level.
   d. Third and Fourth Grade—by 1 1/2 grade levels.
   e. Fifth and Sixth Grade—by at least 2 grade levels.
   f. Seventh and Eighth Grade—by at least 3 grade levels.
   g. Ninth Grade and beyond—by at least 4 grade levels.
2. The child's achievement scores may not be viewed apart from his estimated intellectual capability. The criteria for underachievement given above must be discrepant from the student's expected performance. That is, his/her relative position in the distribution of achievement scores should be reliably lower than his/her relative position in the distribution of intelligence scores than can be accounted for by other factors in his environment.
3. The amount of underachievement may be less as students participate in a learning disabilities program, begin to make academic growth, and eventually reach a stage of maintenance. Consideration of this will help to determine movement along the continuum of service options and assist in targeting appropriate dismissals from special education learning disabilities programs.

Educational History

When an academic discrepancy is identified, it is important to determine if that discrepancy is the result of an extended absence without the provision of a school program, frequent moving, inadequate instruction, a non-English-speaking home, or other external factors. Parent interview and review of relevant school records are useful information gathering techniques. Remedial reading or other general education alternatives may be the most appropriate interventions in these cases, as well as special education consultative support for the student's classroom or content teacher(s). However, a pupil who satisfied all other criteria should not be excluded from services on the basis of learning disabilities merely because he/she comes from an economically impoverished or culturally different home, or one in which support for the school may be lacking.

Learning Skills and Processes or Language Skills and Processes

The assessment of information processing abilities is achieved by instruments which purport to measure modality preferences, perceptual skills (e.g., closure, discrimination, etc.), memory functions, and levels of meaningfulness. The assessment of the linguistic system is achieved through the use of measures of receptive and expressive semantics, syntax, and morphology.

Use of instruments which purport to measure information processing abilities must be coupled with professional judgment. Most of these standardized instruments are still in developmental stages. Persons knowledgeable in learning disabilities will also be able to make clinical judgments of information processing by observation of how the child deals with the task demands of other instruments and through observation of the student in the school setting.

Data in these areas based on observations, standardized instruments, surveys, or clinical judgments extrapolated from instruments primarily designed to assess other variables should be documented in written form.

Other Characteristics

Other characteristics are frequently associated with the learning disabled, such as attention problems, high distractibility, and difficulty in generalizing from past experiences and drawing conclusions. Observations of these behaviors, if used in determining identification, must also be entered in written form indicating on what basis the clinical judgments have been made.

Assessment for Planning Individual Programs for Students with Learning Disabilities

Assessment of instructional needs is accomplished to acquire the necessary information to develop an appropriate comprehensive educational plan for the student with learning disabilities. Although some of this information is collected by the staffing team as part of the identification process, additional information is necessary for instructional purposes. There should be an analysis of the learner in his environment which includes: (a) teacher and parent interview, (b) direct observation in the classroom in a variety of activities, (c) review of relevant school records.

Assessment of specific educational needs should consider: (a) the teacher's written report of the student's specific strengths and weaknesses in the academic and behavioral areas, (b) behavioral checklists completed by those who currently work with the students, (c) criterion-referenced tests, (d) error analysis of the individual student's work, and (e) diagnostic teaching. This type of assessment for instructional purposes should be ongoing and provide the relevant data for follow-up and yearly re-evaluation.

You will note that these suggestions indicate that students with learning disabilities must score above the minus one standard deviation on a major instrument that is recognized as a valid measure of intellectual functioning. If this statement were in a rule which had the effect of law, it would legally prevent the student who scored slightly less than that from eligibility for special educational instructional programs on the basis of learning disabilities. Or if a student did not quite meet the academic discrepancy criteria, although he/she met all other criteria, it would be necessary to wait until the academic performance became worse for he/she to become eligible. Obviously, none of us would consider this reasonable practice.

However, there is a situation in which it might be necessary to put the arbitrary criteria of operational definition in rule procedure. That situation could exist when the financial support for programs for handicapped students was adequate enough to cause districts to overidentify for fiscal purposes only.

For example, in our state handicapped students are assigned a weighted per pupil index to generate the funds necessary to provide them appropriate programs and services. This weighting is determined by the degree of special education intervention necessary to meet the special needs of each handicapped student. That is, children who need resource teaching programs are assigned a weighting of 1.8. The 1.0 of that weighting is retained by general education to support the student in the general education program and the .8 is used to provide the resource teaching program. Children who require a special class with an integration model are also assigned a weighting of 1.8 but the greater portion of the monies generated go to support the special class with integration. Children for whom the least restrictive alternative is a self-contained special class are assigned a weighted per pupil index of 2.2. Students who are severely/profoundly handicapped can be assigned a weighted per pupil index of 4.4. The maximum teacher-pupil ratio ranges by rule from 1:18 in the resource teaching programs to 1:5 in the special classes for youngsters who have severe and profound handi-caps. To this concept add the new federal plan of a set dollar amount per handicapped child, up to 12 percent of students ages 5 through 17, and "headhunting" could occur. This could be particularly true if the federal and state reimbursements for handicapped students were to go directly to the general fund of local school districts.

However, this kind of abuse need not occur. State education agen-cies are charged with the responsibility for monitoring the expenditure of funds as well as the generation of those funds. Hopefully, special educators will not be party to abuses of what we have fought so long and hard to obtain; that is, appropriate programs and services with a sound financial base for children who are handicapped in obtaining an education.

Another major use of operational definitions is to help local and intermediate education agencies to set priorities in service to handi-capped students. Of course, our goal is full services for all handicapped, but it seems clear that there can be no excuse for not serving the out-of-school and most severely handicapped in each disability area first. Operational criteria can be used to help make decisions regarding com-parative severity. If our fiscal resources were unlimited, this priority setting would not be necessary. Unfortunately, that is not the case.

In summary, we can reach full services goals for the handicapped if we state clearly for whom we are primarily responsible, use our fiscal and personnel resources efficiently, and be held accountable to demon-strate the efficacy of our programs and services.

REFERENCES

Bradley, C. *Recommended operational criteria for identification of students with learning disabilities.* Des Moines, Iowa: Department of Public Instruction, 1976.

Code of Iowa (Vol. 1, chap. 281), 1975.

Gillespie, P., Miller, T., & Fielder, V. Legislative definitions of learning disabilities: Roadblocks to effective service. *Journal of Learning Dis-abilities,* 1975, 8, (10), 61-67.

Mercer, J. R. *Labeling the mentally retarded.* Berkeley: University of Cali-fornia Press, 1973.

Public Law 94-142, Education for All Handicapped Children Act of 1975.

Rules of Special Education, State of Iowa, Department of Public Instruction, Des Moines, Iowa, 1974.

9
Competency-Based Special Education Personnel Preparation

A. Edward Blackhurst

A. Edward Blackhurst is currently professor and chairman of the Department of Special Education at the University of Kentucky. His previous professional experiences include that of a teacher of educable mentally retarded children and principal of a school for the mentally retarded, and co-director and director of a regional special education instructional materials center during which he directed a project to develop a prototype competency-based, inservice training program for administrators of special education resource centers.

Dr. Blackhurst received a B.S. degree in general psychology from the Pennsylvania State University in 1960. Graduate study in special education led to the M.Ed. degree in 1964 and Ph.D. in 1966 from the University of Pittsburgh. Dr. Blackhurst's current research interests are in the area of special education personnel preparation, with a particular emphasis on competency-based instruction. A selected bibliography of his work appears on page 182.

One of the most significant forces that is affecting the preparation of special education personnel at the present time is the emphasis that is being placed upon competency-based instruction (CBI). Saettler (1974) reported the results of a study that found that 17 states had incorporated CBI into their certification regulations, 14 others were actively studying this possibility, and two-thirds of the institutions of higher education surveyed had either adopted this approach or were planning to do so. The impetus for this movement has come from increased demands for accountability by funding and regulatory agencies coupled with professional concerns regarding the need for improving the quality of our personnel preparation efforts.

In many cases in which CBI has been mandated by regulatory agencies, considerable controversy and opposition have developed. For example, when the New York State Board of Regents mandated that special education certification programs be competency-based (Gazzetta, 1974), strong union opposition was registered in the New York State United Teachers CBTE Position and Guidelines (1974) statement. Others (e.g., Hirsch, 1975) have criticized CBI on the basis of theoretical considerations.

Regardless of the pros and cons of the arguments, and their validity, the fact of the matter is that CBI is with us. It has been my recent experience that there are numerous differences of opinion, some confusion, and considerable frustration among many persons who are in the process of developing CBI programs.

Since 1970, my colleagues and I at the University of Kentucky have been attempting to revise the special education curricula into CBI formats. The purpose of this chapter is to present the perspectives that I have developed concerning CBI as a result of these six years of experience. Over the six-year period, my attitudes and approach to CBI have gone from a rather narrow and rigid position to one that I believe is more moderate, practical, rational, and realistic. I believe that the concepts that will be presented here are reasonable and can be generalized to any type of competency-based instructional development effort, including preservice, inservice training, and child instruction. Hopefully, sufficient information will be provided in these perspectives to enable readers to directly apply the concepts, if they so desire.

The chapter is organized to first present some of my biases in order to provide a frame of reference for the reader. The characteristics of a rational CBI program will then be described, followed by a model that can be used to guide CBI development activities. Finally, each element of the program development model will be discussed with examples to illustrate the application of principles that are presented.

PERSONAL BIASES ABOUT CBI

I became interested in CBI in a somewhat accidental manner. In attempting to develop a noncategorical special education methods course (Blackhurst, Cross, Nelson, & Tawney, 1973), my colleagues and I discovered that the course approximated a number of the characteristics that were emerging in the relatively new literature on CBI. Consequently, we began to explore this literature in depth and examine other training programs that were moving in this direction. At the same time we began to revise many elements of our curriculum—undergraduate through doctorate.

Although we are far from finished with this task, we have formally and informally experimented with a number of approaches and engaged in a lot of trial-and-error behavior. As a result of these activities, I have developed a number of biases about CBI:

1. I believe that CBI can be an important vehicle for improving the quality of special education personnel preparation programs.

2. As described in the literature, CBI programming is deceptively simple on first study. It is difficult and time-consuming to implement. In fact, it may take years, or decades, to develop programs that fully meet the criteria described in the literature. Consequently, our efforts over the near future should be viewed as approximations to these criteria.

3. The state of our knowledge is such that we don't have all of the answers to all of the questions that can be raised related to CBI. We need to use our best professional judgment and common sense in response to these questions.

4. There are numerous institutional constraints that militate against the development of "ideal" CBI programs. For example, it is difficult to make time variable in a university that is on the semester or quarter system. Similarly, scheduling units of instruction, or modules, presents problems when scheduling systems are set up on traditional systems that conform most closely to the three-credit course. It becomes necessary, therefore, to accommodate to the administrative system that is in operation.

5. The potentially most disruptive forces that are impinging upon the CBI movement are its "casual acquaintances." These are persons who are both its supporters and its critics. For example, I believe that many of the critics are responding to this approach on the basis of erroneous assumptions about what CBI is and

how it can be implemented, or strictly on the basis of theoretical arguments against the theoretical positions that favor CBI in the literature. A good example of this type of criticism is provided by Hirsch (1975), who obviously has made numerous unwarranted assumptions in attacking CBI on theoretical grounds.

Providing fuel for these critics are those "casual acquaintances" who support the approach, yet also have erroneous assumptions about what CBI is. These include the people who may have read one or two handbooks on CBI and then equate it with auto-instructional modules. One person with whom I talked recently said, "If you can say it, you can write it down. If you can write it down, students can read it. If students can read it, there is no need for the instructor to interact with students except, perhaps, to evaluate their performance." To my way of thinking, this attitude, in which the instructor has little personal contact with the students or is fixated on this type of impersonal approach can be just as detrimental to the advancement of CBI as the critics—if not more so.

6. Finally, I believe that CBI is here to stay in some form or another. Demands for accountability by consumers, taxpayers, legislators, regulating agencies, and funding agencies are accelerating and will continue to require that those who are preparing special education personnel provide increasingly more evidence regarding the effectiveness of their preparation programs.

CHARACTERISTICS OF A RATIONAL CBI PROGRAM

Given the fact, then, that we do not have sufficient human and fiscal resources or the extent of knowledge required to fully implement CBI programs in an ideal fashion, it is my opinion that we need to develop an approach to this topic that is moderate, practical, and rational in nature.

The characteristics that I would propose for a rational CBI program differ from the ideal characteristics suggested in the literature (Arends, Masla, & Weber, 1971; Nagel & Richman, 1972; Houston & Howsam, 1973) only in the respect that they are qualified, based upon the perspectives in the previous section.

Before listing these characteristics, it is important to note that CBI is viewed as an instructional delivery system. It is not a theory of learning, as has been suggested by some. As a method for organizing and delivering instruction, it can accommodate to virtually any theory of learning subscribed to by the person employing it. My colleagues and I have employed CBI delivery systems that have incorporated assumptions about the ways in which students learn based upon subsumption learning theory, field theory, inductive and deductive theories, discovery learning, behavior theory, and other learning theories. The point, here, is that the flexibility of a CBI program is limited only by the imagination and creativity of the instructional designer.

With this in mind, I would list the characteristics of a rational CBI program as follows:

1. Competencies are publicly stated. Although we lack considerable information related to the validity of many competencies for many types of special education professions, educators should at least be able to specify those competencies that they believe to be important for the program under consideration, given the present state of the art. As new knowledge becomes available, these should then be subject to revision.

   A rational program will probably not have long lists of hundreds and hundreds of competencies. The problem of evaluating these would be overwhelming. Competencies should represent higher order behaviors, and should be those that are critical for successful performance. An example will be provided later in the chapter to illustrate this point.

2. Objectives are specified as much as possible in behavioral terms. There are five types of objectives that could be included. These are cognitive, performance, affective, consequential, and experiential.

   Cognitive objectives relate to competencies requiring knowledge, such as being able to describe several methods for teaching reading. Performance objectives are those associated with the learner's ability to do something, such as administer, score, and interpret an informal reading inventory. Affective objectives are those involving attitudes, such as a commitment to the use of informal diagnostic techniques in the classroom. Experiential objectives are related to activities for which we may not be able to specify an outcome, yet are considered important experiences for students. This would include such things as observations, home visitations, and informal interaction with exceptional children. Consequential objectives are probably the most important and those that are most frequently omitted from teacher preparation programs. These are objectives related to change in child performance which is a direct result of activities of the students. An example of this would be when a student who has been taught to teach developmental reading then applies these techniques so that a child improves in reading skills. In my opinion, this is the ultimate criterion in evaluating the effectiveness of a teacher preparation program.

3. Criteria for assessing competency are specified and made available to students. This is perhaps the most difficult part of CBI

programming. We obviously have many competencies for which it is extremely difficult, if not impossible, to specify criteria, given our present state of knowledge. This does not mean, however, that these competencies should be overlooked. What we need to do is to acknowledge our inability to specify fully objective criteria and indicate that the instructor's best professional judgment will be used as the criterion. Granted, this is subjective; however, we should not back away from it. After all, instructors supposedly have the training, experience, intelligence, and sensitivity to make this type of judgment. The critical aspects of this are that instructors are able to explain the basis of their judgment to students, provide them with direction for correction of deficiencies, and then work toward generating new knowledge that will gradually move this type of evaluation from subjective to more objective bases.

4. Alternative learning activities and multiple entry points are available to individualize the program for students, when possible. This is an ideal that is difficult to implement because of the institutional and resource constraints mentioned earlier. I advocate, therefore, the development of one viable learning activity for each competency, while providing students with the option of negotiating with the instructor for other alternatives if it is feasible to do so. In addition, if it is possible for students to demonstrate competence on any activity, they should be provided with the opportunity to do so. Once these procedures have been established for the total program, that is the time to go back and attempt to develop an array of learning alternatives for each competency.

5. Where possible, time is variable and achievement is constant. Again, from a theoretical standpoint, this is ideal but unrealistic —particularly if the program is being implemented at a college that is on the semester or quarter system. Implementation would require that students be given incomplete grades if they did not meet criteria. This creates tremendous strains on faculty members who must interrupt their efforts in the new semester to work with those who should have finished their responsibilities during the previous term. The approach that I have found to be successful here is to hold the semester time-frame constant while making time variable within the semester. Thus, some of the flexibility is maintained, although in a limited fashion.

6. Students are held accountable for performance. Most authorities writing about CBI emphasize that the students are more accountable for achievement than in traditional educational programs. I believe that this is the case; however, I would also emphasize that instructors should be held accountable for pro-

gram design. If the program is poorly conceptualized or inappropriately implemented, it would be dishonest to stress student accountability when, in fact, the fault lies with the instructional designer or manager.

These, then, are the major characteristics that are descriptive of rational CBI programs. Perhaps one additional important characteristic should be noted here which will be discussed in more detail later in the chapter. Namely, that CBI programs need not be comprised totally of auto-instructional, self-contained modules. Auto-instructional modules are only one form of delivery. Others are also appropriate, and rational CBI programs include these.

One other major perspective that I have on CBI programming is that its characteristics are quite analogous to the diagnostic-prescriptive instructional model that most special educators support for working with exceptional children. That is, objectives and prerequisites are specified, students are assessed upon entry into the program, appropriate instruction is provided based upon this assessment, performance is evaluated, and students are recycled if they do not meet criteria. It seems to me that those who are involved in CBI programs are actually demonstrating the approach to instruction that their students are asked to apply to exceptional children. In one sense this is an example of "practice what you preach." (In some respects it is unfortunate that this approach was given the name *competency-based*. It would, perhaps, be more appealing to call it something such as *individual-based* instruction.)

A MODEL FOR CBI DEVELOPMENT

It has been my experience that there are often considerable disagreements, confusion, and trial-and-error behavior among those who are developing programs in CBI formats once a decision is made to move in this direction. Differing concepts, biases, and ideas emerge as a function of interest, commitment, prior knowledge, and varying books and articles that have been read by the developers. Some will turn immediately to the problem of revising the courses that they teach. Others will begin by searching for information from other sources that may have relevance. Most often, efforts are on an individual basis, with no overall plan for program development. This usually results in a program that is fragmented and uneven, with little internal consistency in approach or requirements. The consequence is often confusion and frustration on the part of both faculty and students.

In order to guard against this likelihood, it is wise to adopt a model that can be used to guide program development efforts. In this way, developers can be on the same wavelength with respect to the tasks

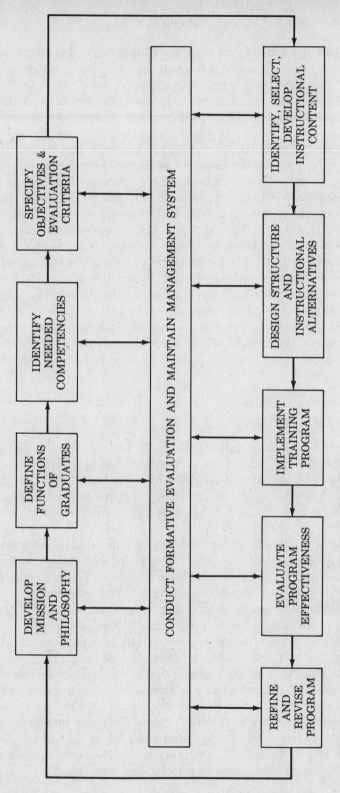

FIGURE 1: Model for CBI program development.

163

that need to be performed, the sequence of these, and their interrelationships. As a result of my involvement in two rather extensive CBI projects, I developed and used a model that I have found to be quite functional and generalizable to virtually any CBI project—whether for teacher education or instruction for children. This model is illustrated in Figure 1.

The entry point for the model is the element in the upper left-hand corner which deals with development of a mission and philosophy. The single-headed arrows then indicate the sequence of activities which should be followed in program development. The model illustrates that CBI development should be flexible and dynamic, as represented by the double-headed arrows. That is, based upon formative evaluation and experience with the system set up to manage program development, revisions can (and should) be made in the elements, as appropriate. Thus, new objectives could be added if an analysis of content indicates that critical objectives have been omitted during the previous step.

Following are my perspectives on some of the activities that should be performed in each element of the model. Although these comments are made within the context of CBI development in a college or university training program, they are equally applicable for inservice or child instruction.

Mission Development

Many CBI developers do not pay sufficient attention to this aspect of their development efforts. Activities here should serve as the philosophical and conceptual underpinning for all other efforts. The mission statement should also serve as the basis for short- and long-range planning and as a guide for faculty members in the implementation of the mission.

Included in the mission should be a specification of the context in which the program operates, the responsibilities that the developers have accepted or been assigned, and the broad goals and specific administrative objectives. The objectives should reflect the commonalities that the particular program shares with other programs, identify its unique features, provide the basis for programmatic decision making, and include both product and process objectives to provide a specification of both what faculty members do and how they do it.

Note that the mission statement should deal with issues much broader than CBI. Major questions should be addressed here such as, "What position do we take on mainstreaming?" "What does noncategorical programming mean to us?" "How does our department view CBI?" Unless these and other questions are discussed and answered to the satisfaction of the faculty, program development activities are bound to be confusing and unsatisfactory to faculty members.

FUNCTION DEFINITION

Activities in this element of the model revolve around the process of defining the general roles and functions that must be performed by graduates of each training program that is offered. These are broad, general statements that will subsume the more specific competencies and objectives. For example, our project to specify competencies of administrators of special education resource centers (Blackhurst, Wright, & Ingram, 1974) identified 15 functions that these administrators should be able to perform if they are to be effective. These included such functions as organizing and managing center operations, selecting and managing personnel, managing fiscal resources, offering inservice training programs, and evaluating center effectiveness.

There are two major values to the identification of functions. First, it provides a broad frame of reference with respect to the direction that the training program should take. Second, it is somewhat easier to reach initial concensus among developers with respect to the general rather than the specific aspects of the program. Function definition can also provide considerable direction for development of the program structure and management system, as will be demonstrated later.

COMPETENCY IDENTIFICATION

Unfortunately, one of the most controversial aspects of CBI programming relates to the specification of competencies that are to be developed as a result of the training. This is due primarily to the fact that we do not have a great deal of evidence regarding the validity of many of the competencies included in various CBI programs. Although this lack of knowledge is a weakness, it is also one of the strengths of this type of training. Because competency statements are made public, we open ourselves for scrutiny and evaluation by our peers and by those to whom we are accountable. We can therefore capitalize on new knowledge, suggestions, and criticisms by revising the competency statements as new evidence becomes available. This assumes, of course, that the developers maintain an open and flexible stance with respect to program modification.

A question that is frequently raised about CBI relates to the definition of what is an acceptable competency statement. An examination of competency lists leads the reader to conclude that there are almost as many different ways to write competencies as there are developers. Some statements appear as phrases, others look more like behavioral objectives which include conditions, behavior, and evaluation criteria. Another problem area concerns the level of generality. Some competency lists include both very general and very specific statements.

In the final analysis, the form of the competency statement and the level of generality is dependent upon what makes sense to the developer.

In my work, I use two or three general rules of thumb as guidelines for writing competency statements: (a) they should be related to, and subsumed by, the general training functions defined in the second step of the model; (b) they should represent higher order behaviors; and (c) they should lend themselves to the development of a manageable program. If the statements are too specific, too many units of instruction will be required which will make the program difficult to manage. If they are too general, they will be too difficult to evaluate. An example might serve to illustrate. In our work to specify teaching and advising competencies for special education professors (Ingram & Blackhurst, 1975), 9 competencies were identified as being critical to the function of advising special education college students. These were stated as follows:

A special education professor, in advising students, must be able to
1. recruit special education students;
2. describe and discuss special education career opportunities;
3. schedule advising sessions;
4. specify regulations, policies, and procedures related to academic programs in special education;
5. identify and utilize resources needed to advise students;
6. plan programs of study with students;
7. provide assistance in implementing and monitoring student programs;
8. communicate with students on a personal level;
9. assist students in the solution of problems.

As a result of the research that identified these competencies, 43 different statements related to students advising were generated. However, it was possible to subsume all of these under the above-mentioned statements. With respect to the three criteria mentioned earlier, these 9 statements (a) were related to the function of student advising; (b) represented higher order behavior, and (c) lent themselves to the development of a manageable program. It was more feasible for us to develop instruction and practice around these 9 statements than around the 43 statements that were identified, although experiences related to all 43 were imbedded in the instructional program.

From my perspective, this more general view of competency statements is a rational one. I get dismayed when I see lists comprised of literally hundreds of competency statements. To my way of thinking, we need to keep the number of statements smaller so that the program is more manageable and so that we can concentrate on insuring that students have mastered those that appear to be most critical for effective performance. Two graduate programs with which I am familiar each have approximately 35 competencies, which seems to be a functional number in both cases.

I do not want to give the impression that the longer lists are ignored. On the contrary, they are included, but in a different fashion. I like to list these more specific statements as tasks and differentiate them from the competencies. By differentiating them and including the functions, a hierarchy of statements can be developed in decreasing order of generality. To illustrate, one of my doctoral advisees (Redden, 1976) recently completed research to identify competencies that elementary teachers need to mainstream handicapped children. The statements were arranged in a hierarchy such as the following excerpt:

FUNCTION 1.0.0 Development of Orientation Strategies for Mainstream Entry

COMPETENCY 1.1.0 *Participate in school-wide planning for mainstreaming activities.*

TASKS:

1.1.1 Work with principal to develop administrative arrangements for effective transition to mainstreaming.

1.1.2 Negotiate with school staff for placement and grouping of students.

1.1.3 Participate in orientation program for regular and special students.

1.1.4 Develop strategies to facilitate the transition of the special student into the regular class.

It should be evident that each of these tasks is important; however, the general competency statement that subsumes these is representative of higher order behavior that is critical for successful performance. The relevance of this type of arrangement will become more evident in the next section.

While on the topic of competencies, I would like to provide a few perspectives on procedures for identifying competencies. Houston, Dodl, and Weber (1973) described six different procedures for identifying competencies. These include translation of existing courses and programs, task analysis, assessment of needs of students in the training program, analysis of needs of school learners, generation from a theoretical base, and cluster analysis. All of these procedures rely primarily upon the use of logic and professional judgment. Shores, Cegelka, and Nelson (1973) criticized procedures for identifying competencies that rely heavily on opinion and subjective judgment. These authors called for greater use of empirical methodologies for competency identification. They made a special plea for procedures that use direct observation to identify those competencies that are valid. Although their position is logical and theoretically defensible, it is obvious that such an approach would present significant logistical problems and be quite expensive and time-consuming to implement.

A competency identification technique that begins to accommodate to some of the concerns of those who recommend more objective procedures is the Critical Incident Technique which was developed by Flanagan (1962). I have been associated with three research projects that have employed this technique (Blackhurst, Wright, & Ingram, 1974); Ingram & Blackhurst, 1975; Redden, 1976), and believe that it has considerable merit.

The Critical Incident Technique is used to obtain descriptions of effective and ineffective behaviors of people who are performing a given job. Persons in a position to observe job performance are asked to report on specific observable incidents that have had either a positive or negative influence. Reporters describe the antecedents that lead up to the incident, the behavior or action that occurred, and the consequence of that behavior that led the observer to conclude that it was either effective or ineffective. The incidents are then translated into succinct statements, redundencies eliminated, and then categorized in much the same way as the functions, competencies, and tasks described earlier. Panels of judges are then used to provide at least content validation of the statements.

The weakness of this technique is that the data are collected on a retrospective basis. There is also the possible danger of contamination by either memory lapses, personal biases, and/or errors in interpretation. Nevertheless, since the data are based upon direct observation and since large numbers of incidents are collected and a validation process is used, the technique probably has greater validity than those procedures that rely solely on personal opinion. It has been my experience that a combination of the above approaches is most functional.

One other major bias that I have concerning competency identification is that we should capitalize on the work of others, as opposed to starting from scratch in identifying competencies. A number of projects in which considerable efforts have been expended to identify competencies in various areas of special education provide useful information to those who are developing CBI programs. They include projects to identify competencies of teachers of the educable mentally retarded (Rotberg, 1968); nurses and attendants in institutions for the retarded (Jacobs, Nichols, & Larsen, 1969; Larsen, Nichols, & Jacobs, 1969); teachers of the secondary level educable mentally retarded (Brolin & Thomas, 1972); special education curriculum consultants (Altman & Meyen, 1974); special education supervisors (Harris & King, 1974); directors of special education (Anderson & Schipper, 1974); directors of special education resource centers (Blackhurst, Wright, & Ingram,

1974); special education professors (Ingram, 1974); clinical teachers (Schwartz & Oseroff, 1975); and classroom teachers involved in mainstreaming (Redden, 1976), to name a few. Dodl (1972) has also prepared an extensive catalog of teacher competencies.

It is obvious that these projects have considerable relevance for persons who may be developing CBI programs in these areas. It should be emphasized, however, that no competency list should be accepted at face value. Developers should examine these carefully within the framework of their philosophy, biases, and knowledge base and select those that appear to be valid for their purposes. It is also quite likely that omissions may have been made, which will require the addition of competencies. At any rate, CBI developers should remain flexible and willing to modify their competencies as new information becomes available. It is important to guard against "hardening of the competencies."

OBJECTIVES AND EVALUATION CRITERIA

Once competencies have been identified, the next set of activities relates to the specification of objectives and the criteria for evaluating these. Although sympathetic to Mager's (1962) suggestions for constructing instructional objectives to include conditions, behaviors, and criteria, I have found this system somewhat unwieldy. The approach that I have found to be most functional is to construct instructional objectives so that only the behavior is clearly specified. Conditions and evaluation criteria are then specified separately.

For example, a "Mager-type" objective might look like this:

> Given a project activity work breakdown structure and PERT chart which includes time estimates for each activity and time constraints, the director of a special education resource center will be able to develop a time schedule for completion of all activities that will include projected early and late start and finish dates for each activity, the amount of float in the schedule, the critical path, and no unfeasible time estimates.

This statement does convey the conditions, behaviors, and criteria for successful performance. However, the statement is so wordy that it tends to become confusing and loses its impact in conveying information to anyone except those who are prepared to really study it. I prefer to use an approach that is illustrated by the following:

> The director of a special education resource center will be able to develop a time schedule for completion of all center activities.

Such an objective only includes the behavior that is desired, yet it conveys quite clearly what this behavior is without imbedding it in a longer, more complex, sentence. It has been my experience that this approach is looked upon more favorably by students in the training program and by those who are unfamiliar with the program but who are interested in its objectives and purposes.

It should not be implied, however, that I advocate ignoring the conditions and criteria. Rather, I prefer to list these separately and in a fashion that is more explicit and understandable. For example, in the objective mentioned above, I would use a statement such as the following:

> In evaluating this objective, students will be given (a) an activity work breakdown structure representative of the activities that would be performed at a typical resource center during one fiscal year; (b) a PERT chart that shows the activities and events, their interrelationships and constraints; (c) the times for starting and finishing the project and at least one time constraint for an interim activity that must be finished or started no later than a given date; (d) a list of nonworking days during the year; and (e) access to the ICES computer-based planning and scheduling system.
>
> They will be required to produce an activity and event schedule that includes the following: (a) a list of the early and late starts and finishes for each activity if the project is to remain on schedule; (b) the date at which each event is to occur; (c) the number of days of float for each activity in the schedule; (d) the critical path; and (e) no unfeasible times. The schedule that is produced must exactly correspond to the criterion schedule that was produced by the instructor using the same input data.

Although the statement is somewhat lengthy, it is my opinion that this writing approach is more explicit and understandable than one that tries to condense all of the information into a single sentence. Thus, the behavioral portion of the instructional objective is briefly stated while the conditions and criteria for evaluation are spelled out in the kind of detail that they deserve.

If this conceptualization of objectives and evaluation criteria is acceptable, then the value of the hierarchical organization of functions, competencies, and tasks which was described in the previous section becomes more apparent. That is, the tasks that have been previously identified become the objectives of the training program, and a statement related to the conditions and evaluation criteria can then be developed for each of these.

Before leaving this topic, one additional point should be made. Since the competencies are representative of higher order behavior, performance related to any given competency may require more than acceptable performance on each of the objectives that it subsumes. This is the Gestaltist notion of the whole being greater than the sum of its parts. If this is the case, then care should be taken to include evaluation of the competency in addition to the evaluation of each objective. If this is not done, there is danger that the student may develop a series of splinter skills without being able to synthesize, interrelate, and integrate these into a meaningful whole.

As mentioned earlier, another problem related to the specification of competencies concerns the fact that many programs include only cognitive and performance objectives. Three other types of objectives should also be considered: affective, experiential, and consequence. Affective objectives relate to attitudes while experiential objectives refer to experiences for which it is almost impossible to predict the outcome (e.g., visitation to a home of an exceptional child, observation of a parent conference). Perhaps the most critical type of objective is the consequence objective. In this particular case, students are required to apply things that they have learned so that the consequence is positive behavior change on the part of an exceptional child.

Perhaps an example will serve to illustrate these different types of objectives and their relationships.

> In a unit on teaching reading to exceptional children, the student may learn about different methods of teaching reading (cognitive) and then observe each method being used (experiential). The student may then be required to demonstrate that he/she can utilize the methods appropriately (performance) in a simulated lesson. During an actual instructional sequence in which the student teaches a reading lesson so that the child learns the material that is presented (consequence), the student may demonstrate sensitivity to the needs of the child (affective) by adjusting the rate or method of presentation according to the responses of the child.

In evaluation, of course, it is desirable to be as objective as possible. However, because we lack sufficient knowledge to clearly specify objective and valid evaluation criteria in many areas, it is frequently necessary to specify that professional judgment of the instructor will be used as the evaluation criterion. This does not bother me as much as it used to. After all, if instructors have had appropriate education and experience, they should be able to employ their best professional judgment for evaluation purposes. When this is done, however, it is incumbent upon the instructors to provide students with explanations for their judgments and positive recommendations for student change when students do not meet their subjective criteria. At the same time, instructors should be attempting to elaborate on their subjective criteria so that they can continue to move in the direction of making these more objective as they gain more experience and collect more data as students progress through their program.

One of my colleagues (Tawney, 1972), has developed and field tested an interesting approach to evaluation of special education teaching behavior. I believe that this has merit for evaluation of both student-teachers and practitioners. He wrestled with the problem of which competencies should be selected for evaluating teacher performance. When one considers the literally hundreds of specific behaviors that could be considered when taking various levels of instruction and subject matter into account, the problem is staggering. After considerable deliberation and experimentation, he concluded that there appear to be three critical questions that should be explored that cut across all subject matter areas. First, does the teacher interact with the child in a humane manner? Second, does the child remain on task when directed to do so by the teacher? Third, does the child exhibit progress on increasingly more complex material over time?

It would seem that if the response to each of these questions was positive, evaluators could feel comfortable in stating that the teacher could, in fact, teach. This position, of course, assumes a number of prerequisite behaviors such as knowledge of subject matter areas, planning skills, classroom management techniques, and others. By incorporating Tawney's concepts with a number of these prerequisites, my colleagues have developed a system for evaluating student teaching performance and have used it on an experimental basis during the past year. Basically, this includes a specification of a number of competencies that are typical of student-teacher evaluation. In addition, we have adapted several of Tawney's observational systems so that direct observational data are taken on humane teacher behavior and on student performance. To date we are quite pleased with the results of this and the responses of both student teachers and their supervising teachers. In my opinion, evaluation systems such as this will eventually reach the point of refinement that will permit us to evaluate teaching behavior with a higher degree of specificity and validity.

Content Selection

Knowledge of potential instructional content for the training program has obviously had some impact on the activities in previous elements of the model. However, if developers are to be systematic about their efforts, they should carefully search for, select, and adapt appropriate instructional materials, texts, and audio-visual materials. It is my impression that portions of many training programs have been too heavily influenced by the available texts that are related to the topic being taught. Many instructors in traditional programs obtain new texts and then structure their courses around the content of these. The approach that I am recommending here deviates from this practice by having the content of the training program being dictated by the competencies and objectives. In this way, content of the training program is determined by the developers and not by the textbook publishing companies.

In addition to publishers' catalogs, there are a few good sources of information about training materials and their location (e.g., Berger et al., 1972; Kincaid, 1972; CEDAR Catalogs, 1972; Houston, 1973). However, these sources are incomplete. There is a real need for a national information system on the availability and location of training materials that are available for loan, rental, or purchase and on those that are in the process of being developed. Perhaps the National Instructional Materials Information System (NIMIS) that is being developed as part of the National Learning Resource System (Blackhurst, 1974b) will eventually meet this need. Perhaps the Learning Resource System could also work with federal agencies and commercial producers to disseminate training materials that have been developed under the auspices of federally funded projects. The new "Unbound Journal" series published by the Teacher Education Division of the Council for Exceptional Children may help to rectify this situation. What is needed, perhaps, is a system for storing and retrieving instructional modules that is modeled after the Instructional Objectives Exchange at the Center for the Study of Evaluation in Los Angeles. It is a constant disappointment to me to become aware of new materials such as those developed by the Center for Innovative Teaching of the Handicapped (*Directory of CITH Training Materials*, n.d.) and then to find that these are unavailable because the projects have no funds for duplication and dissemination.

Although there has been a significant increase in the number of special education training materials in recent years, training program personnel frequently are unable to locate materials that meet their needs. If this is the case, it then becomes necessary to develop one's own materials. Space does not permit an elaboration of techniques to follow in this type of activity. Several excellent resources are available, however, to guide these activities (e.g., Briggs, 1968, 1970; Baker & Schutz, 1971; Thiagarajan, Semmell, & Semmell, 1974; Davis, Alexander, & Yelon, 1974).

PROGRAM STRUCTURE

Earlier, it was mentioned that many people equate CBI with autoinstructional modules. This position is reinforced by handbooks that describe procedures for developing instructional modules (Arends, Masla, & Weber, 1971; Nagel & Richman, 1972; Houston, Hollis, Jones, Edwards, Pace, & White, 1972; Houston, Dodl, & Weber, 1973). These are useful resources for module development; however, they can leave the impression that CBI programs are built solely on self-contained modules. Further reinforcement for this idea is generated by discussions with CBI developers who talk frequently about "modules" that they are using or developing.

It should be emphasized that we are talking about *competency-based* instruction, not *module-based* instruction. The fact remains that the instructional module is a useful way to package and deliver instruction in competency-based programs. It should be emphasized, however, that modules do not need to be auto-instructional. The format and structure of the instructional delivery system should be dictated by the competencies, objectives, and content of the training program. In this way, modules can be lectures, practica, discussions, simulations, seminars, observations, as well as independent or auto-instructional materials.

Use of the term *module* in this context is just a useful way of communicating about a unit of instruction related to a specific competency. It implies that a rationale has been written, objectives and prerequisites have been developed, conditions and evaluation criteria have been specified, content has been identified or developed, alternative learning activities are available, and resources have been listed.

The structure for the delivery of instructional modules can be as varied as the imagination of the developer, within the administrative and physical constraints in which the program is being conducted. The modules in my project related to the inservice preparation of special education resource center directors are in the form of training manuals designed for independent use by the learners. On the other hand, all of the modules in our academic training program at the University of Kentucky are taught within the framework of a traditional course structure.

It is my guess that most colleges and universities will continue to be constrained by administrative considerations such as scheduling, grading practices, and requirements of the registrar's office so that CBI will, of necessity, be delivered through "courses." If this is the case, more universities will probably move to variable credit courses instead of trying to force-fit instruction into standard three-credit courses.

Using the model proposed here to guide program redesign, I have generally found that it is useful to organize courses around the *functions* that were identified. The courses are then composed of instructional modules that are related to the competencies subsumed by the functions. In our recent curriculum revision, for example, we generated new variable-credit courses around functions such as protecting the rights of the handicapped, use of prosthetics, managing the learning environment, providing special education professional services, and others. Very few of the modules in these courses are auto-instructional.

As mentioned previously, it is advisable to have alternative learning activities available to students in order to accommodate to particular styles and preferences for learning. This is desirable, but not always possible in the initial stages of development. Once one good alternative is available for each module (plus the option for individual student design), then it is appropriate to concentrate on the development of other alternatives. Space does not permit a discussion of alternatives such as computer-assisted instruction (Cartwright & Cartwright, 1973; Semmell, 1972), filmstrip-tape programs (*Directory of CITH Training Materials*, n.d.), gaming (Semmell & Baum, 1973), videotapes (Currie, 1976), microteaching (Shea & Whiteside, 1974), or other delivery systems such as multiplier-effect models (Meyen, 1969), dissemination/ change agent models (Anderson, Hodson, & Jones, 1975), use of satellites (Bramble & Ausness, 1976), and large-group, small-group, time-loaded, task-oriented training process models (Watts, 1974). All of these have been successfully applied in the delivery of training to special education personnel. An excellent source of information on various formats for instructional delivery in special education is the text by Thiagarajan, Semmell, and Semmell (1974). If efforts are devoted to the development of learning alternatives which utilize any form of media, it should be realized that these efforts are usually more costly and time-consuming than original projections.

A word of caution is called for before leaving this topic. This relates again to auto-instruction. After several experiences with this type of delivery system, I would advise users not to rely upon it as the sole methodology. If auto-instruction is used, supplement it with seminars so that students have the opportunity to question, discuss, and explore issues related to the content that they have learned independently. Most need and want the opportunity to interact with instructors.

Program Implementation and Management

The structure of the program and institutional constraints will usually dictate the procedures for implementation and management. Since these will most frequently be idiosyncratic to each training program, specific suggestions will not be given here. However, these are a few general principles that should be applied, regardless of the institutional setting. They were generated primarily as a result of negative experiences that I have encountered. Attention to them may help to preclude problems:

1. Develop a realistic plan and timetable for CBI development and implementation.
2. If a course is being changed to a CBI format, every effort should be made to have all necessary materials prepared prior to initiation of the program. It is difficult to conduct a program while continuing to develop materials.

3. Provide a thorough orientation for students and opportunities for additional discussion and dialogue as the program progresses.

4. Be consistent in management, implementation, and evaluation of the program. Students will become disgruntled if there is variance or ambiguity in interpretation of elements of the program.

5. Explain details of the program to administrators (e.g., deans) prior to program implementation—particularly if the new program represents significant departures from previous practice.

6. Develop the simplest possible management and monitoring system. Too much time and resources are often diverted from the instructional program for the maintenance of sophisticated management systems.

7. Provide sufficient inservice and dialogue time for faculty so that understanding and agreement are reached concerning the program. Strive for consistency in faculty interpretation of the program.

8. Be prepared to expend extra resources and "overtime"—particularly in the early phases of implementation.

9. Be sure that there is clear understanding of the respective responsibilities for the implementation of the program.

10. Try to remain flexible, open, and responsive to needed modifications.

Attention to these details will help to minimize problems that are frequently encountered in either developing a new program or in converting an existing one.

EVALUATION

Formative evaluation, in this context, refers to the evaluation of the products that are being developed for use in the training program, the processes used in developing these, and the procedures for delivering instruction to the students. The results of formative evaluations are used by the persons who are responsible for the instructional development and delivery to make revisions before the materials or procedures are finalized.

A very useful two-dimensional structure for the formative evaluation of instructional products is described by Sanders and Cunningham (1973). The first dimension relies on three sources of information: (a) internal information that is generated by an inspection of the instructional product or processes; (b) external information that is concerned with the effects of the program on its users; and (c) contextual information that refers to data related to the context in which the training products are used.

The second dimension of the structure relates to four categories of formative evaluation activities. These are: (a) Predevelopment Activities, such as needs assessment; (b) Evaluation of Objectives, including logical analysis and empirical validation; (c) Formative Interim Evaluation of the development process, content analysis, and unobtrusive measurement; and (d) Formative Product Evaluation including cost analysis, validation studies, and descriptive and goal-free analysis.

This structure appears to have considerable value for identifying the crucial variables to be studied during the development and experimental tryout of CBI programs. Procedures for conducting research on instructional products are also well specified by Baker and Schutz (1972).

The ultimate criterion for program evaluation, however, is the effectiveness of the graduates as determined through follow-up evaluation. This is an area that is in need of considerable research, which is logistically difficult, expensive, and time-consuming. In my opinion, regulatory and funding agencies that are requiring training programs to move toward CBI and account for their effectiveness should realize the cost of this type of evaluation and help to provide the resources necessary to produce valid evaluation data.

While on the topic of evaluation, I should add that the CBI movement opens a number of interesting avenues for research. As previously noted, a number of studies have been done related to competency identification. Other areas such as module effectiveness (Heller & Dale, 1976), student satisfaction (Wixson, 1975), use of alternate forms of media (Donaldson, 1974), and alternate instructional delivery systems (Renne & Blackhurst, 1976) also provide fruitful avenues of inquiry.

Parenthetically, in the area of investigating alternative delivery systems, it is interesting that researchers will be designing studies in which they hope that their results will fail to reject their null hypotheses. This is a departure from the overwhelming majority of intervention studies in which researchers are hopeful that "Method *A*" is superior to "Method *B*." In CBI, this is an important consideration. If we are to offer alternative learning activities to students, we must make sure that each is equally effective.

CONCLUDING COMMENTS

These, then, represent my perspectives on how to proceed in the development of competency-based special education personnel preparation programs. Implementation problems, and suggestions for dealing with these, are described in another publication (Blackhurst, 1974a). As mentioned earlier, the approach represented here is one that is functional and grounded in reality, according to my experience.

The final perspective that I would like to bring to this topic relates to my position concerning some of the issues raised by its critics. CBI has been characterized by some as being mechanistic, rigid, lock-step, nonresponsive to individual differences, narrow in scope, and concerned only with the development of technical skills. As such, it is viewed as a danger to humanistic education (Hirsch, 1975). Although I question some of the assumptions underlying many of these criticisms, the fact of the matter is that there could be some validity to them if developers are not sensitive to the issues and accommodate to them in their programs.

I believe that CBI could become a threat to humanistic education only if its basic premises and characteristics are violated by those who take the wrong approach in using it. Decision makers and evaluators can misuse the system because of basic misunderstandings of what it is and what its capabilities are, given our existing state of knowledge.

I don't necessarily believe that CBI is a panacea for all of the problems that we face in special education personnel preparation. It does have some very attractive features for those who apply its principles in a *rational* fashion. When approached rationally, CBI does provide framework for delivering instruction that is flexible enough to accommodate to issues of technical competence, humanism, and accountability.

If we are truly concerned with the ways in which children are taught, then we should make every effort to identify the best practices that "humanists," "behaviorists," "CBI developers," and persons with other theoretical persuasions have to offer. These practices should then be incorporated into our teacher education curricula, to insure that our students develop the qualities that we have identified as important for effective teaching. This is not an *either-or* situation. We need to prepare competent graduates who can teach exceptional children in a humanistic fashion, and be accountable for our efforts. To argue that one approach is better or worse than any other is polarizing to our profession and nonproductive. We could better spend our time in capitalizing on the strengths of different approaches, working toward overcoming the weaknesses, and devoting our best efforts to the process of preparing better special educators.

REFERENCES

Altman, R., & Meyen, E. L. Some observations on competency based instruction. *Exceptional Children,* 1974, 40, 260-65.

Anderson, D. R., Hodson, G. D., & Jones, W. G. *Instructional programming for the handicapped student.* Springfield: Charles C Thomas, 1975.

Anderson, E. B., & Schipper, W. V. *Functions/tasks of state directors of special education.* Washington, D.C.: National Association of State Directors of Special Education, 1974.

Arends, R. L., Masla, J. A., & Weber, W. A. *Handbook for the development of instructional modules in competency-based teacher education programs.* Buffalo: Center for the Study of Teaching, 1971.

Baker, R. L., & Schutz, R. E. (Eds.). *Instructional product development.* New York: Van Nostrand Reinhold, 1971.

Baker, R. L., & Schutz, R. E. (Eds.). *Instructional product research.* New York: Van Nostrand Reinhold, 1972.

Berger, A. G. et al. *Annotated listing of competency-based modules.* Coral Gables: Florida Center for Teaching Training Materials, University of Miami, 1972.

Blackhurst, A. E. Some practical considerations in implementing competency-based special education training programs. In J. J. Creamer & J. T. Gilmore (Eds.), *Design for competence based education in special education.* Syracuse: Division of Special Education and Rehabilitation, Syracuse University, 1974, 34-71. (a)

Blackhurst, A. E. The learning resource center program—Blueprint for the future. *TEACHING Exceptional Children,* 1974, 6, 216-17. (b)

Blackhurst, A. E., Cross, D. P., Nelson, C. M., & Tawney, J. W. Approximating non-categorical teacher education. *Exceptional Children,* 1973, 39, 284-88.

Blackhurst, A. E., Wright, W. S., & Ingram, C. F. *Competency specifications for directors of special education resource centers.* Washington: Bureau of Education for the Handicapped, U.S. Office of Education Project OEG-0-72-4305(603), 1974.

Bramble, W. J., & Ausness, C. Appalachia's on the beam. *American Education,* 1976, 12, 21-25.

Briggs, L. J. *Sequencing of instruction in relation to hierarchies of competence.* Pittsburgh: American Institutes for Research, 1968.

Briggs, L. J. *Handbook of procedures for the design of instruction.* Pittsburgh: American Institutes for Research, 1970.

Brolin, D., & Thomas, B. *Preparing teachers of secondary level educable mentally retarded: A new model.* Washington: U.S. Office of Education Project OEG-0-4814(603), 1972.

Cartwright, G. P., & Cartwright, C. A. Early identification of handicapped children: A CAI course. *Journal of Teacher Education,* 1973, 24, 128-34.

CEDaR catalogs of selected research and development programs and products. Denver: Council for Educational Development and Research, 1972.

Currie, R. (Project director). *Facilitating educational achievement through telecommunication.* West Lafayette, Indiana: Purdue University, 1976.

Davis, R. H., Alexander, L. T., & Yelon, S. L. *Learning system design.* New York: McGraw-Hill, 1974.

Directory of CITH training materials. Bloomington: Center for Innovation in Teaching the Handicapped, Indiana University (n.d.).

Dodl, N. L. et al. *Catalog of teacher competencies.* Tallahassee: Florida State University, 1972.

Donaldson, J. *Effects of live, video, and audio presentations by a panel of physically disabled individuals on attitudes toward disabled persons.* Unpublished doctoral dissertation, University of Kentucky, 1974.

Flanagan, J. C. *Measuring human performance.* Pittsburgh: American Institutes for Research, 1962.

Gazzetta, V. C. Professional certification and CBTE in New York State. In J. J. Creamer & J. T. Gilmore (Eds.), *Design for competence based education in special education.* Syracuse: Division of Special Education and Rehabilitation, Syracuse University, 1974, 114-32.

Harris, B. M., & King, J. D. *Professional supervisory competencies: Competency specifications for instructional leadership personnel in special education.* Austin: University of Texas Special Education Supervisory Training Project, 1974.

Heller, B., & Dale, M. Traditional teaching and learning modules: A comparative study. *Exceptional Children,* 1976, 42, 231-32.

Hirsch, E. S. Accountability: A Danger to Humanistic Education? *Young Children,* 1975, 31, 57-65.

Houston, W. R. *Resources for performance-based instruction.* Albany: New York State Education Department, 1973.

Houston, W. R., Dodl, N. R., & Weber, W. A. *Competency-based teacher education program design: A simulation.* Westfield, Texas: Competency-Based Instructional Systems, 1973.

Houston, W. R., Hollis, L. Y., Jones, H. L., Edwards, D. A., Pace, A. A., & White, S. J. *Developing instructional modules.* Houston: University of Houston, 1972.

Houston, W. R., & Howsam, R. B. (Eds.). *Competency based teacher education.* Chicago: Science Research Associates, 1972.

Ingram, C. F. *An investigation of instructing and advising competencies of special education professors.* Unpublished doctoral dissertation, University of Kentucky, 1974.

Ingram, C. F., & Blackhurst, A. E. Teaching and advising competencies of special education professors. *Exceptional Children,* 1975, 42, 85-93.

Jacobs, M. A., Nichols, D. G., & Larsen, J. K. *Critical behaviors in the care of the mentally retarded: Behavior of attendents* (Vol. 2). Pittsburgh: American Institute for Research, 1969.

Kincaid, G. H. *A catalog of protocol materials in teacher education.* Tallahassee: Division of Elementary Education, Florida Department of Education, 1972.

Larsen, J. K., Nichols, D. G., & Jacobs, A. M. *Critical behaviors in the care of the mentally retarded: Behavior of nurses* (Vol. 1). Pittsburgh: American Institute for Research, 1969.

Mager, R. F. *Preparing instructional objectives.* Belmont, Calif.: Fearon, 1962.

Meyen, E. L. *Demonstration of dissemination practices on special class instruction for the mentally retarded: Utilizing master teachers as in-service educators.* Washington: Bureau of Education for the Handicapped, U.S. Office of Education Project OEG-3-7-02883-0499, 1969.

Nagel, T., & Richman, P. *Competency-based instruction: A strategy to eliminate failure.* Columbus, Ohio: Charles E. Merrill, 1972.

New York State United Teachers CBTE Position and Guidelines. In J. J. Creamer & J. T. Gilmore (Eds.), *Design for competence based education in special education.* Syracuse: Division of Special Education and Rehabilitation, Syracuse University, 1974.

Redden, M. R. *An investigation of mainstreaming competencies of regular elementary teachers.* Unpublished doctoral dissertation, University of Kentucky, 1976.

Renne, D. J., & Blackhurst, A. E. The effect of adjunct autoinstruction in an introductory special education course. *Exceptional Children,* in press.

Rotberg, J. M. Teacher education: Defining the tasks of teachers of the educable mentally retarded. *Education and Training of the Mentally Retarded,* 1968, 3, 146-49.

Saettler, H. CBTE and the handicapped: A Washington perspective. In J. J. Creamer & J. T. Gilmore (Eds.), *Design for competency based education in special education.* Syracuse: Division of Special Education and Rehabilitation, Syracuse University, 1974. Pp. 8-10.

Sanders, J. R., & Cunningham, D. J. A structure for formative evaluation in product development. *Review of Educational Research,* 1973, 43, 217-36.

Schwartz, L., & Oseroff, A. *The clinical teacher for special education.* Tallahassee: Florida State University, 1975.

Semmell, M. I. Toward the development of a computer-assisted teacher training system (CATTS). *International Review of Education,* 1972, 18, 561-68.

Semmell, M. I., & Baum, R. B. Increasing teachers' understanding through anticipation games. *Viewpoints,* 1973, 49, 59-69.

Shea, T. M., & Whiteside, W. R. *Special education microteaching.* Edwardsville: Southern Illinois University, 1974.

Shores, R., Cegelka, P., & Nelson, C. M. A review of research on teacher competencies. *Exceptional Children,* 1973, 40, 192-97.

Tawney, J. W. *Practice what you preach: A project to develop a contingency-managed "methods" course, and to measure the effects of this course by in-field evaluation.* Lexington: University of Kentucky, 1972.

Thiagarajan, S., Semmell, D. S., & Semmell, M. I. *Instructional Development for Training Teachers of Exceptional Children: A Sourcebook.* Reston, Va.: Council for Exceptional Children, 1974.

Watts, C. A. Time-loaded, task-oriented, large-group, small-group training process. Los Angeles: California Learning Resource System, 1974.

Wixson, S. E. Students' reaction to competency based special education courses. *Exceptional Children,* 1975, **41**, 437.

A SELECTED BIBLIOGRAPHY OF WORKS BY
A. EDWARD BLACKHURST

Blackhurst, A. E. Technology in special education—Some implications. *Exceptional Children,* 1965, 31, 449-56.

Blackhurst, A. E. Mental retardation and delinquency. *Journal of Special Education,* 1968, 2, 379-91.

Blackhurst, A. E. *Effect of an oral advance organizer on the learning and retention of EMR adolescents.* Ann Arbor: Consortium on Auditory Learning Materials for the Handicapped, Michigan State University, 1974.

Blackhurst, A. E. The learning resource center program—Blueprint for the future. *TEACHING Exceptional Children,* 1974, 60, 216-17.

Blackhurst, A. E. Some practical considerations in implementing competency-based special education training programs. In J. J. Creamer & J. T. Gilmore, (Eds.), *Design for competence based education in special education.* Syracuse: Division of Special Education and Rehabilitation, Syracuse University, 1974.

Blackhurst, A. E., Cross, D. P., Nelson, C. M., & Tawney, J. W. Approximating non-categorical teacher education. *Exceptional Children,* 1973, 39, 284-88.

Blackhurst, A. E., Marks, C. H., & Tisdall, W. J. Relationship between mobility and divergent thinking. *Education of the Visually Handicapped,* 1969, 1, 33-36.

Blackhurst, A. E., Wright, W. S., & Ingram, C. F. *Competency specifications for directors of special education resource centers.* Washington: Bureau of Education for the Handicapped, U.S. Office of Education Project OEG-0-72-4305, 1974.

Ingram, C. F., & Blackhurst, A. E. Teaching and advising competencies of special education professors. *Exceptional Children,* 1975, 42, 85-93.

Renne, D. J., & Blackhurst, A. E. Adjunct autoinstruction in an introductory special education course. *Exceptional Children,* 1977, 43, 224-25.

PART 4

Changing
Perspectives in
Programming and
Services

10

Alternative Education for the Mildly and Moderately Handicapped

C. Michael Nelson received a B.S. degree in psychology and English from Kansas State Teacher's College in 1965, a M.S. degree in school psychology from Kansas State Teacher's College in 1967, and an Ed.D. degree in special education from the University of Kansas in 1969. He is presently associate professor and coordinator in the Program for Teachers of the Emotionally Disturbed at the University of Kentucky.

In addition to serving in numerous professional organizations and consultancies, Dr. Nelson has been a third-party evaluator of a Title VI alternative school, a codirector of an assessment clinic, a program direc-

Kathy Boyle, Frank LaBoone, and Debbie Smith assisted in the research for this paper. I wish to express my indebtedness to Bob McLoughlin, who taught me about alternatives.

tor of a school camping program, and a teacher at the junior- and senior-high levels. A selected bibliography of Dr. Nelson's work is found on page 207.

Five years ago, I never would have dreamed of writing a paper on alternative education. My career had pretty much focused on changing children who were considered behaviorally deviant so they could fit back into the educational mainstream. I had no concept of alternative delivery systems, other than those special education interventions designed to get such children back into regular classrooms.

But now I am a staunch advocate of alternative education. The reason goes back to my years as a secondary special education teacher, where, it seems, I had to deal constantly with the reality that school (mainstream and special) had not been kind to many of my pupils; that some were in my special class not for their well-being but for the convenience of a system that could not, or *would* not, adjust to fit their needs.

Since then, I have had a variety of experiences, as a teacher trainer and an intervention strategist, as well as a student desperately trying to keep up with a field changing and expanding in all directions around me. Easily the most significant influence leading me toward alternative education has been my repeated exposure to children such as those I taught years ago; children who have been screened, diagnosed, labeled, and segregated into special "tracts" because their behavior, their achievement, or their culture fails to measure up to the values and expectations of the conventional school. At times, I have felt that special educators are the "hatchet men" for this system—weeding out the "unfit" so the regular classroom teacher can preserve the middle-class standard.

Other influences also have moved me in this direction. My growing awareness of the ecological model and its implications for special education interventions, as well as the opportunity to participate in the development of an intervention system (a Re-ED program) based on this model are very important. My continuing interest in the design and evaluation of special education programs, in labeling, and in secondary education for the handicapped also rank high as influences. This paper gives me a chance to expand on all these subjects and issues as they relate to alternative education.

My purpose then, is to examine alternative education and its relationship to special education for the mildly and moderately handicapped. I will begin with an explication of alternative education: what it is, how and why it developed, who it serves, how it differs from conventional approaches, and whether it works. This will provide the background for an examination of contemporary issues and trends in special education, including how we define and identify our child populations, approaches to the delivery of special education services, evolving roles for special educators, and the place of alternative and special education in the context of our American system of public education.

DEVELOPMENT AND CHARACTERISTICS OF ALTERNATIVE EDUCATION

During the 1960s and into the 70s, a number of scholarly and highly verbal critics of American public education have emerged (e.g. Holt, 1965; Illich, 1971; Kozol, 1967; Postman & Weingartner, 1969; Reimer, 1971; Silberman, 1970). These individuals represent a variety of opinion regarding the source and nature of what is wrong with our educational system. Some—members of what has been called the "counterculture" (Burke, 1974; Fantini, 1973)—see in the educational system the reflection, if not the basis, of social inequities and discrimination in the American culture.

This theme arises again and again in the writings of the counterculturists. They take issue with nearly every facet of contemporary American education—from structure to funding, curriculum, methods and materials, attitudes and values of teachers, and teacher training. The public school is a primary agent of socialization, they argue, which inculcates in children the values of a one-dimensional society (Rhodes, 1975). The educational system is a power structure, facilitating the stratification of society by requiring that citizens accumulate a minimum number of school years to obtain their civil rights. Social entitlements depend on rank achieved in a bureaucratic process; i.e., education. Thus, knowledge is converted to power (Illich, 1973). For many of these critics, schools are the instruments of disorder in the American culture. As Reimer (1972) put it:

> I do not regard schools as truly educational but, more nearly, as an institutional perversion of education. In my opinion, schools not only prevent true education from occurring, they actually miseducate. They teach not what is relevant and true but what is irrelevant and untrue to the interests of their students. They do this, however, in the service of a society of which they are a central institution and a major bulwark. They effectively adjust their students to the requirements of this society [p. 484].

The civil rights movement of the 1960s spawned public action against schools, and with it, other critics, such as Jonathan Kozol (1967, 1972). The reluctance of schools to desegregate led to parent, teacher, and community boycotts of public schools, and the establishment of "freedom schools" in empty buildings and storefronts (Fantini, 1973).

Another impetus for alternative education in America was the British Infant School, based upon John Dewey's concept of progressive education. The open classroom had its beginnings in this model (Fantini, 1973). The concept of a voucher plan, in which families are given educational vouchers redeemable for tuition in any public or private school, also was a factor. Though not adopted in the United States, Fantini (1973) stated that the voucher system has provided sufficient external pressure to stimulate a movement for alternatives within the public schools.

While quite a few critics have expressed the opinion that conventional schools are stultifying environments for children (Goodman, 1969; Illich, 1971; Kozol, 1967; Reimer, 1971), others (e.g., Herndon, 1968; Kohl, 1967) have given first-hand testimony that they are stultifying for teachers as well. Barr (1974) presented the thesis that the school culture mitigates against innovative teaching practices. He observed that new teachers are either driven out by pressures to conform to "routines" or become typical examples of the stereotyped schoolteacher.

Simultaneous with this professional dialogue has been a growth in student and parental dissatisfaction with the type of education afforded by public schools (Gross & Gross, 1969; Moore, 1974; Silberman, 1970). Public dissatisfaction with education is hardly anything new, and professional educators have been criticizing public education since before Dewey. No matter how one evaluates the significance of this outcry and its historical antecedents, the fact remains that public schools have not been uequivocably effective in achieving the basic objective of equalizing opportunity within our culture (Wilkerson, 1969). For example, it is still true that around 30 percent cf those children entering the public school system at age six fail to complete their secondary education (U.S. Bureau of the Census, 1973).

The social context from which alternative education arose, then, was one of dissent, rejection, and disgust, not just with public education, but with the cultural realities that spawned a unidimensional (middle-class) educational model, and enforced conformity to that model. A major outcome of this professional and lay dissent consisted of repeated demands for options to the monolothic educational system.

The most radical of these demands called for "deschooling" society, meaning either to disestablish schools or to deschool the culture (Illich, 1971, 1973). The action advocated by this group of dissenters is to turn over the control formerly exercised by schools to another, more amorphous set of institutions. Taken out of the hands of the school, knowledge would then be more readily available to a larger majority of people (Illich, 1973).

Other measures also have been suggested. For example, Silberman (1970) advocated centralizing control of the schools in the federal government, thereby creating insulation from direct social pressures and allowing schools more freedom to experiment and innovate. Fantini (1971, 1973) suggested establishing options *within* the public school system. Since special education operates primarily within the context of public schools, my analysis of alternative education focuses on public school alternatives.

Smith (1975) described several ways in which such public school-sponsored options could complement the present system:

1. by meeting needs not presently met by conventional schools;

2. by providing places to explore and try out innovations;

3. by prompting conventional schools to re-examine themselves;

4. by emphasizing greater community involvement in the educational process;

5. by providing a vehicle for continuous change and improvement in schools; and

6. by providing educational choice for the consumer and the community, which would result in better local support of schools.

The growth of alternative schools seems to reflect, at last, professional receptiveness to demands for change in the structure of education. In 1962, only one program existed, according to the National Directory of Public Alternative Schools (Mayo, 1974). Sixty-five programs had been started by 1970, and in 1971 alone, 114 schools were opened. The 1975 directory (National Alternative Schools Program, 1975) contained 627 entries, and this was admittedly an incomplete listing. Barr (cited by Shaw, 1975) placed the number of programs, including private alternatives, at well over 5,000. Fantini (1973) identified two broad categories of alternatives. *External free schools* are nonpublic, and therefore "free" from public school bureaucracy. *Alternatives within public schools* consist of a variety of options, all operating within the bureaucracy. Although no complete list of alternative programs exists, it appears to me that the dominant trend leans toward public alternative education programs. Private schools are too expensive for most citizens to support, especially on top of the financial support they must provide for local public schools.

The National Consortium for Options in Public Education (1973) defined an alternative school as any school within a community providing alternative learning experiences to conventional school programs that are available, at no extra cost, to every family in the community desiring its services. While this definition is adequate for programs designed to serve those who *elect* an alternative form of schooling, it does not provide for those children who enter alternative programs by virtue of their *exclusion* from conventional school offerings. The definition adopted for the 1974 and 1975 National Directory of Public Alternative Schools was broadened to include referral-type programs as well.

Various schools appear to entertain other definitions of alternative education, depending upon the purpose of the program and who does the defining. But a common thread in all definitions is the concept of designing educational environments to fit children, rather than providing inflexible learning environments into which children are force-fit. This concept, I think, brings special education squarely into the arena of alternative education, for the major concern of special educators has been the designing of individual learning environments.[1]

Smith (1975) identified four concepts upon which the development of alternative public schools is based:

1. Each person has the democratic right to choose the type of education he/she desires.
2. Different persons learn in different ways.
3. Learning should not be isolated from the world outside the school.
4. The individual school should make the largest portion of the decisions regarding its programs and curricula.

Although until recently, the process by which mildly and moderately handicapped children entered special education programs generally precluded selection of an educational environment by the parent-consumer, these concepts are highly compatible with those held by special educators. Moreover, the main point of alternative programs is to provide a variety of learning environments (National Consortium for Options in Public Education, 1973), including the conventional school itself (Smith, 1975). Consistent with Fantini's (1973) view, special education programs would therefore represent another set of alternatives within the public schools.

Characteristics of Alternative Education Programs

Most alternative schools are developed in response to particular educational needs within their communities. Consequently, no single model or group of models exists. The majority, however, are patterned after one or a combination of the following types (National Consortium for Options in Public Education, 1973):

---

[1] Fantini (1973) pointed out that for special education and other referral tracts, the child is assigned a negative psychological classification. Also, assignment is not based on choice by the consumer.

1. *Open schools* provide for individualized learning activities and are organized around interest centers. This alternative is an outgrowth of the British Infant School.

2. *Schools without walls* emphasize learning activities occurring throughout the community. Accordingly, these schools provide for much community interaction.

3. *Learning centers* concentrate learning resources in one location. These resources are available to all students in the community.

4. *Continuation schools* provide for pupils whose education in conventional schools has, or might be, interrupted. Included are dropout centers, re-entry programs, pregnancy-maternity centers, evening and adult high schools, and street academics.

5. *Multicultural schools* stress cultural pluralism and ethnic and racial awareness. They usually service a multiracial/cultural student body.

6. *Free schools* emphasize greater freedom of choice of curriculum for students and teachers. Generally, free schools operate outside of public school systems.

7. *Schools-within-schools* include a variety of options, such as mini-schools and satellite schools, in which a small number of students and teachers are involved, by choice, in a different kind of learning experience.

Another alternative, described by Moore (1974), is the *freedom school*. Its primary goals include building academic skills, ethnic pride, and community power. The freedom school tends to be more structured than most other alternatives. Kozol (1972) described his experiences with the creation and operation of a freedom school.

It is easy to imagine an alternative school as a very strange environment compared to the traditional school. Certainly many alternative schools tolerate more variation in such matters as dress, curriculum, scheduling, and other routines, but I doubt that one could find examples where clearly inappropriate behavior is supported or condoned. Some alternative programs have, in fact, gone the other way. Called *fundamental schools*, these programs emphasize academic rigor, old-fashioned discipline, patriotism, and teacher control (Shaw, 1975). A number of fundamental schools have sprung up around the country in response to parents dissatisfied with the laxity and lack of scholarship in the regular public schools.

Because of their heterogeneity, the operation of alternative schools is difficult to describe collectively. McLaughlin (1975) listed ten characteristics differentiating an alternative school from the conventional school program:

1. smaller size;

2. increased contact with families;

3. more variety in the curriculum, which is not restricted to the classroom;

4. increased emphasis on "learning by doing";

5. less acceptance or use of the concept of failure;

6. more concerted attempts to create a friendly, humane atmosphere;

7. more concerted attempts to make learning relevant;

8. more relaxed attendance policies, yet seldom are attendance problems manifested;

9. increased emphasis on policy decisions by students and staff; and

10. greater awareness of every facet of a child's environment.

Table 1 presents an analysis of programs reported in the 1975 Directory of Public Alternative Schools (National Alternative Schools Program, 1975).

Although this analysis is subject to the limitations of the information submitted for the directory, it reveals that the majority of alternative schools are indeed small and serve white students in the secondary grades. There are approximately equal numbers of programs in urban, suburban, and inner-city areas.

One of the more interesting characteristics of alternative schools suggested by the directory is the child population served in relation to the general purposes of each program. The directory gives information indicative of two broad categories of programs: those designed to provide enriched or expanded curricula, and those designed to serve children described variously as potential dropouts, dropouts, truants, mentally handicapped, academically retarded, emotionally disturbed, underachievers, or delinquents. (These categories reflect the distinction between optional voluntary programs and referral programs to which I alluded earlier.) Although the reported data were insufficient to classify all programs according to this dichotomy, 251 alternatives could be analyzed. The enrichment type included 120 schools, while 131 were referral programs. Most (69 percent) of the enrichment programs served a predominantly white student body, while the proportion of white to nonwhite students in referral programs was more evenly balanced (44 percent white and 34 percent nonwhite). (Twenty-two percent of the programs in this analysis did not report enough data to determine the racial composition of their populations.) This informal analysis suggests that referral-type programs are serving child popula-

TABLE 1: Description of public alternative schools.

Category	Number	Percent
Serving primarily elementary grades	100	21
Serving primarily secondary grades	365	77
Serving both elementary and secondary	11	2
Total	476[1]	100

Enrollment:

	Number	Percent
0-100 pupils	218	46
100-200 pupils	120	26
200-500 pupils	77	16
over 500 pupils	55	12
Total	470	100

Population:

	Number	Percent
>50% White	283	70
>50% Black	83	20.5
Equally mixed	18	4.5
>50% Spanish	16	4
>50% Indian	5	1
Total	405	100

	Number	Percent
>50% suburban	143	35.1
>50% inner-city	117	28.7
>50% urban	115	28.3
Equally mixed	17	4.2
>50% rural	15	3.7
Total	407	100

[1] Number based on information provided for individual program entries.

Adapted from 1975 directory of public alternative schools. *Applesauce*. Amherst: National Alternative Schools Program, School of Education, University of Massachusetts, 1975.

tions also found in special education programs for the mildly and moderately handicapped.

In describing teacher competencies and roles in alternative programs, again, variability is the only consistent pattern. Barr and Burke (1973) pointed out that different types of alternative schools require different teacher competencies, from highly technical diagnostic and reinforcement skills in schools emphasizing programmed structure, to an ability to transfer responsibility for learning completely to the student in nonstructured programs. Barr and Burke also observed the need for skills in working with a heterogeneous pupil population and emphasized the problems facing teacher training programs attempting to prepare teachers for positions requiring such a wide repertoire of teaching skills.

Not only are a greater variety of skills required, but also the teacher's role in alternative schools is clearly different from that in conventional programs. Armstrong (1973) stressed that the alternative teacher acts as a facilitator, helping students find their own materials and plan learning programs to fit their individual needs. Conventional barriers between the teacher and student are absent. According to Boss (1972), alternative teachers serve as managers of the learning environment, rather than as fountains of knowledge; they demonstrate instead of lecture. Aase and Fiske (1973) added that the teacher's role involves viewing learning from the learner's perspective. Further, the teacher must help students from traditionally structured learning environments adapt to a freer one.

In the alternative school the emphasis on one-to-one interaction, individual guidance, and empathy puts a premium on the personality of the teacher. Whereas the traditional classroom may tend to de-emphasize the teacher's personality, it is a central feature of alternative schools. It is therefore important, according to Burke (1974) "to get hold of the right kind of teachers, who will have helpful personalities, rather than trying to 'train out' the effects of personality" [p. 595]. Just how one goes about identifying helpful personality traits and screening prospective teachers on the basis of these traits has been a thorny problem for all educators. Nevertheless, the small size and informal structure of most alternative programs tends to maximize the effects of teacher personality. Special educators, as a group, are sensitive to the need for teachers strong enough to cope with frustration and with difficult pupils. Alternative teaching would seem to require equally strong personality characteristics.

The curriculums of alternative schools reflect the same diversity that characterizes every other program facet. Nevertheless, general patterns can be identified. One common element seems to be an awareness that formal schooling constitutes only one curriculum, and one part—perhaps the least significant—of a child's education (Cremin, 1974; Silberman, 1970). Alternative educators therefore tend to look beyond the school for curriculum and for teachers (Gross, 1973; Illich, 1971; Jerome, 1973). The ultimate extension of this is doing away with formal institutionalized educational structure entirely (i.e., deschooling society) in favor of educational experiences involving the learner's free choice not only of what he will learn, but of where he will learn it

(Illich, 1973). Others regard curriculum in relation to the specific child population with which they deal. For example, Kozol's (1972) freedom school emphasized academic skills as the survival tools needed by students in the inner-city. Without these skills, Kozol felt that it would be impossible for ghetto dwellers to obtain the political power needed to improve their community and their lives.

In a more general vein, Fantini and Weinstein (1969) listed several curriculum needs for the disadvantaged:

1. flexibility—a curriculum geared to the unique needs of individual schools within a system;
2. an experience base, emphasizing concrete experiences;
3. vertical programming in small-step sequences;
4. orientation to the immediate, as opposed to the past or future;
5. focus on teaching "why" not "what";
6. social participation, or "doing";
7. an attempt to explore reality; and
8. equal emphasis on cognitive (extrinsic) and affective (inner) content.

The curriculum for free schools, in contrast, tends to emphasize its relationship to ongoing life experiences and the activities of the larger community. Direction and aid are offered, but never forced on a child. Grades and standardized measures of achievement or intelligence seldom are employed (Rhodes, 1975).

In view of the widespread endorsement of alternative schools, as seems indicated by their proliferation, it is pertinent to inquire into their effectiveness. The question of efficacy poses some difficult problems for many alternative educators, for effectiveness must be evaluated against anticipated outcomes. The objectives of alternative programs do not necessarily reflect those of conventional schools; e.g., preparation for the assumption of middle-class social and occupational roles. Moreover, many alternative schools emphasize affective goals, such as "improved self-concept" or amorphous process goals like "meeting individual needs." Such ends hardly lend themselves to precise measurement, much less to comparison with control groups. This is not to say that all alternative programs are characterized by ambiguity. Some frankly work toward improved academic performance, reduced delinquency, and other outcomes which can be objectively measured. Fantini (1974) argued that each alternative in a school system should include an evaluation plan. Further, he indicated that each program should be judged by its effects, and a decision to continue that particular option should be made on the basis of these effects.

For the most part, however, effects such as these take years to show up as definite trends in the community; consequently, program evaluation tends to be a relatively arduous and expensive business. It is not surprising that efficacy reports on alternative schools are sparse and permit no generalizations about whether such programs "work" in a statistical sense. Olsen (1974) described several alternative programs, a few of which reported gains in measures of achievement, lower rates of truancy and discipline problems, and improved pupil attitudes. The John Marshall Fundamental School found that students' median scores on end-of-year achievement tests equaled or exceeded median scores for the district on 18 of 21 tests (Shaw, 1975). On the other hand, Barth (1972) described the first years of the Lincoln-Attucks Program as a failure, in that these elementary pupils didn't know what guidelines to use for their behavior, or what to do with materials with which they were given to work. Parents were dissatisfied with the perceived "lack" of teacher control, as well as with the noise, movement, and mess in the classroom. The Los Angeles Alternative School found no changes in the achievement test scores of its pupils either above or below the level expected on the basis of prior school performance (Olsen, 1974).

Since schools generally have close ties, at least on paper, with their local communities, program longevity may bear a relationship to efficacy. By this criterion, the most effective alternative program of which I am aware is the Rose Valley School which began in 1929 (Rotzel, 1971).

In the context of this discussion, I think it is important to consider again the child population of alternative schools, and to ask how effective conventional schools are for them. Recall that over 50 percent of the programs reporting usable data in the 1975 directory were designed for disciplinary problems, truants, delinquents, and the like. Recall also that the so-called "dropout" rate is around 30 percent of those children entering first grade.[2] Ahlstrom and Havighurst (1971) indicated that one-half of this dropout group show serious social maladjustment. These data indicate that many alternative programs are serving a population of children already identified by the educational mainstream as "losers" who probably enter alternative schools with long histories of school misconduct and failure. Thus, alternative schools likely are dealing with a population for whom conventional programs are not effective. From this perspective, even a five percent success rate would be laudable.

Elsewhere (Nelson & Kauffman, in press) I have stressed the need for program evaluation and controlled efficacy studies of special education interventions. This need should be re-emphasized for alternative school programs. However, rigorous, continuous evaluation of conventional schools is badly needed as well, especially for populations similar

---

[2] A conservative estimate by the U.S. Bureau of the Census indicated that, at any given time, 2.4 million children between 7 and 19 years of age are not in school (*U.S. News and World Report*, March 1976).

to those served by alternative programs. Such an evaluation plan would permit direct comparison of various programs, provided agreement on at least some outcome measures (e.g. delinquency rates, achievement, etc.) could be reached.

I feel obligated to conclude this overview of alternative education with a look into the future. Herndon (1968) and Kohl (1967) both held bleak prospects for the futures of children trapped inside the conventional slum school. Wilkerson (1969) and Fantini (1973) observed that compensatory education within the framework of conventional programs has been a failure. What are the chances that those children who fail to thrive in or are suppressed by the regular public school will someday be offered more relevant learning environments? Rhodes (1975), speaking primarily about free schools, saw several possibilities for alternatives: (a) they could be absorbed into the regular public schools; (b) they could maintain a fragile existence outside the public schools; (c) growing public demand for more informal, grassroots education could lead to a decentralization of public schools; or (d) more direct confrontations could occur between public and alternative school advocates. Smith (1975) gave the most optimistic outlook:

> It seems likely that in the forseeable future many different types of schools will exist side by side within the total educational structure, each designed to meet a different set of specific learning and living needs of young people [p. 334].

Fantini (1973) emphasized that alternative schools are more likely to be legitimized if they (a) demonstrate adherence to a comprehensive set of educational objectives; (b) do not cost more than existing programs; (c) do not practice exclusivity; (d) co-exist with the conventional pattern which continues to be legitimate; and (e) refrain from making exaggerated claims. He perceived the greatest danger to alternatives to be that the movement will be regarded as a fad. Given the present size and momentum of alternative education, I doubt that any serious educator would take it so lightly.

RELATIONSHIP OF ALTERNATIVE EDUCATION TO SPECIAL EDUCATION

By this point, if I have done my job, it will be apparent that alternative education is a concept and a process that should very significantly concern special educators for the following reasons. First, alternative programs clearly are serving many children actually or potentially classifiable in one of the traditional disability categories for special education. Second, the current emphasis on mainstreaming of mildly and moderately handicapped children means that special educators will need to work more and more with regular school personnel in designing appropriate learning environments for this population. The concepts and programs in alternative education contain many possibilities for creating such learning environments. Third, there is a need within special education to take another look at our assumptions about educational disabilities. In the past, special education interventions have been based on the assumption that failure to teach a child is largely due to a defect inherent in the pupil. Consequently, our work has emphasized diagnosis and labeling, and placement in segregated special tracts. Several of our colleagues (e.g., Graubard, Rosenberg & Miller, 1971; Lilly, 1970; Rhodes, 1967, 1970) have questioned this assumption and its corollary that it is the child who must change to fit the system. They have emphasized, instead, making the system adapt to the child. This stance is very much in tune with the position of alternative educators. Finally, special educators have the skills and the technology to change the system, to create better environments in which children can learn. These skills need not be restricted to altering classroom environments; they also could be put to use in creating learning environments outside the school proper.

What follows is an examination of a few recent trends in special education and their relationship to the issues just presented. Also, I will describe some special education alternatives—conceptual and programmatic—and several changes in special education practice that could result from the influence of alternative education.

I strongly urge special educators to become involved in alternative education. Our concern for children who flounder and fail in the conventional system dates back to the earliest public school programs for exceptional children. We too have been searching for alternative delivery systems (e.g. Lilly, 1970, 1971; Rhodes, 1967) albeit systems which, for the most part, assume validity for the conventional school model. And, there is no doubt that special educators have the expertise to design learning environments around children's needs.

However, it seems to me that we need to rethink our philosophy and goals. Special educators, for the most part, have worked with handicapped children with the goal of having them function within the existing educational system. Alternative educators are telling us that millions of children are being handicapped *by* that system. As we come to realize that the so-called mildly and moderately handicapped and those children considered intolerable, uneducable, and unreachable represent slices of the same demographic pie, it will be necessary to re-examine our positions on such matters as remediation and mainstreaming. Wilkerson (1969) observed that the theoretical orientation of the slum school and its compensatory programs assumed a deficit-causation hypothesis which encouraged strategies preoccupied with diagnosing and correcting what was "wrong" with the disadvantaged child, whereas the more critical change target may have been the slum school itself. Lilly (1970), responding to the same situation in special education, proposed a definition of an "exceptional school situation" to replace definitions of exceptionality based exclusively upon child characteristics:

> An exceptional school situation is one in which interaction between a student and his teacher has been limited to such an extent that external intervention is deemed necessary by the teacher to cope with the problem [p. 48].

Acceptance of this definition, Lilly went on, would spell the end of special education as we have known it. In its place "would emerge a system in which it is *not* assumed that all school problems are centered in the child and that removal of children from problem situations will be beneficial for everyone involved" [p. 48].

The concept of deviance as inherent in interactions rather than in children is central to the ecological model. This model was used by Rhodes (1967) to conceptualize the phenomenon of "emotional disturbance." Rhodes saw disturbance as transaction between a child and those members of the microcommunity with whom he is in conflict. The disturbance comes as much from the expectations and actions of these others as from the child's behavior itself. The child, being the weakest and least defended person in the conflict situation, is a convenient scapegoat: He is assigned a label because of his microcommunity's inability to cope with him (Rhodes, 1970).

The ecological model is making a tremendous impact on special education. Probably the best-known system of special education interventions based on this model is Re-ED (Hobbs, 1965, 1966). In Re-ED, the focus is on re-educating not only the child, but also the living systems (i.e., microcommunities) of which he is a part. Perhaps the most convincing arguments for the validity of the ecological model is the efficacy of Re-ED. Whereas most interventions directed at "disturbed" children demonstrate no better effect than that of the passage of time (Lewis, 1965), Re-ED has a documented 85-percent success rate (Weinstein, 1969).

Graubard, Rosenberg, and Miller (1971), in a dramatically different application of this model, taught socially deviant children to use behavior modification techniques to change their teachers and peers. Teachers became less punitive and more reinforcing, and peers exhibited less hostility and more approach behavior as a result of reinforcers differentially administered by special education pupils. In a study bearing on this same point, two of my colleagues and I (Nelson, Worell, & Polsgrove, 1971) demonstrated that "disturbed" children of middle-elementary age could function as effective behavior managers for similarly deviant peers.

One of the most important implications alternative education holds for special educators lies in the issue of mainstreaming. Every exceptional child is entitled to the least restrictive environment possible, and such mainstreaming concepts as Lilly's (1971) zero-reject model hold great promise for the total educational system. But the repeated observation that children who do well in experimental or special class programs revert to failure upon return to the regular classroom (Cohen, Filipczak, Slavin, & Boren, 1971; Vacc, 1972; Wilkerson, 1969) raises the question of how much we should continue to emphasize reintegration into a single mainstream. Wilkerson (1969) thought that much of this problem with respect to the disadvantaged lies "in the slum school's failure to provide appropriate learning environments and experiences for the children of the poor" [p. 116]. Cohen et al. (1971) saw the problem in the inability of the child's natural environment (school and home) to support the changes realized in the experimental program.

The solution lies partly in training-based mainstreaming approaches (Lilly, 1971), in which special education staff provide inservice training to regular classroom teachers in whose classes mildly and moderately handicapped children are enrolled. This approach certainly will create more flexible teachers and curricula within the conventional program. But what of those children who own no deficits other than those imposed on them by the middle-class model? For them, the only real solution lies in total alternative learning environments. Mainstreaming would be a viable approach if the mainstream itself were composed not of a single classroom model, but a variety of optional environments.

A further implication for special education has to do with efficacy. The deficit hypothesis, which holds grade-level achievement and middle-class social behavior as the norm, may be entirely inappropriate for some alternative and special education programs. "Success" can also be judged on the basis of idiopathic criteria: Did a child manage to get through a week without resorting to drugs or prostitution? Did he walk away from a fight? Did he go home last night? These questions could be more significant at a given point in time than whether the child was reading at grade level. But, lest I be misunderstood, let me quickly add that I believe education to be the single most important survival tool in our society. I would distrust any program that eschewed academic objectives. It seems to me, though, that academic achievement ought to be put more in the context of children's real living environments than it is presently.

I can't leave the subject of norms without mentioning the issue of labeling. Comparison of children to a standard inevitably results in judgments and labels relative to the standard. In the American culture, there is *one* standard by which we judge virtually all behavior, at least as far as our social institutions are concerned. Special educators have been supremely guilty of perpetuating this standard by assigning labels to deviation, although they purport to adhere to a belief in individual differences. I think that instead of generating labels, we ought to actively campaign against them. Although the results of research on labeling are contradictory, that labels can have deleterious effects has been repeatedly demonstrated (c.f. Dunn, 1968; Graubard, Rosenberg, & Miller, 1971; Rosenthal & Jacobson, 1968). Yet the practice persists, though the labels themselves occasionally change. We need to sensitize the public to the detrimental effects of labels, as well as the capricious way in which they frequently are applied. We also need to alert our colleagues to their irrelevance, as Szasz (1960, 1970) has done with the concept of mental illness. Postman and Weingartner (1969) offered a suggestion that might help put an end to labeling: all teachers should be classified according to their ability, and the lists should be made public. This classification would include not only their teaching ability, but also their IQ and reading scores, and whether they are "advantaged" or "disadvantaged" relative to the knowledge of their students.

Finally, alternative education has underscored the need for an expanded concept of education, extending beyond the school day into all aspects of life (Cremin, 1974; Illich, 1971; Reimer, 1971). Rhodes (1967) proposed a special education delivery system based on this point of view. Also, we are beginning to see an extension of special education programs to the years before and after the normal public school experience. It is possible that in future years, thanks to the influence of alternative education, tax-supported educational programs will be available throughout an individual's lifetime. When this happens, it is more likely that the kind of educational experience one receives at any given time will reflect his real and immediate needs.

CONCLUDING REMARKS

A fair question to ask at this point is what pattern of public school services I would like to see for the mildly and moderately handicapped. Basically, I think the components of an ideal array of special education interventions have already been presented. Deno's (1970) cascade model includes interventions on every level at which such children are found. Lilly's (1971) training-based model improves upon this cascade by the addition of inservice training. Only two additional components are needed.

The first component is a broader context of mainstream options in which special education programs are interwoven. (I know I'm repeating myself, but the point deserves re-emphasis.) If alternatives existed in the mainstream, and if these alternatives recognized the heterogeneity of children in terms of temperament, development, learning style, and culture, the need for remedial special education programs would be greatly reduced.

The second component is a more open and honest perspective on children who have difficulties in school. As a teacher trainer, I have repeatedly witnessed instances in which teacher problems or school problems are translated into child problems, a process greatly facilitated by labeling. The child gets saddled with a categorical label that exonerates those who are really at fault for their participation in his/her difficulties. The child subsequently is shuffled off to some form of "treatment" which, all too often is a dead-end. But the problem is "solved" —or more accurately, removed—and those responsible are "off the hook." In my estimation, we could junk all our diagnostic labeling procedures with little noticeable loss, and probably much gain. An alternative practiced by behaviorists for many years is to identify child (or community) behaviors without recourse to labels. It seems obvious to me that a descriptive account of a child's reading performances is vastly more functional than calling him learning disabled.

The result of adding these components would be a wide assortment of alternative learning environments—regular and special (there would be no purpose in using this distinction, by the way)—available to all children, and open to most by choice. Children would be described in terms of educationally relevant behaviors, "special" educators would be resources to the whole school, and, alas, there would be no special education funding based on the number of handicapped children a psychologists could classify.

This is what I'd *like* to see. Realistically, however, I realize that such reform is a long way off. Therefore, permit me to offer a few recommendations directed at a more immediate future:

1. Special educators should make every effort to learn about alternative education and its potential relationship with special education. Our technology and expertise should then be directed toward the development and evaluation of alternative programs. This should include reconceptualizing and redesigning special education services along the lines I previously mentioned. I fully agree with Lilly (1970) that changes in the underlying structure of special education services are badly needed, and that the new structure "should be supportive of broad experimentation with a variety of new approaches to children with problems in school" [p. 46]. In short, we should explore more of the alternatives we presently only talk about.

2. *All* public education programs—conventional, special, and alternative—should provide plans for objective evaluation relative to their goals. If there were general congruence of objectives for

certain types of programs or schools, these programs could employ similar evaluation measures. This would permit direct comparison of program effectiveness. And, as Fantini (1973) suggested, one effectiveness criterion should be consumer satisfaction. Furthermore, program goals and the results of previous evaluations both should be made public, so that children, parents, and teachers could select from among the available options the program most compatible with, and most effective for, their personal objectives. Freedom of choice involves little real freedom if choices are not made on the basis of all the information available.

3. The use of *mainstream* and *special* to designate the major public school tracts now available should be replaced with the concept of alternative learning environments. The effect would be to facilitate opening such special education alternatives as resource rooms to children not labeled handicapped, and to reduce the stigma attached to such programs. Also, it would stress the need for a plurality of mainstream options, rather than just one.[3] The "least restrictive" environment thus would mean different alternatives for different children, and would eliminate the tendency to make children do all the changing. It is well known that we have the technology to change children's behavior. It is becoming apparent that this technology can be applied to change the system as well. Changing the system entails recognizing that, to some extent at least, we are our own enemy. It seems to me that a crucial factor in the success of public school alternatives is our courage to examine what we are doing so that we can change ourselves.

I hope I've managed to present a strong case for alternative education, and in particular for special education to become actively involved in it. Change within systems, once they become institutionalized, is a slow and arduous process. My feeling is that change should originate from within the field. Unfortunately, the history of education, including special education, indicates that change generally occurs as a result of external forces. But at least it does happen. In my opinion, alternative education has the potential to make it happen faster, and better. Barr (1974) raised the question of what will happen to the alternatives after they have become established. In all likelihood, he observed, they will become institutionalized, and we will begin seeking new alternatives to the old ones. Let us hope that the most enduring educational institution is that of change itself.

[3] This does not imply condemnation of the existing mainstream pattern. The mainstream *is* effective for the majority of children, and most consumers are satisfied with it. This model would continue to be dominant, but it would no longer be the only option available.

REFERENCES

Aase, E., & Fiske, F. M. Teacher adaptation to an informal school. *NASSP Bulletin,* 1973, **57** (369), 1-9.

Ahlstrom, W. M., & Havighurst, R. J. *400 losers.* San Francisco: Jossey-Bass, 1971.

Armstrong, D. G. Alternative schools: Implications for secondary school curriculum workers. *The High School Journal,* 1973, 56, 267-75.

Barr, R. D. School cultures, teacher education, and alternative schools. *Viewpoints,* 1974, 50, 71-87.

Barr, R. D., & Burke, D. J. New teachers for new schools. *Viewpoints,* 1973, 49, 67-75.

Barth, R. S. *Open education and the American school.* New York: Agathon Press, 1972.

Boss, R. Portland's personalized education program. *Educational Leadership,* 1972, 29, 405-7.

Bureau of the Census. *Statistical abstracts of the United States.* Washington D.C.: U.S. Department of Commerce, Social and Economic Statistics Administration, 1973.

Burke, D. Countertheoretical interventions in emotional disturbance. In W. C. Rhodes & M. R. Tracy (Eds.), *A study of child variance: Interventions* (Vol. 2). Ann Arbor: University of Michigan Press, 1974. Pp. 573-659.

Cohen, H. R., Filipczak, Slavin, J., & Boren, J. PICA: *Programming interpersonal curricula for adolescents.* Paper presented at the American Psychological Association Workshop on Delinquent Behavior, Washington, D.C., September 1971.

Cremin, L. A. The free school movement—A perspective. *Today's Education,* 1974, 63, 71-74.

Deno, E. Special education as developmental capital. *Exceptional Children,* 1970, 37, 229-37.

Dropouts and pushouts: The 2.4 million children who aren't in school. *U.S. News and World Report,* March 22, 1976, pp. 43-44.

Dunn, L. M. Special education for the mildly retarded: Is much of it justifiable? *Exceptional Children,* 1968, 35, 5-22.

Fantini, M. D. Options for students, parents, and teachers: Public schools of choice. *Phi Delta Kappan,* 1971, **52**, 541-43.

Fantini, M. D. The what, why, and where of the alternative movement. *National Elementary Principal,* 1973, **52** (6), 14-22.

Fantini, M. D. Alternatives in the public school. *Today's Education,* 1974, 63, 63-66.

Fantini, M. D., & Weinstein, G. Making contact with the disadvantaged. In B. Gross & R. Gross (Eds.), *Radical school reform.* New York: Simon & Schuster, 1969. Pp. 172-78.

Goodwin, P. No processing whatever. In B. Gross & R. Gross (Eds.), *Radical School Reform*. New York: Simon & Schuster, 1969. Pp. 98-106.

Graubard, P. S., Rosenberg, H., & Miller, M. B. Student applications of behavior modification to teachers and environments or ecological approaches to social deviancy. In E. A. Ramp & B. I. Hopkins (Eds.), *A new direction for education: Behavior analysis 1971*. Lawrence, Kansas: University of Kansas Department of Human Development, 1971. Pp. 80-101.

Gross, R. After deschooling, free learning. In A. Gartner, C. Greer, & F. Riessman (Eds.), *After deschooling, what?* New York: Harper & Row, 1973. Pp. 148-60.

Herndon, J. *The way it spozed to be*. New York: Simon & Schuster, 1968.

Hobbs, N. How the Re-Ed plan developed. In N. J. Long, W. C. Morse, & R. G. Newman (Eds.), *Conflict in the classroom* (1st ed.). Belmont, Calif.: Wadsworth, 1965. Pp. 286-94.

Hobbs, N. Helping disturbed children: Psychological and ecological strategies. *American Psychologist*, 1966, 21, 1105-15.

Holt, J. *How children fail*. New York: Pitman, 1965.

Illich, I. *De-schooling society*, New York: Harper & Row, 1971.

Illich, I. After deschooling, what? In A. Gartner, C. Greer, & F. Riessman (Eds.), *After deschooling, what?* New York: Harper & Row, 1973. Pp. 1-28.

Jerome, J. After Illich, what? In A. Gartner, C. Greer, & F. Riessman (Eds.), *After deschooling, what?* New York: Harper & Row, 1973. Pp. 104-11.

Kohl, H. *Thirty-six children*. New York: New American Library, 1967.

Kozol, J. *Death at an early age*. Boston: Houghton Mifflin, 1967.

Kozol, J. *Free schools*. New York: Barton Books, 1972.

Lewis, W. W. Continuity and intervention in emotional disturbance: A review. *Exceptional Children*, 1965, 31, 465-75.

Lilly, S. M. Special education: A teapot in a tempest. *Exceptional Children*, 1970, 37, 43-49.

Lilly, S. M. A training based model for special education, *Exceptional Children*, 1971, 37, 745-49.

McLaughlin, B. An alternative school for Fayette County. Unpublished manuscript, University of Kentucky, 1975.

Moore, B. Counter cultural alternatives to modern institutions. In W. C. Rhodes & S. Head (Eds.), *A study of child variances: Service delivery systems* (Vol. 3). Ann Arbor: University of Michigan, Institute for the Study of Mental Retardation and Related Disorders, 1974. Pp. 595-635.

National Alternative Schools Program. 1975 directory of public alternative schools. *Applesauce*. Amherst: School of Education, University of Massachusetts, 1975.

National Consortium for Options in Public Education. Directory of optional alternative public schools. *Changing Schools* (No. 008). Bloomington: School of Education, Indiana University, 1973.

Nelson, C. M., & Kauffman, J. M. Educational programming for secondary school age delinquent and maladjusted pupils. *Behavior Disorders,* in press.

Nelson, C. M., Worell, J., & Polsgrove, L. Behaviorally disordered peers as contingency managers. *Behavior Therapy,* 1973, 4, 270-76.

Olsen, T. Alternative education programs. *Journal of Reading,* 1974, 18, 190-91.

Postman, N., & Weingartner, C. *Teaching as a subversive activity.* New York: Delacorte Press, 1969.

Reimer, E. *School is dead: Alternatives in education.* Garden City, New York: Doubleday, 1971.

Reimer, E. Unusual ideas in education. In W. C. Rhodes & M. R. Tracy (Eds.), *A study of child variance: Conceptual models* (Vol. 1). Ann Arbor: Institute for the Study of Mental Retardation and Related Disabilities, 1972. Pp. 481-502.

Rhodes, W. C. The disturbing child: A problem of ecological management. *Exceptional Children,* 1967, 33, 637-42.

Rhodes, W. C. A community participation analysis of emotional disturbance. *Exceptional Children,* 1970, 36, 309-14.

Rhodes, W. C. *A study of child variance: The future* (Vol. 4). Ann Arbor: Institute for the Study of Mental Retardation and Related Disabilities, 1975.

Rosenthal, R., & Jacobson, L. *Pygmalion in the classroom: Teacher expectation and pupils' intellectual development.* New York: Holt, Rinehart & Winston, 1968.

Rotzel, G. *The school in Rose Valley: A parent venture in education.* Baltimore: Johns Hopkins Press, 1971.

Shaw, J. S. The new conservative alternative. *Nation's Schools and Colleges,* 1975, 2, 31-39.

Silberman, C. E. *Crisis in the classroom: The remaking of American education.* New York: Random House, 1970.

Smith, V. H. Optional alternative public schools: New partners in education. *North Central Association Quarterly,* 1975, 49, 334-38.

Szasz, T. S. The myth of mental illness. *American Psychologist,* 1960, 15, 113-18.

Szasz, T. S. *The manufacture of madness: The comparative study of the inquisition and the mental health movement.* New York: Harper & Row, 1970.

Vacc, N. A. Long term effects of special class intervention for emotionally disturbed children. *Exceptional Children,* 1972, 39, 15-22.

Weinstein, L. Project Re-Ed schools for emotionally disturbed children: Effectiveness as viewed by referring agencies, parents, and teachers. *Exceptional Children,* 1969, 35, 703-11.

Wilkerson, D. A. The school, delinquency, and the children of the poor. In P. S. Graubard (Ed.), *Children against schools*. Chicago: Follett, 1969. Pp. 107-27.

A SELECTED BIBLIOGRAPHY OF WORKS BY
C. MICHAEL NELSON

Blackhurst, A. E., Cross, D. P., Nelson, C. M., & Tawney, J. W. Special education teacher training: An approximation to a non-categorical approach. *Exceptional Children*, 1973, 39, 284-88.

Nelson, C. M. An evaluation of a non-categorical competency-based special education methods course. In L. M. Bullock (Ed.), *Proceedings of the Annual Fall Conference of Teacher Educators for Children with Behavioral Disorders*. Gainesville: Department of Special Education, University of Florida, 1974. Pp. 29-35.

Nelson, C. M., & Kauffman, J. M. Educational programming for secondary school age delinquent and maladjusted pupils. *Behavioral Disorders*, in press.

Nelson, C. M., Worell, J., & Polsgrove, L. Behaviorally disordered peers as contingency managers. *Behavior Therapy*, 1973, 4, 270-76.

Shores, R. E., Cegelka, P. T., & Nelson, C. M. Competencies needed by special education teachers. *Exceptional Children*, 1973, 40, 192-97.

Worell, J., & Nelson, C. M. *Managing instructional problems: A case study workbook*. New York: McGraw-Hill, 1974.

11
Mainstreaming the Mildly Handicapped Learner

Donald L. MacMillan *Laurence D. Becker*

Donald L. MacMillan's *professional preparation includes a B.A. from Western Reserve University in 1962, a M.A. degree in educational psychology from the University of California at Los Angeles in 1963, and an Ed. D. in exceptional children at U.C.L.A. in 1967. He is presently professor of education at the University of California at Riverside. Dr. MacMillan has published extensively in the areas of behavior modification, motivation, various learning characteristics of the mentally retarded, and mainstreaming. A selected bibliography of works by Donald L. MacMillan is found on pages 226-27.*

Laurence D. Becker *received a B.A. degree in 1969 from the University of California at Los Angeles. His graduate work led to an M.A. in special education in 1971 and a Ph.D. in psychological studies*

208

*in education in 1973 from U.C.L.A. Currently, Dr. Becker is assistant
professor of education at the University of California at Riverside. His
major areas of work include early identification of learning problems and
the regulation of conceptual tempo in educationally high-risk children.
A selected bibliography of works by Laurence D. Becker is found on
page 227.*

INTRODUCTION

The political and social sentiment in America during recent years
has been in opposition to the use of the self-contained special education
class for mildly handicapped children. In prior years, parents, educators,
and legislators argued for specialized services and programs for children
who were failing in the regular education program. In the early 1970s a
series of court decisions concerning mildly handicapped children had
a profound impact on educational programming for them (Ross, De-
Young, & Cohen, 1971). These decisions resulted in legislation mandat-
ing "mainstreaming" special education children back into the regular
education program, a setting which heretofore was deemed inappropriate
for such children since it was in the regular class that they initially
emerged as problem learners. We find this somewhat paradoxical. The
underlying assumption is that the regular classroom and curriculum
have improved over the last decade (see Dunn, 1968), thus making the
present day regular classroom the preferred setting in which to educate
the mildly handicapped child. It is assumed that the regular classroom
teacher can deal with a wide range of individual differences, and that
either the curriculum accommodates a diversity of needs and interests
or can be adapted readily to do so. It is interesting to note that in the
past these children failed in the regular classroom, and now they are
being required to return to the same setting. We question whether
regular education has changed sufficiently to warrant the apparent
optimism regarding the educational plight of the mildly handicapped
learner. One cannot lose sight of the fact that traditionally these have
been "hard to teach" children, and to delabel and mainstream does
nothing to alter that fact.

The basis for decisions made by the courts are a bit unclear, particularly in terms of whether law or evidence was given primary consideration in deciding the cases. In presenting the case for the plaintiffs,
lawyers have presented "evidence" from a number of studies which had
methodological flaws or inconclusive results, which (if the cases were
decided on the basis of evidence) resulted in decisions that negatively
evaluated the self-contained class. One well might question the wisdom
of the precipitous move from the self-contained class to the regular class
to the extent that it has occurred.

We feel that a close examination of mainstreaming is necessary if our concern is with giving each child the best educational program possible. To this end, a number of programmatic options ranging from self-contained classes to total integration should be made available to each child. In our view mainstreaming should be an option for some children, and not a mandatory program for all mildly handicapped children. The focus of this chapter is on several aspects of mainstreaming educable mentally retarded children (EMR). These include: who should be mainstreamed; how mainstreaming might be accomplished; and how mainstreaming should be evaluated. In the following sections we will rely heavily upon the developments in California for a couple of reasons. First, in light of the fact that the early "due process" challenges were located in California, the schools have been very sensitive to the mainstreaming issue. Second, we are more familiar with the California developments given our residence.

MAINSTREAMING DEFINED

Confusion arises over the definition of mainstreaming. Few clearcut definitions can be found in the literature. Dailey (1974) noted a wide variety of definitions, some of which were as simple as delabel and return the child to the regular classroom. A number of terms such as *deinstitutionalize, delabel,* and *integrate* have been used to describe the mainstreaming process. In 1974, the National Advisory Committee on the Handicapped endorsed a policy of placement of exceptional children into the "least restrictive alternative," and recently Congress passed the Education for All Handicapped Children Act (PL 94-142) which also calls for placement in the least restrictive alternative. This measure reaffirms the right of all handicapped children to a "free and appropriate education." Ongoing attempts to define the relationship between mainstreaming, least restrictive alternative, and appropriate educational placement have yet to clarify how the terms translate into educational practice.

Most definitions of mainstreaming emphasize the temporal aspect of the process; i.e., the percentage of time the child will participate in the regular classroom. It is apparent, however, that the process also includes a determination of which children might profit the most from integration, as well as *what* and *how* a child is to be taught. In addition, mainstreaming involves the development of an adequate communication system between special and regular educational personnel for maximum program coordination. Simplistic definitions add to the confusion over mainstreaming in that virtually any activity that involves integration of handicapped learners under any circumstances can qualify as mainstreaming according to one of the existing definitions. A suitable working definition is offered by Kaufman, Gottlieb, Agard, and Kukic (1975).

Mainstreaming refers to the temporal, instructional and social integration of eligible exceptional children with normal peers, based on an ongoing individually determined educational planning and programming process and requires clarification of responsibility among regular and special education administrative, instructional and supportive personnel [pp. 40-41].

This definition points out that mainstreaming is more than just the temporal integration of handicapped pupils; it includes instructional and social integration, as well as educational planning and the clarification of responsibility. MacMillan et al. (1976) added to this definition the additional qualification that categorical labels be removed from children being mainstreamed, given the vehemence with which opponents to the special class singled out labels as having a detrimental effect on children to whom they were given. In essence, we restrict the use of the term mainstreaming to those efforts that include (a) temporal integration, (b) instructional integration, (c) social integration, (d) shared responsibility for programming, and (e) removal of handicap labels. To date, few, if any, programs, meet all of these requirements.

IMPETUS FOR MAINSTREAMING

A number of forces coalesced in the late 1960s that resulted in the demise of the special class and the corresponding push for mainstreaming. Court cases highlighted what special educators had known for some time—namely, that the identification process for mildly handicapped children resulted in disproportionate numbers of minority children being so identified, that the special class did not result in the achievement gains originally anticipated, and that the EMR label was objectionable in that it negatively affected children so labeled. In response to the court decisions, legislation was passed that modified the identification process and provided for the temporal integration of mildly handicapped learners into regular classes.

It is instructive to consider the role of special educators in this entire process. First, sentiment among special educators turned against the special class (Johnson, 1962), reaching a watermark with the publication of Dunn's (1968) position paper. Yet, change could be implemented much more rapidly through the courts than from within the system. As a result, charges leveled in the courts and "evidence" presented by attorneys for the plaintiffs was not countered by attorneys for the defense. For example, Cohen and DeYoung (1973) presented five major arguments: (a) tests used to measure intelligence are inappropriate as they do not accurately measure learning abilities of the plaintiffs, (b) unless the tester is familiar with the cultural background and language of the child, he functions incompetently, (c) parents have not been informed and involved in the placement process, (d) the special class is inadequate and fails to develop adequate educational and vocational skills, and (e) placement and labeling does irreparable personal harm. It is noteworthy that scholarly reviews of existing research data on four of these five points concluded that extant research has failed to support the allegations. Consider the review by Cleary, Humphreys, Kendrick, and Wesman (1975) regarding appropriateness of tests; the reviews by Sattler (1973) and Meyers, Sundstrom, and Yoshida (1974) regarding "incompetent" test administration; that by MacMillan (1971) on the adequacy of the special class; and the review by Mac-Millan, Jones, and Aloia (1974) pertaining to the effects of labeling and placement. It is evident from a research perspective that the preceding arguments have not been fully examined. However, just as clear is the fact that the primary impetus toward mainstreaming did not originate from a compelling evidenciary base, but instead from a social-political one. While we concur with much of the sentiment behind such action, we are at the same time concerned that a considerable number of mildly handicapped learners are going to be adversely affected in the name of the "cause." For example, we have been informed that Diana, over whom a great deal of controversy was generated, is back in a self-contained class, which is now believed to be the preferred placement for her. Let us briefly review the evolution that occurred in California beginning in the late 1960s.

In the late 1960s and early 1970s in several key cases in California, the appropriateness of the self-contained class for EMR children was tested from a legal perspective. A number of class-action suits from minority group members were heard in the courts. Plaintiffs argued that the tests utilized by school psychologists were not accurately measuring learning ability, that parents were not being involved in the placement of their children, and that the harm created by labeling and tracking was irreparable (*Diana* v. *Board of Education*, 1970; *Covarrubias* v. *San Diego Unified School District*, 1971; and *Arreola* v. *Board of Education*, 1968). Decisions, in favor of the plaintiffs, included re-evaluation of all minority group children in California's EMR classes, administration of intelligence tests in the child's home language, more involvement of parents in the placement process, and an examination of the percentage of minority group children in self-contained EMR classes in every school district in California.

These legal decisions were then translated into legislation at the state level. In California, Assembly Bill 1625 (1970) required that all EMR children be re-evaluated and those children with IQ's between 70 and 85 be decertified and placed in regular class programs (Senate Bill 1317, 1970). Senate Bill 33 (1971) required that all children be served in the regular classroom, if possible. More recently, the California Master Plan for Special Education (1974) was enacted. This plan emphasizes mainstreaming and the use of generic labels.

Careful examination of the impetus for mainstreaming indicates that it evolved as a result of several separate forces which existed themselves at a time when the sociopolitical climate was sympathetic to the aims expressed.

WHO SHOULD BE MAINSTREAMED?

Court cases and legislative enactments provide some direction in terms of who should be mainstreamed. Some (Keogh & Levitt, 1976; Mercer, 1974) contend, however, that we do not find in court decisions that kind of precision needed to provide helpful direction to those with responsibility for making the determinations. After the fact, the courts may decide that a given child should or should not have been placed in a certain program, or they will find that the means by which placement was decided was in violation of due process. Furthermore, the courts have sensitized those in the field to the fact that care had best be exercised when considering the case of an ethnic minority child, particularly when the results of an intelligence test are a primary consideration in the decision. The courts, then, have essentially established what should not be done. In realizing a lack of expertise in this area, they have refrained from outlining procedures to be followed in determining who is to be mainstreamed.

In the Education for All Handicapped Children Act (PL 94-142) several broad concepts are upheld (e.g., due process, least restrictive alternative, nondiscriminatory testing) which must be considered in deciding who is to be mainstreamed. The point is that we are still confronted by a major problem in assessment, one that has not been solved by the courts, and one that is multidimensional:

1. For those children who have been classified in one of the mildly handicapped categories (EMR, LD, ED), which ones should be mainstreamed and which maintained in self-contained programs?
2. Who are handicapped learners in need of special educational assistance?
3. How are we to decide the least restrictive alternative for individual students, or the most appropriate alternative program?

As a result of court actions (see Cohen & DeYoung, 1973; Weintraub, 1975; Burt, 1975) the reassessment of children enrolled in special education programs was mandated (e.g., *Diana* v. *Board of Education*) in California resulting in the "decertification" of between 11,000 and 22,000 EMR students (Keogh & Levitt, 1976; Meyers, MacMillan, & Yoshida, 1975). It is interesting to note how decisions were made regarding which EMR children should be returned to the regular class and which were to remain in a self-contained EMR program. The most obvious *bit* of evidence relied on was the child's IQ! Despite the criticism heaped upon the intelligence test in the court cases that precipitated the decertification, these court cases seem to imply that the standard error of measurement of the test is unidimensional; i.e., the IQ score is not to be trusted in identifying EMR children for special programs, but it is very good when it serves to remove children from those same programs. In some cases (exceptions, to be sure), someone simply went down lists of EMR children that gave their most recent IQ scores and checked the children with IQs above 70. Far more care must be exercised in ascertaining child characteristics that are predictive of success in alternative educational service models, suggesting a child-by-situation prediction.

CALIFORNIA EXPERIENCE[1]

In 1970 a series of legislative enactments resulted in programs to "transition" former EMR children into regular classrooms. Hence, with the establishment of lower IQ levels for the upper end of the EMR category (i.e., a shift from one to two standard deviations below the mean) and procedural modifications (e.g., use of nonverbal tests for culturally different students) the wholesale re-evaluation of EMR students was begun. An evaluation of the success of these children has been completed (Meyers et al., 1975), and some of the findings pertinent to child characteristics related to success bear on the present discussion.

Procedurally, the IQ score was the most compelling evidence in deciding which EMR children would be returned to the regular program. IQ cutoffs were established and cases were "reviewed." In some instances, children were retested and a thorough evaluation was undertaken. In others, existing IQ scores (in one case the IQ was obtained seven years before the re-evaluation) were compared to new IQ cutoffs and those above a given IQ were decertified while those with IQs below the cutoff were retained in the EMR program. Interestingly, when the decertified (D) group was compared to the EMR group on the IQ scores obtained when they were initially placed into the EMR program, there was no difference between the groups—although the D group did have higher IQs at the time of decertification. Hence, at the time they were identified initially as EMR there was no indication on the basis of IQ that one group was "psychometrically superior" to the other. One might contend that the D group children benefited from the EMR program in that their IQs ascended while enrolled in that program.

---

[1] Results reported here are based on an investigation funded by BEH (OEG-0-73-5263) and reported by Meyers, MacMillan, and Yoshida (1975).

The second child characteristic that was related clearly to decertification was ethnicity. The decertification action in California was a phenomenon that affected ethnic minority children. Since the investigation was descriptive in nature, it was impossible to establish the reason for the ethnic imbalance. Two obvious possibilities immediately come to mind. First, one would expect more ethnic minority children to be removed from the EMR program when "fair evaluative criteria" were used since these children were the ones against whom the discriminatory criteria operated in the initial identification procedures. Second, one might suspect that school personnel were more inclined to decertify ethnic minority children since the litigation that led to this legislation was brought on behalf of minority children, leading to intimidation of school personnel responsible for the reassessment.

Attempts to relate child characteristics to D or EMR status failed to reveal significant relationships between any of the child variables at the time of initial referral and the status of D or EMR.

NEW ENTRANTS TO THE SYSTEM

In addition to the cohort of EMR children who are returned to regular programs, there is another cohort of children for whom assessment is vital: those children entering school and coming to the attention of school authorities as inefficient learners *after* new guidelines are adopted and mainstreaming is the major programmatic arrangement (MacMillan, Jones, & Meyers, 1976). Determination must still be made concerning which children are in need of special education, or will not benefit maximally from the regular class program without the delivery of support services in some form. In other words, the concerns expressed over the imprecision of assessment procedures when segregated programs abounded have not been answered by mainstreaming. Identification of problem learners must still take place and the attempt to discern the reasons for the problems undertaken. What instruments and/or procedures will be used toward that end?

Recent court decisions (*Larry P.* v. *Riles*) have resulted in California's adopting a policy of prohibiting the use of intelligence tests for purposes of placing children in programs for the retarded. One might hypothesize that this will result in greater proportions of minority children being identified as exceptional by the public schools (Ashurst & Meyers, 1973) as the IQ did serve to prevent placement in the past. The results reported by Ashurst and Meyers (1973) indicated that there was disagreement between the referring teacher and psychologist significantly more often when the child in question was a minority child in comparison to cases of Caucasian children. The point is that the psychologist represents a different perspective than that of the teacher regarding mentally retarded learners. Hence, classification based exclusively on the teacher's perspective will negate the possibility of the IQ score prohibiting classification as mentally retarded in cases where it would be above an established cutoff.

With the passage of the Education for All Handicapped Children Act (PL 94-142), several elements must be incorporated into this assessment process: (a) due process must be assured, (b) testing must be nondiscriminatory, and (c) at some point in the process individual educational plans must be developed for each child. While each of these elements must be operationalized, it is obvious that considerable modification is called for.

POSSIBLE ALTERNATIVES

In the past, undue reliance upon psychometric evidence in determining who needs special education has been noted (Keogh, 1972). Nondiscriminatory testing is difficult to define, as existing tests of achievement (including intelligence tests) do not appear to "underpredict" for minority children (Cleary, Humphreys, Kendrick, & Wesman, 1975). On the other hand, these same tests identify a disproportionate number of minority children as handicapped learners, and this has been a persuasive argument against their continued use for purposes of identifying children in need of special education. Hence, it is clear that alternatives will be sought. Let us consider some possible alternatives to those used previously to identify mildly handicapped learners.

One alternative presently being developed by Mercer (Mercer & Lewis, in press) entails the "correcting" of an IQ obtained in a standardized fashion with data on the child's cultural background, ultimately generating an index of the child's "estimated learning potential" (ELP). Mercer's approach, called the System of Multi-Cultural Pluralistic Assessment (SOMPA) reflects one response to the allegation that psychometric assessment has been biased against cultural minority children. Presumably, some differentiation could be made between children with high ELP scores despite low IQ and children for whom such "correcting" fails to yield an ELP that is much higher than the IQ obtained under standardized testing procedures.

Another possible alternative might result from Jensen's (1970) distinction between *primary* and *secondary* familial retardation. Jensen (1970) has reviewed a body of research on laboratory learning tasks which have been characterized as tapping Level I (associative learning) or Level II (conceptual learning). Low IQ children who perform well on Level I tasks are viewed as capable of higher order learning if approached through their strength in associative learning. *Primary retardation* then refers to a deficiency in both Level I and Level II learning; *secondary retardation* refers to a deficiency in Level II but not in Level I learning.

Does such a dichotomy provide any predictions as to which children with IQs below 70 would succeed in a mainstreaming program? This remains to be determined.

Finally, a third alternative may be found in the work of Budoff and his associates (Budoff, 1967, 1970; Budoff, Meskin, & Harrison, 1971) on the learning-potential hypothesis. Essentially, this hypothesis posits that there are two groups among the EMR population: those who are *educationally* retarded and those who are *mentally* retarded. By means of testing the children with nonverbal reasoning problems, then instructing them in task-relevant principles and retesting them, three types of children were identified according to patterns of response: (a) high scorers, (b) gainers, and (c) nongainers. The *high scorers* and *gainers* are the educationally retarded, while *nongainers* are the mentally retarded in Budoff's typology. Again, it would be interesting to determine whether these subgroupings experience differential success in a mainstream educational program.

In summary, it is clear that some EMR children are more likely to survive educationally in the mainstream than are others. The courts have not provided direction in determining which EMR children will benefit from regular class placement and which ones will be devastated by excessive failure, both academic and social. Clearly, intelligence tests alone do not work in making this distinction. Conversations with school psychologists indicate that there is a reluctance to classify minority children (regardless of whether they will be placed in a segregated EMR class or mainstreamed setting), particularly when a district has its "quota" of minority children in EMR programs. One might well contend that at this point the *cause* begins to have an adverse effect on children.

Determinations of who will be mainstreamed will be made. To date, these determinations have been made by directive of courts, out of fear of litigation, and in efforts to balance ethnic enrollments. Hopefully, we can now move on to make such decisions in the best interest of individual children.

Once we have decided who is to be mainstreamed, the next issue pertains to *how* this will be accomplished.

HOW IS MAINSTREAMING TO BE IMPLEMENTED?

School districts have utilized a variety of techniques for mainstreaming EMR children. In a recent survey of 126 school districts in California, Keogh, Levitt, Robson, and Chan (1974) reported that EMR children are most frequently mainstreamed through (a) regular classes with paraprofessional aides, (b) regular classes in combination with resource rooms, (c) regular classes with special education consultants, (d) tutorial programs, and (e) self-contained classes for educationally handicapped children. Regarding the latter method, Meyers, MacMillan, and Yoshida (1975) question "whether these children are being 'transitioned' or 'recategorized' into alternate special education categories when they could no longer remain classified as EMR" [p. 30]. The *resource model*, although not fully substantiated by research, has been the most popular approach to mainstreaming. This model may vary from a special resource room where the child receives specialized help to a resource consultant or tutor who assists the child and his teacher while the child remains in the regular class full time. Many of the district administrators interviewed by Keogh et al. indicated that they used several program options in combination; i.e., regular class with tutor and part-time participation in a resource room.

The resource model includes both resource rooms and resource specialists. The resource room is a special education setting where a child comes on a regularly scheduled basis for remedial assistance. The facility is staffed by a resource specialist whose role includes working with the child in the resource room, helping the child while in the regular classroom, and assisting the regular classroom teacher. Resource specialists are former special education teachers with master's-level training. The resource room may function as a self-contained unit where children spend a majority of the school day, or as an integrated unit where children spend only brief periods of time with a resource specialist. Children may also be assigned full time to the regular class, thus modifying the role of the resource specialist to that of a consultant who works with both children and teachers in the regular classroom.

An innovative resource room plan for educationally handicapped (EH) and EMR children was developed by Taylor, Artuso, Soloway, Hewett, Quay, and Stillwell (1972). The "Madison Plan" functions both as an integrated and self-contained resource room. The amount of time each child spends in the regular classroom is dependent upon his/her "readiness for regular classroom functioning." Children with severe educational disabilities spend a majority of the school day in a one-to-one setting with a resource specialist. As these children improve, they spend less time in the "learning center" and more time in the regular classroom. Children who are ready to return on a full-time basis to the regular class are first enrolled in a simulated regular class with twelve children to facilitate their transition.

Recently, California enacted a Master Plan for Special Education which calls for the use of a resource specialist program. The program is described as follows in the Master Plan:

> The resource specialist program should provide instructional planning, special instruction, tutorial assistance, or other services to exceptional individuals in special programs and/or in regular classrooms of each school. The program is to be coordinated by a resource specialist, who is a special education teacher with advanced

training in the education of individuals with exceptional needs [p. 30].

The resource specialist program is a school-based program, with one resource specialist for every 600 children in the school.

Proponents of the resource model speak highly of its merits; i.e., it removes labels, reduces segregation, and saves money. Research on the efficacy of the resource model, however, is minimal. The most glaring deficiency in the concept is the lack of attention given to the issue of training regular education and resource personnel to work with mainstreamed children. Curriculum is also ignored. The major focus has been on the mechanism for mainstreaming; i.e. resource room and/or resource teacher. Consideration should be given by those who advocate mainstreaming to the teacher training and curriculum issues.

TRAINING RESOURCE SPECIALISTS

Most reports discussing the resource model are vague as to the training of resource personnel. Prerequisites usually include a special education credential, an advanced degree in special education, and the ability to work with teachers on a consultant basis. Teachers selected for the resource specialist job are frequently described by district administrators as "teachers who can do it all." The question arises as to how this superteacher can be trained. California, like many other states, has turned to competency-based preservice training for special education teachers. Competencies have been delineated by "experts" in the field, and have been incorporated into teacher training programs throughout California. These competencies, however, have not been validated. The competency-based model used for training teachers in other areas of exceptionality is being utilized for the resource specialist. Special educators have spent many hours attempting to define the role of the resource specialist and to delineate valid competencies for that role, but the process has been difficult. Questions arise as to how preservice resource specialists should be taught and what they should be taught.

The training issue also relates to inservice education. If the new role for special education teachers is to act as resource people, how will they be trained on an inservice basis? The task is not an easy one. At the University of California, Riverside, we are attempting to develop a competency-based inservice model for special education teachers. Through this project we have gained insight into the problems of training resource personnel in the field; i.e., developing competency lists, assessing competency levels, and determining the curriculum to be utilized.

The success of mainstreaming will depend, in part, on training special education teachers to assume the role of resource specialists. Results of the survey by Keogh et al. suggest that, to date, school districts have been delinquent in providing inservice training for special education teachers involved in mainstreaming.

TRAINING REGULAR EDUCATION TEACHERS

A related issue is that of training regular class teachers to deal effectively with EMR children. One of the major assumptions underlying mainstreaming is that significant advances have been made in regular education over the past decade. We question that assumption. Training appears to be more organized with competency-based approaches, but evaluation data are lacking. Competencies have not been validated, and their impact on children have not been determined. It is unlikely that regular education teachers have improved to the point where they are now able to deal with these children who are "hard to teach."

Questions arise as to what and how regular classroom teachers should be taught. In addition, the question of the attitudes of regular classroom teachers toward EMR children needs to be addressed by advocates of mainstreaming. Some teachers have expressly stated in their contracts that they will not accept these children in their classes, while others seem more enthusiastic. Should regular education teachers who accept mainstreamed children be required to have a special education credential? Should they be required to student teach in a special class? Is simply completing the introductory course in special education enough? These are all crucial questions that must be carefully considered.

It is evident that our regular educational system is not yet ready for mainstreaming. Regular educators have not developed the skills to use with EMR children, nor do they look upon the process in a favorable light. Special educators must take a leadership role in the training of regular education teachers to function within the mainstreaming process. To ignore the need to re-educate regular class teachers is tantamount to failure for mainstreaming.

CURRICULUM DEVELOPMENT

Consideration must be given to the questions of what and how mainstreamed children should be taught. Regular class methods and procedures have been tried with these children without success, and new curricula that can be utilized in both special and regular classes need to be developed. To mainstream without considering curriculum is not in the best interest of mainstreamed children. Highly individualized programs that are evaluated daily would appear to be valuable. The responsibility for the development and dissemination of new curriculum models to the regular educational system should be that of special educators.

HOW IS MAINSTREAMING TO BE EVALUATED?

Efforts to determine how well mainstreaming works are confronted with a number of thorny problems. First, it must be decided whether the sole concern is with the moral issue of physical segregation, in which case mainstreaming is better than self-contained classes. Second, does one want evidence of greater academic and/or social gains by children in one type of program when compared to those in another? Third, the effect of mainstreaming on groups of children other than those being mainstreamed must be considered. Fourth, the appropriateness of traditional experimental designs for evaluating educational programs must be questioned.

Perspective for evaluation must also be established (MacMillan et al., 1976). From an *administrative* perspective the concern with evaluation is expressed by collecting data on how many children are served, how much money a given program costs, and the extent to which a program avoids negative publicity. From a *child* perspective concerns are reflected by collecting data on child outcomes (e.g., achievement, adjustment) in order to show that children have benefited from a program regardless of how many were served or how many dollars were spent. Within the context of the child perspective, one can use normative- or objective-reference approaches in collecting these data.

It is our contention that if mainstreaming is advocated or advanced on the basis of self-contained classes (with their segregation and labeling) as being morally wrong, or on the basis that the mildly handicapped child is legally guaranteed an education in the regular class if feasible, then there is no need to provide supportive child data demonstrating that he/she is better off in a mainstreamed setting than in a more restricted setting. That is, if there are moral or legal injustices inherent in the self-contained class that do not exist in the mainstreamed setting, then there is no need to show evidence of better achievement or adjustment. However, if the case for mainstreaming is based on the belief that children will benefit academically or socially by being placed in a less restrictive alternative, then it is incumbent upon evaluators to collect the kinds of data that address that belief. Arguments advanced in favor of mainstreaming often include some reference to benefits that will accrue to children presumably as a consequence of no longer being physically segregated, labeled, stigmatized, exposed to an inappropriate curriculum, or some combination thereof. In these cases, those advancing the arguments are compelled to provide corroborating support that these benefits do, indeed, result.

Assuming that there is a belief that there will be academic and/or social benefits derived from being mainstreamed, there are questions regarding how this will be demonstrated. The efficacy studies attempted to show this by means of between-groups research designs wherein one group in a "special class" was compared to a group in a "regular class." The methodological pitfalls of this approach have been discussed widely (Guskin & Spicker, 1968; Kirk, 1964) and most of this discussion is relevant to evaluating mainstreaming programs. Foremost in terms of problems with a between-groups comparison is the fact that the variation within models is as great, or greater, than the variation between mainstreaming models. Hence, it is essential that one consider elements within a model (e.g., instructional strategies, teacher-child interactions) in order to be able to relate increments in performance to factors other than an administrative model itself.

The inappropriateness of between-groups designs is more pronounced in cases of mainstreaming, especially in light of the requirement in PL 94-142 for individual educational plans. If plans are individually tailored, then the "treatment" of mainstreaming will be extremely heterogeneous, thereby violating the assumption that within-treatment variation will be less than between-treatments variation. Hence, group mean scores for outcome measures (e.g., achievement, adjustment) will be exceedingly difficult to attribute to program elements since each child will have been exposed to various programs. Therefore, we do not believe that further efficacy studies comparing mainstreamed students to other groups of children will be at all enlightening.

In evaluating mainstreaming it is essential to realize that the effects of such a program will be felt throughout the entire educational system. In an earlier work (MacMillan et al., 1976), it was suggested that one consider the effect of mainstreaming on several discrete groups, who in California were the following:

(1) Children who were declassified as EMR and mainstreamed as a result of a shift in IQ for defining mental retardation (i.e., shift from 1 to 2 SD below the mean; roughly from IQ 85 to IQ 70).

(2) The EMR children who were not declassified and remain in a self-contained special EMR class with presumably intellectually less capable classmates on the average.

(3) Regular class children into whose classes the declassified EMRs have been placed.

(4) The more recent cohorts of children with IQs between 70-85, a range which in the past permitted classification as EMR had they encountered learning problems, but not now because of change of IQ guidelines [p. 6].

Let us assume that we collect valid achievement and adjustment data on mainstreamed mildly handicapped learners, children left in a self-contained program, and on regular class peers. In all probability the results of such an evaluation are not going to indicate both academic and adjustment benefits across all three groups. Instead, the results will probably be mixed. For example, the mainstreamed EMRs may benefit academically and be adversely affected socially. The point is that unless outcomes are given relative degrees of importance, decisions are going to be difficult to make. In addition, one could encounter beneficial effects for mainstreamed EMRs relative to both achievement and adjustment, but with the additional finding that the nonhandicapped regular class peers are adversely affected. Such a situation confounds direct statements regarding how well mainstreaming works; while it benefits one group, it serves to the detriment of another, forcing policy makers to decide which group should receive primary consideration. We suggest that if the case for mainstreaming presupposes evidenciary support then it will be necessary to prioritize outcomes; further, policy makers may have to choose ultimately between groups of children in the mainstream of education should the evidence suggest the mixed results briefly described. To date, there is little to suggest that much consideration has been given to anticipated outcomes. Instead, the impetus for mainstreaming has been one of compliance to court edicts. Hopefully, special educators do anticipate benefits for children and represent child advocates rather than program advocates. If so, what are the benefits? What are the outcomes of highest priority? What degree of success will be accepted as criteria for academic and adjustment progress?

In the past standardized tests of achievement and various measures of adjustment (e.g., self-concept scales, sociometrics, teacher ratings) have been offered as evidence of the efficacy of special and regular classes. Few studies (e.g., Porter & Milazzo, 1958) have considered the adult status of individuals who have gone through different programs. In efforts to evaluate mainstreaming, longitudinal evidence might clarify the educational and postschool plight of mildly handicapped learners. Such evidence may provide a kind of baseline against which to evaluate "reasonable progress." We suspect that achievement or social success beyond that achieved by the model nonhandicapped learner is unrealistic for the vast majority of children in question. The determination of the success or failure of mainstreaming must be based on evidence that is relevant to the population of children involved.

CONCLUSIONS

The optimism and enthusiasm associated with mainstreaming is laudable, and philosophically we wholeheartedly endorse the move to provide children with academic problems every opportunity possible to remain in a regular classroom. At the same time we are concerned with what we perceive to be unbridled optimism on the part of some who appear to think that mere delabeling and physically returning mildly handicapped learners to the regular class will transform these children into above average students. Such thinking can only be harmful to everyone involved.

It is critical that we not lose sight of the fact that the children in question are hard-to-teach students regardless of whether or not they are labeled, regardless of whether they are placed in the regular class or in a special class, and regardless of whether or not IQ scores are obtained for them. We have not achieved any degree of success in teaching them in any educational setting. A second factor that must be recognized is that mainstreaming is going to be a very difficult process. If we sell it as a simplistic solution, those involved will very likely become quickly discouraged and abandon their commitment to the children involved. Without a philosophical belief in mainstreaming, these children will find that the educational system is a graveyard, not just the special class, regardless of what the court mandates. Let us approach general education with an openness about the difficulties that lie ahead, but instill a conviction that mainstreaming is right.

Finally, we contend that mainstreaming must serve children and not causes. Decisions on the least restrictive alternative must be made in individual cases, not for groups. It cannot be ignored that disproportionate numbers of minority children were classified as retarded; yet today a minority child is often not placed into a self-contained class despite the fact that everyone directly concerned feels that such placement is warranted. The child is not placed because the district has filled its "quota" of that ethnic minority. Surely such actions are not in the best interests of children. Evaluation data should focus on the issue of what effect a given program of mainstreaming is having on children. Child advocates should be insisting on information regarding child benefits, lest the move to mainstreaming be out of fear of possible litigation or because it is politically expedient.

REFERENCES

Ashurst, D. I., & Meyers, C. E. Social system and clinical model in the identification of the educable retarded. *Monographs of the American Association on Mental Deficiency*, 1973, 1, 150-63.

Budoff, M. Learning potential among institutionalized young adult retardates. *American Journal of Mental Deficiency*, 1967, 72, 404-11.

Budoff, M. Social and test data correlates of learning potential status in adolescent educable mental retardates. *Studies in Learning Potential*, 1970, 1, No. 3.

Budoff, M., Meskin, J., & Harrison, R. H. Educational test of the learning potential hypothesis. *American Journal of Mental Deficiency*, 1971, 76, 159-69.

Burt, R. A. Judicial action to aid the retarded. In N. Hobbs (Ed.), *Issues in the classification of children* (Vol. 2). San Francisco: Jossey-Bass, 1975. Pp. 293-318.

California Master Plan for Special Education, California State Department of Education, 1974.

Cleary, T. A., Humphreys, L. G., Kendrick, S. A., & Wesman, A. Educational use of tests with disadvantaged students. *American Psychologist,* 1975, 30, 15-41.

Cohen, J. S., & DeYoung, H. The role of litigation in the improvement of programming for the handicapped. In L. Mann & D. Sabatino (Eds.), *The first review of special education* (Vol. 2). Philadelphia: Journal of Special Education Press, 1973. Pp. 261-86.

Dailey, R. Dimensions and issues in "74": Tapping into the special education grapevine. *Exceptional Children,* 1974, 40, 503-7.

Dunn, L. M. Special education for the mildly retarded—Is much of it justifiable? *Exceptional Children,* 1968, 35, 5-22.

Guskin, S. L., & Spicker, H. H. Educational research in mental retardation. In N. R. Ellis (Ed.), *International review of research in mental retardation* (Vol. 3). New York: Academic Press, 1968. Pp. 217-78.

Jensen, A. R. A theory of primary and secondary familial mental retardation. In N. R. Ellis (Ed.), *International review of research in mental retardation* (Vol. 4). New York: Academic Press, 1970. Pp. 33-105.

Johnson, G. O. Special education for the mentally handicapped—A paradox. *Exceptional Children,* 1962, 19, 62-69.

Kaufman, M., Gottlieb, J., Agard, J., and Kukic, M. Mainstreaming: Toward an explication of the construct. In E. L. Meyen, G. A. Vergason, & R. J. Whelan (Eds.), *Alternatives for teaching exceptional children.* Denver: Love Publishing Co., 1975. Pp. 35-54.

Keogh, B. K. Psychological evaluation of exceptional children: Old hangups and new directions. *Journal of School Psychology,* 1972, 10, 142-44.

Keogh, B., & Levitt, M. L. Special education in the mainstream: A confrontation of limitations? *Focus on Exceptional Children,* 1976, 8(1), 1-11.

Keogh, B., Levitt, M., Robson, G., & Chan, K. *A review of transition programs in California public schools* (Technical report). University of California, Los Angeles, 1974.

Kirk, S. A. Research in education. In H. A. Stevens & R. Heber (Eds.), *Mental retardation: A review of research.* Chicago: University of Chicago Press, 1964. Pp. 57-99.

MacMillan, D. Special education for the mildly retarded: Servant or savant? *Focus on Exceptional Children,* 1971, 2, 1-11.

MacMillan, D. L., Jones, R. L., & Aloia, G. F. The mentally retarded label: A theoretical analysis and review of research. *American Journal of Mental Deficiency,* 1974, 79, 241-61.

MacMillan, D. L., Jones, R. L., & Meyers, C. E. Mainstreaming the mildly retarded: Some questions, cautions, and guidelines. *Mental Retardation,* 1976, 14 (1), 3-10.

Mercer, J. R. *The who, why, and how of mainstreaming.* Paper presented at the Annual Meeting of the American Association on Mental Deficiency, Toronto, June 1974.

Mercer, J. R., & Lewis, J. F. *SOMPA: System of multi-cultural pluralistic assessment.* New York: Psychological Corporation, in press.

Meyers, C. E., MacMillan, D. L., & Yoshida, R. K. *Correlates of success in transition of MR to regular class.* Final report (Grant OEG-0-73-5263), U.C.L.A., NPI-Pacific State Hospital Research Group, 1965.

Meyers, C. E., Sundstrom, P. E., & Yoshida, R. K. The school psychologist and assessment in special education. *School Psychology Monographs,* 1974, 2 (1), 3-57.

Porter, R. B., & Milazzo, T. C. A comparison of mentally retarded adults who attended a special class with those who attended regular school classes. *Exceptional Children,* 1958, 24, 410-12.

Ross, S., DeYoung, H., & Cohen, J. Confrontation: Special education placement and the law. *Exceptional Children,* 1971, 38, 5-12.

Sattler, J. M. Intelligence testing of ethnic minority-group and culturally disadvantaged children. In L. Mann & D. A. Sabatino (Eds.), *The first review of special education* (Vol. 2). Philadelphia: JSE Press, 1973. Pp. 161-201.

Taylor, F., Artuso, A., Soloway, M., Hewett, F., Quay, H., & Stillwell, R. A learning center plan for special education. *Focus on Exceptional Children,* 1972, 4, 1-7.

Weintraub, F. J. Recent influences of law regarding the identification and educational placement of children. In E. L. Meyen, G. A. Vergason, & R. J. Whelan (Eds.), *Alternatives for teaching exceptional children.* Denver: Love Publishing Co., 1975. Pp. 55-72.

A SELECTED BIBLIOGRAPHY OF WORKS BY DONALD L. MACMILLAN AND LAURENCE D. BECKER

Donald L. MacMillan

Guskin, S. L., Bartel, N. R., & MacMillan, D. L. Perspective of the labeled child. In N. Hobbs (Ed.), *Issues in the classification of children* (Vol. 2). San Francisco: Jossey-Bass, 1975.

MacMillan, D. L. Research in Mainstreaming: Promise and reality. In P. H. Mann (Ed.), *Current trends in mainstreaming,* in press.

MacMillan, D. L., Jones, R. L., & Aloia, G. F. The mentally retarded label: A theoretical analysis and review of research, *American Journal of Mental Deficiency,* 1974, 79(3), 241-61.

MacMillan, D. L., Jones, R. L., & Meyers, C. E. Mainstreaming the mildly retarded: Some questions, cautions, and guidelines. *Mental Retardation,* in press.

Yoshida, Roland, K., MacMillan, D. L., & Meyers, C. E. The decertification of minority group EMR students in California: Its historical background and an assessment of student achievement and adjustment. In R. Jones (Ed.), *Mainstreaming and the minority child.* Minneapolis: Leadership Training Institute, University of Minnesota, 1975.

Laurence D. Becker

Becker, L. D. Conceptual tempo and the early detection of learning problems. *Journal of Learning Disabilities,* 1976, 9, 433-42.

Keogh, B. K., Becker, L. D., Kukic, M., & Kukic, S. *Programs for educationally handicapped and educable mentally retarded pupils: Review and recommendations* (Summary report). California State Department of Education, University of California, Los Angeles, 1972.

Keogh, B. K., & Becker, L. D. Early detection of learning problems: Questions, cautions and guidelines. *Exceptional Children,* 1973, 40, 5-12.

Keogh, B. K., Becker, L. D., Kukic, M., & Kukic, S. Programs in EH and EMR pupils: Review and recommendations (Part II). *Academic Theory,* 1974, 9 (5), 325-33.

Loe, D., & Becker, L. D. Research interests of special education administrators. *Phi Delta Kappan,* 1975, 56, 428.

12
New Considerations for the Severely and Profoundly Handicapped

James W. Tawney is currently associate professor in the Department of Special Education and director of the Programmed Environments Project at the University of Kentucky. His previous professional experiences include that of a teacher of educable mentally retarded students and a graduate teaching associate at the University of Illinois.

Dr. Tawney received a B.A. degree in speech from Colorado State College in 1960. Graduate study in special education led to an M.A. degree in 1961 from Colorado State College and a Ph.D. in 1969 from the University of Illinois. Dr. Tawney's major area of work has been in curriculum development and programmed environments pertaining to the severely and profoundly retarded. A selected bibliography of works by Dr. Tawney appears on page 244.

228

ANTECEDENT EVENTS

My introduction to special education came midway in my under-graduate training, when I transferred to Colorado State College (now the University of Northern Colorado) to pursue an interest in speech correction. Once there, the opportunity to observe students in classes for the mildly and moderately retarded shifted my interests, and I graduated with certification to teach the educable retarded. I was fortu-nate to be asked by the late Tony Vaughan to teach in the college's demonstration school, and I remained in Greeley for five years. Thus, with the exception of a brief stint assembling fishing tackle in Miami, I was associated from 1957 to 1965 with one of the college and public school teacher training programs which flourished from the massive infusion of federal funds generated under PL 85-926. The era was noted for the rapid expansion of self-contained classes for the mildly retarded, the beginning of public education for the trainable retarded, and the development of doctoral level programs for training leaders in special education. My roles as student and teacher brought me into daily con-tact with the problems of a rapidly expanding field and the personnel who were being trained to solve them. This was an exciting time in special education. I had the opportunity to meet, or work with, many of those doctoral students who have become leaders in the field including, among others, Richard Schofer and Bill Heller, who have since served in federal and university leadership positions. If memory serves me, it is probably accurate to state that I left Greeley to obtain a doctorate, convinced that I had a fair grasp of the problems in teacher education. I felt that the sooner I obtained a degree and got back to work, the better. Predictably, my first experiences as a doctoral student at the University of Illinois brought about a significant change in my thinking. It was accelerated by my first interview with Sam Kirk who suggested, in his own way, that as long as I was there, I might take advantage of the university's resources. He directed me to Lawrence Stolurow to learn about learning and computers, to Keith Scott to learn about child development, and to Sidney Bijou and Warren Steinman to learn about the experimental analysis of behavior. Dr. Steinman directed my thesis research—my first attempt to develop an "errorless" procedure to train letter discrimination in young children (Tawney, 1972). I recently went through my notes from Dr. Bijou's seminar in natural science approaches to problem solving and found, interestingly enough, no references to what I now believe to be one of the most significant writings on retarda-tion: his functional analysis of retarded development (Bijou, 1963, rev. 1966). Further, it was only after I left Illinois, and gained some per-spective that I became aware of the extent to which Dr. Bijou has influenced the field of retardation. I was fortunate, also, to obtain additional work and curriculum development experience on the Illinois

Down's project and profited from the association with our language team, Lee Wright Hipsher and Kathy Jensen, and Kay Green, a member of the evaluation team. The Distar group (led by Siegfried Engelmann and Carl Bereiter) participated in the earlier phases of the project and made valuable contributions to the *Systematic Language Instruction* (SLI) portion of the curriculum which Ms. Hipsher and I coauthored (Tawney and Hipsher, 1970). This curriculum, completed and field tested during my first year at the University of Kentucky, represented another attempt to develop an "errorless learning" instructional strategy. The general procedure we used and the SLI format has formed the basis, in one way or another, for each of the projects my colleagues and I have initiated since 1971.

In this section I have presented a thumbnail sketch of the persons, events, and circumstances which have influenced my efforts to apply behavioral approaches and technologies to the problems of the education of severely retarded children, their teachers, and the systems which are charged to change both child and teacher behavior. To be complete, I must add the name of Bill Tisdall, the "silver fox" of special education, who enticed me, and others, to Kentucky with the promise of worlds to conquer. His death in 1970, less than six months after my arrival in Kentucky, had a profound effect on the newly formed department which he chaired. To be current, it should suffice to note that my colleagues, A. E. Blackhurst and C. M. Nelson, whose chapters appear elsewhere in this volume, and Patricia Cegelka offer solicited and unsolicited advice which serves to contribute to the overall direction of our projects. Our current project staff and their contributions are too numerous to list here. However, time and publications will identify them. The opportunity to present a personal perspective on special education also provides an opportunity to acknowledge the support and encouragement our efforts received from Norris Haring, Robert Smith, Oliver Hurley, and Bobby Palk.

It does not seem that nearly twenty years have passed since I first sat in a class to listen to the speech and language patterns of mildly and moderately retarded children. It is quite clear, however, that the problems we face as we prepare to develop public educational programs for the severely and profoundly retarded are not appreciably different from those which confronted persons charged to develop classes for the EMR and TMR in the 1950s and early 1960s. As I have stated elsewhere (Tawney, 1975), the major factors which may separate us from our history of failure in special education are simply the *acknowledgement* that we have made major errors and the *determination* to have the good sense not to make these same mistakes again in SMR program development. Events move rapidly, though, and I am less confident now than I was a year ago that we stand in relatively good shape in this endeavor.

I will describe, in the remainder of this chapter, the strategies we employ to develop errorless learning systems and the problems confronting special educators as we develop this "new" field of the severely/profoundly retarded.

THE FOUNDATIONS OF OUR RESEARCH AND DEVELOPMENT EFFORTS

Mental retardation and developmental retardation, despite the similarities of the terms, are not the same thing. The distinction between them is concisely spelled out in Bijou's (1966) functional analysis of retarded development. He described the retarded individual as "one who has a limited repertory of behaviors shaped by events that constitute his history" [p. 2]. We steadfastly adhere to Bijou's definition, and have incorporated it into the majority of our publications and proposals. This is because it (a) directs our attention to observable stimulus-response relationships, (b) encourages us to focus on child-environment interactions, (c) specifies the ways that inadequate environments may retard development, and (d) suggests ways that we can modify environments. Most important, the notion that careful programming of events and arrangement of environment may facilitate development has encouraged us to consider that early intervention may enable us to build or shape a behavioral repertoire for the infant with observable, manifest, and multiple biological defects. This intriguing possibility will undoubtedly shift our attention from the modification of preschool or day care environments to the home and crib environment of the newborn.

A second major influence on our work is the literature on errorless learning. Terrace's (1967) work with pigeons, Sidman and Stoddard's work with normal and retarded subjects, and Bijou's experimental studies (1968) suggested a methodology for developing instructional programs which might enable children with severely limited behavioral repertoires to learn with a minimum of error. My first attempt to develop an errorless program involved the design of slide programs to train experimental and control groups of four-year-old children to discriminate, respectively, critical and noncritical features of letter-like stimuli. This experience convinced me of the necessity for translating laboratory procedures into teaching environments and instructional strategies. As noted, a second attempt resulted in the SLI curriculum, which was structured to develop attending behaviors, establish prerequisite motor responses to enable nonvocal subjects to discriminate through motor (touch) responses, and arrange stimulus materials so that the subject (who did attend, and did possess a mode of responding) was initially presented with only correct instances of a concept. Later, noninstances of a concept were faded into the stimulus array so gradually that current responses, presumably, continued to be emitted. This errorless learning strategy underlies all of our current development efforts. However, we find that, with the passage of time, the phrase *errorless learning* has taken on additional meaning. It now refers to a procedure for the development of instructional materials or methodologies. It has become a goal or criterion statement for the quality of our teaching programs. That is, we are developing materials to enable children to learn without error, and will attempt to validate them so that, when complete, we will be able to say that *n* children have responded "errorlessly" on the programs. This is a hypothetical goal, I should add, and note that responding at or above the 80 percent current level seems attainable, given our present level of skill in programming.

Finally, when we say that children with severe developmental retardation can learn without error, we are expressing a positive view of human potential. In other words, we are stating a conviction that, no matter how severe the handicapping condition, children can learn, and, further, that adults can be taught the strategies to teach so that their level of learning is assured. It goes without saying that the same strategies are used to develop materials for adults and children. And, where we once applied the term to specific aspects of a product or process, we now find that we talk about errorless learning systems. Each component is related to one aspect of the multidimensional set of problems confronting the education of the severely and profoundly retarded in public school settings. The components are described, briefly, and related to the problems with which we must deal immediately.

PROBLEMS AND PRODUCT/PROCESS SOLUTIONS

In 1972, on the heels of the Pennsylvania decision,[1] I proposed to develop teacher- and child-use materials, alternative teacher training models, and a technology-based preschool to address the following set of problems: lack of adequate curricula, lack of adequate manpower and manpower training models, and the potential for misapplication of watered down EMR and TMR curricula in educational programs for what will undoubtedly be called "SMR/PMR" classes. Concurrently, we are developing data management systems for teacher use and have incorporated work begun on another project into a teacher competency evaluation system. In 1974, utilizing our preschool-based computer system, we began the development of a telecommunications system to address the problems of education delivery to a low-incidence population in remote or geographically isolated areas, and to develop, or coordinate, comprehensive social service delivery to the family unit.

[1] *Pennsylvania Association for Retarded Children* v. *Commonwealth of Pennsylvania,* 334 F. Supp. 1257 (E. D. Pa. 1971)

Child-use materials: We are nearing completion, and beginning validation of curriculum in language, self-help, social skills, and motor and concept development appropriate for preschool and developmentally young school-age children. The product, in its final form, will include a scope and sequence matrix, a set of highly task-analyzed instructional programs, and a set of task analyses. Presumably, the teacher who has been appropriately trained will be able to use the program structure, use the task analyses to generate new programs, and use the model to generate curricula in other areas.

The programs were developed in classrooms of children with severe developmental retardation through the intervention of teachers and a curriculum development staff. Field validation efforts are scheduled to take place in those systems which are implementing classes under right-to-education mandates to accomplish two goals: to test the materials and to provide curricula to the environments most in need of them.

Teacher competency development modules: These modules have been designed to provide validation teachers with content and practicum experiences equivalent to those of teachers working at the home site in Lexington. When complete, they will teach a basic set of procedures including program selection, pre- and posttesting, data recording, fading, shaping, prompting, reinforcement, correction strategies, and long-range program planning. One module, presently titled *Decision Making for the Classroom Teacher*, is designed to provide a process for efficient as well as effective instruction within the instructional program format.

Classroom management and data systems: The idea of taking trial-by-trial data is not particularly pleasing to traditionally trained classroom teachers. However, the due process procedures which are emerging from litigation and legislation require parent-teacher interaction with respect to the appropriateness of an educational placement. To facilitate data-based decision making, we are developing systems which enable teachers to code the titles of programs they are using which contain written objectives and collect data on the child's progress through sequentially more complex stages, the amount and percent of time spent in instruction, and the number and percent of correct responses of the child by program area and cumulatively in order to determine whether or not a child is receiving a balanced educational program.

Teacher competency evaluation systems: On an earlier project, entitled *Practice What You Preach*, we began the development of a teacher evaluation system and, as nearly as I can tell, conducted one of the few projects, if not the only one, where teachers received certification through an in-field evaluation procedure based primarily on changes in child performance over time and over increasingly more complex tasks. Our child performance sheets provide one source of data for the current version of our competency assessment system. The final product will, as before, focus on that information, on the extent to which teachers interact positively with children, and on the extent to which they manage efficient and effective instructional environments.

Automated learning environments: Automated instrumentation, once programmed, can present stimuli in a standard manner, record responses from any of a number of response manipulanda, and present consequent events rapidly and consistently. Good classroom teachers approximate this model, but they often are few and far between. The original justification for incorporating instrumentation into preschool environments described the attributes which the automated model would present to teachers in training. Our expectation was that in a brief period of time, children would learn to work independently on response building, discrimination training, and concept learning activities; and that instrumentation would add to the "manpower pool" in the classroom.

With experience, we have learned that an extensive shaping process is necessary to move a child from the level of dependence exhibited when working one-to-one with a teacher who literally prompts or guides the child through a motor response to completely independent work in a learning booth.

We have reassessed the types of instruction which can best be presented, and the ways in which professional staff should interact with the instrumentation in teaching sessions. Presently, we have four active learning stations programmed to teach visual discrimination as well as "reading" behaviors.

Telecommunications systems: The minicomputer system which controls the learning stations in the preschool has been linked to simple response recording devices placed in 18 homes geographically dispersed across the state of Kentucky. During the first year of this project, signal transformation units were developed which enable computer-generated signals to be transformed, transmitted over telephone lines, and reformed to control the home-placed learning devices. Our initial efforts have identified the scope of work which will be required for full-scale implementation of a delivery system which can begin intervention immediately after the birth of an infant with an observable biological defect, and can interact continuously as long as intervention is needed. The full description of the model has recently appeared (Tawney, 1976). In brief, a fully operational system will deliver computer-generated instruction to the infant in his crib, play area, or other "learning station." Liaison personnel will instruct parents to use the system, and to teach their children skills which cannot be taught by computer. These personnel will also assist parents to obtain all the health, legal, and social services necessary to maintain the child in the home or community placement. A system is being developed to store the child's educational history, as well as the types and results of other interventions. Our major task, at the moment, is to obtain a long-term financial support base to continue efforts in infant curriculum development, teaching-machine design, and personnel preparation in this new area.

SUMMARY OF PRODUCT AND PROJECT DEVELOPMENTS

I see each of our activities as a successive approximation to the development of systems which will have a positive influence on the behavior of children with severe and multiple developmental problems. We expect to demonstrate that such children can learn at relatively error-free rates and that it is possible to develop comprehensive systems to train and evaluate teacher performance contingent upon a high level of child performance. The outreach capacity of the telecommunications system enables us to serve rural as well as urban locales, and, to those familiar with the problems of infant research, it represents a breakthrough in the potential for research in home (natural) environments.

As the right-to-education movement continues to gain momentum, new problems will surface. Having described one set of problems, and our approach to some solutions, it is necessary to address a larger set of problems which will influence our further efforts in this newly emerging field.

THE CURRENT STATUS OF THE FIELD

In effect, the current status is disorder bordering on chaos. The fact that, from one perspective, it appears that major development efforts are being initiated on a fairly orderly basis only means that few have conceptualized the dimensions of the problem. And, while I believe there is a commitment to do the job right this time, events may conspire to thwart the best attempts to develop programs of exceptional quality. The problems I am about to discuss do not exhaust the list, but are representative of those which must be confronted.

The normalization and right-to-education movements are an outgrowth of *system failure*, just as the civil rights movement was a response to the failure of our society to provide equal educational opportunity to all children. We have been exposed to the failures of institutions; Professor Burton Blatt has nudged our consciences with descriptions of institutional living conditions for many years. And T.V. has taken us into Willowbrook just as forcefully as it took us into the battlefields of Vietnam. Few really believe that conditions in institutions were diabolically planned by evil people with the sole intent of injuring the souls of the inmates and their caretakers. Instead, we are faced with the disquieting reality that politicians, exercising the will of the people, starved those institutions financially, so that despite the strongest appeals of bureaucrats for additional funds, those well-meaning people who tolerate the impossible cannot succeed under any circumstances. Given that the out of sight–out of mind phenomenon is considered part of the problem, our current solution is to deinstitutionalize individuals, and bring them into daily contact with other members of society. The outcome, presumably, will include better public knowledge of, and support for, programs for the severely and profoundly retarded. I believe this to be a naive view, and would offer that support for regular public education has rarely been sufficient to meet its needs, and that successful integration of the handicapped should make them as anonymous as anybody else.

The source of the problem is money. Current advocacy efforts are garnering funds for public school programs, but the number of suits (approximately sixty at this writing) is testimony that this is not a benevolent outpouring of resources. A new population is competing for resources in a period of retrenchment in commitment to educational and social services. Eventually, parents of the nonhandicapped will realize that sharing resources with the handicapped will reduce the proportion of resources available to their children, and a counteraction can be anticipated. Unless advocates for the severely/profoundly retarded specify clearly the conditions which must exist for these children to perform successfully, and obtain the financial resources to provide those conditions, there is little hope that simply changing arenas/environments will insure that one institution (the schools) will succeed where others have failed.

MULTIPLE REFERENTS FOR THE "SEVERELY RETARDED"

Despite our best efforts, we tend to speak in terms that infer homogeneity. The term *severely retarded* is presently used to refer to children with moderate severe and profound retardation. Since the children who are now enrolled in right-to-education classes were previously excluded children, one can argue that the fact of placement, not the referent, is important. I would agree, but also feel compelled to caution that adequate program development is not likely to occur if heterogeneity is ignored by program planners. In terms of range of functional behaviors, the "severely retarded," excluded, or right-to-education child may be nonambulatory, health impaired, physically debilitated, and manifest nearly a zero behavioral repertoire; or, he may be a high-functioning Down's child whose preschool training is geared to enable him to enter first grade.

The Bureau of Education for the Handicapped describes severely handicapped in the *Federal Register* (40-35-1975) and includes the severely and profoundly retarded. This definition considers that

> "severely handicapped children" (1) may possess severe language and/or perceptual-cognitive deprivations, and evidence abnormal behaviors such as: (i) Failure to respond to pronounced social stimuli, (ii) Self-mutilation, (iii) Self-stimulation, (iv) Manifestation of intense and prolonged temper tantrums, and (v) The absence of rudimentary forms of verbal control, and (2) May also have extremely fragile physiological conditions [p. 7412].

We have found the following set of descriptions helpful in communicating the functional level of children with severe developmental retardation:

1. Little or no vocal behavior.
2. Limited motor gestural behavior.
3. Limited self-help skills.
4. Inconsistent or no bowel or bladder control.
5. No obtained score on a standardized test because none has ever been administered or because these persons were nontestable in the testing situation.
6. Limited social interaction with other children and adults.
7. Inability to follow simple commands.
8. No reciprocal social reinforcement of others in their environment.
9. A high rate of superstitious (stereotyped) behaviors.
10. A high rate of disruptive social behavior.
11. A low rate of behavior that might generally be called "constructive play behavior."
12. Attendant multiple handicaps [Tawney, 1972b, pp. i-ii].

My intent here is not to offer a "best set" of descriptions for this target population, but to point out that professionals have very different populations in mind when they talk about the severely retarded.

SWITCHING SIGNALS ON PARENTS AND OTHER PROFESSIONALS

For the most part, special educators have not expressed positive views of the learning potential of severely retarded children. But other viewpoints are beginning to be heard, and the chorus is growing louder with each positive legal action. The parent advocates who have forced most of the change represent only a fraction of the total population, leaving most special educators, nearly all regular educators, and the majority of parents in the position of trying to understand the reversal of direction. We have switched signals, to all intents and purposes, and left our audiences wondering who to believe. Children previously considered uneducable are now considered to have the potential to learn; the community is now deemed the most appropriate place for those once considered best served by institutionalization. The attitude that institutionalization is a reasonable decision because it eases stress on the family unit is disappearing; parents are now told that their child is their responsibility, and that professional efforts will now be directed toward assisting them with the child in the home and in the community. Parents of "trainable" children have just completed the building programs that have brought them self-contained schools and workshops for their children. Now they learn that "new" thinking dictates that their children should attend schools which provide them maximum opportunity to interact with their nonhand·capped peers, or work in learning stations in competitive employment in preparation for independent living.

These turnarounds have occurred in a very short period of time. The new messages are valid, but we should not be surprised by the confusion they have generated. Our responsibilities lie in explaining the changes, placing them in historical perspective, and communicating realistic expectations for specific individuals who may or may not have access to the opportunities which are likely to facilitate maximal learning.

AMBIGUITIES IN PARENT-PROFESSIONAL RELATIONSHIPS

Parents and public educators are legal adversaries. When the suits are over and children are receiving the education their parents fought for, parents and professionals will be expected to join in a cooperative relationship, to work together for the maximum development of the child. Again, I believe it is naive to assume that this will be other than a superficial alliance. Despite the defendants' verbal statements of sympathy for the plaintiffs, court cases are being bitterly fought. The air of hostility will not dissipate quickly, and within larger systems is likely to be diffused to parents who were not plaintiffs, and to teachers whose systems were not directly involved in litigation.

Further, once parents succeed in getting their child placed, they very likely will discriminate a "placement" from an "appropriate educational program." Mercer and Richardson (1975) have described a multistage process whereby those with a grievance obtain redress, only to find that the original solution is insufficient, and that they must initiate additional action to obtain what they consider to be an equitable solution to the problem.

I am inclined to believe that parents should view the schools with distrust, until they are satisfied that their child is receiving the best education possible. I am concerned that parents will be bought off too easily by such superficialities as "we're doing all our resources will allow." I consider periodic and sustained parent evaluation of classroom environments a necessary condition for achieving quality educational programs. Open disclosure and data exchange must provide the basis for dispassionate, objective discourse on a child's performance. As I previously mentioned, the data systems which we are developing are designed to enable a teacher to indicate, on a daily basis, how much time a child has spent in instruction, who has taught him and under what conditions, the child's rate and percent of correct responses, and the extent to which his/her actual program has met the planned program.

Our curricula are designed to be shared with parents, and to indicate the sequence of increasingly more complex skill acquisition. We will soon begin training teachers to obtain the information and communicate it to parents; and to teach parents to ask for the information and encourage them to sue if they do not get it.

I have suggested earlier that the schools are susceptible to system failure for the same reason that our institutions are in total disgrace: lack of adequate funding. I have stated elsewhere (Tawney, 1974) that after class action suits for equal educational opportunity, and class action suits for failure to educate (e.g., when high school students file suit because they are uneducated and unemployable), that we will see individual suits against the teacher who fails to educate a severely retarded child. Then, we may see teacher suits against the employing district for failure to provide the resources or manpower to enable him/her to do a competent job. And, somewhere in this process, I would not be surprised to find an individual suit against a public school administrator for placing a teacher with a record of marginal performance in a classroom for children with severe developmental retardation.

The prospect of long-term hostility is painful. However, as a field, we are not known for being one-trial learners. When there are both group and individual acknowledgements of responsibility, it may be possible to get down to the business at hand and provide the support to accomplish the task in a direct, open, and accountable manner. When we reach this point, the ambiguities in parent-professional interaction should be removed.

WHO WILL BE THE TEACHERS, AND FROM WHERE WILL THEY COME?

The development of personnel preparation is beginning in the best and worst of times. The same economic and political factors that could work for the establishment of quality training programs also work to retard the growth of these same programs. We are witnessing a decline in school populations, regional surpluses of regular education teachers, surpluses of teachers recently certified in mild learning and behavior disorders, and the initiation of selective admissions policies in teacher education programs. These conditions should argue well for the development of a well-trained cadre of professionals in the area of the severely retarded. On the other side of the coin, however, court orders often carry deadlines for program implementation, thereby creating an instant demand for teachers. Since there are presently few, if any, existing certification programs for teachers of the severely/multiply handicapped, the teacher pool obviously must carry other certification. Where teacher surpluses exist, selecting the potentially most successful ones is not likely to be the primary administrative concern. Immediate need may precipitate disasters like the two- to three-summer recertification programs prevalent in the 1960s and with us still today. Deans are beginning to suggest that their regular educators be retrained in special education to solve their surplus problems. The movement to develop competency-based alternatives to traditional certification strategies, beset by internal confusion and external resistance, is unlikely to provide rational solutions to the problem of temporary certification; nor are the politics of state certification boards likely to support alternatives such as long-term monitoring of temporarily certified persons of sufficient duration to produce a data base which will indicate whether teachers work effectively with severely retarded children or not. Thus, while it appears that the potential for developing model training programs exists, multiple forces which will work against these models are developing with equal momentum.

THE DATA BASE FOR PROGRAM EFFECTIVENESS

The right-to-education movement is based on principle and constitutional guarantees. Consent agreements and consequent legislative changes contain elaborate due process procedures to ensure that these rights are not abrogated. Among the safeguards is a process for determining that a child is receiving an education in an appropriate placement. On an individual basis, this would infer that the child will receive an education, which in turn suggests that he will be presented with instructional tasks and will change (acquire new and more complex behaviors) over time. Collectively, it would seem that broad-based program evaluation will follow current efforts to initiate programs. It is important to note that, as yet, no data-based claims have been made for the effectiveness of right-to-education classes. Instead, reports of the learning potential of severely retarded persons have come from single-subject studies in specific areas (e.g., from the language studies of Guess and Sailor and their associates, from the single-subject and small-group projects reported by Brown and his students, from Gold's learning studies on vocational skill training, and from the emerging data on the Down's project at the University of Washington). To communicate with parents and to monitor the activities in right-to-education classes, it will be necessary to develop comprehensive data systems which are interrelated with the instructional process. The history of efficacy studies in mildly handicapped classrooms should demonstrate the need for data systems and viable evaluation designs.

CURRENT EFFORTS TO DEVELOP PROGRAMS FOR PERSONS WITH SEVERE DEVELOPMENTAL RETARDATION

This section very briefly describes a number of national efforts to attack the multidimensional problems in the field of severe retardation. Such a listing can only claim to be representative, and, obviously, will be outdated rapidly as additional attempts are made to bring a semblance of order to this emerging field.

Brown, at the University of Wisconsin, has begun to train graduate doctoral-level personnel who will direct newly emerging programs in other states. The universities of Kansas, Kentucky, and New Mexico are developing extensive training programs for masters- and doctoral-level personnel. At Kentucky, doctoral-level preparation is, and will continue to be, directed toward developing manpower to engage in research and development activities. Gold, at the University of Illinois, is continuing his long-term research program in vocational skills development. Haring, Hayden, and their associates at the Experimental Education Unit at the University of Washington are engaged in a variety of behaviorally based programs for the severely handicapped. Early intervention projects are also underway at the University of Oregon. Language research and language programming continues to be a highly productive area with significant contributions by the Brickers, Guess and Sailor, and Stremel-Cambell. Vanderheiden, at the Trace Center at the University of Wisconsin, has developed innovative strategies for nonvocal communication. The Bureau of Education for the Handicapped, in addition to supporting most of the activities just described, has initiated a program to develop model demonstration centers for the severely handicapped. Ten were funded in 1974, six in 1975, and approximately six were planned for funding in 1976. As noted, a two-year program in telecommunications technology development was initiated and five projects were funded in 1974. Diverse in nature, they are exploring computer-generated instruction, home training, and interactive television communication.

These efforts represent federal commitments in research training and service. Other efforts (e.g., Head Start-Handicapped, the Early Childhood-Handicapped, and contract research) are also making significant contributions. Collectively, these represent first steps in the development of services to the severely retarded. Much remains to be done.

WHERE SHOULD WE GO FROM HERE?

Litigation precipitated the right-to-education movement. Federal and state legislation has been modified to increase the financial support base for all handicapped persons. The current modification of the Education for All Handicapped Children Act affirms the goal of serving all handicapped by 1980. The law provides a formula for substantial flow-through of funds to local school districts; places stringent requirements on states to develop plans which include due process safeguards; and provides an incentive for serving three- to five-year-old children. However, the law presently excuses states from participation in preschool programs if such participation would conflict with existing state law. The next steps, assuming that a sufficient authorization will be passed, are to include all handicapped children from birth to the present compulsory school age, and to strike the clauses which excuse states from participation in preschool education. These actions, and corresponding changes in state law, are needed to develop the support base for early intervention programs. At the federal level, appropriation should support the following:

1. research in early intervention;
2. development of infant curricula from different theoretical models;
3. future-oriented technologies for research, training, and service delivery;
4. research and development in teacher competence specification and evaluation;
5. planning for comprehensive and community-based service systems;
6. development of data systems for public school environments; and
7. development of curricula which are consistent, and sequential from birth through adult independent work and living skills.

The Bureau of Education for the Handicapped has convened ad hoc advisory groups on two occasions since 1972, and many of the current efforts are the results of suggestions from those groups. In my view, it would be advisable to assemble the leadership personnel for an extended period to develop plans for new comprehensive and coordinated efforts. It makes sense to impact resources and expertise in crisis settings, as we are attempting in our field validation work, in order that several elements of a problem can be explored simultaneously.

At the state and local level, efforts must be directed to remove barriers to the education of all handicapped persons. Those states which are implementing programs under court order have a major task in retraining school personnel and describing what due process is all about. States need technical assistance from the national manpower pool in this area, and particularly in the area of competence alternatives to traditional certification programs.

The next step for colleges and universities is to continue to exercise restraint in the development of personnel preparation programs. Once immediate demands are met, the annual demand for teachers will be relatively low. About a year ago I stated elsewhere (Tawney, 1975) that there were probably less than ten institutions with sufficient resources to establish and maintain training programs over a long period. While that estimate might logically be adjusted upward by the addition of one or two, by no stretch of the imagination will we need fifty to a hundred programs. Multistate planning efforts should begin to identify the next most likely sites for programs.

Finally, as professionals and citizens, we must look carefully at the magnitude of change we have precipitated. A history of exclusion and devaluation is being reversed under conditions that will make it difficult to revert to earlier practices. Such rapid movement calls for us to have a little patience with those who are attempting to sort out the change.

REFERENCES

Bijou, S. W. A functional analysis of retarded development. In N. Ellis (Ed.), *International review of research in mental retardation* (Vol. 1). New York: Academic Press, 1966. Pp. 1-19.

Bijou, S. W. Studies in the experimental development of left-right concepts in retarded children using fading techniques. In N. Ellis (Ed.), *International review of research in mental retardation* (Vol. 3). New York: Academic Press, 1968. Pp. 65-96.

Mercer, J. R., & Richardson, J. G. "Mental retardation" as a social problem. In N. Hobbs (Ed.), *Issues in the classification of children* (Vol. 2). San Francisco: Jossey-Bass, 1975. Pp. 463-96.

Tawney, J. *Program environments for developmentally retarded children: A project for a coordinated program of research, program model develop-*

ment, and curriculum development and dissemination. Original proposal (Project No. 233118). Lexington: University of Kentucky, 1972. (a)

Tawney, J. Training letter discrimination in four-year-old children, *Journal of Applied Behavioral Analysis,* 1972, 5, pp. 455-65. (b)

Tawney, J. *Programmed environments for developmentally retarded children: A project for a coordinated program of research, program model development, and curriculum development and dissemination* (Project No. 443CH50218) Lexington: University of Kentucky, 1974.

Tawney, J. *Prerequisite conditions for the establishment of educational programs for the severely retarded.* Paper presented at the National Association for Retarded Citizens Conference on Education for the Severely Retarded, New Orleans, Spring, 1975.

Tawney, J. Educating severely handicapped children and their parents through telecommunications. In N. Haring & L. Brown (Eds.), *Teaching severely and profoundly multihandicapped children.* New York: Grune & Stratton, 1976.

Tawney, J., & Hipsher, L. *Systematic Language Instruction* (Project No. 7-1205). Washington, D.C.: U.S. Office of Education, 1970.

Terrace, H. Stimulus control. In W. Honig (Ed.), *Operant behavior: Areas of research and application.* New York: Appleton-Century-Crofts, 1967. Pp. 271-344.

A SELECTED BIBLIOGRAPHY OF WORKS BY JAMES W. TAWNEY

Tawney, J. Practice what you preach: An evolving alternative to a summer certification program. *TED Newsletter,* 1973, 10(1), 21-24.

Tawney, J. Acceleration of vocal behavior in developmentally retarded children. *Education and Training of the Mentally Retarded,* 1974, 9(1), 22-27.

Tawney, J. Preliminary observations on teacher-child interactions in a day care setting. *Education and Training of the Mentally Retarded,* 1974, 9(1), 41-43.

Tawney, J. Programmed environments for the developmentally retarded. In P. Mann (Ed.), *Mainstream special education.* Reston, Va.: Council for Exceptional Children, 1974.

Tawney, J. Educating severely handicapped children and their parents through telecommunications. In N. Haring & L. Brown, (Eds.), *Teaching severely and profoundly multihandicapped children.* New York: Grune & Stratton, 1976.

Cegelka, P., & Tawney, J. Decreasing the discrepancy: A case study in teacher re-education. *Exceptional Children,* 1975, 41, 268-69.

13

Federal Legislation for Exceptional Children: Implications and a View of the Future

Martin L. LaVor is currently senior legislative associate for the House Education and Labor Committee of the U.S. Congress. Some of his responsibilities in this position include overseeing all aspects of legislation from introduction to final passage in areas concerned with education of the handicapped, vocational rehabilitation, child abuse, Head Start programs, runaway youth, aging, and others.

Dr. LaVor's professional preparation includes a B.S. degree in industrial arts from Trenton State Teachers College in 1958, an M.A. degree in special education from Seton Hall University in 1962, an M.A. equivalent in rehabilitation counseling from Seton Hall University, and an Ed.D. degree in special education from the University of Alabama in 1969. His early professional positions were with the Southeast Office of Economic Opportunity in Atlanta, Georgia, the Alabama Technical Assistance Corporation in Montgomery, and the Guild Training and Place-

245

ment Service for the retarded and physically handicapped in Newark, New Jersey. A selected bibliography of works by Martin L. LaVor is found on pages 269-70.

On November 29, 1975, the Education for All Handicapped Children Act became Public Law 94-142. This law represents the most complete legislative action ever taken by the federal government in the field of education of the handicapped.[1] Although as many as thirty bills affecting the handicapped have become law in a single year, none has had the scope of this one.

HISTORICAL PERSPECTIVE

The large number of laws in this area indicates a very substantial federal role; however, this movement has only emerged in the last twenty years. Federal laws for the handicapped during the nineteenth century were primarily designed to meet the problems of specific disability groups such as the deaf and the blind. It wasn't until the 1920s that programs designed to provide services for all handicapped persons were enacted. This was achieved primarily through vocational rehabilitation legislation which was the result of the need to assist the great number of people disabled during World War I, or injured while working in the rapidly growing industries. With the exception of periodic extensions to the Vocational Rehabilitation Act, legislation for the handicapped over the next forty years was primarily, though not exclusively, focused on services and special exemptions for the blind.

In 1958, the federal government through the National Defense Education Act, began providing funds for general education. Prior to that legislation, there was virtually no federal money going to finance general education. As part of that law, captioned films for the deaf were authorized.

In 1965, the Elementary and Secondary Education Act became law. As part of that act, a program was established to assist children in state operated or supported schools serving the handicapped.

In 1966, ESEA was amended to establish the Bureau of Education of the Handicapped in the U.S. Office of Education. In addition, funds were provided for states to expand, either directly or through local educational agencies, programs or projects to meet educational and related needs of handicapped children.

[1] The words "disabled" and "handicapped" do not have the same meanings. It happens that in most federal legislation the term "handicapped" has been used in place of or interchangeably with the term "disabled." This chapter will use the term "handicapped" even though "disabled" may be the proper term.

ESEA was amended again in 1967, and Regional Resource Centers to provide testing to determine special educational needs of handicapped children were established.

In 1968, the Handicapped Children's Early Education Assistance Act designed to establish experimental preschool programs for the handicapped became law.

The 1969 amendments to ESEA included the Gifted and Talented Education Assistance Act and the Children with Specific Learning Disabilities Act.

1972 marked the first time in federal history that a law for the handicapped ever received a negative vote in the Congress, and the first time a bill for the handicapped was ever vetoed by the president. The Vocational Rehabilitation Act of 1972 was vetoed, as was its successor in 1973. The revised amendments to the Vocational Rehabilitation Act finally became law (PL 93-112) later in 1973. The Congress that year took significant action in revising the original law by requiring that first priority for rehabilitation services be given to individuals with "the most severe handicaps."

In the Education Amendments of 1974, the Congress significantly increased the authorization level of the basic state aid program for meeting special needs of handicapped children. More importantly, the 1974 law included for the first time language directing states to move toward the goal of guaranteeing the rights of exceptional children and their parents and provided a detailed timetable for achieving this goal.

Fourteen months later, PL 94-142 became law. The purpose of PL 94-142 was to assure

1. that all handicapped children have a free appropriate public education which emphasizes special education and related services designed to meet their unique needs;

2. that the rights of handicapped children and their parents or guardians are protected; and

3. that states and localities provide for the education of all handicapped children.

In order to qualify for assistance under the law, each state must demonstrate that the following conditions are met:

1. It has in effect a policy that assures all handicapped children have the right to a free appropriate public education.

2. It sets forth in detail the policies and procedures which it will undertake or has undertaken in order to assure that:

   (a) there is established (i) a goal of providing full educational opportunity to all handicapped children; (ii) a detailed timetable for accomplishing such a goal; and (iii) a description of the kind and number of facilities, personnel, and services necessary throughout the State to meet such a goal;

(b) a free appropriate public education will be available for all handicapped children between the ages of three and eighteen within the State not later than September 1, 1978, and for all handicapped children between the ages of three and twenty-one within the State not later than September 1, 1980, except that, with respect to handicapped children aged three to five and aged eighteen to twenty-one, inclusive . . .

(c) all children residing in the State who are handicapped, regardless of the severity of their handicap, and who are in need of special education and related services are identified, located, and evaluated, and that a practical method is developed and implemented to determine which children are currently receiving needed special education and related services and which children are not currently receiving needed special education and related services;

(d) it has established . . . procedures to assure that, to the maximum extent appropriate, handicapped children, including children in public or private institutions or other care facilities, are educated with children who are not handicapped, and that special classes, separate schooling, or other removal of handicapped children from the regular educational environment occurs only when the nature of severity of the handicap is such that education in regular classes with the use of supplementary aids and services cannot be achieved satisfactorily;

(e) . . . procedures are established for consultation with individuals involved in or concerned with the education of handicapped children, including handicapped individuals and parents or guardians of handicapped children, and . . . there are public hearings, adequate notice of such hearings, and an opportunity for comment available to the general public prior to adoption of the policies, programs, and procedures required.

These words represent the culmination of years of consideration, extensive hearings, thorough research, debates, trade-offs and compromises by the United States Congress. They reflect an awareness of and concern for handicapped children and their goal of achieving full rights as citizens. The law represents a significant commitment by the federal government to assist them in gaining full educational opportunities; it has been hailed as the most far-reaching legislation for the handicapped ever enacted by the Congress and, in the minds of handicapped individuals, their parents, and persons who work with them throughout the nation, it is.

While PL 94-142 represents a significant national commitment, it should not be perceived as the only one. An earlier amendment (contained in PL 93-112) to the 50-year-old Vocational Rehabilitation Act many would argue is equally potent in its implications. Section 504 of the Rehabilitation Act of 1973 (PL 93-112) parallels and complements PL 94-142. Section 504 has been characterized as a bill of rights for the handicapped. It requires that:

> No otherwise qualified handicapped individual in the United States . . . shall, solely by reason of his handicap, be excluded from the participation in, be denied the benefits of, or be subjected to discrimination under any program or activity receiving Federal financial assistance.

Any student of American statutory law well knows that the gap between a law and its enforcement, between mandate and fulfillment, between promise and practice can be considerable. And where the guarantee of constitutional rights is involved, closing that gap may be aggravating and prolonged.

PL 94-142 set in motion a mandate which *should* guarantee that all handicapped children in America will receive a complete education. As a result of Sec. 504 of the Vocational Rehabilitation Act, the handicapped of America *should* have access to education and jobs, and *should not* be denied anything that any other citizen is entitled to or already receives. Although legislative language can be cumbersome and difficult to understand at time, words in these two laws are not. The laws are sufficiently direct and specific to satisfy anyone interested in the well being of the handicapped. In fact, there are many who, upon reading the laws, will relax in the confidence that everything necessary has been accomplished; that it is just a matter of time until all of the requirements in the law are implemented. This attitude is self-deluding and will hamper the attainment of the goals of meeting the needs of handicapped persons.

It must be noted that for all of the features of these laws which brought satisfaction and hope to so many, PL 94-142 was not received with open arms by everyone. When he signed the law, President Ford said:

> Unfortunately, this bill promises more than the Federal government can deliver and its good intentions could be thwarted by the many unwise provisions it contains. Everyone can agree with the objective stated in the title of this bill—educating all handicapped children in our Nation. The key question is whether the bill will really accomplish that objective.

Even the strongest supporters of this measure know as well as I that they are falsely raising the expectations of the groups affected by claiming authorization levels which are excessive and unrealistic.

Despite my strong support for full educational opportunities for our handicapped children, the funding levels proposed in this bill will simply not be possible if Federal expenditures are to be brought under control and a balanced budget achieved over the next few years.[2]

Criticism was not limited to the White House. In 1977, all of the national organizations representing the governors, legislatures, state school boards, and chiefs of the education agencies responsible for carrying out the new law claimed that it imposed heavy administrative burdens on state and local school districts and did not provide adequate new funds for implementation. For a multitude of reasons, such features as the individualized education program, the due process procedures, the state-local program dollar split, and the relatively low (compared to state) federal funding all found disfavor somewhere. There were claims that the law was so extensive that it could not be enforced. The majority of persons interested in and knowledgeable about the new law, however, viewed it as far-sighted, progressive, and very positive. Only time will tell which side is right and whether PL 94-142 can achieve its purpose.

Similarly, it is not yet clear when or whether Section 504 of the Vocational Rehabilitation Act, which became law on September 30, 1973, will be implemented and its intended impact felt. Final regulations interpreting this Section were not promulgated by the Department of Health, Education and Welfare until May 1977, over three and one-half years after the provision was signed into law. HEW Secretary Califano has promised to "vigorously implement and enforce the mandate."

A major cause of confusion and difficulty in the development of the regulations was the lack of legislative history and specific Congressional intent. As a result the Office of Civil Rights in HEW, which drafted the regulations, had no guidance for interpreting the broadly stated Congressional desire to eliminate discrimination against the handicapped. The regulations became the subject of a national controversy. Opponents claimed they were too wide-ranging and detailed, would cost billions and billions of dollars to implement, and were unenforceable at any cost. HEW projected the cost at 2.4 billion dollars with the total cost to be borne by state and local governments, as well as public and private agencies which receive federal funds. Since Sec. 504 applied to every department and agency of the federal government, it was assumed that similar costs might be necessary for the others as well.

The issue involved in parts of PL 94-142 and Sec. 504 is the capacity or willingness of the federal government to enforce its laws. With these laws, new *civil rights* mandates have been enacted while some

[2] From the veto message signed November 29, 1975.

already on the books remain unenforced. Unlike grants-in-aid, civil rights not only provide a right or benefit to an individual, but they impose a correlative duty on someone else, and enforcing that duty is not easy. If voluntary action could achieve this goal, a law would not have been necessary; therefore, some legal requirement for those who have not complied voluntarily is needed. Such a workable mechanism does not exist at this time.

It is clear that the mere passage of a law does not guarantee that its objectives will be met. It is too early to label these laws "success" or "failure"; they were highlighted here because they represent a new concern and awareness by the Congress about the needs of the handicapped.

ISSUES AND UNRESOLVED QUESTIONS

Through the years, as more and more focus is placed on the needs of the handicapped and as the funds appropriated by the Congress to carry out programs rise, numerous questions and issues are being raised.

ACCOUNTABILITY

It is generally contended that special education is the forerunner of activities and procedures which will eventually be adopted in regular education programs. Small class sizes, supplementary services, special equipment, and individualized education are examples of approaches that started in and are part of special education and have been adopted in varying degrees by regular education. When education is scrutinized, special education is often singled out to justify itself more than any other educational area. Also, when budgets are cut back, special education programs are often the first to be reduced. In spite of the fact that general education cannot prove its cost efficiency and effectiveness, special education is usually asked to do so. Whether this demand is fair or not, one of the most critical issues facing programs for the handicapped over the next few years is accountability. How can taxpayers be assured they are getting the most for their dollars? How can they be assured that greater fiscal investment results in improving the future of handicapped individuals? As more money is made available by federal, state, and local governments, greater fiscal accountability will be required, and it is reasonable to suggest that the demands on special education will increase in direct proportion to the demands it makes on those funding sources.

Questions concerning the best ways of financing, the most effective ways to spend public funds, the degree to which such funds produce desired results, the relationship between the child, learning, and costs involved, and most important, the kinds of benefits that are accrued by society will have to be addressed. One of the vehicles which may provide some answers to accountability questions is a provision in PL 94-142 which calls for an individualized education program. As defined in law:

> The term "individualized education program" means a written statement for each handicapped child developed in any meeting by a representative of the local educational agency or an intermediate educational unit who shall be qualified to provide, or supervise the provision of, specially designed instruction to meet the unique needs of handicapped children, the teacher, the parents or guardian of such child, and, whenever appropriate, such child, which statement shall include (A) a statement of the present levels of educational performance of such child; (B) a statement of annual goals, including short-term instructional objectives; (C) a statement of the specific educational services to be provided to such child, and the extent to which such child will be able to participate in regular educational programs; (D) the projected date for initiation and anticipated duration of such services, and appropriate objective criteria and evaluation procedures and schedules for determining, on at least an annual basis, whether instructional objectives are being achieved.

This requirement in the eyes of many is one of the most important features of the new law in that it should give local education agencies an opportunity to develop plans designed to meet the unique needs of each handicapped child and determine the specific services needed. It is anticipated that through successful implementation of the plans and evaluation of outcomes, it should be possible to find out what children are learning so that a clearer view and judgment as to what the end product in special education is, and whether or not goals are being achieved, can be ascertained.

It is claimed that special education is unique because each child has unique problems. If this statement is true, then special education based on these plans should be able to provide unique results. Unfortunately, as special education works with each individual and his or her problems, the costs for providing extra services may increase at a time when the public is clamorous for greater results with fewer resources. It is possible that costs may decrease as a result of individualized planning.

Accountability in education goes far beyond the education of handicapped children; nevertheless, special education will probably become the laboratory in which the answers will first be sought.

CLASS SIZE

One of the first and most obvious questions about special education relates to class size: Why are classes so small? Or How does one determine the optimum class size? There is no doubt that it is difficult to work with most handicapped children who require special services, but one must also ask, Isn't it just as difficult to handle large classes in regular education? Optimum class size appears to be a relative term. It is generally acknowledged that special education class size should be small because of the unique and often complex needs of the students; but does this mean that it is easier to teach "normal" kindergarten or regular elementary school class students with 25-35 students in each class? Almost any teacher with 35 children in a class would probably say, "If I could only get my class size down to 25, I would really be able to do a first-rate job." A teacher with 25 wants to get down to 20 "in order to reach every individual"; a special education teacher with 15 may want to get down to 10. The question of what constitutes an appropriate class size and the related cost implications will have to be addressed.

Since the largest disability group being educated today is the mentally retarded, focus here will be placed on the class size of educable and trainable children. Table 1 (*page 254*), compiled from the *Digest of State and Federal Laws: Education of Handicapped Children*, illustrates the minimums and maximums, laws, rules, or guidelines, which each state generally follows in serving these populations.

Table 1 clearly shows that the maximums for each group vary significantly from state to state. The question is, Does an educable mentally retarded individual in one state which has a maximum class size of 12 receive a better, the same, or a worse education than an individual with the same disability in another state which allows a maximum of 22 in a class?

The economics of education and the costs of teachers' salaries may force the educational establishment to look at the class size structure particularly with the educable mentally retarded (EMR) to determine what is the best way to work with them. Since no efficacy studies can be found which justify and validate specific class sizes for EMR or trainable mentally retarded (TMR) children; the question of cost may necessitate such consideration. The differences between 10 and 20 students in a class is one teacher's salary and of course, the class sizes of 12, 15, and 18 represent a third, more or less, of a teacher's salary. If a professional teacher with one aide (or paraprofessional) can handle 25 students with results comparable to those achieved in a class half the size with one teacher, what cost savings might occur without diminishing the impact of educational programs for students?

The concept of *segregated* or *special* schools of the handicapped rather than integrated classes in regular schools also warrants consideration in terms of benefits versus economic implications. Another concept, *mainstreaming* (i.e., placing handicapped children in regular classes and providing supplementary services for them), which was once thought to be the obvious way to cut special education costs, is proving to be not necessarily cheaper but in many cases more expensive than special edu-

TABLE 1: Class size of educable and trainable children.

State	Special classes			
	Educable mentally handicapped Class size		Trainable mentally handicapped Class size	
	Minimum	Maximum	Minimum	Maximum
ALABAMA	10	15	10	15
ALASKA	—	15	—	15
ARIZONA	—	15	—	10
ARKANSAS	5	15	5[1]	8
Home economics	5	10	—	—
CALIFORNIA				
(depending on age spread)	—	15-18	—	12
COLORADO				
Elementary—mental age 4 and under	—	15	—	—
mental age 4 and over	—	12	—	—
Jr. & Sr. HS—				
mental age 4 and under	—	18	—	—
mental age 4 and over	—	15	—	—
CONNECTICUT	9	9	9	9
DELAWARE	8[2]	22[2]	6[2]	10[2,3]
DISTRICT OF COLUMBIA	—	—	—	—
FLORIDA				
Primary age	6	12	5	10
Intermediate age	8	15	6	10
Jr. high school age	10	18	8	12
Sr. high school age	12	18	10	15
GEORGIA				
Elementary age 6-9	12	14	—	—
Elementary age 9-13	14	16	—	—
Secondary Jr. high over age 13	16	20	—	—
Secondary Sr. high over age 13	20	20	—	—
HAWAII (based on delivery option)	12	15	5	8
IDAHO	—	12[4]	—	12[4]
Resource room	—	12[5]	—	12[5]
ILLINOIS	—	—	5	10
Age 6-9	8	15[6]	—	—
Age 10 and above	10	15[6]	—	—
INDIANA	10-18-w/para		10	13[7]
Primary	— prof. 18-21		—	—
Intermediate	—14-16-w/para		—	—
	prof. 23-25		—	—
Jr. high	16-18-w/para		—	—

Table 1 *continued*

State	Educable mentally handicapped Class size		Trainable mentally handicapped Class size	
	Minimum	Maximum	Minimum	Maximum
Sr. high		— prof. 26-28		
		16-18-w/para		
		— prof. 26-28		
IOWA	—	—	—	10[8]
KANSAS	—	—	5	9
Age spread 3 yrs. or greater	—	15	—	—
Age spread 2 years	—	16	—	—
Age spread 1 year	—	17	—	—
KENTUCKY	15	20	6	12[9]
LOUISIANA	10	15	8	12
Slow learners	12	18	—	—
MAINE	—	15[10]	—	—
Integrated program	—	20[11]	—	—
Primary C.A. 5-9	—	—	3	6[12]
Intermediate C.A. 10-14	—	—	3	8[13]
MARYLAND				
Primary age	—	10	—	7
Intermediate age	—	15	—	10
Jr. & Sr. high	—	20	—	12
Resource teacher	—	30	—	—
MASSACHUSETTS				
Age range less than 1 year	—	20	—	—
Age range 1 year	—	19	—	—
Age range 2 years	—	18	—	—
Age range 3 years	—	17	—	—
Age range 4 years	—	16	—	—
Age range 5 years	—	15	—	—
Age range 6 years		14	—	—
MICHIGAN	—	15	—	15
MINNESOTA	12	15	5	7
MISSISSIPPI	5	—	5	—
MISSOURI	10	20	10	20
MONTANA	4	15[14]	4	12
NEBRASKA				
Elementary or secondary—general	—	30	—	—
Elementary level with grouping	—	15	—	—
Elementary level without grouping	—	12	—	—

Table 1   *continued*

| State | Special classes | | | |
| | Educable mentally handicapped Class size | | Trainable mentally handicapped Class size | |
	Minimum	Maximum	Minimum	Maximum
Teacher aide	—	—	—	10[15]
Age range 6 years or greater	—	—	5	6
Age range less than 6 years	—	—	5	10
NEVADA				
Preschool	—	8	—	6
Primary	—	10	—	8
Elementary	—	12	—	8
Intermediate	—	14	—	10
Senior high	—	14	—	—
Elementary 2 or more levels comb.	—	8	—	8
Secondary	—	10	—	10
NEW HAMPSHIRE	—	15[16]	—	10
Departmentalized programs	—	30[17]	—	—
NORTH CAROLINA			—	12[18]
Primary grades	12[19]	12[19]	—	—
Elementary grades	16[19]	16[19]	—	—
Resource teacher daily caseload	—	24-30	—	—
NEW JERSEY	—	15	—	10
NEW MEXICO	5	15	5	10
Part-time instructor	—	5	—	—
Primary grades	12[20]	12[20]	—	—
Elementary grades	16[20]	16[20]	—	—
Resource teacher	—	24-30	—	—
NEW YORK				
Elementary	—	15	—	—
Secondary	—	18	—	—
Over 12	—	—	—	12
Under 12	—	—	—	10
NORTH DAKOTA	5	15	6	12
OHIO[21]			5	12
SLOW LEARNERS				
Elementary age range 24 mos. or less	12	20	—	—
Elementary age range 24-48 mos.	12	16	—	—
Secondary age range 24 mos. or less	12	22	—	—
Secondary age range 25-48 mos.	12	20	—	—
Secondary unit work study program	12	30	—	—
OKLAHOMA	8	22[22] 23[23]	5	10

Table 1 *continued*

State	Special classes			
	Educable mentally handicapped Class size		Trainable mentally handicapped Class size	
	Minimum	Maximum	Minimum	Maximum
OREGON				
Elementary	—	15	—	—
Secondary	—	18[24]	—	—
PENNSYLVANIA	—	—	7[25]	18[25]
Primary	10	18	—	—
Work experience ½ day-Secondary	15	18	—	—
Homeroom w/integrated placement-Secondary	15	20	—	—
Resource teacher-Secondary	15	30[26]	—	—
Secondary	15	18	—	—
RHODE ISLAND				
SPECIAL CLASS[27]				
Preschool program	—	10	—	10[28]
Primary group	—	10	—	—
Intermediate group	—	14	—	—
Jr. high	—	16	—	—
Sr. high	—	16	—	—
Elementary age level	—	—	—	12[28]
Elementary age level	—	—	—	8[29]
Secondary C.A. range less than 5 yrs.	—	—	—	12
Secondary C.A. range greater than 5 yrs.	—	—	—	8
SOUTH CAROLINA	10	—	8[30]	—
SOUTH DAKOTA (Recommended)	—	10	—	6
TENNESSEE	—	—	8	16
Primary	12	14	—	—
Intermediate	12	16	—	—
Jr. high	12	16	—	—
Sr. high	12	16	—	—
Sr. high cooperative schools prog.	14	16	—	—
TEXAS				
½ unit/½ day	4	—	4	—
Unit	8	—	8	—
2 units	14	—	14	—
No. children for ea. unit above 2	14	—	14	—
UTAH	8	15	8	12[31]
VERMONT	12	15[32]	—	10
VIRGINIA	—	16	—	12[33]

TABLE 1 *continued*

State	Special classes			
	Educable mentally handicapped Class size		Trainable mentally handicapped Class size	
	Minimum	Maximum	Minimum	Maximum
WASHINGTON				
Preschool-Kindergarten	6	10	—	—
Primary	8	12	—	—
Intermediate	8	12	—	—
Secondary	10	16	—	—
WEST VIRGINIA				
Elementary	10	15	10	15
Secondary	10	15	10	15
WISCONSIN				
General school age	10[34]	20	—	—
Pre-primary age 4-8 years	8	12	—	—
Primary age 7-9 or 7-10 where no pre-primary exists	10[34]	12	—	—
Intermediate 9-12 years	10[34]	15	—	—
Ungraded wide range 8-15 years	10[34]	15	—	—
Jr. high 13-15 years	10[34]	14-16	—	—
Sr. high 16-18	10[34]	20[35], 15[36]	—	—
Full-time	—	—	5	10[37]
Extended day	—	—	5	9
With teacher monitor	—	—	12	15
Homebound	—	—	—	4
WYOMING	13	—	8	—
With instructional assistant	—	—	10	—

[1] Class size may be adjusted downward when multiply handicapped pupils are enrolled, usually on a 2:1 basis. Each multiply handicapped child is counted as 2 pupils.

[2] Implied by unit funding regulations.

[3] Class may be larger if a teacher aide is employed.

[4] Fifteen when teacher has interim certification and full-time aide; 18 when teacher has full certification and full-time aide.

[5] Not available.

[6] Age range of 4 years or less.

[7] Maximum age range—8 years. These figures represent optimum class size. Exceptions may be made when teacher's aide is employed.

[8] Fifteen with matron, if age range does not exceed 8 years.

[9] Smaller classes may be approved.

[10] Twenty with teacher aide.

[11] No more than 15 in a single class at any one time.

[12] Twelve with teacher aide.

13 Twelve with teacher aide.

14 Suggested maximum is 12.

15 Each qualified teacher will be responsible for supervising no more than 5 teacher aides.

16 Age range not to exceed 4 years.

17 No more than 15 pupils are assigned to one teacher at any given time except for music, gym, etc.

18 Sixteen when demand is great. Teacher aide must be employed if class is larger than 7 children. In classes of 13-16 children, two teacher aides must be employed to help the teacher.

19 Approximate class size.

20 Approximate class size.

21 Class size may be adjusted downward for individual units at any age level where pupils with multi-handicaps are enrolled.

22 If equivalent of one half-time aide is used.

23 If one full-time aide is used.

24 In any one scheduled class period.

25 An aide may be employed if class size is greater than 8 pupils and fewer than 15. An aide must be employed when class size is greater than 15 pupils.

26 Not less than 15 children to be in room at any one time.

27 Each class shall have one full-time teacher and a teacher's aide.

28 With aide.

29 No aide.

30 Average daily attendance minimum.

31 Aides may be employed as deemed necessary.

32 A class size of 12 is recommended for early elementary level I educable programs and for programs having one or more children with multiple handicapping conditions.

33 With aide.

34 Minimum number of students may be allowed to drop as low as 8 for no more than two consecutive years.

35 With substantial integration in other nonacademic classes.

36 With limited integration.

37 Smaller class may be approved on a proportionate pro rata.

Adapted from Trudeau, E. (Ed.). *Digest of state and federal laws: Education of handicapped children.* Reston, Va.: Council for Exceptional Children, 1973. Reprinted with permission.

cation classes. The question of costs transcends the classroom to include those children in institutions. Is there any way to serve handicapped children who require institutionalization in a cost-efficient manner, and at the same time provide all of the educational services such children require?

A study entitled *Resource Configuration and Costs* (Rossmiller, Hale, & Frohreich, 1970) illustrated the incredible variation of costs in providing special education for handicapped children within each disability group, and among selected cities throughout the country. Table 2 focuses on only two groups considered in that study: the educable mentally retarded (EMR) and the trainable mentally retarded (TMR).

TABLE 2: Resource configuration and costs.

School district	EMR Exceptional program cost per pupil	TMR Exceptional program cost per pupil	Regular program cost per pupil
A	$ 1,289	$ 871	$ 482
B	708	636	509
C	1,634	1,840	1,114
D	875	562	477
E	1,012	2,321	889
F	1,414	2,629	600
G	1,689	875	795
H	826	1,032	484
I	987	1,701	468
J	1,412	911	860
K	933	1,550	653
L	1,523	1,411	783
M	1,543	1,553	690
N	1,034	2,078	734
P	1,645	912	828
Q	910	1,755	480
R	1,342	1,791	656
T	911	1,010	615
U	1,844	1,739	1,193
V	2,358	2,657	734
W	1,863	2,038	647
X	1,197	1,821	654

Adapted from Rossmiller, R. et al. *Educational programs for exceptional children: Resource configurations and costs.* Madison: University of Wisconsin, 1970, pp. 65, 70.

The obvious question is, For a population which is presumed to be identical as far as disability classification, why should the EMR cost per student vary from $708 in one school district to $2,358 in another, and why should the TMR cost per student vary from $636 to $2,657? On the basis of cost alone, can we assume that a child in the EMR class with an expenditure of $2,358 per student receives a better education than the child in the class with the lower expenditure? Special education must begin to address such issues.

APPROPRIATENESS

Throughout PL 94-142, the requirement of "free appropriate public education" is found. But what is "appropriate" to the education of a child? What does this language mean in terms of what should specifically be provided? What is the yardstick for measuring appropriateness? Children are also required to be served in the "least restrictive environment." What does this really mean in terms of specific services and their settings?

A more important question with the most overwhelming implications is, *What is "appropriate" in terms of dollars?* It must be emphasized that this chapter deals primarily with education and its related costs; it is recognized that health and related expenditures may be far more extensive and that this area should undergo similar questioning and review.

Any parent wants the best money can provide for his or her child. At the same time budget developers have to make hard decisions as to where money should or should not be allocated and as to where cut-offs will be. High costs are receiving considerable attention these days. In Massachusetts, for example, two children are receiving services which cost the public $62,000 per year for each child. The following are examples of some representative per-pupil estimates on high-cost programs compiled in February, 1976 by the Bureau of Education of the Handicapped of the U.S. Office of Education. It is emphasized that not all of these expenses are solely educational, nor are the programs necessarily funded by the Bureau. They are merely examples of costs. *(See Table 3, page 262.)*

It is possible to dismiss these figures as extreme efforts for a limited number of children and as unrepresentative of actual costs of special education. While this may be true to some extent, such figures of the magnitude represented here are those that attract attention and become the basis for questioning all other traditional or excess costs. As emphasized earlier, special education will be in the forefront of education's financial justification.

If society must provide handicapped children with an appropriate education and assume the full costs, then special education is obliged to justify that the appropriate education is being provided for each child in the *most* efficient manner. If the average per pupil cost in a community is $1,500 per student per year, is $1,500 per year for each handicapped child an appropriate expenditure? Is $3,000, $6,000, $12,000, $24,000, or even $62,000 appropriate to spend on an annual basis to meet a child's needs? Since appropriateness has to be considered in the light of desired or expected outcomes, how much more and what kind of services are needed to meet the objectives? Are expectations (desired outcomes) reasonable and achieveable? Is there any limit as to what educational and/or social services should be provided? What should be the extent of society's responsibility? Should all children be supported, regardless of family income, and provided with any services which are

TABLE 3: Representative per-pupil estimates on high-cost programs for the handicapped.

Program (Residential)	Per pupil cost	Handicapping condition
Bell Faire Shaker Heights, Ohio	$ 16,323	Severely emotionally disturbed
Ben Haven New Haven, Conn.	25,000	Autistic
DeVereux Foundations Washington, Conn. Debon, Pa. Kennesaw, Ga.	12,000–18,000	Learning disabled Severely emotionally disturbed
Hillcrest Children's Center Washington, D.C.	18,943	Severely emotionally disturbed
Grove School Madison, Conn.	16,800	Learning disabled Severely emotionally disturbed
National Children's Rehabilitation Leesburg, Virginia	16,200	Severely emotionally disturbed
Christ Child Institute for Children Rockville, Md.	26,299	Severely emotionally disturbed
Perkins School for the Blind Deaf-Blind Department Watertown, Mass.	24,487	Deaf–Blind
New York Institute for the Education of the Blind Bronx, New York	19,000	Deaf–Blind
Oak Hill School for the Blind Connecticut	18,576	Mentally retarded Deaf–Blind
Belchertown State School Massachusetts	21,076	Mentally retarded; Deaf–Blind

required? Finally, the ultimate question is, If a dollar limitation is placed on appropriate expenditures, who will or who should make the judgment as to what is appropriate?

As the issue of what is appropriate in terms of dollars is being considered, the other side of the coin must also be viewed; that is, what will happen when judgments are made on the basis of dollars and parents raise the question that what is proposed to be provided is *not* appropriate or sufficient? Does this portend that future lawsuits against public agencies filed by parents questioning appropriateness will be based on *education malpractice?*

The most significant question that must be answered, however, does not concern what is appropriate in terms of dollars, but whether school systems will be able or willing to provide the broad range of facilities and programs necessary to accommodate the special problems and individual needs of children.

A VIEW FROM THE REAL WORLD

In spite of the new federal and state laws and increased expenditures, some parents are still experiencing difficulty in finding, let alone getting children into, special programs. At the same time, school districts in trying to meet federal and state mandates are experiencing comparable problems, questions, and frustrations. Dr. Gloria Engnoth, Coordinator of Special Education for the Baltimore County (Maryland) schools, in response to my inquiry, provided the following frank and perceptive appraisal of the expenses and problems her school system is facing in attempting to serve *all* handicapped children. Rather than attempt to rewrite or condense her response (with her kind permission), it is inserted with a minimum of change. It should be understood that the concerns noted by Dr. Engnoth are not unique to Baltimore County; similar examples can be found in every state and in almost any school district.

The following is a summary of the philosophical and practical concerns that face a local education agency when trying to implement legislative and judicial directives which state that every handicapped child should be provided with the most appropriate educational program to meet his individual needs. In complying with such a mandate, a local education agency must consider the use of residential facilities as a source of programming for pupils who are severely, profoundly and uniquely handicapped (excerpted from Maryland State Bylaw directive).

As I shared with you, the Board of Education of Baltimore County had appropriated in its 1975–76 special education budget $500,000 to cover the cost of covering such services. This estimate was based on applications during the previous year for this level of service. The figure was derived from the Maryland State Department of Education which directed local education agencies to give priorities to pupils in the following order: (a) to serve all school-age pupils and to finance their educational program in residential settings if this was recommended by the Admission, Review, and Dismissal Committee . . . (b) to continue funding for any handicapped child who had been placed and funded under this service level during the previous year; (c) where possible, to extend residential service appropriate to preschool age levels. I might add that the department in its correspondence indicated that there would be little or no funding support for the infant/preschool group—that this service would need to be provided by finances available through the local county government; i.e., board of education. As of this date, in order to comply with these requests the Board of Education of Baltimore County has expended approximately $735,000 for approximately 156 identified pupils. As you can see, our budgeted amount fell very short of the actual expenditure. This led to my staff and I examining very closely the residential programs for handicapped pupils. Attached you will find a breakdown of costs for 25 pupils whose educational program is being paid for in private schools by the State of Maryland Department of Education and the Baltimore County Board of Education. The board felt that we needed to break apart tuition costs in order to identify specific areas where monies were being spent.

A general explanation of the chart is column 1—child; column 2 is total tuition requested by the nonpublic facility; column 3 is instructional costs; column 4 is therapy costs; column 5 is room and board and any requiring extras; column 6 is the name of the non-

Child	Tuition	Instruction	Therapy	Room and board	School
1.	$15,000	$11,460	$540	$3,000	—A—
2.	11,675	4,800	Inc.	6,875	—B—
3.	11,675	4,800	Inc.	6,875	—B—
4.	11,675	4,800	Inc.	6,875	—B—
5.	11,675	4,800	Inc.	6,875	—B—
6.	11,675	4,800	Inc.	6,875	—B—
7.	14,400	4,800	1,200	8,400	—B—
8.	14,400	4,200	1,800	8,400	—B—
9.	11,675	4,800	Inc.	6,875	—B—
10.	11,675	4,800	Inc.	6,875	—B—
11.	14,400	4,200	1,800	8,400	—B—
12.	11,675	4,800	Inc.	6,875	—B—
13.	11,675	4,800	Inc.	6,875	—B—
14.	12,480	5,800	1,620	3,539	—C—
				1,521 for recreation, extras	
15.	14,760	6,300	1,620	3,539 plus extras	—C—
16.	8,000	3,280	——	4,400 + $320—phys. ed.	—D—
17.	8,000	3,280	——	4,400 + $320—phys. ed.	—D—
18.	8,000	3,280	——	"	—D—
19.	8,000	3,280	——	"	—D—
20.	8,000	3,280	——	"	—D—
21.	18,000	7,020	8,640	2,340	—E—
22.	14,100	6,345	5,640	2,115	—E—
23.	15,600	7,020	6,240	2,340	—E—
24.	13,200	5,940	5,280	1,980	—E—
25.	14,400	6,480	5,760	2,160	—E—

public facility, [changed to letter designation for inclusion in this text]. Perusal of the data raises the following concerns: The Federal Handicap Educational Act, Maryland State Law, and the Special Education Bylaw mandate the payment of educational costs; Question 1—should a board of education direct money intended for instruction to the provision of therapies such as psychiatric treatment? Question 2—when one looks at the total cost to the facility and the costs that parents assume . . . should the use of education monies supplant financial obligations of families toward the rearing of the child? . . . Let me clarify this a little further . . . if a child were living at home, parents would have to pay food costs, transportation, recreation, etc. If one looks at what parents pay in the private facility, it appears that their financial contribution is addressed to laundry, purchase of clothing, spending money.

I think a case consideration needs to be outlined in terms of the dispersal of money across agencies so that educational costs should address instruction and should be paid for through monies allocated to education. Therapy, if it is medical in nature, should be paid for by monies allocated through health and mental health agencies, and room and board at least be partially paid by families requesting service for children in nonpublic schools.

A second aspect deals with a local board of education's obligations to certain categorical types of handicapping conditions. I will describe three special cases, give background data, and then raise the issue that we faced in this particular educational agency.

Case #1 is fourteen years old, is currently being provided with an educational program at School F, and is being supported by funding from the Board of Education of Baltimore County.

Descriptive Diagnosis: This child's handicap can be described as a severe motor expressive aphasia combined with mental retardation. The pupil's educational service summary is as follows:

1966-67	School G*	$ 700.00
1968-69	School H*	800.00
1/1/70-6/70	School F*	-3,331.14
1971-72	School F	8,100.00
1972-73	School F	8,100.00
1973-74	School F	8,100.00
1974-75	School F	8,100.00
1975-76	School F	9,540.00

This case is unique in that the Board of Education of Baltimore County has available classes for children with severe communicative/language disabilities and classes for pupils with communicative/language disorders and mental retardation. However, the child's mother refuses to have the child in the home. When this child returns home, it causes such an upheaval the mother must be hospitalized for psychiatric care. The issue in this case addresses itself to . . . should there again be a shared financial cost across

* Schools F, G, H, I, J, and N are additional schools which do not appear in table.

agencies of the cost of keeping this child in a residential setting? It is a very difficult question to resolve. As you see from the summary cost of School F, if we were to continue this young man through the age of 21, the cost to the educational agency would be $66,500 for these remaining years. This figure is only approximate. It has been our observation that in many cases the tuition cost of nonpublic facilities has arisen several thousand dollars from one fiscal year to the next. The second issue is should a child be continued in a residential program due to the physical and mental health of his family?

Case #2 raises some difficult questions regarding educational programming in nonpublic facilities. This child is twelve years old and is blind and retarded with an estimated IQ of 25. There is a recurrent history of epilepsy and limited speech and communicative abilities. His performance level is limited progress in self-help skills and group skills. He requires strong staff supervision and direction, has a history of adversive behavior, although some improvement has been noted. Investigations have been made for services within the local school district. The Mental Retardation Administration has indicated that they cannot serve this young man because rentro lental fibro plasia has left him too blind to profit from programs for the mentally retarded. The State School for the Blind has rejected their educational planning for him because he is too retarded. The Vocational Rehabilitation service has indicated that this young man is too handicapped, and therefore could not receive their services. Social Services has indicated that he is still of school age and therefore does not fall within their jurisdiction. Therefore, plans for this young man fall to the educational agency. Therefore, he had his educational program delivered at a residential facility in Chicago which provides services for multihandicapped blind. The cost of provisions of service for this young man has been:

1971-72	School I*	$8,500
1972-73	School I	8,900
1973-74	School I	9,195
1974-75	School I	10,500
1975-76	School I	11,000

for a total of $48,095 to date.

We have recently received communication from the family; though the young man will be 21 years of age in November, they are requesting continuation of funding through June of the coming fiscal year. To my knowledge no agency plans to assume responsibility of this young man at the time the educational agency ceases its service. At issue are two aspects: (1) With a young man of age where the educational program is about to cease and little hope of increase in ability to make use of the instructional program, should a local educational agency continue to fund through a year in which the 21st birth date occurs? (2) If there should not again be a coalition of agencies providing service and assuming burdens for services other than educational services, then what services will be available for this child? In this young man's case there are 40 sessions of individual therapy at a cost of $400 and a recreational program of $625. Question: What is a local educational agency's responsibility for continued training of a multihandicapped person till and through the age of 21 who shows minimal progress? Should there be a time when there is realization that the investment of funds for instruction, i.e., $6,835, is not continued and that person continue to have appropriate care? Is every individual entitled to instruction 0–20 years regardless of documentation of progress?

Case #3 involves siblings. The first, Child X, is fifteen years old and has a diagnosis of cerebral dysfunction manifested by mental retardation with performance in the low trainable range. He was seen at School J* and the following behavioral descriptions resulted: (a) biting fingers/wrist at a rate of 6.6 responses per minute; (b) spitting at a rate of 2.1 responses per minute; (c) biting or pinching others at a rate of 0.3 responses per minute; (d) unintelligible sounds at a rate of 1.4 rpm. Total adversive behavioral responses—9.50 rpm.

Educational History: School J Appraisal: Enrollment behavioral modification program—2 months. 1970-71 School K (day center)—released because too difficult to handle. 2/72 enrolled School L (residential center) length of stay 3 hours—too difficult to handle. 8/72 enrolled School M.

This young man has not cost the board of education anything to date, but his father is exploring the possibility of residential placement. This child and his sibling were also plaintiffs in the Maryland Association for Retarded Citizens class action suit against the State of Maryland.

Child Y is fourteen years old and also has a diagnosis of cerebral dysfunction manifested by mental retardation with performance in the low-trainable range.

Behavioral Description: Adversive behavior occurred at the following rates: (a) cries and chews hands at a rate of 2.50 rpm; (b) puts objects in mouth, that is, uses his tongue as a server, at a rate of 3.5 rpm; (c) grabs others; (d) screams at a rate of 3.50 rpm; (e) acceptable behavior could only be elicited if the young man was reinforced at a rate of 0.25 tokens per minute.

This young man parallels his brother except that he appears to have a bit more potential. He is enrolled in a private facility: 1975-76—School N*—$6,000. The Baltimore County Board of Education assumed responsibility as of this year.

This Office of Special Education has had lengthy and frequent contact with the father of the two boys. He is separated from his wife and has custody of the two boys; however, he indicates that he has no way of providing home care for either child and that residential placement will be essential from now on. Since this young man is 15 years of age we can look forward to paying education and care costs for him for the next six years. Both boys show minimal progress. The private nonpublic school and the public institution have indicated that the prognosis for their educational development is poor. Rather they indicate that the youngsters need tender, loving care. Again, I feel that the Baltimore County Board of Education has an obligation to see that some aspect of educational program is continued with both boys, but should a full cost of care fall to an educational agency alone? Also, what should the parent's responsibility be in the provision of some financial contribution toward their care?

Marty, please be aware that I am not in any way trying to minimize the role that education should play in seeing that severely, profoundly and uniquely handicapped children be provided with an educational program. I am in full agreement with legislation and judicial decisions to insure every individual the opportunity for education. The issues and questions I have raised address themselves primarily to whether it is the sole responsibility of a board of education because a child is of school age to provide all services in order for the individual to live and to supplant parental responsibility during the developing years of their child. As further explanation of that statement, let me say that quite often parents call to say "Well, my kid's been kicked out of the last residential school where you sent him—now, what are you going to do for him? Remember he is of school age and it is your responsibility to see that he gets the appropriate education in the most conducive environment—law and court guarantees this as my right."

WORK AND PLACEMENT

It is recognized that every individual should have the opportunity to live the fullest possible life with all of the benefits and pleasures that life has to offer. It is recognized, too, that education is one of the vehicles through which fulfillment comes. After education is completed, however, finding and securing employment is yet another difficulty the handicapped must face.

The questions raised in this chapter go beyond the matter of spending levels and go to the basis of special education itself. Because PL 94-142 requires that handicapped children be educated, a re-evaluation of what they will be educated for must be made. The nation is currently faced with high unemployment, a move toward more and more automation, and an increasing elimination of unskilled jobs. When viewed in the light of the anticipated identification and school enrollment of thousands of new severely handicapped children within the next few years, it is obvious that thought must be given to the future placement of these children and their role in society after the schools have completed their work. Special education will have to re-evaluate its programs to determine whether it is properly meeting the needs in today's changing world.

What should handicapped individuals who cannot work in competitive employment do? In five or ten years if there are as few jobs available as there are today, what will become of these individuals? One possibility is sheltered or limited and restricted work structures which provide settings in which individuals perform work skills at their own rates and within their own abilities. Payment is generally below the minimum wage. The question that must be asked now is whether workshops as they presently exist can adequately accommodate or begin to meet the needs of these severely handicapped individuals who will be brought into special education programs within the next few years.

If one assumes that there will not be any more jobs available in ten years than there are today and many of the lower level jobs which exist today will be eliminated, what will become of the severely handicapped individuals who will not be able to compete with able-bodied persons? Should these individuals be placed in sheltered, restricted, controlled work situations which pay less than the minimum wage? Should these settings be required to pay employees at least the minimum wage because of the reality that an individual earning at that level is below the poverty standard and certainly cannot support himself from those wages alone? Should federal, state and/or local governments supplement salaries of handicapped persons working in sheltered employment? Should financial support be given to the agency or organization providing employment to cover costs and salaries or should they be closed altogether and the money which would have gone to them be given directly to each severely handicapped person who might be "employed," thereby eliminating all overhead and operating costs?

CONCLUSION

In 1954 as the Supreme Court considered the *Brown* v. *Board of Education* case, the problem was unequal access to unequal resources for achieving identical ends. In the early 1960s, we had equal access to equal resources to achieve identical ends. Through compensatory education programs, the move was to equal access to differing resources to achieve identical ends. In the last part of the 1970s, through individualized education, we are entering an era of equal access to differing resources to achieve differing ends.

The old joke, "I have some good news and some bad news," dramatically applies to special education today. The good news is that the dream of having the capacity to serve all handicapped children may finally be realized. The bad news is that there will be greater public scrutiny of how well schools are educating children, how well they are utilizing scarce public resources, and how well handicapped individuals are prepared to lead a meaningful life. To some, these questions may be overwhelming. But it is hoped that those who work with the handicapped will see them as a positive and exciting challenge.

REFERENCES

Rossmiller, R., Hale, J., & Frohreich, L. *Educational programs for exceptional children: Resource configurations and costs.* Madison: University of Wisconsin, 1970. Pp. 65, 70.

Trudeau, E. (Ed.). *Digest of state and federal laws: Education of handicapped children.* Reston, Va.: Council for Exceptional Children, 1973.

A SELECTED BIBLIOGRAPHY OF WORKS BY MARTIN L. LAVOR

LaVor, M. *Ceramics for any hands.* Charlotte, N.C.: Hermitage Press, 1965. (hardback)

LaVor, M. *Ceramics for any hands.* Livonia, Mich.: Scott Advertising & Publishing Co., 1976. (soft back)

LaVor, M. Economic Opportunity Amendments of 1972, Public Law 92-424. *Exceptional Children,* 1972, 39 (8), 249-53.

LaVor, M. History of federal legislation dealing with children with specific learning disabilities. *Journal of the American Speech and Hearing Association,* 1976, 18 (8), 485-90.

LaVor, M. Federal legislation for exceptional persons: A history. In F. Weintraub, A. Abeson, J. Ballard, & M. LaVor (Eds.), *Public policy and the education of exceptional children.* Reston, Va.: Council for Exceptional Children, 1976.

LaVor, M. Martin hatches an egg: A fairy tale describing the way laws are made. In F. Weintraub, A. Abeson, J. Ballard, & M. LaVor (Eds.), *Public policy and the education of exceptional children.* Reston, Va.: Council for Exceptional Children, 1976.

LaVor, M. Time and circumstances. In F. Weintraub, A. Abeson, J. Ballard, & M. LaVor (Eds.), *Public policy and the education of exceptional children.* Reston, Va.: Council for Exceptional Children, 1976.

LaVor, M. You want to change the system—But where do you begin? In F. Weintraub, A. Abeson, J. Ballard, & M. LaVor (Eds.), *Public policy and the education of exceptional children.* Reston, Va.: Council for Exceptional Children, 1976.

LaVor, M., & Duncan, J. Rehabilitation act of 1973. *Exceptional Children,* 1974, 40 (6), 443-49.

LaVor, M., & Duncan, J. Vocational rehabilitation—The new law and its implications for the future. *Journal of Rehabilitation,* 1976, 42 (4), 20-28, 39.

LaVor, M., & Harvey, J. Headstart, Economic Opportunity, Community Partnership Act of 1974. *Exceptional Children,* 1976, 42 (4), 227-30.

LaVor, M., Weintraub, F., Abeson, A., & J. Ballard (Eds.). *Public policy and the education of exceptional children.* Reston, Va.: Council for Exceptional Children, 1976.

PART 5

Changing
Perspectives in
Research

14
Research: The Perpetual Revolution

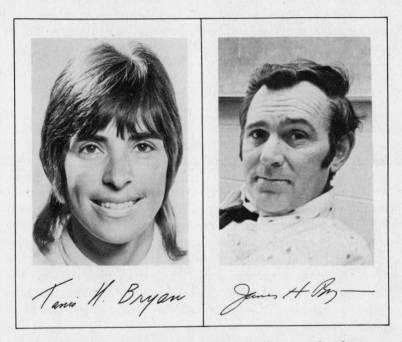

Tanis H. Bryan is associate professor of human development and learning, University of Illinois at Chicago Circle, and research scientist at Illinois State Pediatric Institute, Chicago. She began her professional experience as a speech pathologist in the Chicago public schools, later served as supervisor of the diagnostic clinic at Northwestern University, and then as supervisor of student teachers in learning disabilities at the University of Illinois at Chicago Circle. Dr. Bryan is on the editorial advisory board of the Journal of Learning Disabilities *and serves as a consultant to BEH. She has presented numerous papers at state and national conferences.*

Dr. Tanis Bryan received from Northwestern University the B.S. degree in speech pathology in 1958, the M.A. degree in communication disorders in 1968, and the Ph.D. in communication disorders in 1970.

273

James H. Bryan is professor, Department of Psychology, North-western University. Prior to his appointment at Northwestern, he was assistant professor in residence, Department of Psychiatry, University of California, Los Angeles. In 1966–67 he was visiting research psychologist, Center for Psychological Studies, Education Testing Service, and in 1968–69 he was acting director of clinical psychology at Northwestern University. Dr. Bryan has written many book chapters and has published widely in professional journals.

Dr. James Bryan received the B.A. degree from the University of California in 1954, the M.A. degree from San Francisco State College in 1956, and the Ph.D. from Pennsylvania State University in 1961. A selected bibliography of works by Tanis H. Bryan and James H. Bryan appears on pages 293-94.

INTRODUCTION

There is a United States senator who periodically announces his choices for the "Golden Fleece Award," an "award" given to federally funded research projects whose titles and costs seem outrageous to the senator—outrageous because they are not suggestive of societal benefits, but rather of rip-offs of taxpayers' monies. The reader, too, may find it questionable, if not ridiculous, to have money expended to study donkey urine or the aerodynamics of the frisbee, or to teach mothers to play with their infants. As we understand it, the study of donkey urine provided important information related to the human kidney, the frisbee study was a crashing disaster, and the study of mother-child interactions could have implications for the prevention or alleviation of socio-culturally induced mental retardation.

The senator's attack on research is by no means isolated, as many persons, researchers included, have recently been questioning the value of research in our society (e.g., Elms, 1975; Gadlin & Ingle, 1975).

The feelings expressed indicate that researchers rarely produce answers of any national moment, and if they did it wouldn't make much difference since the national decision makers don't talk to them anyway. The assumptions appear to be that research should have immediate applicability and that researchers should be influential. Given that we do not necessarily adhere to either of these assumptions, we are delighted to have the opportunity to present our ideas concerning the role research can, sometimes does, and ought to play in the field of special education.

The goal of this chapter is to discuss the value of the study of human behavior within the context of special education. The initial section of the chapter will discuss how one goes about doing "science," the purposes and limitations of the procedures which define the usual activities of the researcher. The second section will discuss some research of major consequence.

ON DOING "SCIENCE"

The purpose of science is to arrive at ever-better estimations of the "truth." The purpose of the scientific method is to ensure that those individuals striving for truth proceed in such a fashion as to reduce the possibility that they affect the data being gathered. Truth-seeking hardly separates the scientist from others. Virtually all of mankind seeks some sort of truths, whether of a trivial or profound nature. What separates the researcher from the teacher and clinician is the researcher's scorn of the personal, anxiety about bias, and professionally reinforced skepticism about all "truths." The scientist insists that professional truths, and oftentimes nonprofessional ones, be based on the scientific method which attempts to minimize subjectivity. Most people, including teachers, arrive at their truths through personal experiences which are not constrained by the rules of data collection adhered to by researchers. This differential stance regarding the nature of the evidence necessary for asserting that a truth has been found sharply distinguishes researchers from others; a distinction often leading to considerable misunderstanding and, sometimes, conflict.

It is important to note at the outset that scientists perpetually search for better "truths" than those currently available. They must then attack the beliefs and assumptions of their audience. Moreover, they attempt to make the nonresearcher more critical of social "truths" generated from other than the scientific method. The researcher seeks to replace various faiths with a faith in the scientific method. Insofar as science is always critical, always attacking, even if by refining today's truths, it seeks of its nonresearch audience a radicalism of considerable magnitude. If faiths must be replaced and replacements then attacked, the researcher is asking of the audience the implementation of the unorthodox. If what we say is true, the research movement is and will continue to be in a political struggle to change faiths and to increase skepticism. Much of this radicalism of science remains submerged since a great deal of research is not concerned with issues affecting people's beliefs, competencies, or values. If physicists exhort a radical belief which will allow a faster flight to the moon, the idea is likely to receive scant attention since the public can neither understand it nor feel morally offended. But in the fields which study human behavior, a radical idea is likely to stir considerably more controversy since it is rare that individuals feel either incompetent in assessing others or indifferent as to what is done to them. The layman's humility runs deeper concerning the understanding of physics than of people. It is no wonder that stresses and strains occur between administrators, politicians, clinicians, teachers, and researchers.

Varying perspectives on the nature of reliable and valid evidence affect the current status of special education. Personal experience, the foundation of most people's beliefs and the cornerstone of the attribution of expertise, is belittled. When personal experience as a foundation for belief is supplanted by research, an idea is formulated and then tested empirically. When derived from a formal theory, the idea is generally called a hypothesis. When the idea is not derived from or generated by a formal theory, the researcher attempts to articulate its rationale and then proceeds to test its viability. What is critical in the process, however, is not whether the idea is a formal hypothesis or a hunch, but rather that it is expressed in testable terms before rather than after its empirical evaluation. An idea generated after a peep at the data, a post hoc hypothesis, may be a good idea, but it will not qualify as a truth until it is empirically tested. To do this, questions must be posed which can be answered by observing and quantifying events.

It seems to us that there are several considerations that should be explicated concerning question-posing and the field of special education. In special education, we are generally working with educated guesses about our interests. There are few well-formulated theories that are applicable to the field. It is perhaps because of the lack of substantiated theory that research is more likely to be directed towards assessing experimental programs and meeting governmental concern about social ills than to be directed towards the discovery of more broadly based principles of human conduct which are only peripherally related to the immediate social presses of the times. For instance, research concerned with deinstitutionalization is not often generated from theoretical concerns with the impact of institutional versus community isolation upon behavior; rather there is interest in the characteristics of children and teachers which might affect rates of institutional recidivism. We seem to be more concerned with what we have to do to guarantee the success of current policies and programs than with advancing our understanding of the impact of a handicap. Following the formulation of the hypothesis, data are collected. The procedures followed must be performed so as to minimize the risk that the results are a function of the investigator's biases and expectations. The investigator clearly defines the problem to be studied and the methods which will be used but cannot allow the occurrence of personal influence upon the final set of observations obtained. The desired procedures are those which minimize the number of possible explanations of the results obtained. For example, if one wished to study the effects of sugar level upon learning by giving lots of sweets to a group of mentally retarded and none to a group of nonretarded children, any differences in their learning could be attributable to either sugar effects or differences in intellectual levels. To the degree that studies employ procedures which allow rival explanations of the data, their internal validity is reduced.

The problem of rival and plausible explanations of research data in special education is particularly acute since investigators are frequently concerned with comparing groups of individuals who differ on a number of pre-existing personality and social characteristics. The retarded are compared with the nonretarded, the hyperactive with the lethargic, and the brain damaged with the hyperactive. Any differences found between the performances of such different groups may be a result of a variety of social, personal, or situational factors. A good example of such difficulties within the field of special education is in the study of hyperactive and mentally retarded children. These groups of children are often described as being more distractible (as opposed to having more interests) than nondisabled children. Studies of learning disabled children, however, frequently report that intelligence test scores for the learning disabled and comparison children are different, the latter usually obtaining higher scores. Differences in distractibility, or whatever, can then be explained by differences in intelligence rather than by some hocus pocus characteristic unique to learning disabled children.

Another important feature of a research project or program is the applicability of the results to other populations and in differing situations. The question is asked whether the results from a study can be applied to other groups in other locations. This feature of research is called validity. One cannot speak with authority about the external validity of a particular study until there are a number of other studies conducted in other locations. More often than not, such studies are not conducted, at least not very quickly. Usually the applicability of a research result is a matter of guesswork, and probably depends upon the faiths of the various judges in their intellect and the scientific method.

Following the data collection in a research study, the results are analyzed by prescribed statistical techniques to determine whether or not the data support the hypothesis. The analysis is such that the investigator can say whether the results are due to chance or, in varying degrees, support the hypothesis. Some persons have expressed the belief that it is possible to make any sow's ear into a silk purse through the use of statistics. But, in order to be meaningful, results must be public, and the scientific audience is condemning of stupidity and absolutely intolerant of cheats. There is a consensus about the uses of statistics which limits the freedom of the researcher to manipulate data to obtain desired results.

Furthermore, while the motives of the scientists involving themselves in research are many and varied, most experienced researchers do not expect a definitive answer from any one study. The investigator merely wishes to determine if there is evidence to support the idea and to get new ideas for the next investigation. The end of one study merely signals the beginning of the next. The objective is to study a complex event, piece by piece, step by step, so that ultimately these events are increasingly understood. Whether the initial question concerns training methods for language, deinstitutionalization and mainstreaming, or identification and prevention of learning problems, the researcher seeks to understand the processes and variables involved and realizes at the same time that this understanding will be subsequently changed by more research which leads to new understanding.

LIMITATIONS OF THE SCIENTIFIC METHOD

It is our belief that across time the scientific method of inquiry produces the best, albeit imperfect, estimates of "truth." There are limitations to this method, however, in terms of our need for information within the field of special education.

One limitation pertains to the span of time between the need for a "truth" and the production of a "truth." Nobody expects a child to learn to read in one teaching session. Everyone understands that learning complex skills requires time, effort, and many trials. The same holds true for research. It is not possible to develop a body of knowledge concerning some complex issue within the framework of a single research study. Nonresearchers too often expect a single project to have all-encompassing, definitive, unequivocal results. The accumulation of significant information takes many research studies, however, and to conduct many research studies requires much time. The lengthy time line of research is not easily circumvented or shortened, and this is very difficult for those not involved in research to accept.

A second limitation is that scientists cannot promise results, although there is pressure upon them to do so, particularly when applying for outside financial support. It is unfortunate that researchers are pressed to make promises like used car salesmen, and like used car salesmen they sometimes disappoint and disillusion the consumer when promises are not kept. The press to produce applicable results has increased conservatism at the university level. Kolstoe (1976) expressed this concern very well when he stated, "If I had been on the Wright brothers' dissertation committee I would have said, 'Forget it, it will never get off the ground' " (p. 250).

Even when promised results are forthcoming, there are scientific constraints placed upon investigators related to the presentation of these results. The results should be presented accompanied by all possible interpretations the investigator can conjure up, and caution is often expressed regarding the external validity of the study. The investigator must not make claims which cannot be explicitly and concretely tied to the data. Seeming equivocation and uptightness is scientifically healthy, appropriate, and necessary to obtain fellow researchers' approval of the work. But nonresearchers seem to interpret equivocation as an indication that either the researcher is incompetent or the data worthless. Teacher/clinicians want single answers to complex questions, and multiple possibilities seem to decrease their regard for the value of research.

RESEARCH AND THE GOVERNMENT

Money makes the world go around; it also makes people happy. The cost of research, like everything else, has gone up, leading to an increased reliance of the investigator and perhaps even his university, upon government funds. It would appear that the process by which the government elects which research to support is undergoing some major changes. Until recently, researchers submitted grant applications to government agencies for funds. These applications were reviewed by appropriate persons and the best ones won. "Best" was determined by peer group assessment of a project's scientific merit. The topic, however, was presumed to be a function of the theoretical interests of the investigator.

It now appears that government agencies, rather than individual scientists, are setting policies concerning the topics to be investigated and funded. Government agencies are establishing the areas in which research data is deemed socially relevant, thus desirable. Political and social ideologies are becoming the predominant determinants of research directions. This is unfortunate for a number of reasons.

There is great unwillingness to provide financial support for research which does not promise instant applicability. As Kolstoe (1976) suggested, there are few people who would provide financial support to someone who wanted to teach pigeons how to hit a bar with their beaks. But because an idea appears impractical on the surface does not mean it might not ultimately provide critical and applicable information, just as Skinner's pigeon work did in operant conditioning.

Conversely, just because a project appears to be educationally relevant does not mean that the promises will be fulfilled. Have we not all witnessed millions of dollars wasted on applied projects which failed to provide any new knowledge concerning handicapped persons or educationally relevant information?

A related issue facing research is that the government can, by virtue of holding the purse strings, control not only the topics being investigated but the research methods employed. And this control may be exerted by government administrators who do not reflect either public policy or scientific sophistication. There is little question that government controls are needed. Some medical and psychological research has abused subjects. Moreover, with our increasing ability to control behaviors, be it from M&Ms or brain implants (London, 1970), decisions concerning who the subjects will be, the techniques to be used, for how long, and under what conditions are a matter of public urgency and not simply the sole concern of the investigator. The particular policy decisions concerning the control of research and the procedures by which such decisions will be implemented are still under serious debate and discussion. Until policies are established and procedures debugged, it is likely that the government funding agencies or delegates are going to assume a particularly conservative stance regarding research procedures. As examples of this conservative approach, one investigator was required by a university-appointed committee to obtain informed consent from preschool-age children before initiating his investigation, while another was warned that increasing children's generosity was exposing them to considerable risk. While the intentions of such controls are admirable, it is likely that the progress of reasonable research will be slowed until we all obtain more experience in the area of government control of research.

But there is another problem in this complex government-research relationship. Let us suppose that the government funds research on a currently critical issue such as mainstreaming. And let us suppose that the research findings indicate that government policy is inappropriate and not providing the promised better educational environments and outcomes for disabled children. What happens when results of research studies indicate that policies should be changed in that they are creating problems for many persons? In this instance, we have a conflict between values and data. One can perhaps predict the outcome by recalling politicians' reactions to research results pertaining to the effects of pornography on human behavior.

The researcher who elects to study problems defined by government agencies runs certain risks. Remember there is a lengthy time line for the accumulation of research data, even if the study is focused upon nationally important problems. If public policy shifts, changes values during the term of the study, the researcher may be left holding the bag with diminished financial support and interest in the work. Federal and state institutions can be fickle fellows. An example of research which conceivably may be jeopardized by shifting values is that on the identification of learning disabilities in preschool children. The arguments in favor of early identification must be counterbalanced with arguments against labeling children as defective. On the one hand there are state mandates to provide appropriate educational services to children starting at age three years. About 80 percent of school districts have initiated screening programs to identify potential school failures. Concurrently there are a number of longitudinal research studies to identify characteristics of children and appropriate assessment techniques for early identification (Keogh et al., 1974; Adelman & Feshbach, 1975). On the other hand there is considerable groundswell against testing and labeling children (Mercer, 1973). In addition, there is the problem that if children are tested and identified as needing special services, the special services had better be forthcoming and effective. The past few years have seen an increase in parental legal actions taken against school districts for the districts' failure to provide effective services. In the preschool programs, educators may be able to claim effective interventions, what with maturation and mother nature on their side; nonetheless, we must be concerned with overlabeling, mislabeling, and appropriate followup for any labeling.

Research and policy decisions: The time line necessary in research limits the utilization of research in setting government policy. However, there are many public policy decisions made in special education which have immediate, long-term, observable impact upon the lives of handicapped persons, their families, and communities. It is no minor bureaucratic process, to say the least, which has the effect of opening or closing institutions, moving people about, making demands for services upon communities, and changing lifestyles of the handicapped and their families. By and large, these public policy decisions reflect the current social-political ideologies of those people who are the primary decision makers. Presumably, and hopefully, they are knowledgeable of related research studies and that policies are formed and expedited on the basis of "facts" rather than emotional responses to limited information.

Even if pertinent research data are available when decisions are made, such data are usually fragmented, inconclusive, and most likely to be contradictory. Often, an arbitrary decision is made, and then whatever data are available to support the decision are cited. Research has frequently been used as a handmaiden to legitimize public policy.

An example of this can be seen in the decision to deinstitutionalize and mainstream handicapped persons. There were data to suggest that segregated placements in self-contained classrooms and institutions were not providing the intended benefits for disabled children and adults. There were also data which demonstrated that not all institutions were evil and that many provided very fine services. But all the data were limited and fragmented, and suffered many methodological faults. For instance, it was found that retarded children in regular school classes did as well or better academically and socially than retarded children in segregated classes. However these studies suffered problems in internal validity because the retarded children in the regular classrooms were of higher intelligence than those in the segregated settings. A handful of research studies, and imperfect ones at best, can hardly be used as a basis for the radical shifts in policy toward handicapped persons which are involved in the deinstitutionalization and mainstreaming movements.

THE RESEARCHER

A distinguished scientist advised a new faculty member that one must take a "vow of poverty" in electing to become a researcher. Persons who choose academic careers rather than other professions are well aware of the differential remuneration associated with being a college professor rather than a physician or lawyer. In addition to the low pay, other factors become apparent which operate to prohibit research activity. The difficulties in obtaining government support and the restrictions placed upon scientists by government policies have already been outlined. Also, the nonresearch responsibilities and demands of the university position leave little time for research. By the time a person finishes attending meetings, developing courses and programs, and attending to student needs there is precious little time or energy for research. Although there is the oft-quoted "publish or perish" dictum of university life, it does not appear that publications are a primary determinant of promotion and tenure at most schools. Perhaps our experiences have made us more cynical and perhaps our impressions are incorrect, but the data concerning who publishes support these authors' impression that there are very few Ph.D. psychologists engaging in research.

In special education there are likely to be considerably fewer at the Ph.D. level engaging in scientific studies. In part this is appropriate; this is a service-oriented field. But there should be questions as to whether our brightest, most creative persons are obtaining the training which would allow them to become researchers and the necessary encouragement and support from places of employment to pursue the development of a research program.

THE VALUE OF RESEARCH IN
SPECIAL EDUCATION

There are many ways in which research serves special education. For starters, research efforts contribute to and challenge the ideas of clinicians concerning diagnosis and intervention for handicapped persons, provide a technique to evaluate policies and programs for handicapped children and adults, and contribute to the understanding of our society. Research in other social and medical sciences also adds to our knowledge of the disabled, sometimes serendipitously. In the following section some examples of how research contributes to special education will be outlined. The selections are by no means an attempt to cover all the relevant research literature.

Research is of value in special education when it contributes to our understanding of what affects treament of handicapped and disabled persons.

Behaviorism: The research studies of B. F. Skinner have had a profound impact upon our perspectives of human behavior and our treatment of many kinds of problems. Skinner demonstrated that behavior is controlled by its consequences and that the appropriate use of rewards can serve to strengthen or diminish a wide variety of actions. While teachers, clinicians, and parents have intuitively used rewards to increase the incidence of appropriate behaviors in children for centuries, Skinner's research greatly refined our understanding of how rewards work; how much reward may be necessary, when rewards should be given, and how often they should be given. By focusing upon external observable events, Skinner drew our attention to the impact upon the individual of environmental variables, particularly people, and how these environmental variables elicit and maintain maladaptive as well as adaptive behaviors. Shifting from concern for intraphysic events to environmental variables which increase or decrease adaptive and maladaptive behaviors is particularly critical within special education. Skinner's work has forced us to examine external environmental variables which affect handicapped persons so that we no longer put the blame on the disabled for all the ill effects of a handicap. We instead focus on the role of various agents and events which may increase or decrease these ill effects.

Research is of value in special education when it challenges our stereotypes.

Social behaviors of learning disabled children: Since the work of one of us (Tanis H.) was initially based on clinical descriptions of learning disabled children, it is used as an example here (Bryan, 1974a, 1974b, in press–a, in press–b; Bryan et al., in press).

Every aversive, negative behavior imaginable has been associated with the learning disabilities label. Nowhere in the definition of learning disabilities nor in the typical assessment procedures is there direct acknowledgement or assessment of behavioral characteristics. The question posed in the initial state of the research program was whether there are empirical bases to the negative behavioral attributes associated with learning disabilities. Using observational, experimental, and paper-and-pencil questionnaires, several studies were conducted. The results contradicted some popular stereotypes and revealed some unexpected findings.

To summarize, it has been found that learning disabled children are rejected by classmates on measures of sociometric status. This has been replicated three times. The results of observational studies indicate that the behavioral responses learning disabled children receive from teachers and peers in classrooms are different from those received by their normal classmates, and these differences are suggestive of rejection. Impartial observers viewing videotaped interactions between learning disabled and normal children playing a laboratory bowling game make differential ratings of the learning disabled and comparison children. They rate learning disabled children as less likeable and less likely to do well in school than the comparison classmates. On a test of comparison of nonverbal social communications, learning disabled children obtain significantly lower accuracy than nondisabled peers; a finding which replicated. Studies of children's classroom conversations indicate that learning disabled and normal children tend to say different things to peers and tend to be the recipients of different statements from peers. These differences indicate that peers are more likely to reject learning disabled children, although the sex and race of the children also are important factors.

These data challenge notions of learning disabled children as hyperactive or emotionally liable. They are not troublemakers in the classrooms. There is considerable evidence, however, that a significant number of learning disabled children are experiencing very real problems in their social relationships with others. Their comprehension of the affective states of others and their verbal responsiveness to others may be important factors affecting whether they are accepted or rejected.

At this point it would be desirable if clinical assessments of learning disabled children were expanded to integrate these data. For example, descriptions of the relationships of the child with significant others (parents, teachers, peers, siblings) should highlight the kinds of interpersonal problems learning disabled children are having and provide a beginning to understanding the origins of interpersonal problems. It would be helpful if psychoeducational assessment could reveal whether interpersonal problems occur with particular kinds of learning deficits. We might also get some idea as to the adaptiveness of the behaviors of learning disabled children. Behavior which on the surface appears obnoxious may be quite justifiable if the situation is taken into account. For instance, an incompetent parent or teacher may frustrate a child, respond inappropriately, or in a way which exacerbates a problem.

Research is of value when it has serendipitous outcomes for special education.

Teacher expectancy: Attempts to define characteristics of teachers which affect pupil achievement have had specific implications for our understanding of handicapped children, particularly the learning disabled and educable mentally retarded. Teachers are "gatekeepers" in education in that they frequently are the first ones to identify and make referrals for children with learning problems. There are data to suggest that teachers, themselves—their attitudes, behavior, or competency—may be the source of difficulty for at least some children who develop into school problems. Now that we are heavily involved in mainstreaming handicapped children, it is more important than ever to have some reliable evidence concerning the impact upon children of classroom teachers' attitudes and behavior.

For years educational researchers attempted to define the "good" teacher. Religious and socioeconomic background, age, years of training, and type of teaching style were among the variables studied—to no avail. About all one could say was that intelligent, nurturant people were more likely to be effective teachers than were stupid, mean people. In 1968, a book entitled *Pygmalion in the Classroom* by Rosenthal and Jacobsen helped to open up a new area of investigation on teacher effectiveness. This area is based upon the idea that a teacher's attitude toward individual children affects the teacher's behavior, and this, in turn, affects individual children's attitudes and behaviors.

The impact upon children of teacher expectations was also investigated, and the data were as impressive as they were extensive. Palardy (1969) compared the reading achievement of first-grade boys and girls who had teachers who believed that girls would perform better than boys with those who had teachers who did not believe that there were sex differences in initial reading achievement. He reported that by the end of first grade boys were reading at significantly lower levels than were girls in classes in which teachers believed there were sex differences which favored girls. Boys and girls read equivalently in classes where teachers did not believe there were sex differences. Rist (1970) used interviews and observations to study the stratification of children in black classrooms. He observed that by the eighth day of kindergarten the children were assigned to permanent seats at three tables which varied in their distance from the teacher. It seemed that the teacher had formed expectations concerning the children's academic potential before the children started school on the basis of information which was strictly nonacademic (i.e., whether the family was on welfare). The children's permanent seat assignments (i.e., their proximity to the teacher) were a manifestation of those expectations. By third grade, preferred children belonged to the "tigers" reading group while the nonpreferred children belonged to the "clowns."

There have been a number of studies of teacher expectations specific to special education classes. Willis (1970) asked teachers in five special education classrooms to rank their eight students from most to least efficient as learners. Observations were then made of the teachers' interactions with the children rated highest and lowest. Teachers were more likely to ignore the children ranked as least efficient, and more likely to respond verbally to those ranked most efficient. Veldman (1974), as cited by Brophy and Good (1974), reported on learning disabled and mentally retarded children who had been mainstreamed into regular education classes. The children responded to a questionnaire that their teachers expected less of them and made fewer cognitive demands on them than on their classmates.

In sum, it appears that there is a good deal of empirical support for the hypothesis that teachers form expectations (for the most part, unconsciously) concerning particular children, and they relate to these children differentially so that the children may accept and live up to the expectations. One thing that is striking is that teachers do not use academic performance alone to form their expectations. Indeed, the evidence would suggest that attitudes concerning sex (Palardy, 1969), welfare status, use of Standard English (Rist, 1970), facial responsiveness to teachers (Willis & Brophy, 1974), commonness of the child's name (Harrari & McDavid, 1973), and responsiveness to teacher instruction (Beckman, 1973) all contribute to teacher judgments of and responsiveness to individual children.

Research is of value in special education when it challenges labeling procedures.

Early identification studies: Concern for early identification of learning problems emanated from the idea that we might prevent learning failure if we could detect it and intervene early. The goal was to prevent the occurrence of secondary emotional and learning problems which so often accompany school failure. In light of the data concerning the influence of teacher attitudes and behavior upon the success and failure of children, it can be seen that early prediction efforts need to account not only for characteristics of children which eventuate in school failure, but also characteristics of teachers and schools which might contribute to children's difficulties.

There are a number of ongoing longitudinal research studies which are concerned with early identification of learning problems. These efforts are focused on which tests and techniques predict school failure, as well as on characteristics of children, teachers, and schools which affect children's school performance.

Adelman and Feshbach (1975) have been studying all the kindergarten children in two Los Angeles schools for two years. Their measures have included individual tests of intelligence and reading readiness, teacher ratings, demographic and medical data, questionnaires completed by parents, and classroom observations. When the children reach first, second, and third grades they are administered additional achievement tests. Meanwhile, Keogh and Sbordone (1974) and Keogh, Hall, and Becker (1974) have been studying kindergarten children classified as high risk and nonrisk for school failure. Teacher ratings, experimenter observation of classroom behavior, and a battery of tests are administered in kindergarten and again in first grade.

It appears that these projects will lead to some interesting findings concerning early identification. First it appears that prediction and identification of learning problems can be accomplished, although there are some children who will be falsely labeled as risk or nonrisk. Second, it appears that the risk group is not homogeneous, but consists of at least two types of children. One type appears to have academic aptitude difficulties; whereas the second has problems in behavioral adaptability.

It also appears that teacher characteristics are significant determinants of children's potential success or failure. Teacher attitudes, classroom style, and responsiveness to individual children affect whether children are labeled risk or nonrisk, and whether the children change their status. It would seem from these studies that early identification requires that we expand our current assessment procedures to include new dimensions of child characteristics. In addition, assessment and prediction of learning problems must account for teacher attitudes, teaching styles, and instructional programs.

Research is of value in special education when it challenges teaching techniques.

A primary teaching technique within the field of learning disabilities has been based on the modality-deficit notion. Using scores on tests like the Illinois Test of Psycholinguistic Abilities (Kirk & Kirk, 1972) to determine if a child has an auditory or visual modality information-processing deficit, learning disability teachers have been providing special instruction to remediate these deficits. This approach of matching child characteristics to instruction was recently challenged by Newcomer and Goodman (1976). In their research study fourth graders were divided into two groups—one with auditory deficits and the other with visual deficits—and were then administered two kinds of learning tasks. In one task the children were presented either visually or orally with nonsense syllables; in the second task meaningful categorization problems were presented either visually or orally. The performances of high-auditory, low-auditory, high-visual, and low-visual children were compared. There were no significant group differences on the meaningful learning task, no matter how it was presented. There were significant differences on the nonmeaningful task, as children in the low-auditory group performed more poorly than did the other subject groups when the task was presented orally. High-visual and high- and low-auditory groups did quite well, and the low-visual group was not adversely affected by the visual presentation of material. This data, albeit from but one research study, does suggest that matching academic instruction to modality choices, at least at fourth grade, does not yield academic benefits. By this time, meaningfulness of material is more important than modality of presentation. At the same time, children who have auditory deficits relative to other children may be experiencing bona fide short-term memory problems, at least when they have to deal with nonmeaningful materials.

The results of this study challenge our notions concerning modality deficits and matching instruction to modality preferences. In light of the difference in performance of the groups on meaningful and nonmeaningful material, however, one must challenge the challenge by virtue of the age of the subjects. By fourth grade instruction is content oriented. But in the primary grades, children are involved in skill acquisition, and in the initial stages the tasks are more closely allied to learning nonsense syllables than to meaningful learning. We cannot disregard the modality-deficit approach until research is conducted with considerably younger children.

Research is of value in special education when it helps us evaluate the impact of our policies upon handicapped persons, their families, and communities.

Deinstitutionalization and reintegration of handicapped persons into their home communities is a major goal within special education today. We need information concerning the impact of this policy upon all affected members of the community. We need to know which child, family, school, or community factors contribute to the likely success or failure of the reintegration movement.

Peterson and Kreisman (in preparation) conducted a research study to determine the impact of reintegration upon children, parents, and teachers. The focus of the study was upon parents' and teachers' feelings of adequacy to cope with reintegrated developmentally disabled children and children's status subsequent to reintegration. Nine children were studied when they were removed from the institution and placed in community programs and when the project terminated, three months later. A variety of assessments were made of teacher and parent attitudes toward their ability to cope with deviant behavior upon the children's return and three months later.

It was found that all nine children were being maintained within their homes and community programs at the end of the three-month period. Several factors were found to be related to teachers' final assessment of the likelihood that the child would or would not be successful in reintegration efforts. There was a significant finding for sex, as females received higher ratings from teachers. No other demographic variables were significant. Teachers' attitudes were related to the child's manifestation of asocial, aversive behavior. Children who exhibited aggressiveness, attention-getting behavior, or bizarre actions were considered less likely to be maintained than children who did not exhibit such behavior. It is notable that the children's skill level was not a significant indicator of teacher ratings. It was found that teachers' evaluations of their own ability to cope with a variety of aberrant behaviors was not predictive of teacher ratings; but their initial responses and judgments of the child at the moment of re-entry was significantly predictive of their final ratings. If, for example, a teacher decided upon seeing a child for the first time that he/she would not be able to cope with that child, this judgment tended to remain the same after the three-month period.

Parents' attitudes were related to the child's manifestation of emotional behavior (crying, inability to cope with daily problems) and bodily symptoms (facial grimaces, noises).

The attitudes of teachers of developmentally disabled children were compared with attitudes of teachers of emotionally disturbed children. Both groups defined the same kinds of behaviors as highly aversive and unmanageable.

There were no significant findings of changes in skills or in manifestation of aberrant behavior across the three-month period. However the data indicated a tendency toward a drop in skill level and increased manifestations of aggression, attention-getting, and bizarre behaviors.

The data strongly suggest that labels or even skills of disabled children do not significantly affect whether or not they will be successfully integrated into community programs. The key factor is the behavior of the children; in particular, the degree to which it is aversive or unmanageable.

There are a number of limitations to this study. First, there were only nine children actually reintegrated of a possible eighty children. It would have been far better had the eighty children been randomly assigned to either remain in the institution or be mainstreamed. In that there were no control subjects, we have no way of knowing whether the children remaining within the institutional setting would have shown more or less maladaptive behavior than the reintegrated children. Nor do we know what characteristics or variables affected the particular nine children being reintegrated. In spite of these shortcomings, the data that were collected provide important information concerning what will affect successful reintegration; and it is notable that some of these findings are quite counterintuitive.

Research is of value in special education when it can be translated into instructional techniques and programs.

For a number of years, Meichenbaum (1974) has been studying the role of private speech in mediating behavior. The data suggest that people who use verbal mediators are more efficient and better at learning than people who fail to use verbal mediators. It has also been demonstrated that people can be trained to use verbal mediators with subsequent improvement in performance. With Goodman (1970), Meichenbaum developed a therapeutic program in which people are taught to talk to themselves as a means of controlling their own behavior.

Using Meichenbaum's training program for self-control, Bash and Camp (1975) developed the Think Aloud Program for training young aggressive boys. These boys were found to have adequate verbal ability, but were described as impulsive, quick responders with immature and voluble private speech. It was demonstrated that they have a high threshold for verbal mediation. A variety of techniques are used in the program, among them modeling, overt verbalization, and self-instruction to develop self-control in these boys within the program itself and in other situations. The tasks used with the children include cognitive problems and interpersonal problem situations.

With a firm basis in empirically demonstrated effective methods for changing behavior, such as modeling and rehearsal, this program has particular promise. It is also unique in that it attempts to train children in the *process* of learning, whereas most training programs focus on the *product* of learning. If this program is effective, it should provide the children with the skills to learn independently. The lack of such skills has been associated with many handicapping conditions.

Research is of value in special education when it contributes to a body of knowledge.

Until recently most research on language development has been focused upon young children. This is reasonable insofar as the growth of language skills is obviously greatest during the preschool years. There is increasing recognition, however, that language development continues at least into adolescence (Palermo & Molfese, 1972) and that the language comprehension and expression difficulties which have been observed in young children may persist at least into adolescence. Research is being conducted on language-processing skills of adolescent learning disabled children, and this work should considerably advance our understanding of both language development and language deficits in older children.

In one study, Wiig and Roach (1975) tested immediate recall for semantically and syntactically varied sentences by learning disabled and control adolescents. The rank order of difficulty for the varied sentences was the same for both learning disabled and nondisabled subjects. The groups were discriminated, however, as learning disabled subjects committed significantly more errors in immediate recall than did the control group. Learning disabled subjects had particular difficulty on sentences which were syntactically correct but which violated semantic rules, sentences which were in incorrect order or randomly ordered, and sentences which were structurally complex. Their responses were marked with interfering perseveration, word omissions and substitutions, and, less frequently, normalization of deviant structures. The authors hypothesize that these results indicate that learning disabled adolescents may have short-term memory and sequencing problems.

In another study, Wiig and Semel (1975) assessed learning disabled and comparison adolescents' accuracy and speed on naming tasks, producing sentences, and defining words. They reported that in comparison to control subjects, learning disabled children were verbally less quick and accurate, named fewer items, produced more agrammatical sentences and grammatical sentences of shorter length, had longer response lags in producing sentences, and gave more incorrect word definitions.

A battery of tests was administered to learning disabled subjects to determine the relationship between language comprehension and language production (Wiig, Lapointe, & Semel, 1975). By and large, the results suggest that measures of language reception correlate with one another, measures of language production correlate with one another, but language reception may be fairly independent of language production. The authors distinguish between two types of language deficits which may exist within learning disabled populations. One deficit is characterized as cognitive linguistic-processing deficit; a reduction in morphology and syntax as well as in comprehension of linguistics concepts. The second type of deficit is dysnomia; a verbal paraphasia, word-finding, and retrieval problem. Wiig and Semel suggest that effective remediation may require the accurate assessment of the type of linguistic problem a learning disabled adolescent may have.

We have tried to relate our opinions of the scientific enterprise and how it may relate to the field of special education. Before we conclude, we would like to advance a few further comments. First, in our opinion, it is extremely important that society recognize and support the researcher and scholar. This will mean supporting, at great expense, a lot of bad research, efforts which lead nowhere, and ideas which appear to be grounded in fantasy. But the university setting, in which most research is done, is perhaps the last haven for intellectual freedom, even if it is sometimes exploited by dullards and "crazies." To make the researcher the handmaiden of the political-social structure does a great disservice to the very structure the researcher is presumably serving. We cannot afford to further reduce that limited area of intellectual freedom that this society has so long protected.

In the last analysis, whether or not the researcher makes a meaningful contribution to society or to the international community of scholars (the ultimate audience), and whether or not he/she finds funds, there are two things which sustain the researcher. Research is fun, and it is a living besides.

REFERENCES

Adelman, H., & Feshbach, S. *Early identification of children with learning problems: Some methodological and ethical concerns.* Paper presented at the Society for Research in Child Development meeting, Denver, April 1975.

Bash, M. A., & Camp, B. *Think aloud program: Group manual,* October 1975.

Beckman, L. Teacher's and observers' perceptions of causality for a child's performance. *Journal of Educational Psychology,* 1973, 65, 198-204.

Brophy, J. E., & Good, T. L. *Teacher-student relationships.* New York: Holt, Rinehart & Winston, 1974.

Bryan, T. An observational analysis of classroom behaviors of children with learning disabilities. *Journal of Learning Disabilities,* 1974, 7, 26-34. (a)

Bryan, T. Peer popularity of learning disabled children. *Journal of Learning Disabilities,* 1974, 7, 621-25. (b)

Bryan, T. *Strangers' judgments of children's social and academic adequacy: Instant diagnosis.* Unpublished manuscript, 1975. (Available from University of Illinois at Chicago Circle, P.O. Box 4348, Chicago 60680).

Bryan, T. Learning disabled children's comprehension of nonverbal communication: The kiddiepons. *Journal of Learning Disabilities,* in press. (a)

Bryan, T. Peer popularity of learning disabled children: A replication. *Journal of Learning Disabilities,* in press. (b)

Bryan, T., Wheeler, R., Felcen, J., & Henek, T. "Come on Dummy": An observational study of children's communications. *Journal of Learning Disabilities,* in press.

Elms, A. C. The crisis of confidence in social psychology. *American Psychologist,* 1975, 30, 967-76.

Gadlin, H., & Ingle, G. Through the one-way mirror: The limits of experimental self-reflection. *American Psychologist,* 1975, 30, 1003-9.

Harari, D., & McDavid, R. Name stereotypes and teacher's expectations. *Journal of Educational Psychology,* 1973, 65, 222-25.

Keogh, B. K., Hall, R. J., & Becker, J. D. *Early identification of exceptional children for educational programming* (Tech. Rep. SERP 1974-A6). Los Angeles: Graduate School of Education, University of California, November 1974.

Keogh, B. K., & Sbordone, M. W. *Early identification of high risk and high potential kindergarten children* (Tech. Rep. SERP 1974-A5). Los Angeles: Graduate School of Education, University of California, December 1974.

Kirk, S. A., & Kirk, W. P. *Psycholinguistic learning disabilities: Diagnosis and remediation.* Urbana: University of Illinois Press, 1972.

Kolstoe, O. Comments in *Exceptional Children,* 1976, 42, 250.

London, P. *Personal liberty and behavior control technology*. Paper presented at the conference of the American Association for the Advancement of Science, Chicago, 1970.

Meichenbaum, D. Self-instructional methods. In F. H. Kanfer & A. P. Goldstein (Eds.), *Helping people change*. New York: Pergamon Press, 1974.

Mercer, J. R. *Labeling the mentally retarded*. Berkeley: University of California Press, 1973.

Newcomer, P. L., & Goodman, L. Effect of modality of instruction on the learning of meaningful and nonmeaningful material by auditory and visual learners. *Journal of Special Education*, 1976, 9, 261-68.

Palardy, J. What teachers believe—What children achieve. *Elementary School Journal*, 1969, 69, 370-74.

Palermo, D. S., & Molfese, D. L. Language acquisition from age 5 onward. *Psychological Bulletin*, 1972, 78, 409-28.

Peterson, C., & Kreisman, Evaluation of three school reentry programs for developmentally disabled children. In preparation, 1976.

Rist, A. Student social class and teacher expectations: The self-fulling prophecy in ghetto education. *Harvard Educational Review*, 1970, 40, 411-51.

Rosenthal, R., & Jacobson, L. *Pgymalion in the classroom: Teachers' expectations and pupils' intellectual development*. New York: Holt, Rinehart & Winston, 1968.

Veldman, D. Scale structure of "Your School Days!" In J. E. Brophy & T. L. Good (Eds.), *Teacher-student relationships*. New York: Holt, Rinehart & Winston, 1974.

Wiig, E. H., Lapointe, C., & Semel, E. *Relationships among language processing and production abilities of learning-disabled adolescents*. Paper presented at the conference of the American Speech and Hearing Association, Washington, D.C., 1975.

Wiig, E. H., & Roach, M. A. Immediate recall of semantically worried "sentences" by learning disabled adolescents. *Perceptual and Motor Skills*, 1975, 40, 119-25.

Wiig, E. H., & Semel, E. M. Productive language abilities in learning disabled adolescents. *Journal of Learning Disabilities*, 1975, 8, 578-86.

Willis, B. The influence of teacher expectation on teacher classroom interaction with selected children. *Dissertation Abstracts*, 1970, 30, 5072-A.

Willis, S., & Brophy, J. The origins of teachers' attitudes toward young children. *Journal of Educational Psychology*, 1974, 32, 290-93.

A SELECTED BIBLIOGRAPHY OF WORKS BY TANIS H. BRYAN AND JAMES H. BRYAN

Bryan, J. H. You would be well advised to watch what we do instead of what we say. In D. J. DePalma & J. M. Foley (Eds.), *Moral development: Current theory and research*. Hillsdale, N.J.: Lawrence Erlbaum Associates, 1975.

Bryan, J. H. Children's cooperation and helping behaviors. In M. Hetherington & A. Stein (Eds.), *Review of Child Development Research* (Vol. 5). Chicago: University of Chicago Press, 1975.

Bryan, J. H. Development of prosocial behavior. In I. Benjamin, B. Wolman, and Patricia Keith-Spiegel (Eds.), *International encyclopedia of neurology, psychiatry, psychoanalysis, and psychology,* in press.

Bryan, T. H., & Bryan, J. H. The effect of film material upon behavior. *Psychological Bulletin,* 1971, 75, 50-59.

Bryan, T. H., & Bryan, J. H. Imitation and judgments of children with learning disabilities. *Exceptional Children,* 1971, 38, 157-58.

Bryan, T. H., & Bryan, J. H. *Understanding learning disabilities.* New York: Alfred, 1975.

Bryan, T. H. The effect of forced mediation upon short-term memory of children with learning disabilities. *Journal of Learning Disabilities,* 1972, 5, 605-9.

Bryan, T. H. An observational analysis of classroom behaviors of children with learning disabilities. *Journal of Learning Disabilities,* 1972, 23, 26-34.

Bryan, T. H. Learning disabilities: A new stereotype. *Journal of Learning Disabilities,* 1974, 7, 304-9.

Bryan, T. H. Peer popularity of learning disabled children. *Journal of Learning Disabilities,* 1974, 7, 621-25.

15

Implications of Language
Research

James E. McLean is director of Parsons Research Center in
Parsons, Kansas and research associate of the Bureau of Child Research
at the University of Kansas. Prior to his appointments in Kansas, Dr.
McLean was professor of special education at George Peabody College
for Teachers. In his early public school experience, Dr. McLean was a
speech clinician and director of speech and hearing programs. He has
presented numerous papers and workshops at state and national conferences and, at present, is a consultant to BEH.

Dr. McLean received the B.S. degree in speech pathology from
Indiana University in 1951, the M.A. degree in speech pathology from

The author's research on language intervention has been partially supported
by a contract from the Bureau of Education for the Handicapped (OEC-0-74-9185)
to George Peabody College for Teachers, Nashville, Tennessee.

The author gratefully acknowledges Lee K. Snyder's significant contribution
to the preparation of this chapter.

*the University of Kansas in 1959, and the Ph.D. in speech pathology
and audiology from the University of Kansas in 1965. A selected bibliography of works by James E. McLean is found on pages 316-17.*

INTRODUCTION

My goal in this chapter is to analyze research in language and language acquisition in terms of its implications for the changing perspectives in special education. Rather a formidable task—but one which would seem productive from the point of view of both language researchers and special educators.

At this point in my career, I find myself quite firmly ensconced in a role committed to gaining perspectives about language and language acquisition which will enable more successful intervention programs for children with *severely* deficient language systems. The reader will see that my perspectives have been colored by a wide range of experiences, and I think that they will be found to be relatively nondoctrinaire in the sense that they have not been constrained by any overly rigid disciplinary allegiance. As I have observed the rise and fall of various exclusive schools of thought which at one time or another have seemed to hold a corner on truth in certain areas, I have found that the Haiku written by a dear friend of mine holds more and more true:

> The reds won't win
> Nor will the lily-whites
> It will be a thing
> quite plaid[1]

This metaphor is particularly appropriate for embarking on a discussion of language and research into language since this area has truly been a battleground for the past few years. Indeed, neither the reds nor the lily-whites have won, and the plaid perspectives of today seem to bode well for productive approaches to the problems of severely language-deficient children and adults. In turn, these productive approaches, seemingly, have important implications for special education in terms of service models, service delivery systems and, hopefully, process models of greater scope and rigor. These latter points will be discussed much later in the chapter; for now, it is important to get to the substantive content of this discussion.

---

[1] McLean, Barbara. Ho for the highlands. In *The sky starts just above the soles.* Unpublished master's thesis, University of Kansas, 1965.

CURRENT PERSPECTIVES ON LANGUAGE FORM, FUNCTION, AND ACQUISITION

Current perspectives on language are far from the definitive level we would all like, but they are in such a dynamic state of confrontation and controversy that some very real answers about the entire process appear eminently possible over the next few years. Today's perspectives are swirling about in the eddies and currents created by the confluence of three major streams of thought and research in language. These streams of thought, with their different points of origin, can perhaps best be identified as

1. theoretical and empirical attempts to describe the human language *system;*
2. theoretical and empirical attempts to describe the *function* of the human language system; and
3. theoretical and empirical attempts to describe the *process* by which the human language system is *acquired.*

Today, emerging perspectives reflect the awareness that any satisfactory knowledge about language must certainly include appropriate knowledge about all three aspects—the language system per se, the function of that system, and the process of its acquisition. In addition, these emerging perspectives hold that no one of the aspects of language can be analyzed without consideration of the other two. Thus, it is not just a matter of summing independently derived perspectives on each of the three aspects; rather, it is a matter of integrating all three aspects from the start in order to understand any one of them. This integrative perspective is just emerging, however, so let us first, briefly, look at the three independent streams of thought as they *have* existed in recent years and then look at the effects of their integration on each.

Descriptions of the language system: The language system has been analyzed and described extensively in terms of its several physical properties. The acoustic characteristics of its sound system and the physiological bases for its production have been described by experimental phoneticians. The structural units of the speech system that encode meaning have been fully described at the phonological, morphological, and syntactic levels by linguists. The basic elements of this momentous body of work are empirical and objective.

As work toward the specification of language structure expanded and the full complexity of the system was quantified, attempts were begun to reduce the complexity of the system by identifying new models for synthesizing what was known. Most notable of these reductionistic attempts have been the distinctive feature system for phonology (Jakobson, Fant, & Halle, 1963); the semantic feature system for morphology (Katz & Fodor, 1963); and the transformational grammar system for syntax (Chomsky, 1957, 1965).

The value of these quantifications and analyses of the language system has been significant. For a long time, professionals responsible for intervention in language carried out their efforts with an amazingly superficial body of knowledge about the human language system. In fact, few teachers and/or speech pathologists knew anything that went much beyond the articulation of the speech sound system and/or the outlining of formal grammar rules of a particular language. The work of the descriptive linguists and the linguistic model-builders sensitized all workers in language to the several levels of the spoken language system and the complexities involved at each of these levels. Furthermore, these descriptive efforts produced a relevant and highly systematic set of research variables and/or instructional objectives and thus were both important and productive for everyone involved in language, whether they were involved at theoretical or applied levels.

Problems were created by the language describers, however, when they attempted to move beyond description of the system and began to hypothesize about the origin and/or the acquisition of language. Other problems were created by applied workers in language when they took the descriptive language models created by the theoretical linguists and treated them as though they represented the system as it is operationalized by language users. These problems, and their consequences, will be discussed in later sections of this chapter.

Identification of language functions: The function of language has been consistently defined since the earliest days of philosophical thought as the mode for communication of thoughts and ideas between humans. There has been little reason to dispute this definition; yet, its singularity has been surprisingly constraining on the entire field of language theory and language remediation efforts.

The only effective attempt to go beyond this broad definition in recent times was that of psychologists of the behavioral school. In this movement, the ideas of Skinner (1957) have been the predominant force. Skinner conceptualized language as communication among humans which has as its purpose the attainment of various kinds of reinforcing consequences. This construct of communication function has obvious face validity, and there are few logical bases from which to dispute its basic tenet. Obviously many good consequences accrue to people through language communication. However, it also often evokes events which appear to be punishing rather than positively reinforcing. While it is true that people often cease communication behaviors which are punished, it is also true that people often persist in them. Skinner's constructs would explain this latter phenomenon by positing that, even though a communication attempt is *apparently* punished, its persistence indicates that it is also being reinforced in some fashion that may not be obvious.

Upon reflection, this consideration of reinforcement properties which are beyond those extrinsic types usually sought by behaviorists leads to constructs of communication function which, although they have been around for a long time, have been largely ignored. These constructs were expressed, for example, by DeLaguna (1963) and have been recently rearticulated by Bruner (1975, 1974/75) and Luria (1974/75). The function of communication posited in these views stems from the question, *Why* do people want to communicate their thoughts and ideas? The answer, while expressed in slightly varying ways, is essentially that people want to communicate in order that they might, thereby, engage other people in cooperative and/or joint activities. Thus, communication of thoughts and ideas functions to promote harmonious social interaction.

This concept of language function, obviously, is not counter to Skinner's reinforcement construct—but it extends that construct well beyond its current general application by the behaviorists. In the most simplistic extension, it is suggested that reinforcement of language, whatever its quantifiable, tangible nature, is imbedded in *social* contexts which are perhaps more important than the quantifiable reinforcer(s) per se. Such expanded views of communication function are beginning to have revolutionary impact on ideas about how language is acquired and, therefore, on ideas about treatment of the severe language deficiencies among handicapped children. This impact will be detailed and analyzed later in this chapter.

It is important to note at this point that *describers* of language have pursued their work with little concern for language *function*, save its mechanisms for encoding meaning. The chief model-builder in syntax, Chomsky (1957, 1965), has not even dealt with the meaning function in the sense that he considers meaning and structure essentially independent of one another. It is of equal importance to note that the most radical behaviorists interested in language function have given little attention to understanding the consequences of communication in the broad social contexts of human interactions. Their focus is on tangible "reinforcers" which are not interpreted beyond face value. Interestingly, therefore, the two streams of thought concerning structure and function have been pursued in relative independence of one another, at least in terms of the *substance* of each of their respective tracks. That is, describers of language have largely ignored language function, and analyzers of language function, generally, have chosen to focus on specific language structures that are consonant with their ideas of what reinforces such utterances, rather than on how they fit the models of the linguist-structuralists. Thus, Chomsky toyed with good structures that had no meaning (e.g., "Colorless green ideas sleep furiously") and behaviorists like Guess, Sailor, and Baer (1974) generated structures which specified the reinforcers they had available (e.g., "I want _____"). The point at which these independent streams regarding structure and function met and clashed has been where each has attempted to project its constructs to explain *language acquisition*.

Explanations of language acquisition and related clinical applications: It is the process of language acquisition which has most concerned the applied disciplines in human behavior. The applied schools within such disciplines as speech pathology, special education, and psychology have long been gathering and synthesizing knowledge about various domains of human knowledge and behavior for the purposes of applying these findings in the design of procedures to enhance and/or modify such knowledge and behavior. Thus, it is not surprising that the applied disciplines have been in a state of rather complete frustration as they have attempted to apply the knowledge gained in the past two decades from the independent and disparate tracks of research aimed at the description of language and the analysis of its function. This frustration has occurred in reaction to the fact that neither the descriptive track nor the functional track has provided the theoretical or empirical bases from which language acquisition can be satisfactorily explained and/or from which treatment can be satisfactorily generated.

As an example, the most powerful and dominant theories of the descriptive track have been those in phonology (Jakobson, Fant, & Halle, 1963); lexical morphology (Katz & Fodor, 1963); and in so-called transformational grammar (Chomsky, 1957, 1965). Even though all of these are being utilized extensively as bases for generating clinical intervention attempts, it appears to many of us that none of them have yet been successfully demonstrated as representing anything that is "real" to the language learner/user. Keep in mind, all of these models are descriptive models and, as such, they can be applied to provide after-the-fact descriptions of adult language behaviors. This does not mean, however, that they necessarily describe the processes by which people generate their language behaviors. Thus, to use these describers of the *product* as though they were describers of the *process* by which the product is created is an error of the first order.

The creators of these descriptive constructs do not, themselves, claim that they are models of the process. In fact, Chomsky would vigorously reject the notion that the components of his model can serve as the targets for intervention. When Chomsky seeks to explain how humans can acquire such a complex system of behavior as his transformational grammar model describes, he has eschewed any functional explanation. He (Chomsky, 1968) posits, instead, the notion that language is the product of an *innate* predisposition of the human mind to generate specific linguistic structures of the type his model describes.

Thus, the generators of the most refined descriptive models of the human language system have developed constructs which appear to mitigate against any functional explanation of their acquisition. Furthermore, these systems and their components have appeared to many of us to be incapable of *direct* projection to remedial or compensatory intervention processes. But, even though their originators point out the theoretical-descriptive nature of these models, attempts to extend them into functional applications abound. For example, within the various applied disciplines, many subscribers to the constructs of transformational grammar are using this model as though it were a map of the acquisition process. Interestingly, some of the foremost users of structural grammar maps are applying them in strictly behavioral delivery systems, e.g., Gray and Ryan (1973). Others, although not strictly speaking behaviorists, are nevertheless applying these model structures in functional clinical programs, e.g., Lee, Koenigsknecht, and Mulhern (1975).

The aforementioned programs are being applied most generally to older children who are already language users, albeit, poor ones. One might observe that these clinical subjects are relatively nearer to the mature language model which linguists describe than are the *severely* language-deficient and nonverbal children who are increasingly encountered by special educators as well as language therapists. The fact seems powerfully evident that these models of the mature linguistic system have been essentially useless in their application to an understanding of the process by which a language system is first *acquired* by the normally developing human child and, certainly, the process by which language acquisition might be enhanced for a child who manifests severely disorderd natural processes for such acquisition.

Similar to these problems with the models of language describers, the most dominant of the ideas generated to explain language function have not been totally successful in their translation into clinical and/or educational attempts to modify language. Skinner's (1957) specific constructs (e.g., mands, tacts, etc.) regarding language functions have not been particularly productive in their contribution to the understanding of language and language acquisition; however, some of his more general constructs in operant conditioning (Skinner, 1938; Holland & Skinner, 1961) have found great prominence in their application to language enhancement and/or modification. Indeed, behaviorists such as Guess (1969), Guess and Baer (1973), and Guess, Sailor, and Baer (1974) have empirically demonstrated that verbal behaviors can be modified by programs in which antecedent models are presented and reinforced. These behaviorists have demonstrated that newly conditioned linguistic

responses will generalize to new antecedent conditions and recur even
without specific reinforcement. What the behaviorists have not yet accomplished, however, is a satisfactory demonstration that they have,
indeed, conditioned a productive and truly generative language system
as opposed to a repertoire of well-conditioned adaptive verbal behaviors.

Despite the preceding criticism, the work of the behaviorists has far
surpassed that of the language-model theorists who despair of the value
of any functional (environmental) manipulations toward the purposes
of teaching language. The behaviorists have served us well in their
empirical demonstrations that verbal behaviors are modifiable by functional means. Indeed, were it not for their basic principles and their
demonstrated, albeit limited, effects, in all probability there would be
no language intervention programs at all for severely communicatively
delayed children.

Where it appears to me that the behaviorists have failed to this
point is, ironically, in their overall failure to follow one of the basic
precepts of their progenitor, Skinner, who has said, in essence, that no
one directly *trains* or *teaches* anyone else anything. Rather, what one
does, according to Skinner (1968), is to arrange an environment which
enhances and reinforces the "discovery" of things. Too often, the radical
behaviorists have seemed to think of training and/or conditioning and
not of facilitating discovery. It seems likely that this may be one reason
why generalization of some newly trained responses may be difficult to
achieve and why truly productive language repertoires may not result
from even the most intensive training. To be sure, facilitating "discovery" by a severely developmentally disabled human organism is not
likely to be accomplished through elegant and subtle means, but rather
would most probably still require a rigorous and intensive program of
reinforcement and stimulus control. That fact notwithstanding, the
behaviorists seem to have failed in their identification of variables which
would impact most powerfully on the language discovery process. To
add further to the irony of their relative failure, it appears to me at this
point that the variables that behaviorists have generally missed lie in
the area of the *function* of language—the very area in which their
functional analysis procedures are supposedly most representative. We
shall look at this issue more specifically shortly.

Overall, then, the contributions of the theory and data of the
linguistics model-builders and the behavioral modifiers of language seem
to be less than satisfactory as they have been projected to explain
language acquisition. The model-linguists, essentially, do not attempt
to explain language acquisition. The behaviorists explain the acquisition
of *functional* language behavior as they see it—but they do not deal
adequately, it seems, with the acquisition of the total functional language *system*. Thus, applied workers in the area of language have had a
rather frustrating couple of decades: either they have attempted to use
theoretically derived descriptive language models which seem to have

no reality as models for teaching humans to be actual language users; or they have chosen functional verbal behavior targets which most often seem to fall far short of attaining the status of a true communication *system*.

EMERGING PERSPECTIVES

As I stated in earlier sections of this chapter, ideas about language function which have been around for some time now, and which have been recently restated in compelling fashion, seem to hold great promise for the revision of currently held views about the nature of the language system and the process involved in its acquisition. These are the ideas which consider the function of language as a tool for the establishment of joint human activities. Such new perspectives have a profound effect on all existing perspectives about language. First, they expand the inventory of possible antecedents and reinforcers to language utterances in exponential fashion. When the set of evokers and consequences of language usage is thus expanded, entirely new perspectives on the dynamics of language acquisition open up. These, in turn, give rise to new perspectives about the linguistic structures of child language; and, when new perspectives about child language emerge, new perspectives on adult language are possible. Here, then, is the basis for reconsideration of both language function, as currently postulated by radical behaviorists, and descriptive language models, as currently postulated by theoretical linguists. Here, too, are perspectives which *supplement* current perspectives rather than confront them.

In order to fully appreciate their supplementary functions, we must first look briefly at these emerging perspectives in some detail. After such analysis, we can look at their impact on immediately past perspectives and, in this process, begin to point to their overall important implications for both language intervention in particular and for all of special education in general.

The newer, integrating perspectives in language have crystallized in the relatively short period of five years. Even more amazingly, the newer views are actually an integration of three separate, but related, bursts of empirical data and newly cast theoretical perspectives. Each of these three perspectives is important and each has added an important dimension to language intervention and research. Further, I am confident that these same perspectives will have their concomitant important impact on all of special education. These three perspectives can be identified as

1. the semantic analysis of child language;
2. the cognitive/constructive views of child language; and
3. the socio-constructive views of language.

Semantic analyses of child language: After years of structural description and simplified functional analyses of child language, the *content* of child language finally began to receive some attention with the advent of the *semantic revolution.* For most of us, the semantic revolution began with the concurrent publication of Bloom's first work in that area (1970) and Schlesinger's (1971) paper which focused attention on the semantic intent of early child utterances. These works were immediately followed by important contributions by Bowerman (1973), Slobin (1973), and Brown (1973).

The primary substance of the semantic revolution had two dimensions. First, the data generated indicated that children learning language rather universally refer to the existence of things, the nonexistence of things, and the recurrence of things which have disappeared. Further, children learning language also rather universally mark such relationships as possessor of a thing and location of a thing or of some action. As importantly, in their earliest two-word combinations, children talk about *actions*, and both the instigators (agents) of actions and the receivers (objects) of actions.

The fact that the semantic content of child language was found to be relatively consistent across children (and even across cultures) led to the second dimension of the semantic perspective, namely, that the primary source of such consistency had to reside in children's universal knowledge about the world rather than, as had been suggested, in their universal linguistic-rule predisposition. Children's talk had long been described as "here and now" as opposed to abstract and displaced from its referents. Now, in the semantic data, children's perspectives about the world and the objects, people, and relationships they found important in their world, were becoming clearer. The hypothesized relationship between language and children's cognitive holdings which has resulted from these perspectives is that language maps a child's existing knowledge. This mapping function of language has been widely accepted and stated in one form or another by all of the leaders in the semantic revolution (e.g., Bloom, 1970; Slobin, 1973; Bowerman, 1973; Schlesinger, 1971), and it has given applied workers in language intervention a productive new perspective from which to assess and train child language targets.

It should be noted here that the only highly visible cognitive mapping perspective prior to the semantic revolution was that represented by Bereiter and Engelmann's (1966) language program. Even though they did not speak in the same specific terms of today's cognitive/semantic constructs, Bereiter and Engelmann's programming was undergirded by the construct that one of language's most basic functions is to accurately "map" specific cognitive constructs and/or logical relationships.

Despite its powerful face-validity, however, the semantic view has not fully resolved all of the issues surrounding research in language acquisition and language intervention. While semantic targets have much more reality than purely structural ones, educators and speech clinicians still found themselves without useful guidelines for making many critical decisions, e.g., what specific word-entities, relationships, and structures to teach; what sequential variables might exist; what contexts would lend themselves best to such targets; etc. At this time, however, the second major contributor to today's emerging perspectives was becoming most visible, and it provided important constructs for those who were involved in applying the new semantic perspectives.

Cognitive/constructive views of child language: The semantic perspectives of language as a realization of a child's already existing knowledge provided a receptive environment for the reawakening of interest in the views of cognitive development specialists regarding early stages in language development. This, in turn, led to a rapid integration of the respective views of the developmental semanticists and cognitivists— particularly those cognitivists who were interested in a child's early development of knowledge.

Prominent among the early developmental cognitivists were those who subscribed broadly to the constructionist theories associated with Piaget and the so-called Genevan school. In these theories, the child is seen as an active processor of sensory experiences and as a constructor of knowledge schemata which can accommodate these experiences. Language acquisition theorists soon noted an isomorphism between the Piagetian constructs associated with early cognitive development and the semantic constructs associated with early language development. For example, the Piagetian construct of "object-permanence" seems to correspond closely to the semantic constructs of "existence," "nonexistence," and "recurrence." Similarly, there would seem to be a direct correspondence between the child's attainment of "causality," as posited by Piaget, and his/her marking of such semantic relations as "agent-action" and "instrumental." This apparent isomorphism added strong support to the argument for a cognitive base underlying early language development—a theoretical position offering many advantages over the previously posited innate structure theories as bases for designing intervention programs. Even further, the identification of probable cognitive bases for language began to suggest that, perhaps, language acquisition did not have to be explained solely as an innately determined process incapable of further explanation.

Research investigations of children's early language acquisition in terms of the possible functional determiners involved began to bring more and more substance to the general semantic-cognitive theoretical positions. Among these empirical efforts, Nelson's (1973, 1974) work is particularly noteworthy. Nelson's research indicated that children's earliest words strongly reflect sensorimotor bases in that they are generally related to objects or events which have dynamic properties and with which the child has had direct, manipulative, and/or participatory experience. Other important contributions by MacNamara (1972), Sinclair deZwart (1970, 1973), and Bloom (1970, 1973) strengthened the hypothesis that as children construct their knowledge about their world in the form of cognitive schemata and constructs, they also construct the relationship between this knowledge and the language forms they hear and produce.

From this general body of work has grown still another view which has served to supplement the semantic and cognitive perspectives and complete the integrated perspectives which are emerging today and which, I think, will continue to undergird language research for some time to come. This most recent view is that which perceives in the semantic and developmental dynamics of children's emerging language the important manifestations of its ultimate function—socialization.

Socio-constructive views of child language: As both the product and the process of child language development have been observed and analyzed, attention has again centered on the *why* of language and language acquisition. As long ago as 1927, DeLaguna (1963/1927) explained it as a means toward the attainment of cooperative behaviors among humans. More recently, Bruner (1975, 1974/75) has described the function of language as the attainment of joint actions and joint referents among people. Halliday (1975) has described such functions as instrumental (get me) and heuristic (tell me), among several others. Whatever the specific nature of the explanation, however, the purposes of language use now seem clear—language is a primary tool in the human being's gradual assimilation into the existing social compact of his environment.

Like so many other "discoveries" about human behavior in general, and language behavior in particular, this view of the *why* of language is not all that remarkable. What is remarkable, however, is the extent to which this view has been ignored in our theories and descriptions of language form, language function, and, particularly, language acquisition and/or modification. The structural psycholinguist ignores the *why* of language when he views language as based on innate predisposition for syntactic structures of a certain type. The behaviorist essentially ignores the *why* of language in providing an edible reinforcer when a child says "drink cup" as a label for a picture of a cup. The language clinician ignores the *why* of language as he targets *in*, *on*, and *under* as labels for pictures with a mentally retarded child. By way of contrast, if we were really applying our understanding of the social function of language in combination with the latest semantic and cognitive perspectives, we would be ignoring the innateness hypothesis completely; we would be evoking "drink cup" with a cup of *Coke* and reinforcing it with a drink from that cup; and we would be teaching *in*, *on*, and *under* by having children themselves get into, or on, or under a big box, or find desired goodies which were so located, for example, *under* a table, *in* a cup, etc.

While these examples are simplistic, I hope they make the point that, in general, our contexts and procedures in language intervention have often ignored the social function of language and the general mechanics of that function for young children with severe language deficiencies. To be sure, many of our current techniques are adequate for children and adults who already have a language but who need it refined and brought into more concordance with adult cultural standards. Those advanced (and needed) programs notwithstanding, we have had far from adequate clinical representation of the perspective which views language as a laboriously constructed behavioral repertoire directly related to a similarly constructed set of cognitive schemata which represent the child's organization of his knowledge about the world. We are also still far from the systematic clinical representation of the perspective which views the language acquisition process as a direct correlate of the child's construction and utilization of social concepts and behavioral repertoires which are specific to the interactive processes of socialization.

As these realizations have begun to influence both theoretical and empirical activities in language intervention research with severely developmentally delayed children, however, their eventual effect on both service delivery and service deliverers can be predicted to be significant.

SUMMARY OF PERSPECTIVES ON LANGUAGE

All of the foregoing discussion has been directed toward an understanding of currently emerging perspectives that have implications for research in language and for language intervention with severely language-deficient children. It is hoped that this understanding will also provide the reader with some feel for the processes by which these new perspectives crystallized. Since the research activities in this area have been both varied and prolific, even this cursory exposition of the issues involved has necessarily been somewhat complex and lengthy. Let me here, then, try to pick up the primary points of the foregoing discussion and highlight them in a summary form.

Overall it appears that current research in the area of language is moving to both supplement and integrate past perspectives on language. First, the knowledge about language structures that we have received from the work of structural and theoretical linguists and psycholinguists is being supplemented by important and far-reaching theory and data relating to the semantic content carried by these structures. Thus, we are seeing (and will be seeing much more) work directed toward the attainment of language *content* as well as language *structure*. Secondly, with language content being so obviously controlled by a language user's knowledge about the world (Olson, 1970; Bloom, 1970; Bowerman, 1974), we are seeing language interventionists moving toward the attainment of a better understanding of those activities and processes which result in a child's having knowledge about the world. In this sense, then, language workers will become much more involved with children's construction of their cognitive holdings and the specific conceptual content within those holdings. Thirdly, with language interveners' resensitization to the seemingly solid observation that human language is first and foremost a tool for human socialization in its broadest sense, we are realizing that any attempt to intervene in language must provide a better representation of this social function both in the products and, most importantly, in the *process* of such intervention. The synthesis of these current perspectives, then, would suggest several trends in applied language research for the immediately foreseeable future. In the following section, I will briefly discuss these new directions for language intervention research and look at some broader implications for special education in general.

IMPLICATIONS FOR FUTURE RESEARCH AND INTERVENTION

IMPLICATIONS FOR APPLIED LANGUAGE RESEARCH

Throughout the preceding discussion I have maintained a distinction between the *products* and the *processes* of natural language acquisition, noting the emergence of new perspectives on both aspects of development. Not surprisingly, each of these aspects of natural development has a correlate in the domains of research and intervention. Thus, new perspectives on the *products* of language acquisition have direct implications for the selection of appropriate dependent variables or *treatment targets* in applied research. Similarly, new perspectives on the acquisition *process* have implications for the design of *treatment procedures and contexts*. Accordingly, we will discuss the implications for applied language research in terms of these two aspects.

Treatment targets: In light of the emerging perspectives discussed in this chapter, we would expect that experimental language programs will be increasingly directed toward more multidimensional language response goals. Targets for programs will need to include not only specific grammatical structures, but specific semantic content as well. Thus, for the child who is being trained to produce single-word utterances, we will not simply target "nouns" or "verbs." Rather, our targets will be selected to assure that the child's verbal repertoire allows him to mark a variety of semantic cases such as the agentive (e.g., "mommy"); the objective (e.g., "ball"); and the locative (e.g., "sit chair") as well as such early semantic relationships as recurrence (e.g., "more"); rejection (e.g., "no"); and nonexistence (e.g., "all gone").

In addition, programs will need to include as a specific objective the discovery of the *communication function* of utterances which have been targeted initially in terms of their linguistic form and their semantic content. Thus, children will not only learn to "name things," but will learn to specify desired ends of social interaction by marking objects, events, and/or relationships as a *means* of fulfilling such communicative functions as requesting action (e.g., "Daddy up," "Mommy more"); requesting an answer (e.g., "What's that?" "Where doggie?"); or social greeting (e.g., "Hi," "Bye-bye").

It now seems evident that language intervention procedures must also be expanded to include examination of prelanguage and nonlanguage behaviors which appear to undergird and/or precede specific language usage. For example, concept development, social/interactive development, and development of prelanguage communication repertoires (e.g., gestures, motor-prompts, vocal inflection changes) will all be taken into account. Therefore, language intervention will be more closely tied to such other activity centers of child experience as the home, the school, and the playground.

Treatment procedures and contexts: In the coming years, there should be increased emphasis on social contexts for training that are more "natural." This is not to say that the systematic behavioral procedures will be abandoned. Rather, the current behavioral technology will be used to control and quantify training contexts which utilize human social relationships as a greater source for both independent and dependent variables.

The nature of the changes implied in the modified procedures and contexts just predicted may be seen most clearly by comparing two hypothetical training procedures. Today, a typical behavioral session might consist of evoking a syntactic phrase through imitation in the presence of a picture stimulus and reinforcing it with an extrinsic reward such as a token or an edible; e.g., trainer requests child to say, "boy eat cookie" (shows picture of boy eating cookie); child makes response and trainer says, "good boy" and delivers an edible. The sequence is repeated for "boy drink juice" (with picture). By way of contrast, procedures reflecting our new understandings of the language acquisition process would more likely target this response by setting up a situation in which there is orange juice to drink; a cookie, an M&M, and a bit of sugar cereal to eat. The trainer and the child then might alternately eat one of the various edibles and drink the juice for several weeks while modeling the appropriate syntactic phrase: "Jim eat cookie," "Billy drink juice," "Jim drink juice," etc. Alternative phases of training would bring the child's action (eating/drinking) and the recipient of that action (cookie, juice, M&M) under verbal direction; e.g., "Billy eat cookie," "Billy drink juice," etc. Finally, the child would be required to specify his desire, e.g., "eat cookie," "drink juice," and be allowed to carry out that action upon his appropriate utterance.

While simplistic examples are always dangerous to use in trying to make a point, I would ask that the reader not dismiss the preceding example as trivial in demonstrating differences in procedure. Please look at the *function* of language in the two situations and the *context* of the language utterances. The relationship of the utterance to both the stimulus conditions of the training context and to the consequence of the utterance is vastly different in the two instances, and these differences are of extreme importance.

The second training procedure is obviously closer to a "natural" reciprocal communication situation, albeit still highly structured and highly controlled for desired linguistic form. It is also obvious that this procedure does not represent the ultimate in training excellence. It can be said, however, that it reflects, in primitive form, the *essence* of the differences in procedures and contexts which will be forthcoming in language intervention programs of the near future.

The gestalt of anticipated changes: Implicit in the specific areas of change just discussed is a change in the overall atmosphere in which language intervention programs will most probably be applied. First, although technical specificity will guide the content and contexts of language intervention, the actual intervention process will *seem* less technical in its overall tenor. This is because the variables being manipulated on both the antecedent and consequent ends of the treatment paradigm will be drawn more from the variables which are operative in so-called natural developmental human-interaction patterns. Thus, structured language programs of the future will exist in treatment settings that will allow for richer manipulative interaction with people and things, and, thus, will be more dynamic in their overall context. Second, and related to the first, the need for richer interactive settings will make it impossible to carry out language treatment in contexts which are isolated from a child's natural environment. This will mean that programs will be more frequently applied in settings that are more central to a child's knowledge base and his/her highest potential activity base. This implies that homes, classrooms, and playrooms will most likely supplant the "clinic room" atmosphere in which so much of today's language intervention is carried out.

Thirdly, as we are already seeing (MacDonald, 1975), language intervention programs will utilize a wider range of manpower than is currently the case. Parents, teachers, and others who establish significant interactive relationships with children will be enlisted to structure and apply intervention procedures. Obviously, if social assimilation and social actions are the ultimate functions of communication, the context of language intervention must contain important social dimensions.

When we sum all of the highly probable changes which will occur in the content, the procedures, and the setting contexts for language intervention with severely language-deficient children, we can see important implications for the entire design of special education programs for severely developmentally delayed children. In addition to the straightforward changes in special education already obvious as a result of our discussion to this point, I think there are some less obvious implications in all of this activity in language intervention to which special educators should become sensitive. We will be discussing both the obvious and the less obvious implications in the concluding section of this chapter which follows.

IMPLICATIONS FOR SPECIAL EDUCATION

Each of the three areas of change noted in the preceding discussion seems to me to have specific applications in special education. With the overall goals of both applied language efforts and educational efforts being identical in their espoused desires to attend to the "normalization" of handicapped children, what seems to be important are the basic differences which are implied in the different *implementation* designs in the two areas. The most recent trends in language research seem clearly aimed at designing and implementing a *process* from which the language product emerges. The process, as currently conceptualized, derives from analytic studies directed toward understanding the nature of the human behavioral product desired. The resulting conceptualization of the products of language acquisition reflects a great appreciation for the total behavioral system of the human species. It views this complex behavior as a product only of a complex ethological system. Such an ethological perspective is, essentially, a behavioral perspective, but it is important to note that an ethological perspective is one which views behavior and behavioral products in terms of their broadest *systemic* causes and effects.

While the area of language intervention is moving more and more to broadened perspectives of human process, special education seems to be in great danger of being forced into a design which stresses only product. In this product-oriented design, concern with process often seems limited to an almost complete dependence on so-called technology. This, of course, is consonant with the great American tradition that technology will solve all problems. While I will not demean the great benefits of improved educational technology, it is obvious that technology is only effective when it is implementing appropriate processes.

Today, with our intensive (and appropriate) efforts to correct past derelictions in service to handicapped people, many professionals and societal systems behave as though they think that technology and technology alone will attain the much-needed products of special educational treatment for such people. For some reason, we often still don't appear to fully understand that technology is only a tool for carrying process; it does not provide its substance. As the computer programmer's adage goes, "garbage in—garbage out."

It would be easy to link special education's technologically oriented bent toward behavioral products to the failure of behavioral modification researchers to broaden their view of the overall human behavioral system. This begs the issue, however. Although the behavioral "mod squad" may be accused of having failed to carry out its full responsibility for expanding the brilliant empirical relationships established by Skinner and his followers, I would think that special education has its own concomitant responsibility to contribute to the body of knowledge which is specific to the functional amelioration of the debilitating effects associated with severe mental and/or emotional disabilities. It appears, however, that in its forced march to effect normalizing behavioral *products*, special education, as a whole, is being shunted away from a parallel commitment to establish truly normalizing *processes* which would result in these same products, but would also result in more products within the general cognitive and broad social domains. It is the latter products, of course, which hold the long-term key to eventual integration of the handicapped into the continuum of human social systems.

I know that many will point to "mainstreaming" processes as an obvious and specific rebuttal to the points just outlined. It is my contention, however, that many of the current implementations of mainstreaming designs make my point rather than rebut it. Mainstreaming, I am sure, was intended to describe a process—a process in which handicapped individuals were assured an environment in which the normal elements of human ethological systems would be available to them for acquiring the behavioral and cognitive products required and enabled by such systems. Most special educators recognize this process nature of mainstreaming, and, yet, we see widespread implementation of mainstreaming as a *product* and seem powerless to stop it. In too many instances, it seems that educators have been willing to simply grit their teeth and try to implement mainstreaming in ways that they know are both ill-conceived and dangerous to the eventual accomplishment of true integration of the handicapped into the social system of our culture.

Recent empirical and theoretical perspectives in the area of language seem now to have re-alerted researchers in this area to the critical importance of interactive human process. The fact that this area of research concerns the human species' most complex and unique behavior is probably basic to this discovery. Special educators, too, must reawaken and respond to this need. It is the educational experience of children which provides the cognitive and social bases for language, as for most other human behavior. As the study of natural language acquisition seems to be indicating, however, we can never really understand the educational products we need and desire unless we view them within the context of the experiences which generate them. Just as language researchers have generally failed to attain normalized syntax from severely handicapped children by targeting syntactic form, special educators will most surely fail to attain normalized behavioral repertoires by targeting only the specific end behaviors desired.

The process must be reciprocal: A vital element in the product versus process problems is one other awareness that is becoming clear in language intervention and that should have a concomitant representation in special education. The current views in language all seem to indicate that language is a constructed behavior which is dependent on many other behaviors and knowledges. It is widely postulated, for example, that language is dependent on the child's cognitive holdings and social interaction repertoires. Miller and Yoder (1972) point out that in order to talk, a child must have something to say and a reason for saying it, as well as having a specific way to say it. Mahoney (1975) posits that language begins not with spoken utterances of linguistic form, but rather with relatively extensive nonverbal communication systems which eventually become the bases of formal language conventions. The implications of these views are straightforward. They imply that for language to develop, the child must function within the overall human interactive system. They would indicate that a child who does not function within this system cannot benefit from the system's process. The result of these implications is also straightforward, namely, that language interveners will be working mightily to develop the necessary systemic interaction repertoires for child language targets. Attention and reciprocal-play repertoires will be established. Sensorimotor interactions with environmental objects will be structured. Affective exchanges will be modeled and evoked. All in all, attempts will be made to structure a process in which the child can and will participate. Without such participation, a language acquisition process of any consequence appears to be a remote probability. I am sure that most special educators subscribe to these general views. They must, however, design and implement educational experiences which will truly involve the child as an active participant in the educational process. In this sense, they must resensitize themselves to the fact that, while it is important for the child to learn new or modified behaviors, the too common unilateral process of teacher-imposed surface repertoires will not suffice to ensure truly generative behavioral repertoires. I think our current problems with generalization of newly trained responses is a symptom of the nonreciprocal nature of some of our procedures.

Overall then, it appears most necessary for special education to follow the example of language intervention and enhance its ethological and ecological perspectives. It must look more to human behavioral *systems* for the normalizing products it desires. It must design educational processes which emphasize the fact that people behave as they do because they coexist with other people and, further, because social interactions are important to them and allow them to discover the way to behave.

If educators carry forth such enhancement of ethological and ecological perspectives, I think that they will find, just as language researchers have found, that existing technology is not destroyed. Rather, this technology can now be fed by a greater reservoir of important and functional independent variables. Further, I think that educators will find that the products achieved by these modified processes will also result in behavioral repertoires among severely handicapped children which have more stability and generalizability, based as they are on *discovered* functions within human systems. Please note that this treatise is *in no way* antibehavioral. On the contrary, I would hope that it is more a suggestion that we move forward with our understanding of the control and reinforcement of human behaviors by expanding our perspectives on the dynamics of such behaviors. And, as the latest contributors to language theory now emphasize, we should realize that we cannot truly identify appropriate behavioral products unless we understand better how and why these products emerge in the individual human behavioral repertoire.

REFERENCES

Bereiter, C., & Engelmann, S. *Teaching disadvantaged children in the preschool.* Englewood Cliffs, N.J.: Prentice-Hall, 1966.

Bloom, L. *Language development: Form and function in emerging grammars.* Cambridge: M.I.T. Press, 1970.

Bloom, L. *One word at a time: The use of single word utterances before syntax.* The Hague: Mouton, 1973.

Bowerman, M. F. *Early syntactic development: A cross linguistic study with special reference to Finnish.* Cambridge, England: Cambridge University Press, 1973.

Bowerman, M. F. Discussion summary—Development of concepts underlying language. In R. L. Schiefelbusch & L. L. Lloyd (Eds.), *Language perspectives: Acquisition, retardation and intervention.* Baltimore: University Park Press, 1974.

Brown, R. *A first language: The early stages.* Cambridge: Harvard University Press, 1973.

Bruner, J. S. From communication to language—A psychological perspective. *Cognition,* 1974/75, 3, 255-87.

Bruner, J. S. The ontogenesis of speech acts. *Journal of Child Language,* 1975, 2, 1-19.

Chomsky, N. *Syntactic structures.* The Hague: Mouton, 1957.

Chomsky, N. *Aspects of the theory of syntax.* Cambridge: M.I.T. Press, 1965.

Chomsky, N. *Language and mind.* New York: Harcourt Brace Jovanovich, 1968.

DeLaguna, G. A. *Speech: Its function and development.* Bloomington: Indiana University Press, 1963. (Originally published, 1927.)

Gray, B., & Ryan, B. *A language program for the nonlanguage child.* Champaign, Ill.: Research Press, 1973.

Guess, D. A functional analysis of receptive language and productive speech: Acquisition of the plural morpheme. *Journal of Applied Behavior Analysis,* 1969, 2, 55-64.

Guess, D., & Baer, D. M. An analysis of individual differences in generalization between receptive and productive language in retarded children. *Journal of Applied Behavior Analysis,* 1973, 6, 311-29.

Guess, D., Sailor, W., & Baer, D. To teach language to retarded children. In R. L. Schiefelbusch & L. L. Lloyd (Eds.), *Language perspectives: Acquisition, retardation and intervention.* Baltimore: University Park Press, 1974.

Halliday, M. Learning how to mean. In E. Lenneberg & E. Lenneberg (Eds.), *Foundations of language development: A multidisciplinary approach* (Vol. 1). New York: Academic Press, 1975.

Holland, J. G., & Skinner, B. F. *The analysis of behavior.* New York: McGraw-Hill, 1961.

Jakobson, R., Fant, C. G. M., & Halle, M. *Preliminaries to speech analysis: The distinctive features and their correlates* (2nd ed.). Cambridge: M.I.T. Press, 1963.

Katz, J., & Fodor, J. The structure of a semantic theory. *Language,* 1963, 39, 170-210.

Lee, L. L., Koenigsknecht, R. A., & Mulhern, S. *Interactive language development teaching: The clinical presentation of grammatical structure.* Evanston, Ill.: Northwestern University Press, 1975.

Luria, A. Scientific perspectives and philosophical dead ends in modern linguistics. *Cognition,* 1974/75, 3, 377-85.

MacDonald, J. D. Environmental language intervention. In F. Withrow & C. Nygren (Eds.), *Language, Materials, and Curriculum Management for the Handicapped Learner.* Columbus, Ohio: Charles E. Merrill, 1976.

MacNamara, J. Cognitive basis of language learning in infants. *Psychological Review,* 1972, 79, 1-13.

Mahoney, G. Ethological approach to delayed language acquisition. *American Journal of Mental Deficiency,* 1975, 80, 139-48.

Miller, J., & Yoder, D. A syntax teaching program. In J. E. McLean, D. E. Yoder, & R. L. Schiefelbusch (Eds.), *Language intervention with the retarded: Developing strategies.* Baltimore: University Park Press, 1972.

Nelson, K. Structure and strategy in learning to talk. *Monographs of the Society for Research in Child Development,* 1973, 38 (1-2 Serial No. 149).

Nelson, K. Concept, word and sentence: Interrelations in acquisition and development. *Psychological Review,* 1974, 81, 267-85.

Olson, D. Language and thought: Aspects of a cognitive theory of semantics. *Psychological Review,* 1970, 77, 257-73.

Schlesinger, I. M. Production of utterances and language acquisition. In D. I. Slobin (Ed.), *The ontogenesis of grammar.* New York: Academic Press, 1971.

Sinclair-deZwart, H. The transition from sensori-motor behavior to symbolic activity. *Interchange,* 1970, 1, 119-26.

Sinclair-deZwart, H. Language acquisition and cognitive development. In T. E. Moore (Ed.), *Cognitive development and the acquisition of language.* New York: Academic Press, 1973.

Skinner, B. F. *The behavior of organisms.* New York: Appleton-Century-Crofts, 1938.

Skinner, B. F. *Verbal behavior.* New York: Appleton-Century-Crofts, 1957.

Skinner, B. F. *The technology of teaching.* New York: Appleton-Century-Crofts, 1968.

Slobin, D. I. Cognitive prerequisites for the development of grammar. In C. A. Ferguson & D. I. Slobin (Eds.), *Studies of child language development.* New York: Holt, Rinehart & Winston, 1973.

A SELECTED BIBLIOGRAPHY OF WORKS BY JAMES E. McLEAN

McLean, J. E. Extending stimulus control of phoneme articulation by operant techniques. In F. L. Girardeau & J. E. Spradlin (Eds.), *A functional analysis approach to speech and language behavior.* ASHA Monograph 14, American Speech and Hearing Association, Washington, D.C., January 1970.

McLean, J. E. *Shifting stimulus control: A clinical procedure for articulation therapy.* Lawrence: University of Kansas, Bureau of Child Research, March 1970. (Thirty-minute color film)

McLean, J. E. Developing clinical strategies for language intervention with mentally retarded children. In J. E. McLean, D. E. Yoder, & R. L.

Schiefelbusch (Eds.), *Language intervention with the retarded: Developing strategies*. Baltimore: University Park Press, 1972.

McLean, J. E. Language development and communication disorders. In N. G. Haring (Ed.), *Behavior of exceptional children: An introduction to special education*. Columbus, Ohio: Charles E. Merrill, 1974.

McLean, J. E. Articulation treatment: Strategies and procedures. In L. Lloyd (Ed.), *Communication programming for the developmentally disabled*. Baltimore: University Park Press, in press.

McLean, L. P., & McLean, J. E. A language training program for nonverbal autistic children. *Journal of Speech and Hearing Disorders*, 1974, 39 (2), 186-93.

McLean, L. P., & McLean, J. E. Teaching autistic children. In F. B. Withrow & C. J. Nygren (Eds.), *Language, Materials, and Curriculum Management for the Handicapped Learner*. Columbus, Ohio: Charles E. Merrill, 1976.

Raymore, S., & McLean, J. E. A clinical program for carry-over of articulation therapy with retarded children. In J. E. McLean, D. E. Yoder, & R. L. Schiefelbusch (Eds.), *Language intervention with the retarded: Developing strategies*. Baltimore: University Park Press, 1972.

16
Research on Cognitive Styles

Barbara K. Keogh is presently professor of special education, Graduate School of Education, University of California, Los Angeles. She also serves as director of the Special Education Research Program and co-director of the UCLA USOE Learning Disability Fellowship Training Program at UCLA. Dr. Keogh is a member of the National Advisory Committee to the Handicapped. She is associate editor of Exceptional Children and also serves as consulting editor or reviewer for numerous other professional journals. She is a certified psychologist in the state of California, and prior to her appointment to the UCLA faculty, she held school psychologist and clinical/research psychologist positions.

Dr. Keogh received the B.A. degree in psychology from Pomona College in 1946, the M.A. degree in psychology from Stanford University

318

in 1947, and the Ph.D. in psychology from Claremont Graduate School in 1963. In 1965–66 she was a USPHS postdoctoral fellow, Centre for Child Study, University of Birmingham, England. A selected bibliography of works by Dr. Keogh appears on page 342.

There is something elusive about the concept of cognitive styles, a kind of "now you see it now you don't" quality which sometimes leads researchers to wonder if they are chasing the proverbial will-o-the-wisp. Style elicited by one measure may not appear on another; transfer in predicted directions is inconsistent; individual characteristics in style may vary relative to task and conditions. The consistency and robustness of expression which presumably characterize a number of dimensions of individual differences are clearly not attributes of cognitive style. Yet, researchers and clinicians alike are convinced that there are consistencies in the ways in which individuals interact with their worlds, that these consistencies are reasonably stable perceptual and cognitive attributes, and that they constitute important indicators of individual differences. It is the very will-o-the-wisp nature of cognitive styles that accounts in part for their attraction as a research topic.

Before discussing some substantive aspects of research in cognitive styles as related to exceptional children, it is necessary to put the topic into context. The history of special education may well be viewed as a preoccupation with individual differences. Some parameters of difference were likely identified in order to protect exceptional individuals from other segments of society; some parameters, perhaps, to provide the basis for exclusion from the majority society. In the search for individual differences of relevance to education, special educators borrowed heavily from related disciplines, especially from psychology, medicine, and sociology, applying both the basic constructs and the methodology of those disciplines. Early work on individual differences in special education, thus, involved to a considerable degree the identification, definition, and description of variations on a broad band of essentially child-based characteristics, e.g., intelligence, language, fine- and gross-motor abilities, perception, even social class and ethnicity. There was also extensive descriptive documentation of various aspects of educational achievement, primarily reading, arithmetic, and spelling, usually defined in terms of grade-level norms or expectancies. Historically these summaries were organized to describe pupils' characteristics according to chronological age, sometimes taking into account sex differences and more recently social-cultural differences. Descriptive data provided the basis for categorization and grouping of exceptional children. Consider as example the historical use of IQ to classify mental retardates as idiot, imbecile, or moron; or the more recent IQ distinctions between trainable mentally retarded, educable mentally retarded, normal, and gifted. A trip through the historical literature in the field yields a good deal of information describing a variety of syndromes of atypical development, but very little as to what to do in order to ameliorate or change them.

The point to be made is that for the most part early research in special education was limited to a documentation of individual differences on rather gross child-referenced dimensions, with relatively little effort directed at analysis of intervention programs or, importantly, at specification of the nature of the interactions between pupils and interventions. There has been a spate of studies which document pupils' characteristics, *or* which describe programs, but there is little solid evidence to delineate the nature of the child by program interactions. It seems likely, however, that these Aptitude-Treatment Interactions (ATIs) may be especially critical in educational interventions with exceptional children. It seems likely, too, that individual differences in cognitive styles are influences in the pupil-program interactions.

APTITUDE-TREATMENT INTERACTIONS

Before focusing on a discussion of cognitive styles, it may be wise to consider that also attractive but often slippery concept, Aptitude-Treatment Interaction (ATI). Recognition of the possible power of Aptitude-Treatment Interactions is neither new nor original. Almost twenty years ago Cronbach (1957) suggested that the traditional schism between experimental psychology and the study of individual differences might be reconciled through this approach. As he noted more recently, this "hybrid discipline is now flourishing" [Cronbach, 1975, p. 116], although in his opinion, sometimes not all that effectively. Cronbach suggests that differing results from studies using the same treatment is probably a function of unpredicted and unknown interactions resulting from unspecified variance among sample subjects. He notes: "An ATI result can be taken as a general conclusion only if it is not in turn moderated by further variables. . . . Once we attend to interactions we enter a hall of mirrors that extends to infinity" [Cronbach, 1975, p. 119].

Despite the implicit pessimism in the image of a hall of mirrors extending to infinity, Cronbach's words deserve careful consideration by those special educators conducting research as well as by those involved in implementation of programs for exceptional children. We have tended to base our diagnostic and intervention decisions on children's characteristics assessed on a limited set of variables and with a restricted number of evaluation instruments. We have assumed homogeneity on a number of broad developmental dimensions on the basis of measures which presumably identify commonality on a few. We have provided programs and research interventions directed at single variables, or at category-referenced characteristics, even when these are imprecisely defined. Given the limited nature of our understanding of the range and expression of individual differences and the global definition of most programs of interventions, it is not surprising that the research data are cloudy, and that the nature of the Aptitude-Treatment Interactions are for the most part unknown. It seems reasonable—even likely—that both our conceptual and our methodological limitations have led to oversimplified analyses of complex functions. We measure intelligence with highly standardized tests composed of selected discrete items, draw inferences from this narrow band of information to children's performance in a variety of complex educational settings, and then are surprised when the children do not learn and perform in the ways we anticipated.

The limited predictive or analytic power of the IQ for directing instructional or intervention decisions is widely recognized (Keogh, 1972) and supports the interpretation that many facets of individual differences interact with instructional programs to influence learning and performance. One dimension which has attracted and intrigued researchers and practitioners alike has to do with the broad band of abilities and characteristics subsumed under the general rubric, *cognitive style*. This topic has received extensive study and is viewed as one of the characteristics of individuals which, in relationship with intelligence and other specific abilities, may be a powerful determinant in the interactions between pupils and programs. As individual differences in cognitive styles may influence individual differences in performance and accomplishment on a variety of school-related tasks, they are of concern for the special educator.

COGNITIVE STYLES

What then are these individual stylistic differences and how do they interact with treatment and situational demands, especially with educational programs? Kagan, Moss, and Sigel (1963) as well as Holtzman (1966) refer to "stable, individual preferences in modes of perceptual organization and conceptual categorization of the external environment" [Kagan et al., p. 8]. Messick (1970) defined cognitive styles as a "person's typical modes of perceiving, remembering, thinking, and problem solving" [p. 188]. In an earlier review of this topic (Keogh, 1973), I referred to "individual consistencies in information seeking and information processing across a variety of problem solving situations" [p. 84]. Despite some differences in emphasis, review of various definitions and approaches to the topic suggests that all refer to some qualitative characteristics of perceptual and cognitive processing. We are, thus, not concerned so much with *how much* but with *how*. In this sense, techniques for study of cognitive styles may differ from those used in study of other dimensions of individual differences, as for example traditional psychometric approaches to assessment of intelligence. Almost by definition, measurement of cognitive styles excludes simple quantitative approaches; it is not concerned with objective "correctness" or "incorrectness" of response, but with the kind or style of response. As noted by Nathan Kogan (1971), "Abilities concern level of skill—the more and less of performance—whereas cognitive style gives greater weight to the *manner* and *form* of cognition" [p. 244]. Further, it is likely that most individuals have developed a repertoire of styles, so that particular measurement techniques or approaches may elicit a preferred style, given varying situational demands. Distinctions between capacity and performance, between availability and preference, are important in assessment of many dimensions of individual difference; they may be especially critical in assessment and analysis of cognitive styles, as differences in modes of response may be situationally sensitive. The appropriateness of particular response styles relative to demands of particular situations or tasks is an important consideration for special educators and will be discussed more fully in this chapter.

Although cognitive-style theorists agree as to qualitative aspects of the constructs, there are some differences in emphasis and content which reflect different conceptualizations. Kogan (1971), for example, in adapting an earlier analysis by Messick (1970) describes nine cognitive styles: field independence vs. field dependence; scanning; breadth of categorization; conceptualizing styles; cognitive complexity vs. simplicity; reflectiveness vs. impulsivity; leveling vs. sharpening; constructive vs. flexible control; and tolerance for incongruous or unrealistic experiences. Kogan also added a dimension of risk taking vs. cautiousness as having educational implications. With the exception of the final item, most of these specific constructs have their bases in the work of major theoretical approaches as defined by H. A. Witkin, Jerome Kagan, Riley Gardner, and their colleagues. These positions have been well described in comprehensive reviews (Kagan & Kogan, 1970; Keogh, 1973; Kogan, 1971; Messick, 1970). For purposes of the present chapter, two stylistic constructs, field articulation and reflection-impulsivity, will be discussed in some detail, as both are widely viewed as having implications for educational practice.

FIELD ARTICULATION

Early work by H. A. Witkin and his associates was focused primarily on perceptual abilities, specifically on laboratory tests of perception of the vertical. In the volume, *Personality through Perception*, coauthored with Lewis, Hertzman, Machover, Meissner, and Wapner (1954), Witkin summarized findings on a number of perceptual measures and began to relate these findings to broader cognitive and personality functioning. Further development of the implications of these perceptual findings for other cognitive, affective, and personality functions was synthesized in Witkin's 1962 publication, *Psychological Differentiation*, written in collaboration with Dyk, Faterson, Goodenough, and Karp. This work brought together an extensive series of studies by Witkin and others. The perceptual work by the Witkin group was conceptualized under the rubric of field independence-dependence (FID), referring to individual differences in ways of organizing a perceptual stimulus—"an analytical, in contrast to a global, way of perceiving [which] entails a tendency to experience items as discrete from their backgrounds and reflects ability to overcome the influence of an embedding context" [Messick, 1970, p. 188]. Generalizing from their laboratory tasks, Witkin et al. proposed that the perceptual findings were expressions of a broadly based dimension of individual differences; thus, they opted for the more encompassing concept of field articulation.

The extensive data generated in studying the global-analytic articulation dimension suggested a stability of style over time and task and correlates according to sex of subject, personality patterns, clusters of cognitive abilities or skills, and even to expression of pathology (Witkin et al., 1954, 1962; Witkin, 1964, 1965a, 1965b). Field independence was associated with an active, analytic, differentiated approach to the environment; field dependence, with a more passive, global, less differentiated approach. Witkin and his colleagues demonstrated that differentiation increased with age through childhood and that males were more analytic than were females within age periods. Tentative data allowed some interpretation as to antecedents of style differences, specifically as to the influences of parent-child interactions. The early work by Witkin et al. (1954, 1962) was carried out in the laboratory and involved the Body Adjustment Test and the Rod and Frame Test, both assessing whether the subject organizes his perception of the vertical relative to internal cues or to cues in the visual field. A third measure, the Embedded Figures Test, requires the subject to disembed a figure from the background, does not require laboratory administration, yet is assumed to tap the same dimension as the two laboratory techniques. Both the Rod and Frame and the Embedded Figures Tests have been modified for use with children, and a variety of rod and frame tests are available for use outside of the laboratory. Relationships among the many forms of the FID measures are somewhat variable, and measurement continues to be a problem in research on this topic (Kagan & Kogan, 1971; Keogh, 1973). Implications of the field-organization construct for children with school problems will be discussed in a later section of this chapter.

REFLECTION-IMPULSIVITY

With the possible exception of field independence-dependence, few cognitive-style dimensions have generated as much interest and research as has reflection-impulsivity. Kogan (1971) suggests that this dimension has direct implications for education, as it "involves the child's evaluation of his own cognitive products—that is, his willingness to pause and reflect on the accuracy of his hypotheses and solutions" [p. 266]. The background to understanding of reflection-impulsivity comes from earlier work with children by Kagan, Moss, and Sigel (1963) and by Kagan, Rosman, Day, Albert, and Phillips (1964). These investigators described three major styles of categorization: analytic-descriptive, relational, and inferential-categorical. Response modes were found to have consistency and stability over time and across tasks. Analytic responses were found to increase with age and to be more characteristic of boys than of girls. Further work led to the conceptualization that two *fundamental dispositions* were contributors to the generation of analytic responses. One had to do with a perceptual scanning strategy which analyzed complex visual arrays into components, a second with the tendency to reflect on available solutions before responding. It should be emphasized that individual differences in decision speed and in perceptual strategy presumed to characterize the reflection-impulsivity dimension refer to decisions made in situations of stimulus ambiguity or response uncertainty. A voluminous literature documents that children do, indeed, respond differently to ambiguity, some acting on the first solution that comes to mind, guessing without regard for accuracy or validity of the response; other children appear to evaluate alternative solutions, to evaluate a response for accuracy and correctness before acting on that idea. Such difference in style clearly may affect children's performance in school.

The most common technique for assessing reflection-impulsivity is the Matching Familiar Figures Test (MFFT), a match-to-sample test in which the child is presented with a stimulus and six choices, only one of which is identical with the standard figure. Time to first response and number of incorrect choices are recorded; thus, although the presumed theoretical dimension of reflection-impulsivity is unitary, the operational measurement involves two discrete indices, time and errors. Impulsive children are those with short response latencies and high error rates; reflectives are characterized by longer latencies and fewer errors. For determining impulsivity or reflection in any sample or population, Kagan has opted for a median split on each index, approximately two-thirds of any group expected to fit into the two modal quadrants. The remaining one-third sample subjects would either be in the category of high errors, long response latency, or in that of low errors, low response latency. These children fall outside the reflective-impulsive dichotomy, but nevertheless may be important to consider when planning programs in schools. Despite wide interest and enthusiasm for the construct, the operational aspects of the MFFT have been questioned, the most recent comprehensive criticism and controversy between Block, Block, and Harrington (1974, 1975) and Kagan and Messer (1975).

RESEARCH OF EDUCATIONAL RELEVANCE

The implications of individual differences in cognitive styles for a variety of abilities and achievements have been addressed in an extensive research literature. The volume of research directed at reflection-impulsivity and field articulation is almost overwhelming. A sample of available work may be seen in the following array. It should be emphasized that this represents only a limited proportion of the available published material dealing with these two constructs. Truly these are attractive will-o-the-wisps!

In a series of papers Kagan explicated the reflection-impulsivity construct, drawing applications for education (Kagan, 1965a, 1965b, 1966, 1967, 1973; Kagan, Pearson, & Welch, 1966a, 1966b). Witkin, too, has written extensively as to implications of his field-articulation construct, raising questions as to origins, influences, modifiability, and educational consequences (Witkin, 1964, 1965a, 1965b; Witkin et al., 1954; Witkin et al., 1962; Witkin, Goodenough, & Karp, 1967). The volume of research stimulated by these two cognitive-style constructs precludes review in this paper, but selected research relating them to exceptional children deserves attention. Published research includes that by Witkin, Birnbaum, Lomonaco, Lehr, and Herman (1968) with blind children; Fiebert (1967) with deaf; and Arner (1973), Keogh and Hall (1974), Keogh, Wetter, McGinty, and Donlon (1973), Massari and Mansfield (1973), Nesbit and Chambers (1976), and Witkin, Faterson, Goodenough, and Birnbaum (1966) with mentally retarded pupils. Denny (1974), Gill, Herdter, and Lough (1968), Kalash (1973), King (1972), Peterson and Magaro (1969), and Watson (1969) all related aspects of cognitive-style differences to reading readiness or reading performance. Also of interest is the work with children with learning problems and behavioral disturbances, especially hyperactive children (Campbell, Douglas, & Morgenstern, 1971; Cohen, Weiss, & Minde, 1972; Juliano, 1974; Keogh & Donlon, 1972), and the study of cognitive styles of emotionally disturbed children and adolescents (Barden, 1973; Finch & Montgomery, 1973; Finch, Nelson, Montgomery & Stein, 1974; Montgomery & Finch, 1975; Stein, Finch, Hooke, Montgomery, & Nelson, 1975; and Zern, Kenney, & Karaceus, 1974). Other investigators have focused on aspects of problem-solving skills (Ault, 1973; Becker, 1973; Berzowsky & Ondrako, 1974; Hallahan, Kauffman, & Ball, 1973; Mann, 1973; Siegel, Babich, & Kirask, 1974; Weiner, 1975). Recently there has been some interest in the study of possible relationships between cognitive styles and neurological functioning (Friedman, Guyer, & Tymchuk, 1975; Guyer & Friedman, 1975; Neuringer, Goldstein, & Gallagher, 1975). From this cursory review it may be seen that the cognitive-style constructs as proposed by Kagan and Witkin have generated extensive research and theorizing. For more detailed and comprehensive content the reader is referred to reviews by Epstein, Hallahan, and Kauffman (1975), Kagan and Kogan (1970), Keogh (1973), Kogan (1971, 1973), Tarver and Hallahan (1975), and Wachtel (1972).

Despite the considerable empirical evidence which presumably has implications for both regular and special education, for the most part implications have been formulated globally, and lack specificity or direction for operational interventions in classrooms. A good deal of effort has been focused on delineating or documenting the stylistic characteristics of children according to age and sex groups, or even according to various clinical diagnostic categories. Less attention has been paid to characteristics of the setting, task, or instructional programs which might interact with pupils' styles to produce success or failure. Interestingly, relatively little attention has been paid to the possible influences of cognitive styles on assessment of ability or achievement, i.e., on IQ or norm-referenced achievement tests. Similarly, despite appeal in the notion of teacher style interacting with pupil style, we have only limited evidence to document the effects of presumed matches or mismatches of teachers and pupils on style dimensions. We have few solid data to support the interactive effects of particular instructional techniques for children with particular problem-solving styles.

It is important to emphasize that lack of evidence does not negate the possibility, in some cases even likelihood, that such relationships prevail, and that they might provide insight into instructional interventions. Kogan (1971) notes that "Witkin's analytic-global dimension would appear to be ideally suited for research on the interaction between variables of cognitive style and instructional treatment. Both ends of Witkin's dimension have adaptive properties, though of a distinctly different kind, and it is feasible that educational programs could be devised to profit each of the polar types. Unfortunately, no work of this sort has yet been carried out" [p. 253]. The point to be emphasized is that we have not yet systematically tested the implications of cognitive styles for educational practice. We are, it seems, forced to consider Aptitude-Treatment Interactions. In the case of cognitive styles we are also forced to take into account related influences which interact with these stylistic differences. We may, indeed, have entered Cronbach's "hall of mirrors."

INFLUENCES OF SEX AND CULTURAL DIFFERENCES

In identifying and analyzing characteristics of pupils which might be relevant to an Aptitude-Treatment Interaction, even when that paradigm is loosely defined, both sex and cultural differences require consideration. The vastness of the published literature on these two topics precludes comprehensive review in this chapter, but clear recognition of possible individual differences in learning styles related to sex and socio-cultural background may be pertinent when planning programs for children with special educational needs. Culture and sex-roles as determinants of behavior are not mutually exclusive, as their interactions are complex and confounded; certainly, the very term, *sex-role*, carries a cultural connotation. The appropriateness of particular behaviors for boys and girls varies relative to the age of the child and the culture in which the child lives. Attitudes, motivations, interests, and behaviors in school have both sex and cultural links, and individual differences in cognitive styles may also be expressions of sex-related socialization these styles or modes of interaction with the environment becoming relatively stable characteristics of individuals. The point to be made is that it is probably impossible to speculate about the implications of cognitive styles for special education without recognizing both sex and cultural influences; perhaps more broadly, it is impossible to consider sex-linked aspects of cognitive styles without consideration of the cultural context in which they are defined. The reader is referred to the recent work of Maccoby and Jacklin (1974) for a comprehensive summary and review of the sex-difference literature.

From the viewpoint of the special educator, there is consistent documentation of the discrepancy between numbers of males and females in special education programs, especially programs for the mentally retarded, learning disabled, and emotionally disturbed. It is of interest to note that sex ratios vary according to special educational classification, however. In reviewing programs in California, for example, we found that 60 percent of the pupils in EMR programs were boys, whereas boys comprised 80 percent of the pupils in programs for the educationally handicapped, a special education category which included both learning disabled and mildly emotionally disturbed children (Keogh, Becker, Kukic, & Kukic, 1972). Our findings are consistent with figures from special education programs across the country and support the sex-difference ratio reported for frequency of referral and placement in special programs, at least at the elementary and intermediate school levels. Analysis of numbers of adults in hospital and institutional placement, however, raises some interesting considerations as to age and cultural influences on deviance, as some reports suggest a reversal in sex ratio at older ages, especially for psychiatric disturbances (Chesler, 1975).

In addition to known differences in frequency of referral and placement in special programs relative to the sex of a child, the relationship between socioeconomic status, ethnicity, and school achievement has also been described. In a well-known national study of pupils in regular education status, Coleman, Campbell, Hobson, McPartland, Mood, Weinfeld, and York (1966) demonstrated a relationship between socioeconomic status, ethnicity, and school achievement. Sociologist Jane Mercer (1971) and her colleagues at Riverside have documented the overrepresentation of ethnic minority pupils in special programs for the mentally retarded, as have Chandler and Plakos (1970) on a sample of California pupils. The confounding of ethnicity and educational programming has been the basis for extensive legal, educational, and sociological debate and decision. The reader is referred to the two volumes on classification of children edited by Hobbs (1975) for a comprehensive overview of these issues. Without belaboring the point, there is little doubt that boys and ethnic minorities are overrepresented in special educational placements. The reasons for this overrepresentation are debatable and are, in fact, debated in a broad and varied research literature. Hypotheses include those which stress biologic or genetic differences, those which focus on cultural deficits or cultural differences, and those which emphasize specific language differences. Some investigators "explain" the sex and ethnic differences in terms of the kinds of identification procedures used to select pupils, and still others place responsibility on teachers and on the instructional characteristics of school systems.

Realistically, it seems likely that the differential referral and placement findings are not a function of single effects or conditions. That is, there may be subtle differences in learning styles related to sex role and culture which influence how a child performs in school and in school-related activities. These differences in cognitive style may not be demonstrated directly on psychometric tests or on usual achievement-based assessments in the classroom. On the contrary, differences in style may actually influence how a child performs on standard tests, or how he performs in the classroom, thus increasing the likelihood of his identification as "atypical." Culturally based, sex-linked modes of approach to problem solving, to new learning situations, and to the social and cognitive demands of the formal educational setting may be important to achievement in school. The influences of culturally determined experience may lead to characteristic approaches to school and school learning by children from different cultural groups. Said directly, some cognitive styles probably enhance success in the traditional instructional program; others may increase the probability of failure in school. Thus, examination of some of the findings relative to cultural differences in cognitive styles seems appropriate. It is interesting to note that such a review requires search of the research literature in a number of professional disciplines. Because of the volume and scope of material, the content reviewed in this chapter will for the most part be focused on the cognitive-style dimension of field independence-dependence (FID).

COGNITIVE STYLES AND EDUCATIONAL PROGRAMS

The essence of the cultural-difference argument as to the interactive nature of individual characteristics in cognitive styles and the demands of the educational program is that pupils and programs often operate in different social and cognitive systems. Anthropologist Rosalie Cohen, in an article in the *American Anthropologist* (1969) noted that the middle-class school, like the standardized intelligence tests used to assess children in those schools, requires a particular background of general information, as well as abilities for analytic abstraction and field independence. Cohen stressed that the overall orientation of the school is compatible with an analytic rather than a relational cognitive style, leading her to observe that the relational cognitive style and its "sociobehavioral correlates" are frequently viewed as deviant in the environment of the school where the analytic style is emphasized. Her observations are consistent with those of Witkin (1965b) and become especially telling if we think in terms of achievement as a function of the "match" or "mismatch" between pupils and programs.

Cross-cultural findings: Cohen (1969) suggests that "systematic variations [in style] . . . may have arisen as a result of different social environments that stimulate, reinforce, and make functional the development of one style of conceptual organization and constrain and inhibit others" [p. 498]. This interpretation of the cultural influences on cognitive styles finds independent support in a number of investigations. A few examples will demonstrate the thrust of the argument. Berry (1966) found characteristic differences in performance among samples of Edinburgh Scots, Temnes of Sierra Leone, and Eskimos of Baffin Island on perceptual tests, tests of discrimination, and tests of spatial organization and skills. In his opinion performance differences among the subgroups were consistent with differences in ecology and in socialization practices of the societies. Berry's findings were replicated by MacArthur (1967) with other Eskimo groups. Differences in cognitive styles relative to rural and urban environments have been identified by Okonji (1969) in Nigeria, and more recently by Park and Gallimore (1975) in Korea. In both studies urban subjects were more field independent than were rural subjects, and in the Park and Gallimore study they had higher analytic scores. Consistent findings were also reported by S. Kagan (1974) in Mexico. Comprehensive discussion of the evidence as to the hypothesized effects of culture and ecology on development of individual differences in cognitive styles may be found in reviews by Witkin (1967), Witkin and Berry (1975), and in a report of research by Witkin, Price-Williams, Bertini, Christiansen, Oltman, Ramirez, and Van Meel (1974). Aspects of cognitive styles are also reviewed and interpreted in the intriguing volume *Culture and Thought* by Cole and Scribner (1974). On the basis of the published evidence it seems reasonable to conclude that there are interactive effects of culture, ecology, and style, at least when assessed across clearly different social groups. What is of more direct relevance to us in this chapter is consideration of possible subcultural effects within the American society, and especially the speculation as to the relevance of such individual differences for success or failure in school.

Subcultural findings: Differences among subcultural groups in ability patterns have interested American psychologists and sociologists for a number of years. Lesser, Fifer, and Clark (1965) found that samples drawn from four ethnic groups (Black, Chinese, Jewish, Puerto Rican) in New York City had characteristically varied patterns of primary mental abilities. Hertzig, Birch, Thomas, and Mendez (1968) described differences in approach to IQ testing taken by Puerto Rican and Anglo-American preschoolers, and Sarason (1973) presented a sensitive personal view of culturally determined influences on achievement orientation. Some research has been directed specifically at identification of possible effects of subcultural socialization practices on cognitive styles of American children. Dershowitz (1971), for example, documented differences between orthodox and nonorthodox Jewish boys in field independence, and Ramirez and Price-Williams (1974) found cultural differences in styles among three American subgroups: Anglo-American, Black, and Mexican. Although a considerable amount of work has been focused on cognitive styles of Mexican children, for the special educator, both practitioner and researcher, three related questions must be asked if we are to make use of this body of research: Are there consistent differences in field articulation between Mexican-American children and Anglo-American peers? Are these differences related to achievement in school? How may these stylistic differences be used to enhance instructional success?

Field articulation: Whereas consistent differences in cognitive styles have been documented in comparisons of children in markedly different cultures, the question of concern for American educators is whether there are consistent within-culture differences. It might be argued that exposure to the majority culture (as through television, radio, and movies) might override subcultural experiences leading to particular cognitive styles. Research already reviewed has suggested differences in Mexican and American children in home countries; of interest is possible differences between Mexican-American and Anglo-American children in this country.

Canavan (1969), using a portable apparatus for assessment of field articulation, reported that elementary school Mexican-Americans were more field dependent than were their Anglo-American peers. Ramirez and Price-Williams (1974) also found differences in field dependence between Mexican and Anglo-American children, and Kagan and Zahn (1975) found Mexican-American children in grades two, four, and six more field dependent than their Anglo-American classmates. In an effort to tease out the interaction between style and socialization, Buriel (1975) compared Mexican-American and Anglo-American subjects but differentiated among first-, second-, and third-generation Mexican families. He reported significant differences between Mexican and Anglo-American children for first- and third-generation subjects. Buriel's findings are complex, as the curvilinear relationship between generation and style was unpredicted. They are consistent with the findings of Kagan (1974) and with the results of a study by Ramirez, Castenada, and Herold (1974), the latter investigators finding Mexican-American children from traditional Mexican families to be more field dependent than were children from dualistic or atraditional families. Taken as a whole, there does appear to be some evidence to support differences, albeit frequently subtle ones, in problem-solving or cognitive styles between children raised in predominantly Anglo- or Mexican-American cultures. Following the suggestion of Ramirez and Castenada (1974) Buriel proposes that these differences reflect differences in early experiences within the family. Describing Mexican childrearing practices he notes that they "typically emphasize adherence to convention, respect for authority, and a continued identity with the family. . . . [They are] in opposition to the usual childrearing practices of 'mainstream' Anglo-American culture, which typically emphasize greater assertiveness, autonomy, and a more individualistic sense of self-identity" [p. 418]. Buriel points out the similarity of the Mexican emphases to the characteristics of family structure described by Witkin et al. (1974) as leading to field dependence. The "set" that many Mexican-American children bring to school, thus, may be inconsistent with the requirements of the Anglo-American school. It is this question which deserves consideration by majority educators.

Style and achievement in school: Assuming that stylistic patterns reported for cultural subgroups within the United States represent real and functional dimensions of individual differences, it is reasonable to assume that these differences may be influences in an Aptitude-Treatment Interaction affecting school performance. Theoretically at least, pupils' cognitive styles are interactive with instructional materials, teachers' styles, and the nature of social and educational reinforcers. In this regard, Ramirez and Price-Williams (1974) refer to DiStefano's (1970) work in which it was demonstrated that teachers tended to prefer and to grade positively pupils with cognitive styles similar to their own. This is especially pertinent when coupled with Ramirez's (1973) finding that teachers were more field independent than were their Mexican-American pupils. To add another dimension to the possible dissonance, Ramirez, Taylor, and Peterson (1971) found that Mexican-American junior and senior high school students had less-positive attitudes toward school than did their Anglo-American counterparts.

As noted in an earlier review (Keogh, 1973), given the nature of the program in most American middle-class schools, there is little doubt that an analytic, field-independent style is preferred. Despite claims as to the "value-free" aspect of stylistic dimensions, and despite reports of particular tasks or accomplishments which are done more easily and effectively by those with field-dependent, relational approaches, it seems clear that in a school program where accuracy, speed, and task-oriented behaviors are rewarded, the field-independent, analytic, reflective child is advantaged (Keogh, 1973; Keogh & Donlon, 1972; Kagan, 1965a, 1965b; Kogan, 1971). Said simply, the match between the middle-class, Anglo-American pupil and the school he attends may be more optimal than is the match for the Mexican-American pupil. Whereas the achievement findings have usually been "explained" in terms of the language patterns of Mexican-American pupils, the cognitive-style literature allows consideration of even broader and more pervasive dimensions of difference. Mexican-American children may be disadvantaged in the usual school program not only because of language but because they approach learning tasks in a manner or style which is discrepant from the style of the teacher and the curriculum. Recent work by Kagan and Zahn (1975) is relevant, as they report a higher relationship between field dependence and math than between field dependence and reading for elementary school Mexican-American pupils. These investigators propose that math is more culture free than is reading and that individual differences in cognitive styles may therefore be especially strong influences on achievement in that school subject. The Kagan and Zahn work is especially interesting as it delineates accomplishments within the general achievement domain and demonstrates differential relationships between field independence and particular subject-matter areas.

On the basis of still tentative evidence it seems reasonable that there are consistencies in individual differences in cognitive styles which affect or at least are related to achievement in educational programs. It seems reasonable, too, that there may be strong cultural influences on cognitive styles which work to the disadvantage of children from cultural minority backgrounds. As it is still unclear as to whether cognitive styles represent relatively permanent basic cognitive and personality characteristics or whether they are expressions of learned and changing functions, the specific implications for educational programming are uncertain. As noted by Kogan (1971),

> It makes a great deal of difference whether variation in a particular form of cognitive functioning is attributed to primary ego structure on the one hand, or to acquired habits of processing information on the other. In the former case, efforts would focus on the design of educational treatments intended to take maximum advantage of the child's innate capacities. In the latter case consideration can be given to possible modification of the child's modes of information processing so that he will better profit from current educational treatments. [p. 245]

The issue of whether and how to treat individual differences, including differences in cognitive style, is one of the important issues in educational programming.

Intervention considerations: Whether to try to change the pupil or to modify the program to fit the pupil is the basic issue, although surely an issue not limited to discussion of cognitive styles. The assumption has been that because the school is a major socializing force on children, that because it serves the society at large by preparing pupils for life in the majority culture, it should be the child who makes the major accommodations to the relatively stable educational system. Events of the past ten years have placed these assumptions in doubt, however, and have led to suggestions of drastically changed school programs. Castenada and Gray (1974/75), for example, stress that some children, usually those from culturally different families, are forced to function in two separate social systems. They suggest that schools can no longer assess children within the majority set or continue to provide instruction which is compatible with only one social cultural system. They propose instead that the kinds of characteristics already described as characterizing the Mexican-American child, i.e., relational, field sensitive, be incorporated into the educational program so that there is exposure to compatible instruction and materials. Ramirez and Castenada (1974) suggest that there are "two cognitive styles" and that we must think in terms of "bicognitive development." On the basis of a number of parameters of instructional programs (relationships to peers, personal relationships to teacher, instructional relationship to teacher, characteristics of curriculum that facilitate learning), they have designed a program for "field-sensitive" pupils.

The Ramirez and Castenada approach is compatible with the point of view taken by Mercer (Mercer, 1971, 1973; Mercer & Brown, 1973; Mercer & Lewis, 1976; Soeffing, 1975) who argues for a multiple approach to assessment of children. Mercer is well known for her position on psychometric testing for special education placement, and she has been one of the most outspoken critics of the standardized IQ test for this purpose. In her current work she is developing pluralistic norms for assessment, building into the system consideration of family and cultural influences as well as normative, modal requirements of performance. She stresses that it is important for the child from the cultural minority background to master the competencies of the majority culture, but not at the cost of giving up the values, strengths, and unique abilities inherent in his own cultural system. In her view it is, in part at least, the educational system which must make accommodations to culturally different pupils. Although Professor Mercer has come to her conclusions outside the cognitive-style arena, her findings and interpretations are at least consistent with the point of view of Witkin, Faterson, Goodenough, and Birnbaum (1966) who point out the narrowness of the "psychometric net." Our own data (Keogh & Hall, 1974) support this view, as there are clearly differences in cultural subgroups in special education placement relative to verbal-comprehensive, analytic, and attentional skills, these differences among children also observed in clinic subgroups (Keogh, Wetter, McGinty, & Donlon, 1973). There is, thus, at least some preliminary evidence to support a stylistic approach to assessment. Ramirez (1973), Ramirez and Castenada (1974), and Castenada and Gray (1974/75) argue for far more sweeping changes than assessment alone, however, as in their view the very substance of most educational programs is culturally laden in ways which disadvantage the Mexican-American pupil. The argument is made explicitly:

> (a) Public education tends to favor a teaching style that is more appropriate to one cognitive style than the other; (b) Many children from ethnic minorities come from homes which tend to teach in a style more appropriate to the other cognitive mode; and (c) Equal educational opportunity is denied when educational policy and practice favor one teaching and cognitive style over the others. [Castenada & Gray, 1974/75, p. 204]

Given the tenor of that argument, it appears likely that future issues relating to cognitive styles may be both academic and political.

SOME OBSERVATIONS

Despite the intuitive appeal of the notion of individual differences in cognitive styles, the topic is fraught with inconsistencies which frequently confuse and frustrate researchers. We continue to be plagued with problems of measurement and methodology. Reliability of assessment techniques is frequently not high, and validity, if estimated at all, may be defined in terms of strength of relationship to another measure which is, itself, of questionable reliability and validity. Variations on equipment, administrative methods, and scoring systems make it difficult to generalize from one study to another. More fundamentally, the constructs which provide the theoretical basis for measurement are somehow slippery or at least are interpreted freely by different investigators. A number of writers on this topic have cautioned against equating the constructs in one theoretical system with those in another, as there may be no logical or necessary relationships across systems.

While there is considerable enthusiasm for applying cognitive styles to educational programs, for the most part there is lack of systematic evidence on which to delineate the nature of the presumed Aptitude-Treatment Interaction, and almost no evidence on which to determine program efficacy. It seems safe to make the generalization that educational programs are developed by advocates not skeptics; programs utilizing cognitive-style constructs are no exceptions. The very advocacy which is required to implement a program may get in the way of a systematic evaluation of its effectiveness. The point to be made is that we are forced to accept or reject a cognitive-style approach to educational programming more on faith than on evidence. There is need for careful delineation of appropriateness and effectiveness of a given intervention for particular children.

Finally, too often, interpreters and implementors of the various positions have tended to adopt *either-or* positions. A given child is viewed as being either impulsive *or* reflective, field dependent *or* field independent, analytic *or* global. On the contrary, it seems likely that most children have a variety of responses at their disposal but that they prefer certain strategies and may overlearn given strategies. It may be productive for both researchers and practitioners to think in terms of hierarchies of styles, to determine when and under what conditions children use certain strategies of styles, and when and under what conditions styles can be modified. In our research at UCLA on the early identification of high-risk pupils we have seen indication that they are less able than low-risk pupils to modify their strategies of problem solving. High-risk pupils tend to overuse some approaches, even when the outcomes are negative. Because these children seem to have difficulty in modifying their styles they are especially vulnerable to the instructional program. The ability to be analytic is of value a good deal of the time in educational settings, but global articulation is beneficial in some situations. Where instruction is either one or the other, and where the child does not utilize his repertoire appropriately, the educational program fails. It may not be enough, therefore, to determine if a given child is impulsive or field dependent; it is important to determine if he has a variety of strategies available, and if he can regulate his response styles relative to the task to be accomplished. In this analysis both the child's preferred mode or style and the requirements of the task must be taken into account.

Having raised some cautionary points, I would like to conclude this review with some argument as to the value of an approach to educational programming which incorporates cognitive-style constructs. One of the major benefits in such an approach has to do with assessment of pupils. Recognition of individual differences in cognitive styles has made us more sensitive to individual differences on many dimensions and has sensitized us especially to the limitations of standard psychometric tests for assessing children with school problems. Classroom teachers will recall those children whose learning and achievement were not consistent with their scores on tests, some achieving far beyond their scores, others at a far lower level. Clearly other factors than a narrowly defined IQ influence how a child performs in school. The awareness of individual differences in cognitive styles has helped to remind us that the *how* as well as the *how much* of school performance is important.

Sensitivity to cognitive-style differences has also helped to make sense out of the broad array of evidence coming from the study of sex and cultural differences. It could be argued that recognition of the nature of cultural and sex roles may provide insight into differences among children which can be interpreted but not devalued. We have too long viewed the modal behavior and learning pattern to be the best, sometimes the only one of value, at the same time equating difference with deficit. Consideration of possible differences in style may allow us to be more understanding and supporting of difference.

Recognition of differences in cognitive styles may also lead us to consider Aptitude-Treatment Interactions rather than focusing exclusively on the pupil, especially on presumed pupil deficits. That a child fails in school or that he has social adjustment problems should not be viewed as the *fault* of the child or the *fault* of the teacher. It may indeed be a function of the interactions between teacher and child, between the particular instructional system and the child's learning style. Too often we tend to lay blame when we, in fact, should be seeking reasons. An approach which recognizes individual differences in styles may allow us more confidence in this approach. Closely related, the recognition of individual differences in learning styles argues for a variety of instructional and curricular opportunities within the regular classroom.

Finally, from a research point of view, the constructs have sparked controversy, discussion, and more refined theory—and they have generated an extraordinary amount of empirical evidence. Not all of that evidence is solid, but taken as a whole the research directed at cognitive styles allows some tentative generalizations and applications to instructional programs for children. The study of cognitive styles is stimulating and provocative, challenging the researcher to careful yet creative efforts. Will-o-the-wisps have a long history of attraction. The will-o-the-wisp known as cognitive styles is no exception.

REFERENCES

Arner, M. A study of cognitive style and its concomitant traits and characteristics in adolescent educable mental retardates. *Dissertation Abstracts International*, 1973, 33 (7-B), 3276-77.

Ault, R. Problem-solving strategies of reflective, impulsive, fast-accurate, and slow-inaccurate children. *Child Development*, 1973, 44, 259-66.

Barden, E. A. Object sorting and defining styles of emotionally disturbed and normal children. *Dissertation Abstracts International*, 1973, 33 (10-B), 5046.

Becker, L. D. Regulation of conceptual tempo in educationally "high risk" children (SERP A12). University of California, Los Angeles, 1973.

Berry, J. W. Temne and eskimo perceptual skills. *International Journal of Psychology*, 1966, 1 (3), 207-29.

Berzonsky, M. D., & Ondrako, M. Cognitive style and logical deductive reasoning. *Journal of Experimental Education*, 1974, 43 (1), 18-24.

Block, J., Block, J. H., & Harrington, D. M. Some misgivings about the matching familiar figures test as a measure of reflection-impulsivity. *Developmental Psychology*, 1974, 10, 611-32.

Block, J., Block, J. H., & Harrington, D. M. Comment on the Kagan-Messer reply. *Developmental Psychology*, 1975, 11, 249-52.

Buriel, R. Cognitive styles among three generations of Mexican-American children. *Journal of Cross-Cultural Psychology*, 1975, 6 (4), 417-29.

Campbell, S., Douglas, V., & Morgenstern, G. Cognitive styles in hyperactive children and the effect of methylphenidate. *Journal of Child Psychology and Psychiatry*, 1971, 12, 55-67.

Canavan, D. Field dependence in children as a function of grade, sex, and ethnic group membership. Paper presented at the annual meeting of the American Psychological Association, Washington, D.C., 1969.

Castaneda, A., & Gray, T. Bicognitive processes in multicultural education. *Educational Leadership*, 1974/75, 66, 203-7.

Chandler, J. T., & Plakos, J. *Spanish-speaking pupils classified as educable mentally retarded*. Mexican-American Research Project. Sacramento: California State Department of Education, 1970.

Chesler, P. Women as psychiatric and psychotherapeutic patients. In R. K. Unger & F. L. Denmark (Eds.), *Woman: Dependent or independent variable*. New York: Psychological Dimensions, 1975. Pp. 138-62.

Cohen, R. A. Conceptual styles, culture conflict, and nonverbal tests of intelligence. *American Anthropologist*, 1969, 71 (Pt. 2), 828-36.

Cohen, N. J., Weiss, G., & Minde, K. Cognitive styles in adolescents previously diagnosed as hyperactive. *Journal of Child Psychology and Psychiatry*, 1972, 13, 203-9.

Cole, M., & Scribner, S. *Culture and thought: A psychological introduction*. New York: Wiley, 1974.

Coleman, J. J., Campbell, E. Q., Hobson, C. J., McPartland, J., Mood, A. M., Weinfeld, F. D., & York, R. L. *Equality of educational opportunity* (GPO No FS S 278:38000). Washington, D.C.: U.S. Department of Health, Education and Welfare, Office of Education, 1966.

Cronbach, L. J. The two disciplines of scientific psychology. *American Psychologist*, 1957, 12, 671-84.

Cronbach, L. J. Beyond the two disciplines of scientific psychology. *American Psychologist*, 1975, 26, 116-27.

Denney, D. R. Relationship of three cognitive style dimensions to elementary reading abilities. *Journal of Educational Psychology*, 1974, 66 (5), 702-9.

Dershowitz, Z. Jewish subculture patterns and psychological differentiation. *International Journal of Psychology*, 1971, 6 (3), 223-31.

Epstein, M. H., Hallahan, D. P., & Kauffman, J. M. Implications of the reflectivity-impulsivity dimension for special education. *Journal of Special Education*, 1975, 9 (1), 11-25.

Fiebert, M. Cognitive styles in the deaf. *Perceptual and Motor Skills,* 1967, 24, 319-29.

Finch, A., & Montgomery, L. Reflection-impulsivity and information seeking in emotionally disturbed children. *Journal of Abnormal Child Psychology,* 1973, 1 (4), 358-62.

Finch, A., Nelson, W., Montgomery, L., & Stein, A. Reflection-impulsivity and locus of control in emotionally disturbed children. *Journal of Genetic Psychology,* 1974, 125, 273-75.

Friedman, M. P., Guyer, B. L., & Tymchuk, A. *Cognitive styles and specialized hemispheric processing in learning disability.* Paper presented at the NATO conference on the Neuropsychology of Learning Disorders: Theoretical Approaches, Korsor, Denmark, June 1975.

Gill, N. T., Herdtner, T., & Lough, L. Perceptual and socio-economic variables, instruction in body orientation, and predicted academic success in young children. *Perceptual and Motor Skills,* 1968, 26, 1175-84.

Guyer, L., & Friedman, M. Hemispheric processing and cognitive styles in learning-disabled and normal children. *Child Development,* 1975, 46, 658-68.

Hallahan, D. P., Kauffman, J. M., & Ball, D. W. Selective attention and cognitive tempo of low achieving and high achieving sixth grade males. *Perceptual and Motor Skills,* 1973, 37, 179-88.

Hertzig, M. E., Birch, H. G., Thomas, A., & Mendez, O. A. Class and ethnic differences in the responsiveness of preschool children to cognitive demands. *Monographs of the Society for Research in Child Development,* 1968, 33 (1, Serial No. 117).

Hobbs, N. (Ed.). *Issues in the classification of children* (Vols. 1, 2). San Francisco: Jossey-Bass, 1975.

Holtzman, W. H. Intelligence, cognitive style, and personality: A developmental approach. In O. Brim, R. Crutchfield, & W. Holtzman (Eds.), *Intelligence perspectives, 1965: The Terman-Otis memorial lectures.* New York: Harcourt Brace Jovanovich, 1966.

Juliano, D. Conceptual tempo, activity, and concept learning in hyperactive and normal children. *Journal of Abnormal Psychology,* 1974, 83, 629-34.

Kagan, J. Reflection-impulsivity and reading ability in primary grade children. *Child Development,* 1965, 36, 609-28. (a)

Kagan, J. Impulsive and reflective children: Significance of conceptual tempo. In J. D. Krumboltz (Ed.), *Learning and the educational process.* Chicago: Rand McNally, 1965. (b)

Kagan, J. Reflection-impulsivity: The generality and dynamics of conceptual tempo. *Journal of Abnormal Psychology,* 1966, 71 (1), 17-24.

Kagan, J. Biological aspects of inhibition systems. *American Journal of Disturbed Children,* 1967, 114, 507-12.

Kagan, J. Impulsive and reflective children: Significance of conceptual tempo. In S. G. Sapir & A. C. Nitzburg (Eds.), *Children with learning problems.* New York: Brunner-Mazel, 1973.

Kagan, J., and Kogan, N. Individual variation in cognitive processes. In P. Mussen (Ed.), *Carmichael's manual of child psychology* (Vol. 1). New York: Wiley, 1970.

Kagan, J., & Messer, S. A reply to "Some misgivings about the Matching Familiar Figures Test as a measure of reflection-impulsivity." *Developmental Psychology*, 1975, 11 (2), 244-48.

Kagan, J., Moss, H. A., & Sigel, I. E. Psychological significance of styles of conceptualization. In J. C. Wright & J. Kagan (Eds.), Basic cognitive processes in children. *Monographs of the Society for Research in Child Development*, 1963, 28 (2, Serial No. 86).

Kagan, J., Pearson, L., & Welch, L. Conceptual impulsivity and inductive reasoning. *Child Development*, 1966, 37, 583-94. (a)

Kagan, J., Pearson, L., & Welch, L. Modifiability of an impulsive tempo. *Journal of Educational Psychology*, 1966, 57 (6), 359-65. (b)

Kagan, J., Rosman, B., Day, D., Albert, J., & Phillips, W. Information processing in the child: Significance of analytic and reflective attitudes. *Psychological Monographs*, 1964, 78 (1, Whole No. 578), 35-36.

Kagan, S. Field dependence and conformity of rural Mexican and urban Anglo-American children. *Child Development*, 1974, 45, 765-71.

Kagan, S., & Zahn, G. L. Field dependence and the school achievement gap between Anglo-American and Mexican-American children. *Journal of Educational Psychology*, 1975, 67 (5), 643-50.

Kalash, B. D. The relationships of preferred learning modalities and conceptual tempo to reading readiness of first grade disadvantaged children. *Dissertation Abstracts International*, 1973, 33, 5552-53.

Keogh, B. K. Psychological evaluation of exceptional children: Old hang-ups and new directions. *Journal of School Psychology*, 1972, 10 (2), 49-53.

Keogh, B. K. Perceptual and cognitive styles: Implications for special education. In L. Mann and D. A. Sabatino (Eds.), *The first review of special education* (Vol. 1). Philadelphia: JSE Press, 1973.

Keogh, B. K., Becker, L. D., Kukic, M., & Kukic, S. Programs for EH and EMR pupils: Review and recommendations (SERP A11). University of California, Los Angeles, 1972.

Keogh, B. K., & Donlon, G. Field dependence, impulsivity and learning disabilities. *Journal of Learning Disabilities*, 1972, 5, 331-36.

Keogh, B. K., & Hall, R. J. WISC subtest patterns of educationally handicapped and educable mentally retarded pupils. *Psychology in the Schools*, 1974, 9 (3), 296-300.

Keogh, B. K., Wetter, J., McGinty, A., & Donlon, G. Functional analysis of WISC performance of learning-disordered, hyperactive, and mentally retarded boys. *Psychology in the Schools*, 1973, 10 (2), 178-81.

King, I. B. An experimental investigation of the potential of reflection-impulsivity as a determinant of success in early reading achievement. *Dissertation Abstracts International*, 1972, 33 (1-A), 191-92.

Kogan, N. Educational implications of cognitive styles. In G. Lesser (Ed.), *Psychology and educational practices*. Chicago: Scott Foresman, 1971.

Kogan, N. Creativity and cognitive style in a life-span perspective. In P. B. Baltes & K. W. Schaie (Eds.), *Life-span-developmental psychology: Personality and socialization.* New York: Academic Press, 1973.

Lesser, G. S., Fifer, G., & Clark, D. H. Mental abilities of children from different social class and cultural groups. *Monographs of the Society for Research in Child Development.* 1965, 30 (4, Serial No. 102).

MacArthur, R. Sex differences in field dependence for the Eskimo: Replication of Berry's findings. *International Journal of Psychology,* 1967, 2 (2), 139-40.

Maccoby, E. M., & Jacklin, C. N. *The psychology of sex differences.* Stanford: Stanford University Press, 1974.

Mann, L. Differences between reflective and impulsive children in tempo and quality of decision making. *Child Development,* 1973, 44, 274-79.

Massari, D., & Mansfield, R. Field dependence and outer-directedness in the problem solving of retardate and normal children. *Child Development,* 1973, 44, 346-50.

Mercer, J. R. Institutionalized anglocentrism: Labeling mental retardates in the public schools. In P. Orleans & W. R. Willis, Jr. (Eds.), *Race, change, and urban society: Urban affairs annual reviews* (Vol. 5). Beverly Hills, Calif.: Sage, 1971.

Mercer, J. R. *Labeling the mentally retarded: Clinical and social system perspectives on mental retardation.* Berkeley: University of California Press, 1973.

Mercer, J. R., & Brown, W. C. Racial differences in IQ: Fact or artifact? In C. Senna (Ed.), *The fallacy of IQ.* New York: The Third Press, 1973.

Mercer, J. R., & Lewis, J. F. *SOMPA: System of multi-cultural pluralistic assessment.* New York: Psychological Corporation, in press.

Messick, S. The criteria problem in the evaluation of instruction: Assessing possible not just intended outcomes. In M. C. Wittrock & D. E. Wiley (Eds.), *The evaluation of instruction: Issues and problems.* New York: Holt, Rinehart & Winston, 1970.

Montgomery, L., & Finch, A. Reflection-impulsivity and laws of conflict in emotionally disturbed children. *Journal of Genetic Psychology,* 1975, 126, 89-91.

Nesbit, W. C., & Chambers, J. Performance of MA-matched nonretarded and retarded children on measures of field-dependence. *American Journal of Mental Deficiency,* 1976, 80 (4), 469-72.

Neuringer, C., Goldstein, G., & Gallagher, R. B. Minimal field dependency and minimal brain disfunction. *Journal of Consulting and Clinical Psychology,* 1975, 43, 20-21.

Okonji, M. O. The differential effects of rural and urban upbringing on the development of cognitive styles. *International Journal of Psychology,* 1969, 4 (10), 293-305.

Park, J. Y., & Gallimore, R. Cognitive style in urban and rural Korea. *Journal of Cross-Cultural Psychology,* 1975, 6(2), 227-37.

Peterson, S., and Magaro, P. A. Reading and field dependence: A pilot study. *Journal of Reading*, 1969, 12 (4), 287-94.

Ramirez, M. Cognitive styles and cultural democracy in education. *Social Science Quarterly*, 1973, 53 (4), 895-904.

Ramirez, M., & Castaneda, A. *Cultural democracy, bicognitive development, and education*. New York: Academic Press, 1974.

Ramirez, M., Castaneda, A., & Herold, P. L. The relationship of acculturation to cognitive style among Mexican-Americans. *Journal of Cross-Cultural Psychology*, 1974, 5 (4), 424-33.

Ramirez, M., & Price-Williams, D. R. Cognitive styles of children of three ethnic groups in the United States. *Journal of Cross-Cultural Psychology*, 1974, 5 (2), 212-19.

Ramirez, M., Taylor, C., & Paterson, B. Mexican-American cultural membership and adjustment to school. *Developmental Psychology*, 1971, 4 (2), 141-48.

Sarason, S. B. Jewishness, blackishness, and the nature-nurture controversy. *American Psychologist*, 1973, 28 (11), 962-71.

Siegel, A., Babich, J., & Kirasic, K. Visual recognition memory in reflective and impulsive children. *Memory and Cognition*, 1974, 2, 379-84.

Soeffing, M. Y. New assessment techniques for mentally retarded and culturally different children—A conversation with Jane R. Mercer. *Education and Training of the Mentally Retarded*, 1975, 10 (2), 110-16.

Stein, A. B., Finch, A. J., Hooke, J. F., Montgomery, L. E., & Nelson, W. M. Cognitive tempo and the mode of representation in emotionally disturbed and normal children. *Journal of Psychology*, 1975, 90, 197-201.

Tarver, S. G., and Hallahan, D. P. Attention deficits in children with learning disabilities: A review. *Journal of Learning Disabilities*, 1974, 7 (9), 36-45.

Wachtel, P. Field dependence and psychological differentiations: Re-examination. *Perceptual and Motor Skills*, 1972, 35, 179-89.

Watson, B. L. Field dependence and early reading achievement. Unpublished doctoral dissertation, University of California, Los Angeles, 1969.

Weiner, A. Visual information processing speed in reflective and impulsive children. *Child Development*, 1975, 46, 998-1000.

Witkin, H. A. Origins of cognitive style. In C. Scheeres (Ed.), *Cognition: Theory research, promise*. New York: Harper & Row, 1964.

Witkin, H. A. Psychological differentiation and forms of pathology. *Journal of Abnormal Psychology*, 1965, 70 (5), 317-36. (a)

Witkin, H. A. Some implications of research on cognitive style for problems of education. *Archivio di Psicologia, Neurologia, e Psichiatria*, 1965, 26, 27-55. (b)

Witkin, H. A. A cognitive-style approach to cross-cultural research. *International Journal of Psychology*, 1967, 2 (4), 233-50.

Witkin, H. A., & Berry, J. W. Psychological differentiation in cross-cultural perspective. *Journal of Cross-Cultural Psychology*, 1975, 6 (1), 4-87.

Witkin, H. A., Birnbaum, J., Lamonaco, S., Lehr, S., & Herman, J. L. Cognitive patterning in congenitally totally blind children. *Child Development,* 1968, 39, 767-86.

Witkin, H. A., Dyk, W., Faterson, H., Goodenough, D., & Karp, S. *Psychological differentiation.* New York: Wiley, 1962.

Witkin, H. A., Faterson, H., Goodenough, D., & Birnbaum, J. Cognitive patterning in mildly retarded boys. *Child Development,* 1966, 37, 301-16.

Witkin, H. A., Goodenough, D., & Karp, S. Stability of cognitive style from childhood to young adulthood. *Journal of Personality and Social Psychology,* 1967, 7 (3), 291-300.

Witkin, H. A., Lewis, H. B., Hertzman, M., Machover, K., Neissner, P. B., & Wapner, S. *Personality through perception.* New York: Wiley, 1954.

Witkin, H. A., Price-Williams, D., Bertini, M., Christiansen, B., Oltman, P. K., Ramirez, M., & VanMeel, J. Social conformity and psychological differentiation. *International Journal of Psychology,* 1974, 9 (1), 11-29.

Zern, D., Kenney, H. J., & Karaceus, W. C. Cognitive style and overt behavior in emotionally disturbed adolescents. *Exceptional Children,* 1974, 41, 194-95.

A SELECTED BIBLIOGRAPHY OF WORKS BY BARBARA K. KEOGH

Keogh, B. K. A compensatory model for psychoeducational evaluation of children with learning disorders. *Journal of Learning Disabilities,* 1971, 4, 544-48.

Keogh, B. K. Hyperactive and learning disorders: Review and speculation. *Exceptional Children,* 1971, 38, 101-10.

Keogh, B. K. Psychological evaluation of exceptional children: Old hang-ups and new directions. *Journal of School Psychology,* 1972, 10, 49-53.

Keogh, B. K. Perceptual and cognitive styles: Implications for special education. In L. Mann & D. A. Sabatino (Eds.), *The first review of special education* (Vol. 1). Philadelphia: JSE Press, 1973.

Keogh, B. K., & Becker, L. D. Early detection of learning problems: Questions, cautions, and guidelines. *Exceptional Children,* 1973, 40, 5-11.

Keogh, B. K., & Donlon, G. Field dependence, impulsivity and learning disabilities. *Journal of Learning Disabilities,* 1972, 5, 331-36.

Keogh, B. K., & Hall, R. J. WISC subtest patterns of educationally handicapped and educable mentally retarded pupils. *Psychology in the Schools,* 1974, 9, 296-300.

Keogh, B. K., Tchir, C., & Windeguth-Behn, A. Teachers' perceptions of educationally high risk children. *Journal of Learning Disabilities,* 1974, 7, 367-74.

Keogh, B. K., Wetter, J., McGinty, A., & Donlon, G. Functional analysis of WISC performance of learning disordered, hyperactive, and mentally retarded boys. *Psychology in the Schools,* 1973, 10, 178-81.

PART 6

Future
Perspectives

17

Where the Change
Is Taking Us

Rebecca Dailey Kneedler received a B.A. degree in elementary education from the University of North Carolina in 1967, an M.A. in special education from the George Washington University in 1968, and an Ed.D. in special education from the University of Virginia in 1975. She is currently assistant professor in special education at the University of Virginia. Dr. Kneedler's experiences include teaching behavior-disordered children in both resource and special-class settings and working on the publication staff at the Council for Exceptional Children.

The preceding chapters in this volume, particularly the historical chapter by Tarver, describe or reflect the profound changes which have characterized the developing field of special education. The profession continues to be in a state of flux, with conflicting attitudes and efforts in such areas as mainstreaming, teacher preparation, and research directions. In 1971, James Gallagher noted, "It is one of those times when substantial change seems to be in the wind. What we really have to decide is whether the change will be improvement" [p. v]. Where is this change taking us? Since it is difficult to predict how external social and political events or internal shifts will influence the future direction of special education, projections obviously are tentative and speculative. However, in order to ensure that we react responsibly to changes as they occur, it is extremely important that we constantly examine the possible consequences of our present actions and the directions in which our current perspectives may lead us.

As a starting point, it is apparent that special education as a profession will remain dynamic and receptive to change. As Michael Nelson[1]

[1] References to authors' chapters included in this volume are not followed by a date or listed in the References section.

notes in the closing sentences of his chapter, this is a desirable and essential trait: "Let us hope that the most enduring educational institution is that of change itself" [p. 203]. Although changes undoubtedly will occur, the widely fluctuating shifts in emphases and approaches which have characterized the past thirty years probably will not be as evident in the future. The field of special education has passed from adolescence, with its accompanying moodiness and insecurity, to a more demanding, more responsible adulthood. This stabilizing trend was apparent in a telephone survey in which this author was involved (Dailey, 1974), in which participants were asked to describe their own work and to identify major issues and trends. Most of the eighty-odd participants viewed the work by their colleagues and themselves with careful scrutiny, constructive criticism, and a healthy caution. They were extremely leary about educational "bandwagons" and cures, and tended to define successful efforts in terms of small achievements in a particular area rather than broad solutions to a problem. The expectations and demands of special educators have never been higher or stronger. This new level of sophistication and skepticism enables special educators to resist the temptation to abandon their current areas of interest for ones which may be more fashionable. As a result, the field of special education should now begin to reap the benefits of much-needed longitudinal efforts and to meet the twenty-first century with new knowledge, more solid directions, and the "improvement" which Gallagher was urging.

The contributing authors in this book are representative of special educators who have been involved in the most current and innovative changes in special education in the 1970s. Indicative both of special education as a discipline and of exceptional children, themselves, the work of these contributors varies widely and reflects their uniqueness and creativity. However, an examination of their divergent perspectives reveals three major themes which permeate the areas of methodology, evaluation, programming, and research, and which hold promise of a continuing impact on the future: (a) an increased emphasis on the interaction of multiple factors, (b) a redefinition of the teacher's preparation and role, and (c) increasing pressures for accountability exerted by external economic and legislative forces and by the internal demands of special educators themselves.

INTERACTION OF MULTIPLE FACTORS

When studies were conducted in special education only a decade or two ago, the purpose frequently was to isolate and understand a unitary factor, such as a test, a learning characteristic, a physical deficit, or a method of behavior modification. As new levels of knowledge and sophistication have been reached, the focus has shifted from the study of one variable in isolation to that of the *process* by which that variable interacts with another. A recurring theme throughout this volume is the new emphasis on the manner in which multiple factors impinge upon one another in methodology, evaluation, programming, and research.

Many of the outstanding educators in methods and curriculum development advocate the study of the interaction of numerous variables in the comprehensive planning of a child's program (Cawley, Goodstein, Fitzmaurice, Lepore, Sedlak, & Althaus, 1976; Mayer, 1975; Meyen, 1972). No longer is the focus on a single program of instruction; the demand now exists for comprehensive curriculum plans—ones which relate learning objectives to a child's needs for his entire day and, whenever possible, for his whole school experience of several years. In this volume, both Cawley and Engelmann state that too much effort has been expended in assessing the solitary learner via formal evaluation methods and too little effort in designing and/or organizing the task for that learner. As the emphasis becomes more balanced and includes the task as well as the learner, Cawley predicts that future curriculum developers will further improve the systems of instruction by linking the "how" (methods) with the "what" (curriculum) and by linking both more closely to the learner.

One area of methodology which has been conspicuously isolated as a separate entity in the minds of special educators is educational technology. As Cartwright points out, to this point educational technology has been most frequently defined in terms of "hardware" and viewed as an appendage to instruction rather than an integrated part of the teaching approach. We all undoubtedly have witnessed the incongruous showing of a film to a class with no rationale other than that the film was available. Cartwright points to a more comprehensive view that is emerging in which the *processes* of technology will be stressed. The programming, "software," as well as specific types of media, "hardware," will be well integrated with the teaching objectives and will be used only when they truly facilitate teaching the task to the learner. As knowledge of the interaction between learner and task increases, the benefits of the correct use of educational technology will inevitably grow.

In no other area is the trend of taking interaction factors into account clearer than in the area of diagnosis and evaluation. First, there is practically universal agreement that diagnosis in isolation is of dubious value. The four authors who address evaluation in this volume adhere to the view that in order to be worthwhile, evaluation must be tied into and directly lead to instructional programming. In addition to examining the relationship of the child's diagnosis to his instruction, diagnosticians also are broadening diagnosis to encompass the child's interaction with certain aspects of his particular environment. Larsen, for example, advocates that evaluation include the interaction of the student with his teacher, his curriculum, his peers, and any other factors which appear significant in his learning environment. Logan also emphasizes the multiple ways in which students must be evaluated and discusses Mercer and Lewis' (in press) "pluralistic assessment" as one of his examples.

Current research efforts are too diverse to permit many generalizations. However, scanning recent research in almost any area reveals that increased attention is being given to the interaction of variables. In this volume, for example, Keogh explores one dimension which affects the interaction between the learner and his learning task, i.e., cognitive style. She looks forward to the time when we can effectively "match" the learner's style with the teacher's style and can consider the style of the learner in presenting or developing the instructional task.

THE TEACHER'S ROLE

The role of the special educator has never been an easy one. In the past, the special-class teacher was expected to "individualize" instruction without always being taught either the precise measurement skills or the correct instructional approaches needed for such a formidable goal. As the move to mainstreaming has gathered momentum, the special educator often has been placed in the even more demanding position of a resource specialist who must work with regular education teachers as well as the special learner. Most of the proponents of mainstreaming concur that the most critical factor for its success is the teacher's performance and that the most pressing charge in special education today is the preparation of teachers for this new role (Connor, 1976; Hewett & Forness, 1974; MacMillan & Becker).

The demands now being placed on teachers as a result of new alternative and integrated programs for the mildly handicapped such as those described by Nelson in his chapter, and MacMillan and Becker in theirs, have had a direct impact on the needs of and approaches to teacher training. One of the most widespread effects of these changing needs has been the proliferation of noncategorical, competency-based programs (a development which is fully discussed in Blackhurst's chapter). According to one HEW report, the move toward competency-based teacher education presently is evident in 32 states (Connor, 1976). Longevity for this competency-based emphasis appears to be assured at this time, due largely to the current demands of accountability (Blackhurst).

Teacher preparation programs have an increasingly arduous task as the expectations for teacher performance continue to rise. In the future, teachers will be expected to learn about and utilize the newest developments in curriculum planning and design, task analysis, and behavioral research such as those described by Cawley, Engelmann, and White. In the area of evaluation, Larsen and Logan both call for the teacher to play the central role in the educational diagnosis of each child. The successful implementation of changes in programming such as those described by Nelson, MacMillan and Becker, Tawney, and LaVor is largely dependent on the teacher's ability. The research achievements reported by McLean, Keogh, and the Bryans encounter a dead-end unless they are understood and utilized by the practitioner. Thus, the crucial link in the total process of educational change and improvement is the teacher.

In addition to responding to these changes, the teacher must go one step further: He/she must become an active participant in the change process. As Simches (1970) puts it,

> If we are desirous of change, then the teacher must begin to realize the important role he can play as a catalyst. Too often one has the feeling that the special education teacher, like most teachers, is identified not as a producer of new knowledge or the dissemination of knowledge, but only as a utilizer of knowledge; not as an active person instrumental in bringing about change, but mainly as a reactor to change. [p. 12]

INCREASING DEMANDS OF ACCOUNTABILITY

The term *accountability* has already become overworked and somewhat hackneyed. However, one of the surest predictions which can be made is that the pressures for accountability will continue to increase and to influence education as we enter the 1980s. At the same time that developments and innovations in special education seem most constructive and promising, the field is faced with unrelenting and stringent demands from three different sources.

First, current legislative actions are making new and compelling demands that special educators enlarge the scope of their services. As a result of PL 94-142, the states have been required to provide special education services to handicapped persons between the ages of 3 and 21 years. In addition, more teachers and programs are now being required to serve the severely and profoundly handicapped. The specific court cases and legislative actions which pertain to special education have been fully documented and discussed (Trudeau, 1973; Turnbull, 1975). However, as both LaVor and MacMillan and Becker point out in their chapters, these actions alone do not ensure that adequate services for the handicapped will be provided. It is up to the parents and educators of exceptional children to see that the laws and decisions receive full implementation.

A second source of the current demands on special education is the restrictive economic atmosphere of the 1970s. Taxpayers and politicians have become increasingly conservative about the allocation of funds for anything which even hints at "frills" or nonessentials. In his chapter on programming for the severely handicapped, Tawney vividly describes the present situation:

> The source of the problem is money. Current advocacy efforts are garnering funds for public school programs, but the number of suits . . . is testimony that this is not a benevolent outpouring of resources. A new population is competing for resources in a period of retrenchment in commitment to educational and social services. Eventually, parents of the nonhandicapped will realize that sharing resources with the handicapped will reduce the proportion of resources available to their children, and a counteraction can be anticipated. [p. 236]

This bleak economic situation has a potentially negative impact on virtually every area of special education. Tanis and James Bryan lament the fact that lack of sufficient funds affects not only the amount of research conducted, but also influences the nature of the topics studied and the methodologies employed. Moreover curtailed funding, in limiting the development and purchase of new, sophisticated materials and equipment, retards the implementation of research findings. The negative effects of financial constraints are compounded when they are accompanied by the dangerous trend to evaluate programs primarily in terms of cost efficiency. It is a most difficult task to convince the taxpayer that educating ten mentally handicapped children at a much greater expense than that of educating ten nonhandicapped children is a sound expenditure of public funds. In addition, the results of special education (as well as general education) do not lend themselves to cost analysis. LaVor notes that

> when education is scrutinized, special education is often singled out to justify itself more than any other educational area. Also, when budgets are cut back, special education programs are often the first to be reduced. In spite of the fact that general education cannot prove its cost efficiency and effectiveness, special education is usually asked to do so. [p. 251]

Thus, while certain pressures for accountability are beneficial to special education and the students it serves, those which are born of economic concerns are counterproductive. However, regardless of whether the economic demands are fair, realistic, or productive, they undoubtedly will persist in the coming decade.

The third and more positive pressure for accountability is, in many ways, both the most uncomfortable and the most valuable. It emerges from the internal scrutiny by and judgment of fellow colleagues within special education. As described earlier in this chapter, increased expectations are a natural accompaniment to the maturation of a profession. While the legislative and economic demands for accountability never have been stronger, neither has the ability of special educators to meet such demands. Although it still lags behind that of many other countries, the national commitment to handicapped people in the United States has grown enormously during the past twenty years. It is incumbent upon practitioners, administrators, and researchers in special education to be accountable by responding to this commitment with the application of sound knowledge to programs demonstrating growth and progress.

OTHER CHANGES IN THE FUTURE

Within the general areas of methodology, evaluation, programming, and research, other minor trends appear inevitable as an extension of current emphases and developments. The teaching/learning process will be enhanced by further efforts in curriculum development, task analysis, instructional technology, and the application of behavioral and other types of research. The efforts in identification and diagnosis will continue to increase in reliability and will be more closely aligned with the instructional process itself. Although the issue of mainstreaming will continue to be a focal point for debate, future changes in programming, if monitored by parents and other advocates, will be determined more often according to the benefits to the child rather than to the dictates of court action, philosophical views, or economic constraints. Finally, continued emphasis on original research will provide scientifically sound direction for future programs in special education and help to ensure the most effective education of exceptional children.

Perhaps this future view seems too rosy. It is difficult, however, in spite of present problems and mistakes, to make a negative prognosis for special education at this time. The progress may seem agonizingly slow and the obstacles insurmountable; however, the field has grown enormously during the past few decades and shows all indications of continued growth. The most solid foundation on which to build this hope for the future is on the people working in special education today. Marie Skodak Crissey (1975), in projecting the future of mental retardation, made this observation:

> I realize that there has been one consistent omission from my discussion. I have discussed "the retarded" movements, trends, and developments. This is the objective approach we think is appropriate. Sadly, we mislead ourselves. It is people, individual people, who make the difference in other people. It was Seguin's enthusiasm that

inspired his teachers to work, to invent, and to influence from 5:30 in the morning when the children awoke to 8:30 at night when they went to bed. [p. 807]

In a similar vein, it will be individuals such as those who contributed to this volume whose ability, vision, and hard work will fortunately determine where the changes in special education will take us in the future.

REFERENCES

Cawley, J. F., Goodstein, H. A., Fitzmaurice, A. M., Lepore, A., Sedlak, R., & Althaus, V. *Project MATH*. Tulsa: Educational Progress Corporation, 1976.

Connor, F. P. The past is prologue: Teacher preparation in special education. *Exceptional Children*, 1976, 42, 366-78.

Crissey, M. S. Mental retardation: Past, present, and future. *American Psychologist*, 1975, 30, 800-808.

Dailey, R. F. Dimensions and issues in '74: Tapping into the special education grapevine. *Exceptional Children*, 1974, 40, 503-7.

Gallagher, J. J. Quoted in P. L. McDonald, E. R. Blum, & P. E. Barker (Eds.), *Kaleidoscope: Emerging patterns in media*. Arlington, Va.: Council for Exceptional Children, 1971.

Hewett, F. M., & Forness, S. R. *Education of exceptional learners*. Boston: Allyn & Bacon, 1974.

Mayer, W. *Planning curriculum development*. Colorado: Biological Sciences Curriculum Study, 1975.

Mercer, J. R., & Lewis, J. F. *SOMPA: Systems of multi-cultural pluralistic assessment*. New York: Psychological Corporation, in press.

Meyen, E. *Developing units of instruction: For the mentally retarded and other children with learning problems*. Dubuque: W. C. Brown Co., 1972.

Simches, R. F. The inside outsiders. *Exceptional Children*, 1970, 37, 5-15.

Trudeau, E. (Ed.), *Digest of state and federal laws: Education of handicapped children*. Reston, Va.: Council for Exceptional Children, 1973.

Turnbull, H. R. Accountability: An overview of the impact of litigation on professionals. *Exceptional Children*, 1975, 41, 427-33.

INDEX

Aase, E., 194
Ability training, 111–12
Adelman, H., 281, 286
Agard, J., 210
All Handicapped Children Act, 242
Alternative education
  characteristics of, 190–97
  development of, 187–90
  relationship to special education, 197–201
Applied Behavior Analysis (ABA), 137, 138
Aptitude—Treatment Interaction (ATI), 320
Armstrong, D. J., 194
Ashurst, D. I., 215
Association for Children with Learning Disabilities, 11
Attridge, C., 135

Baer, D. M., 69, 71–5, 301
Baker, R. L., 177
Barr, R. D., 193, 194, 203
Bartel, 127
Barth, R. S., 196
Bash, M. A., 290
Becker, D. B., 208–9
Becker, J. D., 286
Becker, L. D., 327, 348
BEH (Bureau of Education for the Handicapped), 3, 92, 237

Early Childhood-Handicapped, 243
  Head Start-Handicapped, 242
Behavioral methodology
  Groups vs. single subject, 75–78
Behaviorism, 63–79
Behavior Resource Guide, 36
Bereiter, C., 304
Berry, J. W., 329
Bijou, S. W., 231
Binet, A., 9
Blackhurst, A. E., 156, 158, 165, 166, 168, 178, 348
Bloom, L., 304
Boothroyd, A., 94
Boss, R., 194
Bowerman, M. F., 304
Bradley, C., 143
Brophy, J., 135, 286
Brown, R., 304
Bruner, J. S., 299, 306
Bryan, J. H., 274, 350
Bryan, T. H., 273–74, 350
Budoff, M., 217
Burke, D. J., 193, 194

Camp, B., 290
Campbell, D. T., 75, 76
Cartwright, G. P., 84, 347
Castenada, A., 333, 334
Cattell, R. B., 13, 14
Cawley, J. F., 4, 7, 21, 33, 39, 347, 348